TRACING YOUR IRISH ANCESTORS
THE COMPLETE GUIDE

Tracing Your Irish Ancestors
The Complete Guide

JOHN GRENHAM

Published in Ireland by Gill and Macmillan Ltd.
Goldenbridge, Dublin 8, Ireland

Published in the USA and Canada, 1993, by
Genealogical Publishing Co., Inc.
1001 N. Calvert Street / Baltimore, MD 21202
Published by arrangement with Gill and Macmillan Ltd.

Library of Congress Catalogue Card Number 92-74687
International Standard Book Number 0-8063-1369-2
Printed and bound in the United States of America

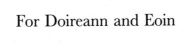

For Doireann and Eoin

Contents

Part 2 Other Sources

Part 3 A Reference Guide

List of Illustrations

Acknowledgments

My greatest debt is to Mr Donal Begley, Chief Herald of Ireland; without his encouragement and endless patience this work would never have been started. I also owe a great deal to the other members of staff at the Genealogical Office, in particular Colette O'Flaherty and Willie Buckley of the Consultation Service, and the Assistant Chief Herald, Fergus Gillespie. My former colleagues in Hibernian Research, Tom Lindert, Anne Brennan, Eileen O'Byrne and Éilis Ellis have all generously shared their knowledge and experience, and contributed very welcome advice and suggestions. I am also grateful to the staff of the National Library, the General Register Office, the Public Record Office of Northern Ireland and the National Archives for all their help to me over the years; I am particularly indebted to Jim O'Shea of the National Library for his help with Chapter 13. The member centres of the Irish Family History Foundation were also of great assistance, especially Dr Chris O'Mahony of Limerick Archives, Seán O Súileabháin of Leitrim County Library, Brian Mitchell of Derry Inner City Trust, and Theo McMahon of Monaghan Ancestral Research, as was Noel Reid of the Irish Family History Society. I owe special thanks to my father, Seán Grenham, who drew the parish maps, and to Jonathan Hession, who took the photographs and helped out with rest and recreation. Needless to say, none of those who helped me have any responsibility for the errors and omissions: these are all my own. Finally, I thank my wife Breda Kearney for all her tolerance and encouragement.

Abbreviations

AH	*Analecta Hibernica*
C. of I.	Church of Ireland
DKPRI	Deputy Keeper of Public Records in Ireland
GRO	General Register Office
GO	The Genealogical Office
IA	*The Irish Ancestor*
IG	*The Irish Genealogist*
IGRS	Irish Genealogical Research Society
ILB	Irish Large Book (National Library)
IMA	*Journal of the Association for the Preservation of the Memorials of the Dead in Ireland*
IMC	Irish Manuscripts Commission
Ir.	Irish (National Library prefix)
IUP	Irish University Press
J	Joly Collection pamphlet (National Library)
JCHAS	*Journal of the Cork Historical and Archaeological Society*
JCLAS	*Journal of the Co. Louth Archaeological and Historical Society*
JGHAS	*Journal of the Galway Historical and Archaeological Society*
JKAHS	*Journal of the Kerry Archaeological and Historical Society*
JKAS	*Journal of the Co. Kildare Archaeological Society*
JLB	Joly Large Book (National Library)
JNMAS	*Journal of the North Munster Antiquarian Society*
JRSAI	*Journal of the Royal Society of Antiquaries of Ireland*
LC	Local Custody
LO	Library Office (National Library)
mf	Microfilm
MS.	Manuscript
MSS.	Manuscripts
MFCI	Microfilm of Church of Ireland records (National Archives)
MP	Member of Parliament

n.d.	no date
NA	National Archives
NL	National Library
O'K	*O'Kief, Coshe Mang etc.* (ed. Albert Casey)
P.	Pamphlet (National Library)
Ph.	Phillimore publication
Pos.	Positive (microfilm)
pr. pr.	privately printed
PRONI	Public Record Office of Northern Ireland
PRS	Parish Register Society Publication
RCBL	Representative Church Body Library
RDKPRI	Report of the Deputy Keeper of Public Records of Ireland
RIA	Royal Irish Academy
TCD	Trinity College Dublin
Unpub.	Unpublished

DOWN & CONNOR DIOCESE

1	Aghagallon & Ballinderry	1828
2	Ahoghill	1833
3	Antrim	1874
4	Armoy	1848
5	Ballintoy	1872
6	Ballyclare	1869
7	Ballymoney	1853
8	Belfast city:	
	Belfast	1798
	Holycross	1868
	St Joseph	1872
	St Malachy	1858
	St Mary	1867
	St Patrick	1875
	St Peter	1866
9	Blaris	1845*
10	Braid & Glenravel	1825
11	Carnlough	1869
12	Carrickfergus	1821
13	Culfeightrin	1825
14	Cushendall	1837
15	Cushendun	1834
16	Derryaghy	1877
17	Duneane	1835
18	Dunloy	1860
19	Glenavy	1848
20	Glenarm	1825
21	Greencastle	1854
22	Kirkinriola	1847
23	Larne	1821
24	Loughguile	1845
25	Portglenone	1864
26	Portrush & Bushmills	1844
27	Ramoan	1838
28	Randalstown	1825
29	Rasharkin	1848

*Local custody

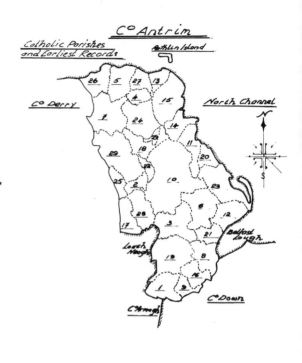

Co Antrim

Catholic Parishes and Earliest Records

ARMAGH DIOCESE

1	Armagh	1796
2	Ballymacnab	1820*
3	Ballymore & Mullaghbhrac	1798*
4	Clonfeacle (Moy)	1814
5	Creggan Lr	1845
6	Creggan Upr	1796
7	Derrynoose	1814*
8	Drumcree	1844
9	Dungannon	1783*
10	Eglish	1862
11	Faughart	1851
12	Forkhill	1844
13	Killeavy Lr	1835
14	Killeavy Upr	1832
15	Kilmore	1845
16	Loughgall	1833
18	Loughgilly	1825
19	Tynan	1822

DROMORE DIOCESE

20	Magheralin	1815
21	Newry	1818
22	Seagoe	1836
23	Shankill (Lurgan)	1822

*Earliest records in Armagh Diocesan Archives

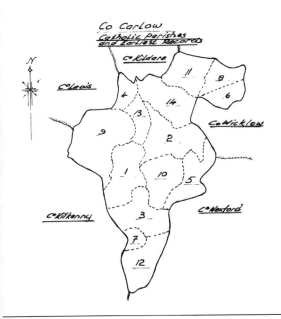

KILDARE & LEIGHLIN DIOCESE

1	Bagenalstown	1820
2	Ballon & Rathoe	1782
3	Borris	1782
4	Carlow	1787
5	Clonegall	1833
6	Clonmore	1813
7	Graiguenamanagh	1818
8	Hacketstown	1820
9	Leighlinbridge	1783
10	Myshall	1822
11	Rathvilly	1797
12	St Mullin's	1813
13	Tinryland	1813
14	Tullow	1763

ARDAGH & CLONMACNOISE DIOCESE

1	Drumlumman North	1859
2	Drumlumman South	1837
3	Scrabby	1833

MEATH DIOCESE

4	Carnaross	1805
5	Kilbride	1832
6	Kingscourt	1838

KILMORE DIOCESE

7	Annagh	1845
8	Ballintemple	1862
9	Castlerahan	1752
10	Castleterra	1763
11	Corlough	1877
12	Crosserlough	1843
13	Denn	1856
14	Drumgoon (Cootehill)	1829
15	Drumlane (Staghall)	1836
16	Drung (see Kilsherdony)	—
17	Drumreilly	1867
18	Glangevlin	1867
19	Kildallon (Ballyconnell)	1867
20	Killan (Bailieboro)	1835
21	Killeshandra	1835
22	Killinagh	1860*
23	Killinkere	1766
24	Kilmainhamwood & Moybologue	1867
25	Kilmore	1859
26	Kinawley (Swanlinbar)	1835
27	Knockbride	1835

28	Kilsherdony	1803
29	Laragh	1876
30	Lavey	1867
31	Lurgan (Virginia)	1755
32	Mullagh	1842
33	Templeport	1827
34	Urney & Annegeliff	1812

*Earliest records in Cavan Heritage Centre

GALWAY DIOCESE

1 Beagh	1849
2 Ennistymon (Kilmanaheen & Cloony)	1823*
3 Glanaragh (Ballyvaughan)	1854
4 Kilcronin & Kilcorny	1853
5 Kilfenora	1836
6 Kilshanny	1870
7 Liscannor (Kilmacrehy & Killaspuglonane)	1843
8 Lisdoonvarna	1854
9 New Quay (Glanamanagh)	1836*

KILLALOE DIOCESE

10 Broadford	1844
11 Carrigaholt	1852
12 Clarecastle	1834*
13 Clondegad	1846
14 Clonrush (Mountshannon)	1846
15 Corofin	1818
16 Crusheen	1860
17 Doonass & Truagh	1851
18 Doora & Kilraghtis	1821
19 Dysart	1845
20 Ennis	1837
21 Feakle	1860
22 Inagh	1850
23 Inch & Kilmaley	1828
24 Kilballyowen	1878
25 Kildysart	1829
26 Kilfarboy (Milltownmalbay)	1831
27 Kilfidane	1868
28 Kilkee	1836*
29 Kilkeedy	1833
30 Killaloe	1828
31 Killanena (Flagmount)	1842
32 Killard	1855
33 Killimer	1859

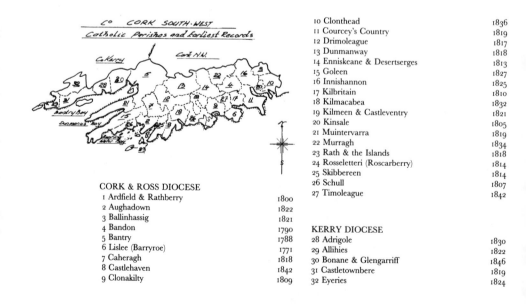

Co Clare
Catholic Parishes and Earliest Records

34 Kilmacduane	1853
35 Kilmihil	1849
36 Kilmurry-Ibrickane	1839
37 Kilmurry-McMahon	1837
38 Kilnoe & Tuamgraney	1832
39 Kilrush (St Senan's)	1827
40 Newmarket	1828
41 O'Callaghan's Mills	1835
42 Ogonnelloe	1832
43 Quin & Clooney	1816
44 Scarriff & Moynoe	1852
45 Sixmilebridge	1828
46 Tulla	1819

LIMERICK DIOCESE

47 Cratloe	1802
48 Parteen & Meelick	1814

*Earliest records in Clare Heritage Centre

Co CORK SOUTH-WEST
Catholic Parishes and Earliest Records

CORK & ROSS DIOCESE

1 Ardfield & Rathberry	1800
2 Aughadown	1822
3 Ballinhassig	1821
4 Bandon	1790
5 Bantry	1788
6 Lislee (Barryroe)	1771
7 Caheragh	1818
8 Castlehaven	1842
9 Clonakilty	1809
10 Clonthead	1836
11 Courcey's Country	1819
12 Drimoleague	1817
13 Dunmanway	1818
14 Enniskeane & Desertserges	1813
15 Goleen	1827
16 Innishannon	1825
17 Kilbritain	1810
18 Kilmacabea	1832
19 Kilmeen & Castleventry	1821
20 Kinsale	1805
21 Muintervarra	1819
22 Murragh	1834
23 Rath & the Islands	1818
24 Rosseletteri (Roscarberry)	1814
25 Skibbereen	1814
26 Schull	1807
27 Timoleague	1842

KERRY DIOCESE

28 Adrigole	1830
29 Allihies	1822
30 Bonane & Glengarriff	1846
31 Castletownbere	1819
32 Eyeries	1824

Co Cork East
Catholic Parishes and Earliest Records

Co Tipperary

Co Waterford

C° Cork N.W.

C° Cork S.W.

Youghal Bay

10 Conna	1834
11 Doneraile	1815
12 Fermoy	1828
13 Glanworth & Ballindangan	1836
14 Glountane	1829
15 Imogeela	1833
16 Kildorrerry	1803
17 Killeagh	1822
18 Kilworth	1829
19 Lisgoold	1807
20 Mallow	1757
21 Midleton	1819
22 Mitchelstown	1792
23 Rathcormac	1792
24 Youghal	1801

CORK & ROSS DIOCESE

25 Carrigaline	1826
26 Cork city:	
Blackrock	1810
St Finbarr (South)	1756
St Mary	1748
St Patrick	1831
SS Peter & Paul	1766
27 Douglas	1812
28 Glanmire	1803
29 Glounthaune	1864
30 Monkstown	1875
31 Passage West	1795
32 Tracton Abbey	1802
33 Watergrasshill	1836

WATERFORD & LISMORE DIOCESE

34 Lismore	1820

*Earliest records in Mallow Heritage Centre

CLOYNE DIOCESE

1 Aghada	1785*
2 Annakissy	1805
3 Ballymacoda	1835
4 Blarney	1778
5 Carrigtohill	1817
6 Castlelyons	1791
7 Castletownroche	1811
8 Cloyne	1786
9 Cobh	1812

CLOYNE DIOCESE

1 Aghabulloge	1820
2 Aghinagh	1848
3 Ballyclough	1805
4 Ballyhea	1809
5 Ballyvourney	1825
6 Banteer (Clonmeen)	1847
7 Buttevant	1814
8 Castlemagner	1832
9 Charleville	1774
10 Clondrohid	1807
11 Donaghmore	1790
12 Freemount (Milford)	1827
13 Glountane	1829
14 Grenagh	1840
15 Inniscarra	1814
16 Kanturk	1822
17 Kilnamartyra	1803
18 Liscarroll	1812
19 Macroom	1780
20 Mourneabbey	1829
21 Newmarket	1821
22 Rock & Meelin	1866
23 Shandrum	1829

CORK & ROSS DIOCESE

24 Ballincollig	1820
25 Iveleary	1816
26 Kilmichael	1819
27 Kilmurry	1786
28 Ovens	1816

KERRY DIOCESE

29 Ballydesmond	1868*
30 Boherbue	1833

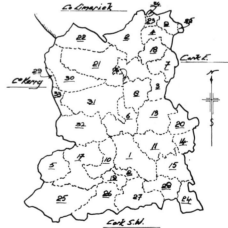

Cork North West
Catholic Parishes and Earliest Records

Co Limerick

Co Kerry

Cork E.

Cork S.W.

31 Dromtariffe	1832
32 Millstreet	1853
33 Rathmore	1837

LIMERICK DIOCESE

34 Ballyagran	1841
35 Kilmallock	1837

*Local custody

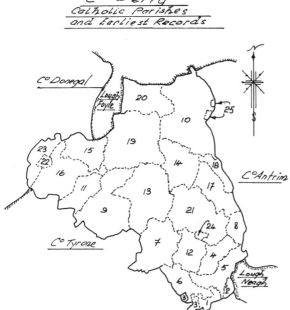

ARMAGH DIOCESE
1	Arboe	1827
2	Ballinderry	1826
3	Cookstown (Desertcreight)	1827
4	Magherafelt	1834
5	Moneymore	1832
6	Lissan	1839

DERRY DIOCESE
7	Ballinascreen	1825
8	Ballyscullion (Bellaghy)	1844
9	Banagher	1848
10	Coleraine (Killowen)	1843
11	Cumber Upr	1863
12	Desertmartin	1848
13	Dungiven	1847
14	Errigal (Garvagh)	1846
15	Faughanvale	1860
16	Glendermot	1864
17	Greenlough	1846
18	Kilrea	1846
19	Limavady	1855
20	Magilligan	1863
21	Maghera	1841
22	St Eugene's (Derry city)	1873
23	Templemore (Derry city)	1823
24	Termoneeny	1837

DOWN & CONNOR DIOCESE
25	Ballymoney	1853
10	Coleraine	1848

CLOGHER DIOCESE
1	Carn (Pettigo)	1836
2	Inishmacsaint	1847

DERRY DIOCESE
3	Burt	1856
4	Clonca	1856
5	Clonleigh	1773
6	Clonmany	1852
7	Culdaff	1838
8	Desertegney	1864
9	Donagh	1847
10	Donaghmore	1840
11	Iskaheen (Moville Upr)	1858
12	Moville Lr	1847
13	Urney	1829

RAPHOE DIOCESE
14	All Saints	1843
15	Annagry	1868
16	Ardara	1867
17	Aughnish	1873
18	Clondahorky	1877
19	Clondavaddog	1847
20	Conwal & Leck	1853
21	Drumholm	1866
22	Glencolumbkille	1880
23	Gortahork (Raymunterdoney)	1849
24	Gweedore	1868
25	Inishkeel (Glenties)	1866
26	Inver	1861
27	Kilbarron	1854
28	Kilcar	1848
29	Killaghtee	1845
30	Killybegs	1850
31	Killygarvan	1868

32	Killymard	1874
33	Kilmacrennan	1862
34	Kilteevogue	1855
35	Lettermacaward (Dungloe)	1876
36	Mevagh	1871
37	Raphoe	1876
38	Stranorlar	1860
39	Tawnawilly	1872
40	Termon & Gartan	1862

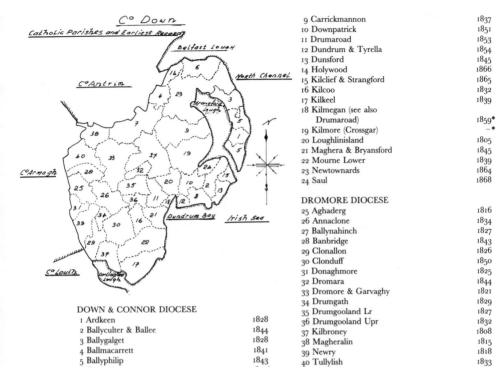

Co Down
Catholic Parishes and Earliest Records

9 Carrickmannon		1837
10 Downpatrick		1851
11 Drumaroad		1853
12 Dundrum & Tyrella		1854
13 Dunsford		1845
14 Holywood		1866
15 Kilclief & Strangford		1865
16 Kilcoo		1832
17 Kilkeel		1839
18 Kilmegan (see also Drumaroad)		1859*
19 Kilmore (Crossgar)		—*
20 Loughlinisland		1805
21 Maghera & Bryansford		1845
22 Mourne Lower		1839
23 Newtownards		1864
24 Saul		1868

DROMORE DIOCESE

25 Aghaderg		1816
26 Annaclone		1834
27 Ballynahinch		1827
28 Banbridge		1843
29 Clonallon		1826
30 Clonduff		1850
31 Donaghmore		1825
32 Dromara		1844
33 Dromore & Garvaghy		1821
34 Drumgath		1829
35 Drumgooland Lr		1827
36 Drumgooland Upr		1832
37 Kilbroney		1808
38 Magheralin		1815
39 Newry		1818
40 Tullylish		1833

*Local custody

DOWN & CONNOR DIOCESE

1 Ardkeen		1828
2 Ballyculter & Ballee		1844
3 Ballygalget		1828
4 Ballmacarrett		1841
5 Ballyphilip		1843
6 Bangor		1855*
7 Blaris (Lisburn)		1880*
8 Bright		1856

CLOGHER DIOCESE

1 Aghavea		1862
2 Aughalurcher (Lisnaskea)		1835
3 Carn (Pettigo)		1836
4 Cleenish		1835
5 Clones		1821
6 Derrygonnelly		1853
7 Drumully		1845
8 Enniskillen		1818
9 Galloon		1847
10 Garrison		1860
11 Inishmacsaint		1847
12 Irvinestown		1846
13 Magheraculmany		1836
14 Roslea		1862
15 Tempo		1845

KILMORE DIOCESE

16 Drumlane		1836
17 Kildallan		1867
18 Killesher		1855
19 Kinawley		1835
20 Knockninny		1855

Co Fermanagh
Catholic Parishes and Earliest Records

East Galway
Catholic Parishes and Earliest Records

CLONFERT DIOCESE

1 Abbeygormican & Killoran	1846
2 Aughrim & Kilconnell	1828
3 Ballymacaward & Cloonkeenkerrill	1841
4 Ballinakill	1839
5 Ballinasloe (Creagh & Kilcloony)	1820
6 Clonfert	1829
7 Clontuskert	1827
8 Duniry & Ballinakill	1839
9 Fahy & Kilquain	1836*
10 Fohenagh & Kilgerill	1827
11 Kilconickney	1831
12 Kilcooley & Leitrim	1815
13 Killallaghten	1809
14 Killimorbologue	1831
15 Killimordaly (Kiltullagh)	1830
16 Kilmallinogue (Portumna)	1830
17 Killeenadeema	1836
18 Kiltormer	1834
19 Loughrea	1827
20 New Inn	1827
21 Tynagh	1809
22 Woodford	1821

ELPHIN DIOCESE

23 Ahascragh	1840
24 Athleague & Fuerty	1807
25 Dysart & Tisrara	1850
26 Glinsk & Kilbegnet	1836
27 Killian & Killeroran	1804
28 Oran (Cloverhill)	1845*

GALWAY DIOCESE

29 Ardrahan	1839
30 Ballindereen (Kilcolgan)	1854

31 Beagh	1856
32 Claregalway	1849
33 Clarenbridge (Kilcornan)	1837
34 Craughwell	1847
35 Gort (Kilmacduagh)	1848
36 Kilbeacanty	1854
37 Kilchreest	1855
38 Oranmore (Kilcameen & Ballynacourty)	1833
39 Peterswell (Kilthomas)	1854
40 Kinvarra	1831

KILLALOE DIOCESE

41 Mountshannon (Clonrush)	1846

TUAM DIOCESE

42 Abbeyknockmoy	–
43 Addergoole & Liskeevy	1858
44 Annaghdown	1834
45 Athenry	1858
46 Boyounagh	1838
47 Donaghpatrick & Kilcloona	1844
48 Dunmore	1833
49 Kilconly & Kilbannon	1872
50 Kilkerrin & Clonberne	1855*
51 Killascobe	1807
52 Killererin	1851
53 Killursa & Killower	–
54 Kilmeen	–
55 Kilmoylan & Cummer	1813
56 Lackagh	1841
57 Mountbellew (Moylough)	1848
58 Tuam	1790

*Local custody only

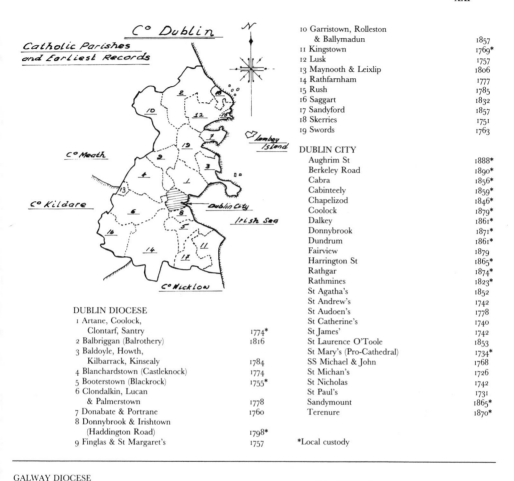

Cº Dublin

Catholic Parishes and Earliest Records

10 Garristown, Rolleston & Ballymadun	1857
11 Kingstown	1769*
12 Lusk	1757
13 Maynooth & Leixlip	1806
14 Rathfarnham	1777
15 Rush	1785
16 Saggart	1832
17 Sandyford	1857
18 Skerries	1751
19 Swords	1763

DUBLIN CITY

Aughrim St	1888*
Berkeley Road	1890*
Cabra	1856*
Cabinteely	1859*
Chapelizod	1846*
Coolock	1879*
Dalkey	1861*
Donnybrook	1871*
Dundrum	1861*
Fairview	1879
Harrington St	1865*
Rathgar	1874*
Rathmines	1823*
St Agatha's	1852
St Andrew's	1742
St Audoen's	1778
St Catherine's	1740
St James'	1742
St Laurence O'Toole	1853
St Mary's (Pro-Cathedral)	1734*
SS Michael & John	1768
St Michan's	1726
St Nicholas	1742
St Paul's	1731
Sandymount	1865*
Terenure	1870*

DUBLIN DIOCESE

1 Artane, Coolock, Clontarf, Santry	1774*
2 Balbriggan (Balrothery)	1816
3 Baldoyle, Howth, Kilbarrack, Kinsealy	1784
4 Blanchardstown (Castleknock)	1774
5 Booterstown (Blackrock)	1755*
6 Clondalkin, Lucan & Palmerstown	1778
7 Donabate & Portrane	1760
8 Donnybrook & Irishtown (Haddington Road)	1798*
9 Finglas & St Margaret's	1757

*Local custody

GALWAY DIOCESE

1 Castlegar	1827
2 Galway (St Nicholas')	1690
3 Killanin (see also Oughterard)	1875
4 Moycullen	1786
5 Oranmore (Kilcameen & Ballynacourty)	1833
6 Oughterard (Kilcummin)	1809
7 Rahoon	1819
8 Rosmuck (see also Oughterard)	1840
9 Salthill	1840
10 Spiddal	1861

TUAM DIOCESE

11 Aran Islands	1872
12 Ballinakill	1875
13 Clifden (Omey & Ballindoon)	1838
14 Cong	1872
15 Clonbur (Ross) (see also Leenane)	1853
16 Killeen (Lettermullen & Carraroe)	1853
17 Leenane (Kilbride)	1853
18 Moyrus	1852
19 Roundstone (see also Moyrus)	1872

West Galway Catholic Parishes and Earliest Records

KERRY DIOCESE

1 Abbeydorney — 1835
2 Annascaul (Ballinvoher) — 1829
3 Ardfert — 1819
4 Ballybunion & Ballydonohoe — 1831
5 Ballyferriter — 1807
6 Ballyheigue — 1857
7 Ballylongford — 1823
8 Ballymacelligot — 1868
9 Boherbue — 1833
10 Bonane — 1846
11 Brosna — 1868
12 Cahirciveen — 1846
13 Cahirdaniel — 1831
14 Castlegregory — 1828
15 Castleisland — 1822
16 Castlemaine — 1804
17 Causeway — 1782
18 Dingle — 1821
19 Dromod (Waterville) — 1850
20 Duagh — 1819
21 Firies — 1830
22 Fossa — 1857
23 Glenbeigh — 1830
24 Glenflesk — 1821
25 Kenmare — 1819
26 Kilcummin — 1821
27 Kilgarvan — 1818
28 Killarney — 1792
29 Killeentierna — 1801
30 Killorglin — 1800*
31 Knocknagoshel — 1850*
32 Listowel — 1802
33 Lixnaw — 1810
34 Milltown — 1821
35 Moyvane — 1830*
36 Prior (Ballinskelligs) — 1832*
37 Rathmore — 1837
38 Sneem — 1845

Co Kerry
Catholic Parishes and Earliest Records

39 Spa — 1866
40 Tarbert — 1859
41 Tralee — 1772
42 Tuogh — 1843
43 Tuosist — 1844
44 Valentia — 1825

*Earliest records in local custody

Co Kildare
Catholic Parishes and Earliest Records

KILDARE & LEIGHLIN DIOCESE

1 Allen & Milltown — 1820
2 Baltinglass — 1807
3 Balyna (Johnstown) — 1785
4 Caragh (Downings) — 1849
5 Carbury — 1821
6 Carlow — 1787
7 Clane — 1785
8 Clonbulloge — 1808
9 Curragh Camp — 1855
10 Kilcock — 1770
11 Kildare & Rathangan — 1815
12 Kill — 1840
13 Monasterevin — 1819
14 Naas & Eadestown — 1813
15 Newbridge — 1786
16 Robertstown — 1852*
17 Suncroft (Curragh) — 1805

DUBLIN DIOCESE

18 Athy — 1753**
19 Ballymore Eustace — 1779
20 Blessington — 1852
21 Castledermot — 1789
22 Celbridge — 1768*
23 Kilcullen — 1777
24 Maynooth & Leixlip — 1806
25 Narraghmore — 1827

*Local custody
**Earliest records in Kildare Heritage Centre

Cº Kilkenny
Catholic Parishes and Earliest Records

6 Clara (see Gowran)	1809
7 Clough	1858
8 Conahy	1832
9 Danesfort	1819
10 Dunamaggan	1821*
11 Freshford	1773
12 Galmoy	1805
13 Glanmore	1831
14 Gowran	1809
15 Inistioge	1810
16 Johnstown	1814
17 Kilkenny city:	
St Canice's	1768
St John's	1809
St Mary's	1754
St Patrick's	1800
18 Kilmacow	1786*
19 Kilmanagh	1845
20 Lisdowney	1771
21 Mooncoin	1772
22 Muckalee	1801
23 Mullinavat	1843
24 Rosbercon	1817
25 Slieverue	1766
26 Templeorum	1803
27 Thomastown	1782
28 Tullaherin	1732*
29 Tullaroan	1843
30 Urlingford	1805
31 Windgap	1822

KILDARE & LEIGHLIN DIOCESE

32 Graiguenamanagh	1818
33 Paulstown	1824

OSSORY DIOCESE

1 Agahviller	1847
2 Ballyhale	1823
3 Ballyragget	1856
4 Callan	1821
5 Castlecomer	1812

*Earliest records in Kilkenny
Archaeological Society

DUBLIN DIOCESE

1 Athy	1779

KILDARE & LEIGHLIN DIOCESE

2 Abbeyleix	1824
3 Arles	1821
4 Ballinakill	1794
5 Ballyadams	1820
6 Ballyfin (Cappinrush)	1819
7 Clonaslee	1849
8 Doonane	1843
9 Emo	1875
10 Graigue (Killeshin)	1819
11 Leighlinbridge	1783
12 Mountmellick	1814
13 Mountrath	1823
14 Portarlington	1820
15 Portlaoise	1826
16 Raheen	1819
17 Rosenallis	1765
18 Stradbally	1820

KILLALOE DIOCESE

19 Roscrea	1810

OSSORY DIOCESE

20 Aghaboe	1794
21 Ballyragget	1856
22 Borris-in-Ossory	1840
23 Camross	1816

Cº Laois
Catholic Parishes
and Earliest Records

24 Castletown	1794
25 Durrow	1789
26 Galmoy	1805
27 Lisdowney	1771
28 Rathdowney	1763

ARDAGH & CLONMACNOISE DIOCESE

1	Aughavas	1845
2	Annaduff	1849
3	Bornacoola	1824*
4	Cloone-Conmaicne	1820
5	Drumshanbo (Murhan)	1861
6	Fenagh	1825
7	Gortleteragh	1826
8	Killenummery & Killery	1827
9	Kiltoghert	1826
10	Kiltubbrid	1841
11	Mohill-Manachain	1836

KILMORE DIOCESE

12	Ballinaglera	1883*
13	Ballymeehan	1844
14	Carrigallen	1829
15	Clooneclare	1841
16	Drumlease (Dromahair)	1859
17	Drumreilly Lr	1867
18	Drumreilly Upr (Corlough)	1870
19	Glenade	1867
20	Inishmagrath	1830
21	Killargue	1852
22	Killasnet	1852
23	Kinlough	1835
24	Oughteragh (Ballinamore)	1841*

*Earliest records in Leitrim Heritage Centre

Co. Leitrim
Catholic Parishes and Earliest Records

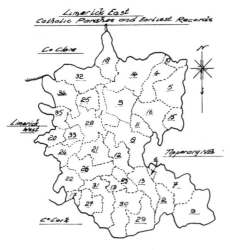

Limerick East
Catholic Parishes and Earliest Records

CASHEL & EMLY DIOCESE

1	Ballybricken	1800
2	Ballylanders	1849
3	Caherconlish	1841
4	Cappamore	1843
5	Doon	1824
6	Emly	1809
7	Galbally	1809
8	Hospital	1810
9	Kilbehenny	1824
10	Kilcommon	1813
11	Kilteely	1815
12	Knockaney	1808
13	Knocklong	1809
14	Murroe & Boher	1814
15	Oola	1809
16	Pallasgreen	1811

CLOYNE DIOCESE

17	Charleville	1774

KILLALOE DIOCESE

18	Castleconnell	1850

LIMERICK DIOCESE

19	Ardpatrick (see Kilfinane)	1861
20	Banogue (see Croom)	1861
21	Bruff	1781*
22	Bruree & Rockhill	1826*
23	Bulgaden	1812
24	Croom	1770
25	Donaghmore	1827
26	Dromin & Athlacca	1817
27	Effin	1843
28	Fedamore	1806
29	Glenroe & Ballyorgan	1853
30	Kilfinane	1832
31	Kilmallock	1837
32	Limerick city:	
	St John's	1788
	St Mary's	1745
	St Michael's	1772
	St Munchin's	1764
	St Patrick's	1805
33	Manister (see Fedamore)	–
34	Mungret & Crecora	1844
35	Patrickswell & Ballybrown	1801

*Earliest registers in Limerick Archives

Limerick West
Catholic Parishes and Earliest Records

LIMERICK EAST

C° Kerry

C° Cork

LIMERICK DIOCESE

1 Abbeyfeale	1829
2 Adare	1832
3 Ardagh	1845
4 Askeaton	1829
5 Athea	1827
6 Ballingarry & Granagh	1825
7 Ballyagran & Colmanswell	1841
8 Cappagh (see Kilcornan)	1841
9 Castlemahon (Mahoonagh)	1810
10 Croagh	1836
11 Drumcollogher	1830
12 Feenagh & Kilmeedy	1833*
13 Glin	1851
14 Kilcolman & Coolcappa	1827
15 Kilcornan (Stonehall)	1825
16 Kildimo (Pallaskenry)	1831
17 Killeedy (Raheenagh)	1840
18 Knockaderry & Clouncagh	1838
19 Loughill & Ballyhahill	1855
20 Monagea	1777
21 Newcastle West	1815
22 Rathkeale	1811
23 Shanagolden & Foynes	1824
24 Templeglantine (see Monagea)	1864
25 Tournafulla & Mountcollins	1867

CLOYNE DIOCESE

26 Freemount	1827

ARDAGH & CLONMACNOISE DIOCESE

1 Abbeylara	1854
2 Ardagh & Moydow	1793
3 Cashel	1850
4 Clonbroney	1849
5 Clonguish	1829
6 Columcille	1845
7 Dromard	1835
8 Drumlish	1834
9 Granard	1779
10 Kilcommuck	1859
11 Kilglass (Legan)	1855
12 Killashee	1826
13 Killoe	1826
14 Mostrim	1838
15 Mohill-Manachain	1836
16 Rathcline (Lanesboro)	1850
17 Scrabby	1833
18 Shrule (Ballymahon)	1820
19 Streete	1820
20 Templemichael & Ballymacormick	1802
21 Taghshiney, Taghsinod & Abbeyshrule	1835

MEATH DIOCESE

22 Drumraney	1834
23 Moyvore	1831

C° Longford
Catholic Parishes and Earliest Records

C° Leitrim
C° Cavan
C° Roscommon
C° Westmeath

ARMAGH DIOCESE

1 Ardee — 1763
2 Carlingford — 1835
3 Clogherhead — 1742
4 Collon — 1772*
5 Cooley — 1811
6 Creggan Upr — 1796
7 Darver — 1787
8 Dunleer — 1772
9 Dundalk — 1790
10 Faughart — 1851
11 Kilkerley — 1752
12 Kilsaran — 1809
13 Lordship — 1833*
14 Louth — 1833
15 Mellifont — 1821
16 Monasterboice — 1814
17 St Peter's (Drogheda) — 1744
18 Tallanstown — 1804
19 Termonfeckin — 1823
20 Togher — 1791

CLOGHER DIOCESE

21 Carrickmacross — 1837
22 Inniskeen — 1837

MEATH DIOCESE

23 St Mary's (Drogheda) — 1835

*Earliest records in Armagh Diocesan Archives

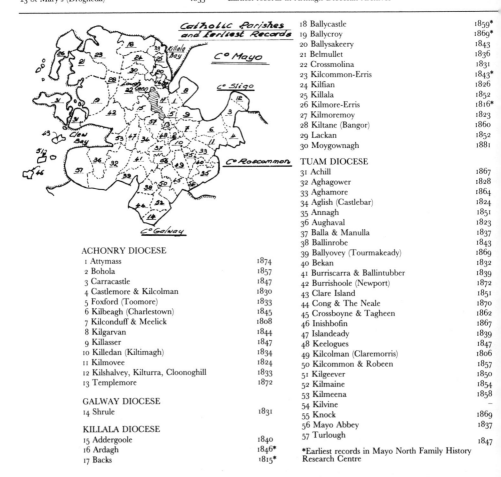

18 Ballycastle — 1859*
19 Ballycroy — 1869*
20 Ballysakeery — 1843
21 Belmullet — 1836
22 Crossmolina — 1831
23 Kilcommon-Erris — 1843*
24 Kilfian — 1826
25 Killala — 1852
26 Kilmore-Erris — 1816*
27 Kilmoremoy — 1823
28 Kiltane (Bangor) — 1860
29 Lackan — 1852
30 Moygownagh — 1881

TUAM DIOCESE

31 Achill — 1867
32 Aghagower — 1828
33 Aghamore — 1864
34 Aglish (Castlebar) — 1824
35 Annagh — 1851
36 Aughaval — 1823
37 Balla & Manulla — 1837
38 Ballinrobe — 1843
39 Ballyovey (Tourmakeady) — 1869
40 Bekan — 1832
41 Burriscarra & Ballintubber — 1839
42 Burrishoole (Newport) — 1872
43 Clare Island — 1851
44 Cong & The Neale — 1870
45 Crossboyne & Tagheen — 1862
46 Inishbofin — 1867
47 Islandeady — 1839
48 Keelogues — 1847
49 Kilcolman (Claremorris) — 1806
50 Kilcommon & Robeen — 1857
51 Kilgeever — 1850
52 Kilmaine — 1854
53 Kilmeena — 1858
54 Kilvine — –
55 Knock — 1869
56 Mayo Abbey — 1837
57 Turlough — 1847

ACHONRY DIOCESE

1 Attymass — 1874
2 Bohola — 1857
3 Carracastle — 1847
4 Castlemore & Kilcolman — 1830
5 Foxford (Toomore) — 1833
6 Kilbeagh (Charlestown) — 1845
7 Kilconduff & Meelick — 1808
8 Kilgarvan — 1844
9 Killasser — 1847
10 Killedan (Kiltimagh) — 1834
11 Kilmovee — 1824
12 Kilshalvey, Kilturra, Cloonoghill — 1833
13 Templemore — 1872

GALWAY DIOCESE

14 Shrule — 1831

KILLALA DIOCESE

15 Addergoole — 1840
16 Ardagh — 1846*
17 Backs — 1815*

*Earliest records in Mayo North Family History Research Centre

Co Meath — Catholic Parishes and Earliest Records

8	Beauparc (Blacklion)	1815
9	Bohermeen	1831
10	Carnaross	1805
11	Carolanstown	1810
12	Castletown	1805
13	Clonmellon	1757
14	Curraha	1802
15	Drumconrath	1811
16	Duleek	1852
17	Dunboyne	1787
18	Dunderry	1837
19	Dunshaughlin	1789
20	Enniskeen	1838
21	Johnstown	1839
22	Kells	1791
23	Kilbride	1832
24	Kilmessan & Dunsany	1742
25	Kilskyre	1784
26	Lobinstown	1823
27	Longwood	1829
28	Moynalty	1829
29	Moynalvy	1783
30	Navan	1782
31	Nobber	1754
32	Oldcastle	1789
33	Oristown	1757
34	Rathcore & Rathmolyon	1878*
35	Rathkenny	1784
36	Ratoath	1780
37	Rosnaree & Donore	1840
38	St Mary's (Drogheda)	1835
39	Skryne	1841
40	Slane	1851
41	Stamullen	1830
42	Summerhill	1812
43	Trim	1829

*Earliest records in Meath Heritage Centre, Trim

ARMAGH DIOCESE
1 Collon — 1789

KILMORE DIOCESE
2 Kilmainham & Moybologue — 1867

MEATH DIOCESE
3 Ardcath — 1795
4 Athboy — 1794
5 Ballinabracky — 1826
6 Ballivor & Kildalkey — 1759*
7 Batterstown — 1836

ARDAGH & CLONMACNOISE DIOCESE
1 Banagher (Gallen & Reynagh) — 1797
2 Clonmacnoise — 1826
3 Lemanaghan & Balnahown — 1821
4 Ferbane (Tisaran) — 1819

CLONFERT DIOCESE
5 Lusmagh — 1824

KILDARE & LEIGHLIN DIOCESE
6 Clonbulloge — 1808
7 Daingean — 1850
8 Edenderry — 1820
9 Killeigh — 1844
10 Portarlington — 1820
11 Rhode — 1829

KILLALOE DIOCESE
12 Birr — 1838
13 Bournea (Couraganeen) — 1836
14 Dunkerrin — 1820
15 Kilcolman — 1830
16 Kinnitty — 1833
17 Roscrea — 1810
18 Shinrone — 1842

MEATH DIOCESE
19 Ballinabrackey — 1826
20 Clara & Horseleap — 1821
21 Eglish — 1807
22 Kilcormac — 1821

Co Offaly — Catholic Parishes and Earliest Records

23 Rahan — 1810
24 Tubber — 1821
25 Tullamore — 1801

OSSORY DIOCESE
26 Seirkeiran — 1830

CLOGHER DIOCESE

1	Aghabog	1871
2	Aughnamullan East	1857
3	Aughnamullan West	1841
4	Ballybay (Tullycorbet)	1862
5	Carrickmacross (see also Magheracloone)	1838
6	Castleblayney (Muckno)	1835
7	Clones	1821
8	Clontibret	1861
9	Donagh (Glasslough)	1836
10	Donaghmoyne	1863
11	Drumully	1845
12	Drumsnat & Kilmore	1836
13	Ematris (Rockcorry)	1848
14	Errigal Truagh	1835
15	Killany	1857
16	Killeevan (Newbliss)	1871
17	Mahgeracloone	1826
18	Monaghan & Rockwallis	1827
19	Tydavnet	1825
20	Tyholland	1827

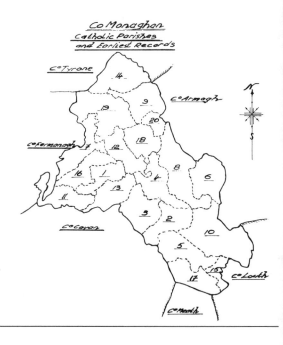

CLONFERT DIOCESE

3	Creagh	1820
4	Taghmaconnell	1842

ELPHIN DIOCESE

5	Aghanagh	1800
6	Ardcarne & Tumna (Cootehall)	1843
7	Athleague & Fuerty	1807
8	Ballintober & Ballymoe	1830
9	Boyle & Kilbryan	1792
10	Cloontuskert	1865
11	Dysart & Tisrara	1850
12	Elphin & Creeve	1808
13	Geevagh	1851
14	Kilbegnet & Glinsk	1836
15	Kilbride (Fourmilehouse)	1835
16	Kilcorkery & Frenchpark	1865
17	Kilglass & Rooskey	1865
18	Kilkeevan (Castlerea)	1804
19	Killukin & Killumod (Croghan)	1811
20	Kilmore & Aughrim	1816
21	Kilnamanagh & Estersnow	1859
22	Kiltoom (Ballybay)	1835
23	Loughglynn (Lisacul)	1817
24	Ogulla & Baslick	1864
25	Oran (Cloverhill)	1845*
26	Roscommon & Kilteevan	1820
27	St John's (Knockcroghery)	1841
28	St Peter's & Drum (Athlone)	1789
29	Strokestown	1830
30	Tarmonbarry	1865
31	Tibohine (Fairymount)	1833

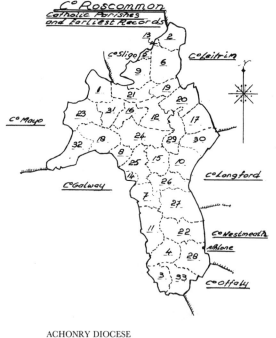

ACHONRY DIOCESE

1	Castlemore & Kilcolman	1830

ARDAGH & CLONMACNOISE DIOCESE

2	Kilronan (Arigna)	1823

TUAM DIOCESE

32	Kiltullagh	1860
33	Moore	1876

*Local custody only

Co Sligo
Catholic Parishes
and Earliest Records

Atlantic Ocean

Sligo Bay

Co Leitrim

Co Mayo

Co Roscommon

8 Kilfree & Killaraght		1844
9 Killoran		1846
10 Kilmacteigue		1845
11 Kilshalvey, Kilturra, Cloonoghill		1840

ARDAGH & CLONMACNOISE DIOCESE
12 Killenummery & Killery		1827

ELPHIN DIOCESE
13 Aghanagh (Ballinafad)		1800
14 Ahamlish		1796
15 Drumcliffe		1841
16 Geevagh		1851
17 Riverstown		1803
18 Sligo		1831*

KILLALA DIOCESE
19 Castleconnor		1835*
20 Easkey		1864
21 Kilglass		1825
22 Kilmacshalgan		1868
23 Kilmoremoy		1823
24 Skreen & Dromard		1817
25 Templeboy		1815

ACHONRY DIOCESE
1 Achonry		1865
2 Ballysadare & Kilvarnet		1842
3 Castlemore & Kilcolman		1830
4 Cloonacool		1859
5 Curry		1867
6 Drumrat		1842
7 Emlafad & Kilmorgan		1824

KILMORE DIOCESE
26 Glenade		1867
27 Kinlough		1835

*Earliest records in Sligo Heritage Centre

CASHEL & EMLY DIOCESE
1 Anacarty (Donohill)	1821
2 Ballingarry	1814
3 Bansha & Kilmoyler	1820
4 Boherlahan & Dualla	1810
5 Cashel	1793
6 Clerihan	1852
7 Clonoulty	1798*
8 Drangan	1811
9 Emly	1809
10 Fethard & Killusty	1806
11 Galbally & Aherlow	1809
12 Golden	1833
13 Killenaule	1742
14 Knockavilla	1834
15 Lattin & Cullen	1846
16 Mullinahone	1809
17 New Inn	1798
18 Oola & Solohead	1809
19 Tipperary	1793

WATERFORD & LISMORE DIOCESE
20 Ardfinnan	1809
21 Ballylooby	1828
22 Ballyneale	1839
23 Ballyporeen	1817
24 Cahir	1776
25 Carrick-on-Suir	1784
26 Clogheen	1778
27 Kilsheelan (Gambonsfield)	1840
28 Newcastle	1814
29 Powerstown	1808

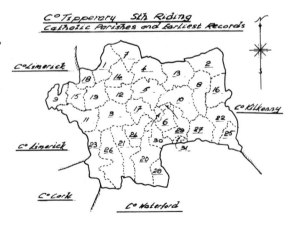

Co Tipperary Sth Riding
Catholic Parishes and Earliest Records

Co Limerick

Co Kilkenny

Co Limerick

Co Cork

Co Waterford

30 St Mary's, Clonmel	1790
31 SS Peter & Paul, Clonmel	1836

*Earliest records in local custody

CASHEL & EMLY DIOCESE

1	Ballina	1832
2	Ballinahinch	1839
3	Borrisoleigh	1814
4	Cappawhite	1804
5	Doon	1824
6	Drom & Inch	1809*
7	Gortnahoe	1805
8	Holycross (Ballycahill)	1835
9	Kilcommon	1813
10	Loughmore	1798
11	Moycarkey	1793
12	Newport	1795
13	Templemore	1807
14	Templetouhy & Moyne	1804
15	Thurles	1795
16	Upperchurch	1829

KILLALOE DIOCESE

17	Birr	1838
18	Borrisokane	1821
19	Castleconnell	1850
20	Castletownarra	1849
21	Cloughprior & Monsea	1834
22	Cloughjordan	1833
23	Couraganeen (Bournea)	1836
24	Dunkerrin (Moneygall)	1820
25	Kilbarron (Terryglass)	1827
26	Kilnaneave & Templederry	1839
27	Kyle & Knock	1845
28	Lorrha & Dorrha	1829
29	Nenagh	1792
30	Shinrone	1842

31	Silvermines (Kilmore)	1840
32	Toomevara	1830
33	Youghalarra	1820
34	Roscrea	1817

*Earliest records in local custody

Co Tipperary Nth Riding Catholic Parishes and Earliest Records

Co Galway

Offaly

Co Clare

Co Laois

Co Kilkenny

Co Limerick

Co Tipperary Sth Riding

Co Tyrone Catholic Parishes and Earliest Records

Co Derry

Co Donegal

Co Armagh

Co Monaghan

ARMAGH DIOCESE

1	Aghaloo	1832
2	Ardboe	1827
3	Artrea (Magherafelt)	1830
4	Ballinderry	1826
5	Ballintacker	1832
6	Clonfeacle (Moy)	1814
7	Clonoe	1806
8	Coagh	1865
9	Coalisland (see also Donaghenry)	1861
10	Cookstown (Desertcreat & Derryloran)	1827*
11	Donaghenry (Coalisland)	1822
12	Donaghmore (see Killeeshil)	1816
13	Dungannon	1783*
14	Errigal Kieran	1834*
15	Kildress	1835
16	Killeeshil	1816
17	Lissan	1822*
18	Pomeroy	1837
19	Termonmaguirk	1834

*Earliest records in Armagh Diocesan Archives

CLOGHER DIOCESE

20	Aghalurcher	1835
21	Clogher	1825
22	Donaghcavey	1857
23	Dromore	1833
24	Errigal Truagh	1835
25	Fivemiletown	1870
26	Kilskeery	1840

DERRY DIOCESE

27	Ardstraw East	1860
28	Ardstraw West	1843
29	Bodoney Lr	1865
30	Badoney Upr	1866
31	Camus (Strabane)	1773
32	Cappagh	1843
33	Donaghedy (Dunamanagh)	1854
34	Drumragh	1846
35	Langfield	1846
36	Learmount	1863
37	Leckpatrick (Strabane)	1863
38	Mourne (see also Camus)	1870
39	Termonamongan	1863
40	Urney	

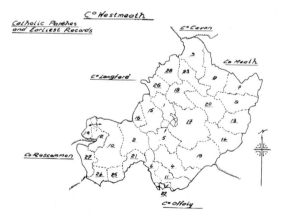

C° Waterford
Catholic Parishes and Earliest Records

C° Tipperary Sth Rd.

C° Kilkenny

C° Cork

9 Clashmore & Kinsalebeg			1810
10 Dungarvan			1787
11 Dunhill & Fenor			1829
12 Kilgobnet			1848
13 Kill (Rossmore)			1797
14 Kilrea (Dunmore East)			1780
15 Kilrossanty			1822
16 Kilsheelan (Gambonsfield)			1840
17 Knockanore			1816
18 Lismore			1820
19 Modeligo			1815*
20 Newcastle (Fourmilewater)			1814
21 Portlaw (Ballyduff)			1809
22 Rathgormuck (Mothel)			1831
23 Ring (Old Parish)			1813
24 St Mary's, Clonmel			1790
25 SS Peter & Paul, Clonmel			1829*
26 Stradbally (Ballylaneen)			1797*
27 Tallow			1797
28 Touraneena			1852
29 Tramore			1786
Waterford city:			
30	Ballybricken		1797
31	Holy Trinity		1729
32	St John's		1759
31	St Michael's		1732
31	St Patrick's		1731
31	St Peter's		1737
31	St Stephen's		1731

CLOYNE DIOCESE

1 Kilworth	1829

OSSORY DIOCESE

2 Slieverue	1766

WATERFORD & LISMORE DIOCESE

3 Abbeyside & Ring	1828
4 Aglish	1831*
5 Ardmore & Grange	1816*
6 Ballyduff	1849
7 Cappoquin	1807
8 Carrickbeg	1807

*Earliest records in Waterford Heritage Survey

MEATH DIOCESE

1 Ballinacargy	1837
2 Ballymore	1824
3 Castlepollard (Lickblea)	1763
4 Castletown-Geoghegan	1829
5 Churchtown (Dysart)	1825
6 Clara & Horseleap	1821
7 Clonmellon	1757
8 Collinstown	1784
9 Delvin	1785
10 Drumraney	1834
11 Kilbeggan	1818
12 Kilkenny West	1829
13 Killucan	1821
14 Kinnegad	1827
15 Milltown	1781
16 Moyvore	1831
17 Mullingar	1737
18 Multyfarnham	1824
19 Rochfortbridge	1816
20 Taghmon	1781
21 Tubber	1821
22 Tullamore	1801
23 Turbotstown	1777

ARDAGH & CLONMACNOISE DIOCESE

24 Lenmanaghan & Ballynahown	1821
25 Moate (Kilcleagh & Ballyloughloe)	1824*

C° Westmeath
Catholic Parishes and Earliest Records

C° Cavan

C° Longford

C° Meath

Co Roscommon

C° Offaly

26 Rathaspick & Russagh	1819
27 St Mary's Athlone	1813
28 Streete	1820

*Local custody only

DUBLIN DIOCESE

1	Arklow	1809

FERNS DIOCESE

2	Adamstown	1807
3	Ballagh (Oulart)	1825*
4	Ballycullane (Tintern)	1827
5	Ballindaggin	1871
6	Ballygarrett	1828
7	Ballymore (Mayglass)	1840
8	Ballyoughter	1810
9	Blackwater (Killilla)	1815
10	Bree	1837
11	Bunclody (Newtownbarry)	1834
12	Camolin	1853
13	Carrick-on-Bannow	1830
14	Castlebridge (Screen)	1832
15	Clongeen	1847
16	Cloughbawn	1816
17	Craanford & Ballymurrin	1856
18	Crossabeg	1856
19	Davidstown	1805
20	Enniscorthy	1794
21	Ferns	1819
22	Glinn	1817
23	Gorey	1845
24	Kilanerin	1852
25	Kilaveny & Annacorra	1800
26	Kilmore	1752
27	Kilrush & Askamore	1841
28	Lady's Island	1737
29	Litter	1789
30	Marshalstown	1854
31	Monageer (Boolavogue)	1838
32	Monamolin	1834
33	New Ross	1789
34	Old Ross (Cushinstown)	1759
35	Oylegate & Glenbrien	1803
36	Piercetown & Murrinstown	1811
37	Ramsgrange	1835

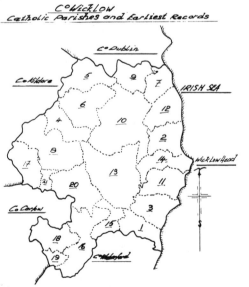

Co Wexford
Catholic Parishes and Earliest Records

38	Rathangan (Duncormuck)	1803
39	Rathnure & Templeludigan	1846
40	Suttons (Ballykelly)	1824
41	Taghmon	1801
42	Tagoat & Kilrane	1853
43	Templetown	1792
44	Tomacork (Carnew)	1785
45	Wexford	1671

KILDARE & LEIGHLIN DIOCESE

46	Borris	1782
47	Clonegal	1833
48	St Mullin's	1796

*Earliest records in local custody

Co Wicklow
Catholic Parishes and Earliest Records

DUBLIN DIOCESE

1	Arklow	1809
2	Ashford	1864
3	Avoca	1778
4	Ballymore Eustace	1779
5	Blessington	1852
6	Boystown (Valleymount)	1860
7	Bray	1800
8	Dunlavin	1815
9	Enniskerry	1825
10	Glendalough	1807
11	Kilbride & Barnderrig	1852
12	Kilquade & Kilmurry	1826
13	Rathdrum	1795
14	Wicklow	1747

FERNS DIOCESE

15	Kilaveny & Annacorra	1800
16	Tomacork (Carnew)	1785

KILDARE & LEIGHLIN DIOCESE

17	Baltinglass	1807
18	Clonmore	1813
19	Clonegal	1833
20	Hacketstown	1820
21	Rathvilly	1797

Introduction

The aim of this book is to provide a comprehensive guide for those who wish to trace their ancestors in Ireland. Because the individual circumstances of each family can be so different, the areas of research which may be relevant vary widely from case to case. None the less there are some areas which are important for the vast majority of people, and some which, though less widely relevant, can be extremely important in particular cases. This work is structured to reflect that division, with Part 1 examining the most basic sources, and Part 2 detailing those which have a narrower application. Part 3 then consists of a reference guide to permit quick access to a range of research materials, including county-by-county source lists, printed family histories, occupations and Church of Ireland records.

How the book is to be used depends very much on individual circumstances. For someone with no experience of genealogical research in Ireland, it would be best to start from this Introduction and work through Part 1, leaving Parts 2 and 3 until the basic materials have been exhausted. Someone who has already covered parish registers, land records, census returns and the state records of births, marriages and deaths may wish to start from Part 2. Others may simply want to use the reference guide. As anyone who regularly uses Irish records will know, however, one of the pleasures of research is the constant discovery of new sources of information, and new aspects of sources long thought to be familiar. The information in this book is the product of more than ten years of such discovery in the course of full-time professional research, and it is quite possible that even a hardbitten veteran will find something new in the account of the basic records given in Part 1.

WHERE TO START

The first question to ask before embarking on ancestral research is, 'What do I need to know before I start?' The answer, unhelpfully, is 'As much as possible'. Although, in the long term, the painstaking examination of original documents can provide much pleasure, in genealogy it is usually better to arrive than to travel hopefully. Theoretically it is of course possible to start from your own birth and work back through records of births, marriages and deaths, parish records and census records. In practical terms, however, the more that can be gleaned from older family members or from family documents the better; there is no point in combing through decades of parish records to uncover your great-grandmother's maiden name if you can find it out simply by asking Aunt Agatha. Nor does the information need to be absolutely precise. At this point quantity is more important than quality. Later on in the research, something that seemed relatively insignificant— the name of a local parish priest, a story of a contested will, someone's unusual occupation, even a postmark—may be a vital clue enabling you to follow the family further back. In any case, whether or not such information eventually turns out to be useful, it will certainly be of interest, helping to flesh out the picture of earlier generations. For most people, the spur to starting research is curiosity about their own family, and the kind of anecdotal information provided by the family itself rarely emerges from the documents.

To enable you to use the records to their fullest, three kinds of information are vital: *dates, names* and *places.* Dates of emigration, births, marriages and deaths; the names of parents, siblings, cousins, aunts, in-laws; addresses, townland names, parishes, towns, counties . . . Needless to say, not all of this is essential, and absolute accuracy is not vital to start out with. A general location and siblings' names can be used to uncover parents' names and addresses, and their parents' names. A precise name and a date can be used to unlock all the other records. Even the name alone, if it is sufficiently unusual, can sometimes be enough. In general, though, the single most useful piece of information is the precise locality of origin of the family. The county of origin would normally be the minimum information necessary, though in the case of a common surname (of which there are only too many), even this may not be enough. For the descendants of Irish emigrants, the locality is often one of the most difficult things to discover. There are ways of doing this, however, and the best time to do it is generally before starting research in Ireland. The Australian and American sources which are most useful for uncovering the locality of origin of Irish emigrants are detailed at the end of this Introduction.

The only cast-iron rule in carrying out research is that you should start from what you know and use that to find out more. Every family's circumstances are different, and where your research will lead you depends very much on where you start from. Thus, for example, knowing where a family lived around the turn of the century will allow you to uncover a census return with the ages of the individuals, leading to birth or baptismal records giving parent's names and residence, leading on in turn to early land records which may permit the identification of generations before the start of parish records. At each stage of such research, what the next step should be is determined by what you have found out. Each discovery is a stepping-stone to the next. Because of this it is simply not possible to lay down a route which will serve everyone. It is possible, however, to say that there is no point in taking, for example, a seventeenth-century pedigree and trying to extend it forward to connect with your family. Although there may very well be a connection, the only way to prove it is in expanding your own family information, working backwards.

WHAT YOU CAN EXPECT TO FIND

What you will uncover depends on the quality of the surviving records for the area and, again, on what you start out with. In the majority of cases, that is, for the descendants of Catholic tenant-farmers, the limit is generally the starting date of the local Catholic parish records, which varies widely from place to place. It would be unusual, however, for records of such a family to go back much earlier than the 1780s, and for most people the early 1800s is more likely to be the limit. In Gaelic culture, genealogy was of crucial importance, but the collapse of that culture in the seventeenth century and the subsequent impoverishment and oppression of the eighteenth century have left a gulf which is almost unbridgeable. This much said, exceptions immediately spring to mind. One Australian family, starting with only the name of their great-grandfather, his occupation and the date of his departure from Ireland, uncovered enough information through parish registers and state records of deaths, marriages and births to link him incontestably to the Garveys of Mayo, for whom an established pedigree is registered in the Genealogical Office stretching back to the twelfth century. Another family, American, knowing only a general location in Ireland and a marriage that took place before emigration, discovered that marriage in the pedigree of the McDermotts of Coolavin, which is factually verified as far back as the eleventh century. Discoveries like this are rare, however, and much likelier in the case of the Anglo-Irish than for those of Gaelic or Scots Presbyterian extraction.

Whatever the outcome, genealogical research offers pleasures and insights which are unique. The desire which drives it is simple and undeniable: it is the curiosity of the child who asks, 'Where did I come from?' All history starts from here, and genealogy is the most basic form of history, tracing the continual cycle of family growth and decay, uncovering the individual strands of relationship and experience which weave together to form the great patterns of historical change. Reconstructing the details of our own family history is a way of understanding, immediately and personally, the connection of the present with the past.

US SOURCES TO IDENTIFY IRISH PLACE OF ORIGIN

NATURALISATION RECORDS

These may contain the date and place of birth, occupation, place of residence, and the name of the ship on which the immigrant arrived. The records are still for the most part in the courts where the naturalisation proceedings took place. Some records are now in Federal Record Centres. Indexes for the states of Maine, Massachusetts, New Hampshire and Rhode Island before 1906, are available at the National Archives, Washington.

CEMETERY AND BURIAL RECORDS

There are two kinds of potentially valuable records: gravestone inscriptions and sextons' records. These vary enormously in usefulness, but may sometimes specify the exact place of origin.

IMMIGRATION RECORDS AND PASSENGER LISTS

The largest single collection is in the National Archives in Washington. The Customs Passenger Lists, dating from 1820, usually give only the country of origin. The Immigration Passenger Lists, from 1883, include details of the last place of residence.

PRINTED OBITUARIES

Around the turn of the century it became common practice to have an obituary printed in a local newspaper, particularly if a senior member of the family died. These are often useful for the information they give regarding the place of origin of the deceased.

MILITARY RECORDS

There are two kinds of records of possible value: service records and veterans' records. Depending on the date and branch of service, these may specify the place or country of origin. See *Guide to Genealogical Records in the National Archives* by Meredith S. Colket, Jnr and Frank E. Bridges (1964).

CHURCH RECORDS

Depending on the date, these can provide a great deal of information on baptisms, marriages and deaths. In particular, the marriages of newly arrived immigrants may specify precise places of origin. Most Catholic records are still in the parishes and, in most cases, only the priest may search them. For other denominations, records may be in local custody or deposited with a variety of record-holding institutions, including public libraries, universities and diocesan archives.

OTHER SOURCES

Vital records and census records are of great genealogical interest, but only rarely give the Irish place of origin. See Val. D. Greenwood's *The Researcher's Guide to American Genealogy* (Baltimore, 1973). Directories and local histories published by subscription sometimes give full information about the subscribers' families. See Clarence S. Peterson's *Consolidated Bibliography of County Histories in Fifty States in 1961* (Baltimore, 1963). Land records are held both federally and locally, and wills are mostly registered in the counties where they are probated.

CANADIAN SOURCES TO IDENTIFY IRISH PLACE OF ORIGIN

NATIONAL AND PROVINCIAL ARCHIVES

The vast bulk of information of genealogical interest can be found in the National and Provincial Archives of Canada, which are familiar with the needs of genealogical research and very helpful. The National Archives, 395 Wellington Street, Ottawa ON K1A ON3 (Tel. 613-995-5138) publishes a useful twenty-page booklet, *Tracing Your Ancestors in Canada*, which is available by post. Some of the information held in the Provincial Archives, in particular the census records, is also to be found in Ottawa, but in general the Provincial Archives have a broader range of information relating to their particular areas.

CIVIL RECORDS

In general the original registers of births, marriages and deaths, which have widely varying starting dates, are to be found in the offices of the Provincial Registrars General, although microfilm copies of some may also be found in Provincial Archives.

CENSUS RECORDS

Country-wide censuses are available for 1851, 1861, 1871, 1881 and 1891. There are, however, many local returns available for earlier years which record a wide variety of information. The largest collection is in the Ottawa National Archives.

OTHER SOURCES

Cemetery and burial records, passenger lists, Church registers and land records may all be of value. The best comprehensive guide is in Angus Baxter's *In search of your Canadian roots* (Baltimore, 1989), which gives details of a wide range of records to be found in the National and Provincial Archives.

AUSTRALIAN SOURCES TO IDENTIFY IRISH PLACE OF ORIGIN

CONVICT TRANSPORTATION RECORDS

There are very comprehensive records relating to convict transportees, originals in possession of Australian archives, microfilm copies of the British Public Record Office records, and Dublin Castle records of those transported from Ireland to Australia, which were computerised and presented to Australia as part of the Bicentennial celebrations of 1988. These last often include details of the conviction and place of residence, and are widely available, with copies in the National Library in Canberra and the genealogical library of Kiama, New South Wales, to name only two repositories.

IMMIGRATION RECORDS

Records of free and assisted immigration are less extensive than convict records, but are substantial. Material dealing with the period before 1901 is held in the State Archives Offices in the various state capitals, with the principal repositories being the New South Wales Archives Office, the Archives Section of the State Library of Victoria, and the J. S. Battye Library of Western Australia. See the NSW State Archives' *Guide to Shipping and Free Passenger Lists*.

CIVIL RECORDS

Civil registration of all births, deaths and marriages became compulsory at different times in the different colonies, as they then were. The information supplied is variable, in the early years in particular, but can include a great deal of secondary material that is very useful, including very often precise places of origin. The original registers and indexes are to be found in the Registrar-General's Offices of the states. These Offices sometimes also have copies of earlier Church registers.

CENSUS RECORDS

The earliest true census took place in 1828, in New South Wales, and has now been published in full. Earlier convict musters also exist. Because of the history of the creation of the various states, the best single records repository for early census returns remains the New South Wales Archives Office.

PART 1

MAJOR SOURCES

1

Civil Records

State registration of non-Catholic marriages began in Ireland in 1845. All births, deaths and marriages have been registered in Ireland since 1864. In order to appreciate what precisely these records consist of, it is necessary to have some idea at least of how registration began. It was, in fact, an offshoot of the Victorian public health system, in turn based on the Poor Law, an attempt to provide some measure of relief for the most destitute. Between 1838 and 1852, 163 workhouses were built throughout the country, each at the centre of an area known as a Poor Law Union. The workhouses were normally situated in a large market town, and the Poor Law Union comprised the town and its catchment area, with the result that the Unions in many cases ignored the existing boundaries of parishes and counties. This had consequences for research which we shall see later. In the 1850s a large-scale public health system was created, based on the areas covered by the Poor Law Unions. Each Union was divided into Dispensary Districts, with an average of six to seven Districts per Union, and a Medical Officer, normally a doctor, was given responsibility for public health in each District. When the registration of all births, deaths and marriages then began in 1864, these Dispensary Districts also became Registrars' Districts, with a Registrar responsible for collecting the registrations within each District. In most cases the Medical Officer for the Dispensary District now also acted as the Registrar for the same area, but not in every case. The superior of this local Registrar was the Superintendent Registrar responsible for all the Registers within the old Poor Law Union. The return for the entire Poor Law Union (also known both as the Superintendent Registrar's District and, simply, the Registration District) were indexed and collated centrally, and master indexes for the entire country were produced at the General Register Office in Dublin. These are the indexes which are now used for public research.

Because of the history of the system, responsibility for registration still rests with the Department of Health. The arrangement at present is that the local Health Boards hold the original registers, with the General Register Office, at 8–11 Lombard St, Dublin 2, holding the master indexes to all thirty-two counties up to 1921, and to the twenty-six counties of the Republic of Ireland after that date. For Northern Ireland, from 1921, the indexes and registers are held at Oxford House, Chichester St, Belfast.

As well as the master indexes for the entire country, the General Register Office also contains microfilm copies of all the original registers, and is the only part of the registration system which permits public research. The indexes are available to the public on the first floor of 8 Lombard St, at a fee of £1.50 per five years searched, or £12 for a general search. It is important to note that only the indexes are open to the public; to obtain the full information contained in the original register entry, it is necessary to purchase a printout from the microfilm, at £1.50 per entry. These printouts are supplied for information only, and have no legal standing. Full certificates, for use in obtaining passports or in testamentary transactions, cost £5.50. Limited research, covering five years of the indexes, is carried out by the staff in response to postal queries only, for the same fee, £5.50.

INFORMATION GIVEN

One of the peculiarities of the system of registration is that, although the local Registrars were responsible for the Registers themselves, the legal obligation to register births, deaths and marriages actually rested with the public, and was enforced with hefty fines. The classes of people required to carry out registration in each of the three categories is given in what follows, along with a detailed account of the information they were required to supply. It should be remembered that not all of this information is relevant to genealogical research.

Births

Persons required to register births were:
1. the parent or parents, or in the case of death or inability of the parent or parents:
2. the occupier of the house or tenement in which the child was born; or
3. the Nurse; or
4. any person present at the birth of the child.

The information they were required to supply was:
1. the date and place of birth;
2. the name (if any);
3. the sex;
4. the name, surname and dwelling place of the father;
5. the name, surname, maiden surname and dwelling place of the mother;
6. the rank, profession or occupation of the father.

The informant and the Registrar were both required to sign each entry, which was also to include the date of registration, the residence of the informant and his or her 'qualification' (for example, 'present at birth'). Notice to the Registrar of the birth was to be given within twenty-one days, and full details within three months. It should be noted that it was not obligatory to register a first name for the child. The very small proportion for which no first name was supplied appear in the index as, for example, 'Kelly (male)' or 'Murphy (female)'.

Deaths

Persons required to register deaths were:
1. some person present at death; or
2. some person in attendance during the last illness of the deceased; or
3. the occupier of the house or tenement where the death took place; or
4. someone else residing in the house or tenement where the death took place; or
5. any person present at, or having knowledge of the circumstances of, the death.

The information they were required to supply was:
1. the date and place of death;
2. the name and surname of the deceased;
3. the sex of the deceased;
4. the condition of the deceased as to marriage;
5. the age of the deceased at last birthday;
6. the rank, profession or occupation of the deceased;
7. the certified cause of death and the duration of the final illness.

Again, the informant and the Registrar were both required to sign each entry, which was also to include the date of registration, the residence of the informant and his or her 'qualification' (for example, 'present at death'). Notice to the Registrar of the death was to be given within seven days, and full details within fourteen days.

INDEX to BIRTHS REGISTERED in IRELAND in 1866.

District.	Vol.	Page
....	7	411
....	18	328
....	20	266
....	6	991
...lin. Lisburn	1	659
....	17	715
....	11	893
rth	7	572
....	5	140
....	11	212
....	20	104
....	11	782
....	7	937
....	7	732
....	3	447
...erick	20	432
....	19	500
....	14	82
....	14	476
....	10	128
....	6	178
North	7	549
....	15	394
....	20	154
....	10	735
....	2	728
....	11	112
....	6	613
....	14	376
....	1	173
....	3	701
...thdown	17	889
....	5	232
....	1	264
H. Parsonstown	18	599
...atrick	11	531
....	11	834
....	2	483
....	17	386
....	7	655
blin, South	17	622
....	10	665
South	7	672
....	16	281
....	12	892
....	2	750
....	15	244
k	20	179
....	14	905
....	9	950
....	19	655
r	9	379
rth	7	571
....	11	82
South	7	813
....	1	757
im, North	2	690
...agh	11	82
....	8	503
....	17	38
im, North	2	630
North	12	547
....	1	838
....	16	788
....	11	43
...es	9	871
....	5	175

Name and Registration District.	Vol.	Page
PELL, John Joseph. Dublin, North	12	584
PELLETT, Anna Maria. Dublin, South	12	656
PELLICAN, John. Listowel	10	500
PELLY, Catherine. Ballinasloe	19	37
—— Catherine Evangiline. Dublin, South	2	745
—— John Joseph. Dublin, South	2	737
—— Mary. Portumna	14	946
PEMBERTON, Marian Sydney. Dublin, North	17	527
—— (female). Dublin, South	7	811
PEMBROKE, Ellen. Tralee	20	627
—— Ellen. Tralee	15	596
—— Margaret. Kilkenny	8	603
—— Mary. Dingle	15	207
—— Mary Eliza. Kilkenny	3	609
—— Patrick. Listowel	10	501
PENDER, Anne. Enniscorthy	14	725
—— Bernard. Carrick-on-Shannon	18	65
—— Bridget. Enniscorthy	4	814
—— Bridget. Enniscorthy	9	753
—— Daniel. Gorey	7	876
—— Daniel. Gorey	7	877
—— Elizabeth. Nenagh	3	651
—— Elizabeth. Carlow	13	447
—— Ellen. Ballymoney	6	194
—— Ellen. Rathdown	12	920
—— Ellen. Enniscorthy	19	764
—— James. Waterford	9	951
—— John. Carlow	8	507
—— John. Enniscorthy	14	722
—— John. Mullingar	13	317
—— Joseph. Athy	13	406
—— Laurance. Carlow	13	436
—— Mary. Wexford	14	911
—— Mary Anne. Carlow	3	505
—— Mary Catherine. Carlow	18	427
—— Mathew. Wexford	14	910
—— Michael. Carlow	3	494
—— Peter. Rathdrum	2	1061
—— Thomas. Ballinasloe	19	31
—— William. Waterford	19	925
—— (female). Limerick	10	454
PENDERGAST, Anne. Roscommon	18	333
—— Bridget. Tulla	19	606
—— Catherine. Swineford	4	579
—— Ellen. Castlereagh	19	161
—— Margaret. Castlereagh	19	162
—— Margaret. Killarney	5	400
—— Mary. Bawnboy	3	51
—— Mary. Castlebar	19	133
—— Myles. Wexford	19	935
—— Pat. Ballinrobe	4	51
—— Patrick. Rathdown	17	891
—— Patrick. Monaghan	8	330
PENDERGAST, Anne. New Ross	4	969
—— Ellen. Killarney	15	315
—— Michael. Killarney	15	316
PENDERS, Mary. Nenagh	13	584
PENDLETON, Essie. Lurgan	16	673
PENGELLY, Michael James. Cork	20	193
PENNAFATHER, (male). Rathkeale	10	621
PENNAMEN, Mary Jane Fraser. Belfast	11	277
PENNEFATHER, John Thomas. Dublin, North	2	608
—— Richard Dymock. Cashel	3	531
PENNELL, (male). Cork	15	101
PENNINGTON, Charles. Banbridge	16	229
PENNY, John. Ballymena	11	113
—— (male). Wexford	14	922

Name and Reg...		
PERCY, Robert Henry		
—— William. Antrin		
PERDUE, John. Calla...		
—— Mary Anne. Tip...		
PERIL, Patrick. Gort...		
PERKINS, Cornelius.		
—— Joseph John. D...		
—— Patrick. Naas ...		
—— Robert Henry.		
—— Thomas. Ought...		
—— (female). Ballin...		
PERKINSON, Barkly. A...		
PERKISSON, Briget. T...		
PERRILL, Patrick. Cli...		
PERRIN Ellen. Dublin...		
—— Henrietta. Rath...		
—— William Alexande...		
—— (female). Cavan...		
PERROT, Catherine. D...		
—— Sarah. Clonakilt...		
PERROTT, Margaret.		
—— Robert. Cork ...		
—— William Cooke C...		
—— William Thomas.		
PERRY, Agnes. Belfas...		
—— Agnes. Lisburn ...		
—— Angelina Margare...		
—— Ann. Downpatri...		
—— Ann Jane. Bally...		
—— Anthony. Ennis...		
—— Catherine. Balti...		
—— Eliza. Ballymah...		
—— Eliza. Naas		
—— Eliza. Belfast ...		
—— Elizabeth. Bally...		
—— Elizabeth. Larn...		
—— Ellen. Ballymen...		
—— Etheld Letitia. ...		
—— Hannah. Larne...		
—— Helena Jane. L...		
—— Henry. Newry ...		
—— James. Dundalk...		
—— James. Dublin, ...		
—— James. Baltingl...		
—— Jane. Banbridge...		
—— Jane Eleanor. B...		
—— John. Lisburn ...		
—— John. Naas		
—— Joseph. Ballym...		
—— Letitia Anne. D...		
—— Martin. Newtow...		
—— Mary. Ballymah...		
—— Mary Anne. Ba...		
—— Rebecca. Ballyn...		
—— Robinson Gale. ...		
—— Sarah. Downpa...		
—— Sarah. Newtow...		
—— Sarah. Ballyme...		
—— Susanna. Down...		
—— Thomas. Trim ...		
—— Thomas. Belfast...		
—— Thomas Shanklin...		
—— William. Tippe...		
—— William Gardine...		
—— William Richard...		
—— William Robinso...		
—— (male). Clonm...		

Marriages

From 1864 any person whose marriage was to be celebrated by a Catholic clergyman was required to have the clergyman fill out a certificate containing the information detailed below, and forward it within three days of the marriage to the Registrar. In practice, as had already been the case for non-Catholic marriages from 1845, the clergyman simply kept blank copies of these certificates, filled them in after the ceremony and forwarded them to the registrar. It is still important to remember, though, that legal responsibility for the registration actually rested with the parties marrying, not the clergyman.

The information to be supplied was:
1. the date when married;
2. the names and surnames of each of the parties marrying;
3. their respective ages;
4. their condition (i.e. bachelor, spinster, widow, widower);
5. their rank, profession or occupation;
6. their residences at the time of marriage;
7. the name and surname of the fathers of each of the parties;
8. the rank, profession or occupation of the fathers of each of the parties.

The certificate was to state where the ceremony had been performed, and to be signed by the clergyman, the parties marrying, and two witnesses.

GENEALOGICAL RELEVANCE

From a genealogical point of view, only the following information is of genuine interest:

BIRTHS
The name, the date of birth, the place of birth; the name, surname and dwelling place of the father; the name, surname and dwelling place of the mother; and, occasionally, the name, residence and qualification of the informant.

MARRIAGES
Parish in which the marriage took place; names, ages, residences and occupations of the persons marrying; names and occupations of their fathers.

DEATHS
Place of death, age at death and, occasionally, the name, residence and qualification of the informant.

Of the three categories, the most useful is probably the marriage entry, both because it provides fathers' names, thus giving a direct link to the preceding generation, and because it is the easiest to identify from the indexes, as we shall see later. Birth entries are much more difficult to identify correctly from the indexes without precise information about date and place, and even with such information, the high concentrations of people of the same surname within particular localities of the country can make it difficult to be sure that a particular birth registration is the relevant one. Unlike many other countries, death records in Ireland are not very useful for genealogical purposes; there was no obligation to record family information, and the 'age at death' is often very imprecise. This much said, these records can sometimes be of value. The 'person present at death' was often a family member, and the relationship is sometimes specified in the register entry. Even the age recorded may be useful, since it at least gives an idea of how old the person was thought to be by family or neighbours.

A general word of warning about civil registration is necessary: a certain proportion of all three categories simply went unregistered. It is impossible to be sure how much is not there, since the thoroughness of local registration depended very much on local conditions and on the individuals responsible, but experience in cross-checking from other sources such as parish and census records suggests that as much as 10 to 15 per cent of marriages and births simply do not appear in the registers.

RESEARCH IN THE INDEXES

In carrying out research in all three areas, a large measure of scepticism is necessary with regard to the dates of births, marriages and deaths reported by family members before 1900. This is especially true for births: the ages given in census returns, for example, are almost always inaccurate, and round figures—50, 60, 70—should be treated with particular caution. The true date of birth is almost always well before the one reported, sometimes by as much as fifteen years. Why this should be so is a matter for speculation, but it seems unlikely that vanity or mendacity were to blame. It would appear more probable that, up to the start of this century, very few people actually knew their precise date of birth. Since, at least after middle age, almost no one feels as old as they actually are, a guess will usually produce an underestimate. Whatever the explanation, charitable or otherwise, it is always wiser to search a range of the indexes before the reported date, rather than after.

From 1864 to 1877 the indexes consist of a single yearly volume in each category—births, marriages and deaths—covering the entire country and recording all names in a straightforward alphabetical arrangement. The same arrangement also applies to the non-Catholic marriages registered from 1845. From 1878 the yearly volume is divided into four quarters, with each quarter covering three months and indexed separately. This mean that a search for a name in, for example, the 1877 births index means looking in one place in the index, while it is necessary to check four different places in the 1878 index, one in each of the four quarters. From 1903, in the case of births only, the indexes once again cover the entire year, and only from this year also supply the mother's maiden surname. In all three categories each index entry gives surname, first name, registration district, volume and page number. The deaths indexes also give the reported age at death. The 'volume and page number' simply make up the reference for the original register entry, necessary in order to obtain a photocopy of the full information given in that entry. The remaining three items, surname, first name and registration district, are dealt with in detail below.

SURNAME

The order followed in the indexes is strictly alphabetical, but it is always necessary to keep possible variants of the surname in mind. In the late nineteenth century, when a large majority of the population was illiterate, the precise spelling of their surname was a matter of indifference to most people. Thus members of the same family may be registered as, for example, Kilfoyle, Gilfoyle or Guilfoile. The question of variants is particularly important for names beginning with 'O' or 'Mac'. Until the start of the Gaelic Revival at the end of the last century, these prefixes were treated as entirely optional and, in the case of the 'O's particularly, more often omitted than included. Until well into the twentieth century, for instance, almost all of the O'Briens are recorded under 'Brien' or 'Bryan'. Before starting a search in the indexes, therefore, it is essential to have as clear an idea as possible of the variants to be checked. Otherwise it may be necessary to cover the same period as many as three or four times.

FIRST NAME

Among the vast majority of the population, the range of first names in use in the nineteenth century was severely limited. Apart from some localised names—'Cornelius' in south Munster, 'Crohan' in the Caherdaniel area of the Iveragh Peninsula, 'Sabina' in the east Galway/north Roscommon area— the anglicisation of the earlier Gaelic names was restrictive and unimaginative. John, Patrick, Michael, Mary and Bridget occur with almost unbelievable frequency in all parts of the country. Combined with the intensely local nature of surnames, reflecting the earlier tribal areas of the country, this can present intense difficulties when using the indexes. For example, a single quarter of 1881, from January to March, might contain twenty or more John (O')Reilly (or Riley) registrations, all in the same registration district of Co. Cavan. A further obstacle is the fact that it is very rare for more than one first name to be registered. Thus someone known to the family as John James (O')Reilly will almost certainly appear in the index as a simple John. It is of course possible to purchase photocopies of all the original register entries, but unless some other piece of information such as the parents' names or the townland address can be used to cross-check, it will almost certainly not be possible to identify which, if any, of the original register entries is the relevant one. This uncertainty is compounded still further by the persistent imprecision regarding ages and dates of birth, which means that over the seven- or eight-year period when the relevant birth could have taken place, there might be fifty or sixty births of the same name in the one county. One way to surmount the problem, if the precise district is known, is to examine the original registers themselves to build a picture of all families in which the relevant name occurs. As already mentioned, the originals are still kept in the local registrars' offices. Although the situation varies from district to district, people visiting the offices in person are usually allowed to examine the original books. The relevant addresses can be found in local telephone directories, under the Health Board. Even in the country-wide indexes, however, despite all of these problems, there are a number of ways in which the births indexes can be used successfully, by narrowing the area and period to be searched with information obtained from other sources, as we shall see.

REGISTRATION DISTRICT

As a result of the original arrangements for administering the system, the registration districts used were, and still are, largely identical with the old Poor Law Unions. Since these were based on natural catchment areas, normally consisting of a large market town and its rural hinterland, rather than on the already existing administrative divisions of townland, parish and county, registration districts for births, marriages and deaths cut right across these earlier boundaries, a fact which can be very significant for research. Thus, for example, Waterford registration district, centred in the town of Waterford, also takes in a large part of rural south Co. Kilkenny. The only comprehensive guide to which towns and townlands are contained in each registration district is to be found in a series of pamphlets produced in the nineteenth century by the Registrar-General's Office for the use of each of the local registrars. These are collected as *Townlands in Poor-law Unions*, copies of which can be found in the National Library (reference: Ir. 9141 b 35) or in the reading room of the National Archives. This is particularly useful when a problem arises identifying a variant version of a townland name given in the original register entry for a marriage, birth or death. By scanning the lists of townlands in the relevant district in which the entry is recorded, it is almost always possible to identify the standard version of the name and, from this, go on to census, parish and land records. To go in the other direction, to find out what registration district a particular town or townland is in, the standard source is the *Alphabetical Index to the Towns, Townlands and Parishes of*

Ireland. Three editions of this were published, based on the census returns for 1851, 1871 and 1901. In the first two, the registration district is recorded as the Poor Law Union; in the 1901 Index it does not appear in the body of the work, but may be found as an appendix. Copies of these can be found on open access in the National Library, the National Archives, the General Register Office itself or in any library. If the original townland or address of the family being researched is known, and the search narrowed to a single registration district, then some at least of the problems picking out the relevant entry, in the births indexes particularly, can be significantly reduced.

RESEARCH TECHNIQUES

BIRTHS

As pointed out above, it is important to approach the birth indexes with as much information as possible from other sources. If the birth took place between 1864 and 1880, the family was Catholic and the relevant area known, it may be best to try to identify a baptism from parish records first, and in many cases, if information rather than a certificate is the aim of the research, the parish record itself will be enough. If the area is known, but not the date, it may be useful to search the 1901 and 1911 census returns to obtain at least an approximate age and, hence, date of birth. If the names of siblings and the order of their birth are known, but the area and date are not, it may be necessary to search a wide range of years in the indexes, noting all births of the names which occur in the family, and then try to work out which births of the relevant names occur in the right order in the same registration district. If the name is unusual enough, of course, none of this may be necessary. In Ireland, however, few of us are lucky enough to have an ancestor called Horace Freke-Blood or Euphemia Thackaberry.

MARRIAGES

As long as care is taken over the question of surname variants, and the names of both parties are known, research in the marriage indexes is straight-forward. If two people married each other, then obviously the registration district, volume and page number references for them in the indexes have to be the same. It is simply necessary to cross-check the two names in the indexes, working back from the approximate date of birth of the eldest child if this is known, until two entries are found in which all three references correspond. Marriage records are especially important in the early years of civil registration, since they record the names of the fathers of people born *c*.1820 to *c*.1840, as well as their approximate ages, thus providing evidence which can be used to establish earlier generations in parish records. For non-Catholic families, the value of these records is even greater, since the records of non-Catholic marriages start in 1845.

DEATHS

As in the case of births, it is essential to uncover as much information as possible from other sources before starting a search of the death indexes. Thus, if a date of birth is known from parish or other records, the 'age at death' given in the index along with the registration district provides at least a rough guide as to whether or not the death recorded is the relevant one. If the location of a family farm is known, the approximate date of death can often be worked out from the changes in occupier recorded in the Valuation Books of the Land Valuation Office (see Chapter 4). Similarly, if the family possessed property, the Will Calendars of the National Archives after 1858 (see Chapter 5) can be the easiest way to pin-point the precise date of death. With such information, it is then usually a simple matter to pick out the relevant entry from the indexes. Information from a marriage entry may also sometimes be useful: along with the names of the fathers of the parties marrying, the register entry sometimes also specifies that one or both of the fathers is deceased. There is no rule about this, however. The fact that a father is recorded as, say, 'John Murphy, labourer', does not necessarily mean that he was alive at the time of the marriage. If an individual is recorded as deceased, this does at least provide an end-point for any search for his death entry. As already pointed out, however, death records give no information on preceding generations, and only occasionally name a surviving family member.

LIVING RELATIVES

It is very difficult to use the records of the General Register Office to trace descendants, rather than forebears, of a particular family. As pointed out above, the birth indexes after 1902 do record the mother's maiden name as well as the name and surname of the child, so that it may be possible to trace all the births of a particular family from that date forward. Uncovering the subsequent marriages of those children without knowing the names of their spouses is a much harder proposition, however. To take one example, the likely range of years of marriage for a Michael O'Brien born in 1905 would be 1925 to 1940; there are certainly hundreds of marriages recorded in the indexes under that name. One could, of course, purchase copies of all the original register entries in the hope that one entry might show the relevant address and father's name, and then investigate births of that marriage, but in most cases the work involved makes the task impracticable. There are, however, other ways of tracking descendants through land, census, voters' and, sometimes, parish records (Chapters 2, 3 and 4).

LATE REGISTRATIONS, ARMY RECORDS, ETC.

LATE REGISTRATIONS

A significant proportion of all births, marriages and deaths were simply not registered, as mentioned above. When the individuals concerned or their relatives later needed a certificate for official purposes, it became necessary to register the event. The index references for these late registrations are included in the volume for the year in which the event took place. Thus, for example, the index reference for someone born in 1880, but whose birth was not registered until 1900, is to be found in the index for 1880. In the case of births and deaths, these references are indexed separately from the main body of the index, at the back of the volume. For marriages, late registrations are written in by hand at the relevant point in the main body of the index. Although the chances of finding a missing registration among these is quite slim, it is still necessary to include them in any thorough search of the indexes.

MARITIME RECORDS

From 1864 up to the present, the General Register Office has kept a separate 'Marine Register' of births and deaths of Irish subjects which took place at sea. From 1886 only, a printed index to this register is bound into the back of the births and death index for each year. For earlier registers, the indexes have to be requested from the staff in the Office. No separate register was kept for marriages at sea.

ARMY RECORDS

The Births, Deaths and Marriages (Army) Act of 1879 required these events to be registered with the Office of the Registrar-General in Dublin, where they affected Irish subjects serving in the British Army abroad. Separate indexes bound into the back of the main yearly indexes start from 1888 and continue until 1930 for births, and 1931 for marriages and deaths. The deaths index for 1902 also contains an index to 'Deaths of Irish Subjects pertaining to the South African War (1898–1902)'.

THE FOREIGN REGISTER

From 1864 the General Register Office was required to keep a separate register of births of Irish subjects abroad, where such birth were notified to the relevant British consul. There is no index to this register, which is small, and is not available in the public research room. It may be requested from the staff of the Office.

THE SCHULZE REGISTER

The General Register Office also holds the 'General Index to Baptisms and Marriages purported to have been celebrated by the Rev. J. G. F. Schulze,

1806–1837'. This records 55 baptisms and *c.*8,000 marriages celebrated in Dublin by this clergyman, without a licence. When some of the marriages were later challenged in court, they were held to be legal, and the volume was acquired by the Register Office. The bulk of the marriages, celebrated at the German Lutheran Church in Poolbeg St, Dublin, are for the years 1825 to 1837, and record only the names of the contracting parties.

USING CIVIL RECORDS WITH OTHER SOURCES

Some of the areas in which information from other sources may be used to simplify research in civil records have already been outlined. What follows is an expanded guide to the ways in which civil records can supplement or be supplemented by those other sources.

BIRTHS

Ages recorded in 1901 and 1911 census returns (see Chapter 2) can be used to narrow the range of years to be searched. If the birth registration is uncovered first, it records the precise residence of the parents, which can then lead to the relevant census returns, providing fuller information on other members of the family.

MARRIAGES

The 1911 census records the number of years a couple have been married, the number of children born and the number of those children still living. This information is obviously very useful in narrowing the range of years to be searched for a particular marriage. In the case of names which are common in a particular area, the fathers' names supplied in the marriage record are often the only firm evidence with which to identify the relevant baptismal record in the parish registers. Once a marriage has been located in civil records, thus showing the relevant parish, it is always worthwhile to check the church record of the same marriage. As church marriage registers were standardised from the 1860s on, they became more informative, in many cases supplying the names, addresses and occupations of both the mother and father of the parties marrying. In the case of most Dublin Catholic parishes, this information is recorded from around 1856.

DEATHS

The records of the Land Valuation Office (Chapter 4), or the testamentary records of the National Archives (Chapter 5) can be used to pin-point the year of death, thus making a successful search more likely. The place of death given, if it is not the home of the deceased person, may be the home of a relative. This can be investigated firstly through land records (Chapter 4), and then through parish and census records, and may provide further information on other branches of the family.

2

Census Records

1. COUNTRY-WIDE

Full government censuses were taken of the whole island in 1821, 1831, 1841, 1851, 1861, 1871, 1901 and 1911. The first four, for 1821, 1831, 1841 and 1851 were largely destroyed in 1922 in the fire at the Public Record Office; surviving fragments are detailed below. Those for 1861 and 1871 were completely destroyed earlier by order of the government. This means that the earliest surviving comprehensive returns are for 1901 and 1911. Because of this the normal rule that census returns should not be available to the public for 100 years has been suspended in the Republic of Ireland, and the original returns can be consulted in the National Archives. (Absurdly, although the original returns for the six northern counties of Antrim, Armagh, Derry, Down, Fermanagh and Tyrone are freely available in the south, copies of these returns held in the Public Record Office of Northern Ireland will not be open to the public until 2001 and 2011.)

1901 and 1911

A. INFORMATION GIVEN
Although these returns are obviously very late for most purposes, the information they contain can still be extremely useful. The 1901 returns record the following:
➢ name;
➢ relationship to the head of the household;
➢ religion;
➢ literacy;
➢ occupation;
➢ age;
➢ marital status;
➢ county of birth;
➢ ability to speak English or Irish.

The returns also record details of the houses, giving the number of rooms, outhouses and windows, and the type of roof. Members of the family not present when the census was taken are not given. The same information was collected in 1911, with one important addition: married women were required to state the number of years they had been married, the number of children born alive and the number of children still living. Unfortunately widows were not required to give this information, although a good number obliged in any case. Only the initials, not the full names, of policemen and inmates of mental hospitals are recorded.

B. USES

(i)   *Age.* The most obviously useful information given in 1901 and 1911 is age. Unfortunately this is also the information which needs to be treated with the most caution. Very few of the ages given in the two sets of returns actually match precisely. In the decade between the two censuses, most people appear to have aged significantly more than ten years. Of the two, 1901 seems to be the less accurate, with widespread underestimation of age. None the less, if used with caution the returns do provide a rough guide to age which can help to narrow the range of years to be searched in earlier civil records of births, marriages and deaths, or in parish records.

(ii)   *Location.* When the names of all or most of the family are known, along with the general area, but not the precise locality, it is possible to search all the returns for that area to identify the relevant family and thus pinpoint them. This can be particularly useful when the surname is very common; the likelihood of two families of Murphys in the same area repeating all of the children's names is slight.

(iii)   *Cross-checking.* At times, again when a name is common, it is impossible to be sure from information uncovered in civil or parish records that a particular family is the relevant one. In such cases, when details of the subsequent history of the family are known—dates of death or emigration, or siblings' names, for instance—a check of the 1901 or 1911 census for the family can provide useful circumstantial evidence. More often than not, any certainties produced will be negative, but the elimination of fake trails is a vital part of any research. An illustration will show why: Peter Barry, born Co. Cork *c.*1880, parents unknown, emigrated to the US in 1897. A search of civil birth records shows four Peter Barrys recorded in the county between 1876 and 1882, with no way of distinguishing which, if any, is the relevant one. A search of the 1901 census returns for the addresses given in the four birth entries shows two of the four still living there. These can now be safely eliminated, and research concentrated on the other two families.

CENSUS OF IRELAND, 1901.

(Two Examples of the mode of filling up this Table are given on the other side.)

FORM A.

RETURN of the MEMBERS of this FAMILY and their VISITORS, BOARDERS, SERVANTS, &c., who slept or abode in this House on the night of SUNDAY, the 31st of MARCH, 1901.

No. on Form B. _9_

Number.	NAME and SURNAME.	RELATION to Head of Family	RELIGIOUS PROFESSION.	EDUCATION	AGE	SEX	RANK, PROFESSION, OR OCCUPATION.	MARRIAGE	WHERE BORN	IRISH LANGUAGE	If Deaf and Dumb; Dumb only; Blind; Imbecile or Idiot; or Lunatic.
1	Bernard McEvoe	Head of Family	Ro Catholic	Read & Write	60	M	Farmer	Married	Co Laois	Irish & English	
2	Mary McEvoe	Wife	Ro Catholic	Read & Write	48	F	Farmers Wife	Married	Co Laois	Irish & English	
3	Marie McEvoe	Daughter	Ro Catholic	Read & Write	23	F	Farmers Daughter	Not married	Co Laois	English	
4	Ellen McEvoe	Daughter	Ro Catholic	Read & Write	19	F	Farmers Daughter	Not married	Co Laois	English	
5	John McEvoe	Nephew	Ro Catholic	Read & Write	6	M	Scholar	Not married	Co Laois	English	
6											
7											
8											
9											
10											
11											
12											
13											
14											
15											

I hereby certify, as required by the Act 63 Vic, cap. 6, s. 6 (1), that the foregoing Return is correct, according to the best of my knowledge and belief.

Michael Killeen *(Signature of Enumerator.)*

I believe the foregoing to be a true Return.

Bernard McEvoe *(Signature of Head of Family.)*

CENSUS OF IRELAND, 1911.

FORM A.

Two Examples of the mode of filling up this Table are given on the other side.

RETURN of the MEMBERS of this FAMILY and their VISITORS, BOARDERS, SERVANTS, &c., who slept or abode in this House on the night of SUNDAY, the 2nd of APRIL, 1911.

No. on Form B. 11

Number	NAME AND SURNAME		RELATION to Head of Family	RELIGIOUS PROFESSION	EDUCATION	AGE (last Birthday) and SEX		RANK, PROFESSION, OR OCCUPATION	PARTICULARS AS TO MARRIAGE				WHERE BORN	IRISH LANGUAGE	If Deaf and Dumb; Dumb only; Blind; Imbecile or Idiot; or Lunatic.
	Christian Name	Surname				Age of Males	Age of Females		Whether "Married," "Widower," "Widow," or "Single."	Completed years the present Marriage has lasted	Total Children born alive	Children still living			
1	Patrick	Head	Head of Family	Roman Catholic	Read and write	65		Farmer	Married				County Down	Irish and English	
2	Patrick	Head	Son	Catholic	Read and write	23		Farmer's Son	Single				County Down	English	
3	Alice	Head	Daughter	Catholic	Read and write		21		Single				County Down	English	
4	Mary Ayd	Head	Daughter	Catholic	Read and write		18		Single				County Down	English	
5	John	Head	Son	Catholic	Read and write	12		Scholar	Single				County Down	English	
6	James	Head	Son	Roman Catholic	Read and write	10		Scholar	Single				Co. Down	English	
7															
8															
9															
10															
11															
12															
13															
14															
15															
16															

I hereby certify, as required by the Act 10 Edw. VII., and 1 Geo. V, cap. 11, that the foregoing Return is correct, according to the best of my knowledge and belief.

Patrick Head Signature of Enumerator.

I believe the foregoing to be a true Return.

Patrick Head Signature of Head of Family.

(iv) *Marriages.* The requirement in the 1911 census for married women to
      supply the number of years of marriage is obviously a very useful aid
      when subsequently searching civil records for a marriage entry. Even in
      1901 the age of the eldest child recorded can give a rough guide to the
      latest date at which a marriage is likely to have taken place.

(v)   *Living Relatives.* Children recorded in 1901 and 1911 are the parents or
      grandparents of people now alive. The ages—generally much more
      accurate than those given for older members of the family—can be
      useful in trying to uncover later marriages in civil records. When used
      together with Land Valuation Office records (see Chapter 4), or the
      voters' lists of the National Archives, they can provide an accurate
      picture of the passing of property from one generation to another.
      Luckily the Irish attitude to land means that it is quite unusual for rural
      property to pass out of a family altogether.

C. RESEARCH TECHNIQUES

The basic geographical unit used in carrying out both the 1901 and 1911
censuses is the District Electoral Division, a subdivision of the county used,
as the name implies, for electoral purposes. To use the returns, ideally the
relevant street or townland should be known. The *1901 Townland Index*, based
on the census returns, supplies the name and number of the DED in which
the townland is situated. County-by-county volumes, on open shelves in the
National Archives Reading Room, go through the DEDs in numerical order
for both 1901 and 1911, giving the name and number of each of the townlands
they contain. To order the returns for a specific townland, it is necessary to
supply the name of the county, the number of the DED and the number of
the townland, as given in these volumes. For the cities of Belfast, Cork,
Dublin and Limerick, separate street indices have been compiled, and are
also on open shelves in the Reading Room. Again, each street or part of a
street is numbered, and these numbers are necessary to order specific
returns. Between 1901 and 1911 some changes took place in the District
Electoral Divisions, and their numbering is different in some cases. There is
no separate townlands index for 1911, but the changes are minor, so that a
DED numbered 100 in 1901 may be 103 in 1911, and can be found simply by
checking the Divisions above and below 100 in the 1911 volume for the
county.

The returns for 1901 have been bound into large volumes, while those for
1911 are still loose and in boxes. In each case all the returns for a townland
or street are grouped together and preceded by an enumerator's abstract
which gives the details of the houses and lists the names of the heads of
households. These lists can be very useful if the precise townland or street is
not known, and it is necessary to search a large area, checking all households
of a particular surname, though such a procedure is of course less precise

than a check on each of the returns themselves. One problem which can
arise in searching a large area is the difficulty of translating from the earlier
geographical division of a parish, for instance, to the relevant District
Electoral Divisions, since these latter cut across the earlier boundaries. The
most straightforward, though cumbersome, way to cover a large area is to
take all the townlands in particular civil parishes and check their District
Electoral Divisions in the *1901 Townlands Index*. The *1841 Townlands Index*, also
known as *Addenda to the 1841 Census*, and available on request from the
National Archives Reading Room staff or in the National Library (Ir. 310 c
1), organises townlands alphabetically within civil parishes

2. NINETEENTH-CENTURY CENSUS FRAGMENTS

1821
This census, organised by townland, civil parish, barony and county, took
place on 28 May 1821, and aimed to cover the entire population. It recorded
the following information :
➢ name;
➢ age;
➢ occupation;
➢ relationship to the head of the household;
➢ acreage of landholding;
➢ number of storeys of house.
Almost all the original returns were destroyed in 1922, with only a few
volumes surviving for parts of Counties Cavan, Fermanagh, Galway, Meath
and Offaly (King's County). These are now in the National Archives, and
full details of call-numbers and areas covered will be found in Chapter 12
under the relevant county. The overall reliability of the population figures
produced by the 1821 census has been questioned recently, but there is no
doubt as to the genealogical value of the returns. Once again, however, the
ages given need to be treated with scepticism.

1831
Again organised by townland, civil parish, barony and county, this census
recorded the following:
➢ name;
➢ age;
➢ occupation;
➢ relationship to the head of the household;
➢ acreage of landholding;
➢ religion.
Very little of this survives, with most of the remaining fragments relating to
Co. Derry. Details of locations and call-numbers are in Chapter 12 under the
relevant county.

No. 38   Townland of *Nappaleen*   in the Parish of *Castlerahan*   Ba

N. B.—In Counties where Plowlands or other denominations or sub-denominations are in use, the word "Townland"   is to be

Col. 1. No. of House.	Col. 2. No. of Stories	Column 3. NAMES OF INHABITANTS.	Col. 4. AGE.	Column 5. OCCUPATION.	Col. 6. No. of Acres.
		Eliza Fitzsimmons Daughter	15	Spinner	
8	1	Garrett Fitzsimmons	60	Farmer	12
		Cath Fitzsimmons his Wife	57	Spinner	
		Patrick Fitzsimmons his Son	32	Labourer	
		Thos Fitzsimmons Do	27	Labourer	
		John Fitzsimmons Do	23	Labourer	
		Mary Smyth	20	House Servt	
9	1	John Gilroy	39	Farmer	16
		Mary Gilroy his Wife	33	Spinner	
		Patrick Gilroy his Son	10		
		Owen Gilroy his Son	1		
		Mary Gilroy Daughter	15	Spinner	
		Mary Gilroy Do	13	Same	
		Bridget Gilroy Do	7		
		Anne Gilroy Do	5		
10	1	Peter Lynch	64	Farmer	15
		Eliza Lynch his Wife	61	Spinner	
		Hugh Lynch his Son	32	Labourer	
		James Lynch his Son	16	Labourer	
		Anne Lynch Daughter	25	Spinner	
		Mary Lynch Daughter	23	Spinner	
		John Lynch his Nephew	1		
11	1	John Flood	33	Farmer	4½
		Anne Flood his Wife	30	Spinner	
		John Flood his Son	8		
		Mary Flood Daughter	10		
		Cath Flood Do	6		
		Anne Flood Do	3		
12	1	John Smyth	55	Mason	
		Peter Smyth his Son	25	Labourer	
		James Smyth his Son	22	Labourer	
		Patk Smyth Do	15	Labourer	

1841

Unlike the two earlier censuses, the returns in 1841 were filled out by the householders themselves, rather than government enumerators. The information supplied was:
➤ name;
➤ age;
➤ occupation;
➤ relationship to the head of the household;
➤ date of marriage;
➤ literacy;
➤ absent family members;
➤ family members who died since 1831.

Only one set of original returns survived 1922, that for the parish of Killeshandra in Co. Cavan. There are, however, a number of transcripts of the original returns. The 1841 census was the earliest to be of use when state Old Age Pensions were introduced in the early twentieth century, and copies of the household returns from 1841 and 1851 were sometimes used as proof of age. The forms detailing the results of searches in the original returns to establish age have survived and are found in the National Archives for areas in the Republic of Ireland, and the Public Record Office of Northern Ireland for areas now in its jurisdiction. County-by-county indexes to the areas covered, giving the names of the individuals concerned, are found on open shelves in the Reading Room. A number of other miscellaneous copies, some also related to the Old Age Pension, and mostly relating to Northern counties, are detailed (though not indexed) in the pre-1901 census catalogue of the National Archives, on open shelves in the Reading Room. For the counties with significant numbers of these copies, details will be found under the relevant county in Chapter 12. As well as these copies, there are also a number of researchers' transcripts and abstracts compiled from the original returns before their destruction, and donated to public institutions after 1922 in an attempt to replace some of the lost records. Since the researchers were usually interested in particular families rather than whole areas, these are generally of limited value. The most significant collections are the Walsh-Kelly notebooks, which also abstract parts of the 1821, 1831 and 1851 returns, and relate particularly to south Kilkenny, and the Thrift Abstracts in the National Archives. Details of dates, areas covered and locations for the Walsh-Kelly notebooks will be found under Co. Kilkenny in Chapter 12. The Thrift Abstracts are listed in detail in the National Archives pre-1901 census catalogue under 'miscellaneous copies'. Counties for which significant numbers exist are given under the relevant county in Chapter 12.

1851

This recorded the following:

➢ name;
➢ age;
➢ occupation;
➢ relationship to the head of the household;
➢ date of marriage;
➢ literacy;
➢ absent family members;
➢ family members who died since 1841;
➢ religion.

Most of the surviving returns relate to parishes in Co. Antrim, and details will be found in Chapter 12. The comments above on transcripts and abstracts of the 1841 census also apply to 1851.

1861 and 1871

The official destruction of the returns for these two years was commendably thorough. Virtually nothing survives. The only transcripts are contained in the Catholic registers of Enniscorthy (1861), and Drumcondra and Lough-braclen, Co. Meath (1871). Details appear in Chapter 12.

3. CENSUS SUBSTITUTES

Almost anything recording more than a single name can be called a census substitute, at least for genealogical purposes. What follows is a listing, chronological where possible, of the principal such substitutes. It is intended as a gloss on some of the sources given county by county under 'Census Returns and Substitutes' in Chapter 12, and as a supplement covering sources which do not fit the county-by-county format. Any material given in the source-lists of Chapter 12 which is self-explanatory is not dealt with here.

SEVENTEENTH CENTURY

1612–13

Undertakers: The *Historical Manuscripts Commission Report*, 4 (Hastings MSS.) gives lists of English and Scottish large landlords granted land in the northern counties of Cavan, Donegal and Fermanagh.

1630

Muster Rolls: These are lists of large landlords in Ulster, and the names of the able-bodied men they could assemble to fight if the need arose They are arranged by county, and by district within the county. The Armagh County Museum copy is available in the National Library (Pos. 206). Published lists are noted under the relevant county in Chapter 12, along with later lists in the Public Record Office of Northern Ireland

1641

Books of Survey and Distribution: After the wars of the mid-seventeenth century, the English government needed solid information on land ownership throughout

Ireland to carry out its policy of land redistribution. The Books of Survey and Distribution record ownership before the Cromwellian and Williamite confiscations, c.1641, and after, c.1703–4. The Books for Clare, Galway, Mayo and Roscommon have been published by the Irish Manuscripts Commission. For other counties manuscript copies are available at the National Library. Details will be found under the relevant counties in Chapter 12.

1654–56
The Civil Survey: This too was a record of land ownership in 1640, compiled between 1655 and 1667, and fuller than the Books of Survey and Distribution. It contains a great deal of topographical and descriptive information, as well as details of wills and deeds relating to land title. It has survived for twelve counties only: Cork, Derry, Donegal, Dublin, Kildare, Kilkenny, Limerick, Meath, Tipperary, Tyrone, Waterford and Wexford. All these have been published by the Irish Manuscripts Commission. Details will be found under the relevant counties in Chapter 12.

1659
'Pender's Census': This was compiled by Sir William Petty, also responsible for the Civil Survey, and records the names of persons with title to land ('tituladoes'), the total numbers of English and Irish living in each townland, and the principal Irish names in each barony. Five counties, Cavan, Galway, Mayo, Tyrone and Wicklow, are not covered. The work was edited by Seamus Pender and published in 1939. (NL I 6551 Dublin)

1662–66
Subsidy Rolls: These list the nobility, clergy and laity who paid a grant in aid to the King. They supply name and parish, and sometimes, amount paid and occupation.They relate principally to counties in Ulster.

1664–66
Hearth Money Rolls: The Hearth Tax was levied on the basis of the number of hearths in each house; these Rolls list the householders' names, as well as this number. They seem to be quite comprehensive. Details of surviving lists will be found under the relevant counties in Chapter 12. For copies of the Hearth Money Rolls listed in the Public Record Office of Northern Ireland under 'T.307', an index is available on the Public Search Room shelves.

VARIOUS DATES, SEVENTEENTH CENTURY
Cess Tax Accounts: 'Cess' (from an abbreviation of 'assessment') was a very elastic term which could be applied to taxes levied for a variety of reasons. In Ireland it was very often to support a military garrison. The accounts generally consist of lists of householders' names, along with amounts due.

EIGHTEENTH AND NINETEENTH CENTURIES
1703–1838
The Convert Rolls, ed. Eileen O'Byrne, Irish Manuscripts Commission, 1981 (NL Ir.). A list of those converting from Catholicism to the Church of Ireland. The bulk of the entries dates from 1760 to 1790.

1740
Protestant householders are listed for parts of Counties Antrim, Armagh, Derry, Donegal and Tyrone. Arranged by barony and parish, it gives names only. Parts are at the Public Record Office of Northern Ireland, the Genealogical Office, the National Library and the Representative Church Body Library. Details will be found under the relevant counties in Chapter 12.

1749
Elphin Diocesan Census, arranged by townland and parish, and listing householders, their religion, the numbers, sex and religion of their children, and the numbers, sex and religion of their servants. Details of the parishes covered will be found under the relevant counties in Chapter 12.

1766
In March and April of this year, on the instructions of the government, Church of Ireland rectors were to compile complete returns of all householders in their parishes, showing their religion, and giving an account of any Catholic clergy active in their area. The result was extraordinarily inconsistent, with some rectors producing only numerical totals of population, some drawing up partial lists, and the most conscientious detailing all householders and their addresses individually. All the original returns were lost in 1922, but extensive transcripts survive for some areas and are deposited with various institutions. The only full listing of all surviving transcripts and abstracts is in the National Archives Reading Room on the open shelves. However, this does not differentiate between those returns which supply names and those which merely give numerical totals. The details given under the relevant counties in Chapter 12 refer only to those parishes for which names are given.

1795–1862
Charlton Trust Fund marriage certificates. As an encouragement to Protestant population growth, the Charlton Trust Fund offered a small marriage gratuity to members of the Protestant labouring classes. To qualify, a marriage certificate recording occupations and fathers' names and signed by the local Church of Ireland clergyman had to be submitted, and these are now in the National Archives. They are particularly useful for the years before the start of registration of non-Catholic marriages in 1845. The areas covered by the Fund were mainly in Counties Meath and Longford, but a few certificates exist for parts of Counties Cavan, King's (Offaly), Louth and Westmeath, as well as Dublin City. They are indexed in NA Accessions Vol. 37.

1796
Spinning-wheel Premium Entitlement Lists. As part of a government scheme to encourage the linen trade, free spinning-wheels or looms were granted to individuals planting a certain area of land with flax. The lists of those entitled to the awards, covering almost 60,000 individuals, were published in 1796, and record only the name of the individual and the civil parish in which he lived. As might be expected, the majority, over 64 per cent of the total, were in Ulster, but some names appear from every county except Dublin and Wicklow. In the county-by-county source-lists only those counties with significant numbers (more than 3,000 names) include a reference. A microfiche index to the lists is available in the National Archives, and the Public Record Office of Northern Ireland.

1798
Persons who suffered losses in the 1798 Rebellion. A list of claims for compensation from the government for property destroyed by the rebels during the insurrection of 1798. Particularly useful for the property-owning classes of Counties Wexford, Carlow, Dublin, Kildare and Wicklow. (NL I 94107)

1824–38
Tithe Applotment Books. See Chapter 4.

1831–1921
National School Records. In 1831 a country-wide system of primary education was established under the control of the Board of Commissioners for National Education. The most useful records produced by the system are the school registers themselves, which record the age of the pupil, religion, father's address and occupation, and general observations. Unfortunately, in the Republic of Ireland no attempt has been made to centralise these records; they remain in the custody of local schools or churches. The Public Record Office of Northern Ireland has a collection of over 1,500 registers for schools in the six counties of Northern Ireland. The administrative records of the Board of Commissioners itself are now held by the National Archives in Dublin. These include teachers' salary books, which can be very useful if an ancestor was a teacher.

1848–64
Griffith's Valuation. See Chapter 4.

1876
Landowners in Ireland: Return of owners of land of one acre and upwards . . ., London: Her Majesty's Stationery Office, 1876 [reissued by the Genealogical Publishing Company, Baltimore, 1988]. This records 32,614 owners of land in Ireland in 1876, identifying them by province and county; the entries

record the address of the owner, along with the extent and valuation of the property. Only a minority of the population actually owned the land they occupied, but the work is invaluable for those who did.

VARIOUS DATES, EIGHTEENTH AND NINETEENTH CENTURIES

➤ **Freeholders**: Freehold property is held either by fee simple, with absolute freedom to dispose of it, by fee tail, in which the disposition is restricted to a particular line of heirs, or simply by life tenure. From the early eighteenth century freeholders' lists were drawn up regularly, usually because of the right to vote which went with freehold of property over a certain value. It follows that such lists are of genealogical interest only for a small minority of the population. Details of surviving lists will be found under the relevant counties in Chapter 12.

➤ **Voters' Lists and Poll Books**: Voters' lists cover a slightly larger proportion of the population than Freeholders' lists, since freehold property was not the only determinant of the franchise. In particular, freemen of the various corporation towns and cities had a right to vote in some elections at least. Since membership of a trade guild carried with it admission as a freeman, and this right was hereditary, a wider range of social classes is covered. Details of surviving lists will be found under the relevant counties in Chapter 12. Poll books are the records of votes actually cast in elections.

➤ **Electoral Records**: No complete collection of the electoral lists used in the elections of this century exists. This is unfortunate, since they can be of great value in tracing living relatives, listing as they do all eligible voters by townland and household. The largest single collection of surviving electoral registers is to be found in the National Archives, but even here the coverage of many areas is quite skimpy.

➤ **Valuations**: Local valuations and revaluations of property were carried out with increasing frequency from the end of the eighteenth century, usually for electoral reasons. The best of these record all householders. Again, details are given under the relevant counties in Chapter 12.

3

Church Records

THE PARISH SYSTEM

After the coming of the Reformation to Ireland in the sixteenth century, the parish structures of the Catholic Church and the Church of Ireland diverged. In general the Church of Ireland retained the older medieval parochial divisions and, as the administrative units of the state Church these were also used for administrative purposes by the secular authorities. Thus civil parishes, the basic geographical units in early censuses, tax records and land surveys, are almost identical to Church of Ireland parishes. The Catholic Church on the other hand, weakened by the confiscation of its assets and the restrictions on its clergy, had to create larger and less convenient parishes. In some ways, however, this weakness produced more flexibility, allowing parishes to be centred on new growing population centres, and, in the nineteenth century, permitting the creation of new parishes to accommodate this growth in population. The differences in the parish structures of the two Churches are reflected in their records. Even allowing for the fact that members of the Church of Ireland were almost always a small minority of the total population, the records of each parish are proportionally less extensive than Catholic records, covering a smaller area, and are thus relatively easy to search in detail. Catholic records, by contrast, cover the majority of the population and a much larger geographical area, and as a result can be very time consuming to search in detail. The creation of new Catholic parishes in the nineteenth century can also mean that the registers relevant to a particular area may be split between two parishes. Both Catholic and Church of Ireland parishes are organised on the diocesan basis first laid out in the Synod of Kells in the Middle Ages, and remain almost identical, although the Catholic system has amalgamated some of the small medieval dioceses.

(1) CATHOLIC RECORDS

Dates

Before the start of civil registration for all in 1864, virtually the only direct sources of family information for the vast majority of the population are the local parish records. However, because of the disadvantages suffered by the Catholic Church from the sixteenth to the nineteenth centuries, record-keeping was understandably difficult, and very few registers survive from before the latter half of the eighteenth century. The earliest Catholic parish records in the country appear to be the fragments for Waterford and Galway Cities dating from the 1680s. Generally speaking, early records tend to come from the more prosperous and anglicised areas, in particular the towns and cities of the eastern half of the island. In the poorest and most densely populated rural parishes of the West and North, those which saw most emigration, the parish registers very often do not start until the mid- or late nineteenth century. However the majority of Catholic registers begin in the first decades of the nineteenth century, and even in poor areas, if a local tradition of Gaelic scholarship survived, records were often kept from an earlier date.

The only way to be sure of the extent of surviving records is to check the individual parish. The National Library catalogue, available at the counter in the main reading room, is the only comprehensive county-wide account of Catholic registers, and records in detail the period covered by each set of registers, including gaps, up to 1880. The catalogue is not entirely accurate—some of the omissions are given below—but it remains the only detailed survey available.

Nature of the records

Catholic registers consist almost exclusively of baptismal and marriage records. Unlike the Church of Ireland, very few parishes kept a register of burials, and in the case of those that did, it is almost always intermittent and patchy. Baptisms and marriages are recorded in either Latin or English, never in Irish. Generally parishes in the more prosperous areas, where English was more common, tended to use English, while in Irish-speaking parishes Latin was used; there is no absolute consistency, however. The Latin presents very few problems, since only first names were translated, not surnames or placenames, and the English equivalents are almost always self-evident. The only difficulties or ambiguities are the following: *Carolus* (Charles); *Demetrius* (Jeremiah or Dermot); *Hugones* (Hugh); *Ioannes* (John or Owen). Apart from names, the only other Latin needing explanation is that used in recording marriage dispensations. These were necessary when the two people marrying were related, *consanguinati*, and the relationship was given in terms of degrees, with siblings first degree, first cousins second degree, and second cousins third degree. Thus a couple recorded as *consanguinati in tertio grado* are second cousins, information which can be of value in disentangling earlier generations. A less frequent Latin comment, *affinitatus*, records an earlier relationship by marriage between the families of the two parties.

BAPTISMS

Catholic baptismal registers almost invariably contain the following information:
➤ date;
➤ child's name;
➤ father's name;
➤ mother's maiden name;
➤ names of sponsors (godparents).

In addition most registers also record the residence of the parents. A typical Latin entry in its full form would read: *Baptisavi Johannem, filium legitimum Michaeli Sheehan et Mariae Sullivan de Lisquill. Sponsoribus, Danielus Quirk, Johanna Donoghue.*

Much more often the entry is abbreviated to: *Bapt. Johannem, f.l. Michaeli Sheehan et Mariae Sullivan, Lisquill, Sp: Daniel Quirk, Johanna Donoghue.* Translated, this is simply 'I baptised John, legitimate son of Michael Sheehan and Mary Sullivan of Lisquill, with godparents Daniel Quirk and Johanna Donoghue.' In many cases even the abbreviations are omitted, and the entries simply consist of dates, names and places.

MARRIAGES

The information given in marriage records is more variable, but always includes at least the following:
➤ date;
➤ names of persons marrying;
➤ names of witnesses.

Other information which may be supplied includes: residences (of all four people); ages; occupations; fathers' names. In some rare cases the relationships of the witnesses to the people marrying are also specified. A typical Latin entry would read: *In matrimonium coniunxi sunt Danielum McCarthy et Brigidam Kelliher, de Ballyboher. Testimonii: Cornelius Buckley, Margarita Hennessy.* Abbreviated, the entry reads: *Mat. con. Danielum McCarthy et Brigidam Kelliher, Ballyboher. Test. Cornelius Buckley, Margarita Hennessy.* 'Daniel McCarthy and Brigid Kelliher, of Ballyboher, are joined in matrimony; witnesses, Cornelius Buckley, Margaret Hennessy.'

Locations

In the 1950s and early 1960s, the National Library carried out a project to microfilm the surviving Catholic parish registers of the entire island. Out of more than 1,000 sets of registers, this project missed only a tiny percentage. Parishes whose records it does not include are: Crossgar (Co. Down); Kilmeen, Clonfert, Fahy, Clonbern (Co. Galway); Killorglin (Co. Kerry); Lanesboro (Co. Longford); Kilmeena (Co. Mayo); Rathcore and Rathmolyon (Co. Meath); Moate (Co. Westmeath); Bray (Co. Wicklow); and the Dublin City and county parishes of Booterstown, Clontarf, Donnybrook, Dun Laoghaire (Kingstown), Naul, St Mary's (Pro-Cathedral), Sandyford and Santry. Almost all these appear to have registers earlier than 1880 in local custody. In addition, the parishes of St John's (Sligo town), Cappawhite (Co. Tipperary) and Waterford City have registers held locally which are fuller than those microfilmed by the Library. Not all of the microfilmed registers in the Library are available to the public; permission for public research has not been granted by the bishops of Ardagh and Clonmacnoise, Cloyne, Down and Connor, Galway, Kerry, and Limerick. In the case of parishes in these dioceses, it is necessary to obtain written permission from the local parish priest before the Library can allow access to the records, although full details of the extent of the surviving registers can be found in the reading room catalogue.

Apart from research in the original records or microfilm copies, one other access route exists to the information recorded in parish registers. This is through the network of local heritage centres which has come into being throughout the country since c.1980. These are engaged, as part of the Irish Genealogical Project, in indexing and computerising all the surviving parish records for the country. At the moment of writing, June 1991, about 40 per cent of all Catholic records have been indexed manually, and about 15 per cent are on computer. These records are not directly accessible to the public, but the centres do carry out commissioned research. Full details of the Project and the centres will be found in Chapter 15.

Research in Catholic records

Because the records are so extensive, and there are so many parishes, the first step in any research must be to try to identify the relevant parish. In the ideal case, where a precise town or townland is known, this is relatively simple. Any of the Townland Indices, from 1851, 1871 or 1901 will show the relevant civil parish. There are then a number of ways to uncover the corresponding Catholic parish. Lewis' *Topographical Dictionary of Ireland* (1837), available on open access at most libraries, gives an account, in alphabetical order, of all the civil parishes of Ireland, and specifies the corresponding Catholic parish.

Brian Mitchell's *Guide to Irish Parish Records* (Genealogical Publishing Co., Baltimore, 1987), contains a county-by-county alphabetical reference guide to the civil parishes of Ireland and the Catholic parishes of which they are part. The National Library 'Index of Surnames' (or 'Householders Index') includes a map of the civil parishes in each county, and a key, loosely based on Lewis, to the corresponding Catholic parishes. A guide which is less reliable, though useful if the exact position of the church is required, is *Locations of Churches in the Irish Provinces*, produced by the Society of Latter-day Saints (NL Ir. 7265 i 8). For Dublin City the procedure is slightly different. Where the address is known, the relevant civil parish can be found in the street-by-street listings of the Dublin directories, Pettigrew and Oulton's *Dublin Almanac and General Register of Ireland* (yearly from 1834 to 1849), and Thom's *Irish Almanac and Official Directory* (yearly from 1844). More details of these will be found in Chapter 10. The corresponding Catholic parishes can then be found in Mitchell's *Guide* or in James Ryan's *Tracing your Dublin Ancestors* (Flyleaf Press, 1988).

Unfortunately, in most cases a precise address is not known. How this is to be overcome depends, obviously, on what other information is known. Where a birth, death or marriage took place in the family in Ireland after the start of civil registration in 1864, state records are the first place to look. When the occupation is known, records relating to this may supply the vital link (see Chapter 11). For emigrants, the clue to the relevant area might be provided by passenger and immigration lists, naturalisation papers, burial or death records, or even the postmarks on old family letters. In general, unless the surname is quite rare, the minimum information needed to start research on parish records with any prospect of success is the county of origin. Knowing the county, the areas to be searched in the registers can then be narrowed with the help of the early and mid-nineteenth-century land records, the Tithe Books (*c.*1830), and Griffith's Valuation (*c.*1855) (see Chapter 4). The National Library 'Index of Surnames' provides a guide, on a county basis, to the surnames occurring in these records in the different civil parishes, giving at least an indication of the areas in which a particular surname was most common. For some counties, indexes are now available which give the full names of the householders appearing in Griffith's, and these can be invaluable in narrowing still further the areas of potential relevance. Where such indexes exist, this is noted under the county in Chapter 12.

Because of the creation of new Catholic parishes in the nineteenth century, the apparent starting dates of many Catholic registers can be deceptive. Quite often, earlier records for the same area can be found in the registers of what is now an adjoining parish. To take an example, the Catholic parish of Abbeyleix, Co. Laois (Queen's), has records listed in the National Library catalogue as starting in 1824. In fact the parish was only created in that year, and before then its records will be found in Ballinakill which has records from '1794. Where surviving records appear too late to be of interest, therefore, it is always advisable to check the surrounding parishes for earlier registers. The maps of Catholic parishes accompanying this chapter are intended to simplify this task. It cannot be emphasised too strongly that these maps are not intended to be geographically precise; their aim is merely to show the positions of Catholic parishes relative to each other. Along with the county lists of parishes, they are based on the National Library catalogue which stops at 1880, and thus reflect the position in that year. Since the only published source of information on nineteenth-century Catholic parishes is Lewis' *Topographical Dictionary of Ireland*, which was published in 1837, and the power and public presence of the Church expanded greatly after Catholic Emancipation in 1836, many of the currently available parish lists have serious omissions and need to be used cautiously.

At first sight, parish registers, particularly on microfilm, can appear quite daunting. A mass of spidery abbreviated Latin, complete with blots and alterations, and cross-hatched with the scratches of a well-worn microfilm can strike terror into the heart of even the most seasoned researcher. Some registers are a pleasure to use, with decade after decade of carefully laid out copperplate handwriting; many more, unfortunately, appear to have been intended by local clergymen as their revenge on posterity. The thing to remember is that it is neither possible nor desirable to read every word on every page. The aim is to extract efficiently any relevant information, and the way to do this is by scanning the pages rather than reading them. In general, each parish takes a particular format and sticks to it. The important point is to identify this format, and where in it the relevant information is given. For most purposes, the family surname is the crucial item, so that in the baptismal example given above, the best procedure would be to scan fathers' surnames, stopping to read fully, or note, only those recording the relevant surname. For other formats, such as: 'John Maguire of Patrick and Mary Reilly; Sp. Thos McKiernan, Rose Smith', in which the family surname is given with the child's name rather than with the father's, it is the child's surname which must be scanned. Even with very efficient scanning, however, there are registers which can only be deciphered line by line, which change format every page or two, or which are simply so huge that nothing but hours of eye strain can extract any information. The most notorious are the registers for Cork City, Clonmel, and Clifden, Co. Galway.

In searching parish records, as for census returns and state records of births, marriages and deaths, a large measure of scepticism must be applied to all reported ages. In general, a five-year span around the reported date is the minimum that can be expected to yield results, and ten years is better if time allows, with emphasis on the years before the reported date. An open mind should also be kept on surname variants—widespread illiteracy made consistency and spelling accuracy extremely rare. It is essential, especially if searching more than one parish, to keep a written note of the precise period searched; even the best memory blurs after a few hours in front of a microfilm screen, and it is perfectly, horribly possible to have to search the same records twice. Duplication of research such as this is an endemic hazard of genealogy, since the nature of the research is such that the relevance of particular pieces of evidence often only emerges with hindsight; this is especially true of research in parish records. Take an example: a search in parish records for Ellen, daughter of John O'Brien, born c.1840. The search starts in 1842 and moves back through the baptismal registers. There are many baptisms recording different John O'Briens as father, but no Ellen recorded until 1834. If it is then necessary to check the names of her siblings, much of what has already been researched will have to be covered again. The only way to guard against having to duplicate work like this is to note all the baptisms recording John O'Brien as father, even though there is a possibility (and in many cases a probability) that none of them will ultimately turn out to have been relevant.

Apart from the obvious family information they record, Catholic parish registers may also include a wide variety of incidental information: details of famine relief, parish building accounts, marriage dispensations, local censuses, even personal letters. Anything of immediate genealogical interest is noted under the relevant county in Chapter 12.

(2) CHURCH OF IRELAND RECORDS

Dates

Records of the Established Church, the Church of Ireland, generally start much earlier than those of the Catholic Church. From as early as 1634 local parishes were required to keep records of christenings and burials in registers supplied by the Church authorities. As a result, a significant number, especially of urban parishes, have registers dating from the mid-seventeenth century. The majority, however, start in the years between 1770 and 1820; the only country-wide listing of all Church of Ireland parish records which gives full details of dates is the National Archives catalogue, copies of which are also to be found at the National Library and the Genealogical Office.

The nature of the records

BURIALS
Unlike their Catholic counterparts, the majority of Church of Ireland clergymen recorded burials as well as baptisms and marriages. These burial registers are

often also of interest for families of other denominations; the sectarian divide appears to have narrowed a little after death. The information given for burials was rarely more than the name, age and townland, making definite family connections difficult to establish in most cases. However, since early burials generally record the deaths of those born well before the start of the register, they can often be the only evidence on which to base a picture of preceding generations, and are particularly valuable because of this.

BAPTISMS

Church of Ireland baptismal records almost always supply only:
➤ the child's name;
➤ the father's name;
➤ the mother's christian name; and
➤ the name of the officiating clergyman.

Quite often, the address is also given, but this is by no means as frequent as in the case of Catholic registers. The omission of the mother's maiden name can be an obstacle to further research. From about 1820, the father's occupation is supplied in many cases.

MARRIAGES

Since the Church of Ireland was the Established Church, the only legally valid marriages, in theory at least, were those performed under its aegis. In practice, of course, *de facto* recognition was given to marriages of other denominations. None the less, the legal standing of the Church of Ireland meant that many marriages, of members of other Protestant Churches in particular, are recorded in Church of Ireland registers. The information given is not extensive, however, consisting usually of the names of the parties marrying and the name of the officiating clergyman. Even addresses are not usual, unless one of the people is from another parish. After 1845, when non-Catholic marriages were registered by the state, the marriage registers record all the information contained in state records, including occupations, addresses and fathers' names.

As well as straightforward information on baptisms, marriages and burials, Church of Ireland parish records very often include vestry books. These contain the minutes of the vestry meetings of the local parish, which can supply detailed information on the part played by individuals in the life of the parish. These are not generally with the parish registers in the National Archives, but the Public Record Office of Northern Ireland and the Representative Church Body Library in Dublin have extensive collections.

Locations

After the Church of Ireland ceased to be the Established Church in 1869, its marriage records before 1845 and baptismal and burial records before 1870

1857

24

Richard son of Richard Cidderley & Ellen his wife
Born February 28th. Baptised April 19a 1857.

Andrew, son of Robert & Jeannette Rutherford
Born 13th May. Baptised 6th June 1857 —

Thomas Eld son of Thomas Heffernan of Newtown Esqre &
Rose his wife, Born February 18th 18?? on Received
into Church November 22d 1857 when —

Sponsors { Thomas Eld
          { Thomas Heffernan & Fanny Eld.

Mary Eld daughter of Thomas Heffernan of
Newtown Esq. & Rose his wife Born Novr 10th 1857
Baptised November 22d 1857.

Sponsors { Mary Bernard
          { Rose Heffernan & Thomas Heffernan

George Thomas son of Edward Thomas of
Corstown Parish of Drumdowney & Marianne
his wife. Born Novr 29th Baptised Decr 20th
1857.

1858 John, son of Michael Farmer & Anne his wife
      Baptised March 21st 1858.

William John, son of Denis Lynch of Ballinasloe and
Ellen his wife Born April 8th Baptised April 24th 18??

were declared to be the property of the state, public records. Unless the local clergyman was in a position to demonstrate that he could house these records safely, he was required to deposit them in the Public Record Office. By 1922 the original registers of nearly 1,000 parishes, more than half the total for the country, were stored at the Public Record Office, and these were all destroyed in the fire at the Office on 28 June of that year.

Fortunately a large number of registers had not found their way into the Office; local rectors had, in many cases, made a transcript before surrendering the originals, and local historians and genealogists using the Office before 1922 had also amassed collections of extracts from the registers. All these factors mitigated, to some extent, the loss of such a valuable collection. However, it has also meant that surviving registers, transcripts and extracts are now held in a variety of locations. The Appendix to *The Twenty-eighth Report of the Deputy Keeper of Public Records in Ireland* lists the Church of Ireland parish records for the entire island, giving full details of the years covered, and specifying those which were in the Public Office at the time of its destruction. No information on locations is included. A more comprehensive account is supplied by the National Archives catalogue of Church of Ireland records, available in the National Archives reading room at the National Library and in the Genealogical Office. Only the copy in the Archives is fully up to date. As well as the dates of the registers, this catalogue also gives some details of locations, but only when the Archives hold the originals, a microfilm copy, a transcript or abstracts on open access, when the Representative Church Body Library in Dublin holds original registers for dates which make them public records, or when they are still held in the parish. The catalogue does not indicate when microfilm copies are held by the Representative Church Body Library, the Public Record Office of Northern Ireland or the National Library, simply specifying 'local custody'. This is accurate in that the originals are indeed held locally, but unhelpful to researchers. Chapter 14 gives a county-by-county listing of Church of Ireland registers, microfilm and published copies, transcripts and extracts to be found in Dublin, with locations and reference numbers.

In general, for the northern counties of Antrim, Armagh, Cavan, Derry, Donegal, Down, Fermanagh, Leitrim, Louth, Monaghan and Tyrone, surviving registers have been microfilmed by the Public Record Office of Northern Ireland, and are available to the public in Belfast. For those counties which are now in the Republic of Ireland, Cavan, Donegal, Leitrim, Louth and Monaghan, copies of the Public Record Office of Northern Ireland microfilms are available to the public at the Representative Church Body Library in Dublin. For parishes further away from the border, 'local custody' is generally accurate, and it is necessary to commission the local clergyman to search his registers. The current *Church of Ireland Directory* will supply the relevant name and address.

The experience of 1922 has left the Church of Ireland understandably protective of its records, although the legal position remains that its early registers are state property. The National Archives have started a microfilming programme to cover the surviving registers in the Republic, which has covered the dioceses of Glendalough and Meath to date. However, for the moment, these records are not available to the public on request. It is necessary to obtain written permission from the local clergyman before the Archives can allow access.

(3) PRESBYTERIAN RECORDS

Dates

In general, Presbyterian registers start much later than those of the Church of Ireland, and early records of Presbyterian baptisms, marriages and deaths are often to be found in the registers of the local Church of Ireland parish. There are exceptions, however; in areas which had a strong Presbyterian population from an early date, particularly in the north-east, some registers date from the late seventeenth and early eighteenth centuries. The only published listing remains that included in Margaret Falley's *Irish and Scotch-Irish Ancestral Research* (repr. Genealogical Publishing Co., 1988). This, however, gives a very incomplete and out of date picture of the extent and location of the records. For the six counties of Northern Ireland and many of the adjoining counties, the Public Record Office of Northern Ireland Parish Register Index and appended list of Presbyterian Registers in Local Custody provides a good guide to the dates of surviving registers. The Local Custody list covers all of Ireland, but is much less comprehensive for the south than for the north.

Nature of the records

Presbyterian registers record the same information as that given in the registers of the Church of Ireland (see above). It should be remembered that after 1845 all non-Catholic marriages, including those of Presbyterians, were registered by the state. From that year, therefore, Presbyterian marriage registers contain all the invaluable information given in state records.

Locations

Presbyterian registers are in three main locations: in local custody, in the Public Record Office of Northern Ireland, and at the Presbyterian Historical Society in Belfast. The Public Record Office also has microfilm copies of almost all registers in Northern Ireland which have remained in local custody, and also lists those records held by the Presbyterian Historical Society. For the rest of Ireland, almost all of the records are in local custody. It can be very difficult to locate these since many congregations in the south have moved, amalgamated or simply disappeared over the last sixty years. The very congregational basis of Presbyterianism further complicates matters, since it means that Presbyterian records do not cover a definite geographical area; the same town often had two or more Presbyterian churches drawing worshippers from the same community and keeping distinct records. In the early nineteenth century especially, controversy within the Church fractured the records, with seceding and non-seceding congregations in the same area often in violent opposition to each other. Apart from the PRONI listing, the only guide is *History of Congregations* (NL Ir. 285 h 8) which gives a brief historical outline of the history of each congregation. Lewis' *Topographical Dictionary of Ireland* (1837) records the existence of Presbyterian congregations within each civil parish, and Pettigrew and Oulton's *Dublin Almanac and General Register of Ireland* of 1835 includes a list of all Presbyterian ministers in the country, along with the names and locations of their congregations. *Locations of Churches in the Irish Provinces*, produced by the Society of Latter-day Saints (NL Ir. 7265 i 8), flawed as it is in many respects, can be useful in trying to identify the congregations in a particular area. A brief bibliography of histories of Presbyterianism is given under 'clergymen' in Chapter 11.

(4) METHODIST RECORDS

Despite the hostility of many of the Church of Ireland clergy, the Methodist movement remained unequivocally a part of the Established Church from the date of its beginnings in 1747, when John Wesley first came to Ireland, until 1816, when the movement split. Between 1747 and 1816, therefore, records of Methodist baptisms, marriages and burials will be found in the registers of the Church of Ireland. The split in 1816 took place over the question of the authority of Methodist ministers to administer sacraments, and resulted in the 'Primitive Methodists' remaining within the Church of Ireland, and the 'Wesleyan Methodists' authorising their ministers to perform baptisms and communions. (In theory, at least up to 1844, only marriages carried out by a minister of the Church of Ireland were legally valid.) The split continued until 1878 when the Primitive Methodists united with the Wesleyan Methodists outside the Church of Ireland. What this means is that the earliest surviving registers which are specifically Methodist date from 1815/16, and relate only to the Wesleyan Methodists. The information recorded in these is identical to that given in the Church of Ireland registers.

There are a number of problems in locating Methodist records which are specific to that Church. First, the origins of Methodism, as a movement rather than a Church, gave its members a great deal of latitude in their attitude to Church membership, so that records of the baptisms, marriages and burials of Methodists may also be found in Quaker and Presbyterian registers, as well as the registers of the Church of Ireland. In addition, the ministers of the Church were preachers on a circuit, rather than administrators of a particular area, and were moved frequently from one circuit to another. Quite often the records moved with them. For the nine historic counties of Ulster, the Public Record Office of Northern Ireland has produced a county-by-county listing of the surviving registers, their dates and locations, appended to their Parish Register Index. No such listing exists for the rest of the country. Again, Pettigrew and Oulton's *Dublin Almanac and General Register of Ireland* of 1835 and subsequent years provides a list of Methodist preachers and their stations, which will give an indication of the relevant localities. The next step is then to identify the closest surviving Methodist centre, and enquire of them as to surviving records. Many of the local county heritage centres also hold indexed copies of surviving Methodist records (see Chapter 15).

(5) QUAKER RECORDS

From the time of their first arrival in Ireland in the seventeenth century, the Society of Friends, or Quakers, kept rational and systematic records of the births, marriages and deaths of all their members, and in most cases these continue without a break up to the present. Parish registers as such were not kept. Each of the local weekly meetings reported any births, marriages or deaths to a larger Monthly Meeting, which then entered them in a register. Monthly Meetings were held in the following areas: Antrim, Ballyhagan, Carlow, Cootehill, Cork, Dublin, Edenderry, Grange, Lisburn, Limerick, Lurgan, Moate, Mountmellick, Richhill, Tipperary, Waterford, Wexford and Wicklow. For all but Antrim and Cootehill registers have survived from an early date, and are detailed below.

The entries for births, marriages and deaths do not themselves contain information other than the names and addresses of the immediate parties involved, but the centralisation of the records and the self-contained nature of the Quaker community make it a relatively simple matter to establish family connections; many of the local records are given in the form of family lists in any case.

There are two main repositories for records, the libraries of the Society of Friends in Dublin and Lisburn. As well as the records outlined below, these also hold considerable collections of letters, wills, family papers, as well as detailed accounts of the discrimination suffered by the Quakers in their early years.

Births, marriages and burials

Ballyhagan Marriages. Library of the Society of Friends, Lisburn, also NL
    Pos. 4127

Bandon, 1672–1713, in Casey A. (ed.), *O'Kief, Coshe Mang*, Vol. 11, Ir. 94145 c 12

Carlow births, marriages and deaths up to 1859, Library of the Society of
    Friends, Dublin, also NL Pos. 1021

Cork, births, marriages and deaths up to 1859, Library of the Society of
    Friends, Dublin (NL Pos. 1021), see also Cork (seventeenth to nineteenth
    centuries) NL Pos. 5530

Dublin, births, marriages and deaths up to 1859, Library of the Society of
    Friends, Dublin, also NL Pos. 1021 (births and marriages) and 1022
    (burials)

Edenderry, births, marriages and deaths up to 1859, Library of the Society of
    Friends, Dublin, also NL Pos. 1022; 1612–1814 (in the form of family
    lists), NL Pos. 5531

Grange, births, marriages and deaths up to 1859, Library of the Society of
    Friends, Dublin, also NL Pos. 1022

Lisburn, births, marriages and deaths up to 1859, Library of the Society of
    Friends, Dublin, also NL Pos. 1022

Limerick, births, marriages and deaths up to 1859, Library of the Society of
    Friends, Dublin, also NL Pos. 1022

Lurgan, births, marriages and deaths up to 1859, Library of the Society of
    Friends, Dublin (NL Pos. 1022), see also Lurgan Marriage Certificates,
    Library of the Society of Friends, Lisburn (NL Pos. 4126)

Moate, births, marriages and deaths up to 1859, Library of the Society of
    Friends, Dublin, also NL Pos. 1022

Mountmellick, births, marriages and deaths up to 1859, Library of the
    Society of Friends, Dublin, also NL Pos. 1023, NL Pos. 5530

Mountrath, Library of the Society of Friends, Dublin, also NL Pos. 5530

Richhill, births, marriages and deaths up to 1859, Library of the Society of
    Friends, Dublin, also NL Pos. 1023

Tipperary, births, marriages and deaths up to 1859, Library of the Society of
    Friends, Dublin, also NL Pos. 1024

Waterford, births, marriages and deaths up to 1859, Library of the Society of
    Friends, Dublin, also NL Pos. 1024

Wexford, births, marriages and deaths up to 1859, Library of the Society of
    Friends, Dublin, also NL Pos. 1024

Wicklow, births, marriages and deaths up to 1859, Library of the Society of
    Friends, Dublin, also NL Pos. 1024

Youghal, births, marriages and deaths up to 1859, Library of the Society of
    Friends, Dublin, also NL Pos. 1024

Births, Marriages and Deaths throughout Ireland 1859–1949, Library of the
    Society of Friends, Dublin, also NL Pos. 1024

Leinster Province, births, marriages and deaths, seventeenth century, Library
    of the Society of Friends, Dublin (NL Pos. 5530)
Munster Province, births, marriages and deaths 1650–1839, Library of the
    Society of Friends, Dublin (NL Pos. 5531)
Ulster Province Meeting Books, 1673–1691, Library of the Society of Friends,
    Lisburn (NL Pos. 3747)
Ulster Province Meetings Minute Books to 1782, Library of the Society of
    Friends, Lisburn (NL Pos. 4124 and 4125)

Other records

(1) PUBLISHED
Eustace, P. B. and Goodbody, O., *Quaker Records, Dublin, Abstracts of Wills* (2
    vols, 1704–1785) Irish Manuscripts Commission, 1954–58
Goodbody, Olive, *Guide to Irish Quaker Records 1654–1860*, IMC, 1967, Ir. 2896 g 4
Grubb, Isabel, *Quakers in Ireland*, London, 1927
Leadbetter, *Biographical Notices of the Society of Friends*, NL J 2896
Myers, A. C., *Immigration of Irish Quakers into Pennsylvania*, Ir. 2896 m 2 and 4
Wright and Petty, *History of the Quakers 1654–1700*, Ir. 2896 w 1

(2) MANUSCRIPT
Quaker Pedigrees, Library of the Society of Friends, Dublin, also NL Pos.
    5382, 5383, 5384, 5385
Quaker Wills and Inventories, Library of the Society of Friends, Lisburn,
    also NL Pos. 4127
Manuscript records of the Quaker Library (see *Guide* above), Swanbrook
    House, Bloomfield Avenue, Donnybrook, Dublin 4.
    Tel. 687157, Thurs. 11 a.m. to 1 p.m.

CATHOLIC PARISH MAPS

The most important point to be kept in mind about the maps (see pages xiv
to xxxii) is that they are intended as research aids, *not* as precisely accurate
depictions of the details of parish boundaries. They aim to show the relative
positions of the Catholic parishes which existed up to c.1800, and are based
largely on the information contained in Lewis' *Topographical Dictionary of Ireland*
(1837), and the National Library of Ireland catalogue of Catholic parish
registers, which details the records up to 1880. Since this forty-three-year
period saw great changes in the Catholic Church in Ireland, many com-
promises have had to be made; I have erred, consistently I hope, on the side
of inclusiveness. Neither of the two major sources used is free of mistakes. As
far as possible, where other sources existed I have attempted to cross-check
with these. None the less, some mistakes undoubtedly remain.

The starting dates given for the parish registers are the dates of the earliest known surviving record. In some cases, where for example only a few pages of an early register survive, this can be misleading. A full account of the extent of all the surviving records is simply beyond the scope of this book, however. Unless otherwise stated, the dates given are those in the National Library catalogue. Where earlier records are known to have survived locally, or are available in a local heritage centre (see Chapter 15), this is noted. It is very possible that other examples of registers not filmed by the Library exist.

4

Land Records

Because of the destruction of nineteenth-century census returns, surviving land and property records from the period have acquired a somewhat unnatural importance. Two surveys cover the entire country, the Tithe Applotment Books of c.1823–38, and Griffith's Valuation dating from 1848 to 1864. Both of these employ administrative divisions which are no longer in widespread use and need some explanation. The smallest division, the *townland*, is the one which has proved most enduring. Loosely related to the ancient Gaelic 'Bally betagh', and to other medieval land divisions such as ploughlands and 'quarters', townlands can vary enormously in size, from a single acre or less to several thousand acres. There are more than 64,000 townlands in the country. They were used as the smallest geographical unit in both Tithe Survey and Griffith's, as well as census returns, and are still in use today. Anything from five to thirty townlands may be grouped together to form a *civil parish*. These are a legacy of the middle ages, pre-dating the formation of counties and generally coextensive with the parishes of the Established Church, the Church of Ireland. They are not to be confused with Catholic parishes which are usually much larger. In turn, civil parishes are collected together in *baronies*. Originally related to the tribal divisions, the *tuatha*, of Celtic Ireland, these were multiplied and subdivided over the centuries up to their standardisation in the 1500s, so that the current names represent a mixture of Gaelic, Anglo-Norman and English influences. A number of baronies, from five in Co. Leitrim to twenty-two in Co. Cork, then go to make up the modern county. Baronies and civil parishes are no longer in use as administrative units.

TITHE APPLOTMENT BOOKS

The Composition Act of 1823 specified that tithes due to the Established Church, the Church of Ireland, which had hitherto been payable in kind, should now be paid in money. As a result, it was necessary to carry out a

41   PARISH OF *Castlerahan*

TOWNLANDS AND LAND-LORDS.	OCCUPIERS.	1st Quality			2nd			3rd			4th		
		A.	R.	P.	A.	R.	P.	A.	R.	P.	A.	R.	P.
Aghlien	Forwarded	52	1	20	73	2	25	10	0	05	4	0	00
"	Peter Lynch &c:	4	2	~	5	~	~	2	2	~	~	~	~
"	T. B. & I. Lynch	10	~	~	17	~	~	5	~	~	~	~	~
"	T. & P. Keogans	3	~	~	26	1	~	4	~	~	~	~	~
"	J. Kilroy & Brady	4	~	~	12	~	~	3	~	~	7	2	~
"	Garret Fitzsimons	3	~	~	7	~	~	1	1	15	~	~	~
"	Jno. Fitzsimons	4	~	~	7	~	~	~	2	15	~	~	~
"	John Brady	~	~	1	~	~	~	~	~	~	~	~	~
"	Luke Magenis	1	0	30	4	~	~	~	~	~	1	~	~
"	Rich.d Glennon	1	~	~	1	~	~	~	~	~	~	~	~
		83	1	10	150	3	25	26	1	35	12	2	~

valuation of the entire country, civil parish by civil parish, to determine how much would be payable by each landholder. This was done over the ensuing fifteen years up to the abolition of tithes in 1838. Not surprisingly, tithes were fiercely resented by those who were not members of the Church of Ireland, and all the more because the tax was not payable on all land; the exemptions produced spectacular inequalities. In Munster, for instance, tithes were payable on potato patches, but not on grassland, with the result that the poorest had to pay most. The exemptions also mean that the Tithe Books are not comprehensive. Apart from the fact that they omit entirely anyone not in occupation of land, certain categories of land varying from area to area are simply passed over in silence. They are *not* a full list of householders. None the less they do constitute the only country-wide survey for the period and are valuable precisely because the heaviest burden of tithes fell on the poorest, for whom few other records survive.

From a genealogical point of view the information recorded in the Tithe Books is quite basic, consisting typically of townland name, landholder's name, area of land, and tithes payable. In addition many Books also record the landlord's name and an assessment of the economic productivity of the land; the tax was based on the average price of wheat and oats over the seven years up to 1823, and was levied at a different rate depending on the quality of the land.

The original Tithe Books for the twenty-six counties of the Republic of Ireland are available in the National Archives. Those for the six counties of Northern Ireland were transferred to the Public Record Office of Northern Ireland in 1924. Photostat copies of these are available at the National Archives, and microfilm copies in the National Library.

The usefulness of the Tithe Books can vary enormously depending on the nature of the research. Since only a name is given, with no indication of family relationships, any conclusions drawn are, inevitably, somewhat speculative. However, for parishes where registers do not begin until after 1850, they are often the only early records surviving. They can provide valuable circumstantial evidence, especially where a holding passed from father to son in the period between the Tithe survey and Griffith's Valuation. The surnames in the Books have been roughly indexed, in the National Library 'Index of Surnames', described more fully below.

GRIFFITH'S VALUATION

In order to produce the accurate information necessary for local taxation the Tenement Act, 1842 provided for a uniform valuation of all property in Ireland to be based on the productive capacity of land and the potential rent of buildings. The man appointed Commissioner of Valuation was Richard Griffith, a Dublin geologist, and the results of his great survey, the *Primary*

Valuation of Tenements.

ACTS 15 & 16 VIC., CAP. 63, & 17 VIC., CAP. 8.

COUNTY OF CAVAN.

BARONY OF CASTLERAHAN.

UNION OF OLDCASTLE.

PARISH OF CASTLERAHAN.

No. and Letters of Reference to Map.		Names.		Description of Tenement.	Area.			Rateable Annual Valuation.						Total Annual Valuation of Rateable Property.		
		Townlands and Occupiers.	Immediate Lessors.					Land.			Buildings.					
					A.	R.	P.	£	s.	d.	£	s.	d.	£	s.	d.
		AGHALION.														
		(Ord. S. 39.)														
1	a	John Lynch,	C. T. Nesbit,	House, offices, and land,	14	2	28	6	5	0	0	10	0	6	15	0
–	b	C. T. Nesbit,	In fee,	Land,	0	3	30	0	5	0	–			0	5	0
2	∫ a	Bryan M'Donald,	C. T. Nesbit,	Herd's house & land,	19	3	22	4	0	0	1	5	0	5	5	0
	∖ –	John Fitzsimon,		Land,				4	0	0	–			4	0	0
3		John Fitzsimon,	Same,	House, offices, and land,	5	1	34	2	0	0	1	0	0	3	0	0
4		John Fitzsimon,	Same,	Land,	4	1	34	2	0	0	–			2	0	0
–	a	Rose Fitzsimon,	Same,	House,	–			–			0	10	0	0	10	0
5	a	John Fitzsimon, jun.,	Same,	House, offices, and land,	8	1	35	4	0	0	1	0	0	5	0	0
–	b	John Fitzsimon,	Same,	Land,	0	2	15	0	5	0	–			0	5	0
	c			Land (gardens),	0	1	24	0	5	0	–			0	5	0
6	– {	John Flood,	Same,	House, offices, and land,	17	2	8	8	0	0	1	15	0	9	15	0
7			Same,	House, offices, and land,	31	0	12	10	0	0	1	5	0	} 14	0	0
8	}	Michael Cogan,	Same,	Land,	7	2	16	2	15	0						
			Same,	House, offices, and land,	5	0	22	1	18	0	0	10	0			
9	a	Peter Lynch,	Same,	Bog,	7	0	17	0	7	0	–			2	15	0
				Ho., off., & sm. garden,	–			–			0	10	0	0	10	0
–	b }	Joseph Brady,	Same,	Land,	1	1	33	0	10	0	–			0	10	0
10			Same,	House and land,	2	0	4	0	10	0	0	5	0	0	15	0
11		Catherine Fitzsimon,	Same,	House, office, and land,	13	0	9	4	10	0	0	10	0	5	0	0
12		Matthew Cogan,	Same,	Land,	11	0	24	4	0	0	–					
13			Same,	House, offices, and land,	23	3	18	12	0	0	1	5	0	} 22	5	0
14	{	Patrick Cogan,	Same,	Land,	8	2	21	4	0	0	–					
15				Land,	1	2	2	1	0	0						
16				Land,	0	1	24	0	4	0				0	4	0
–	a	John Lynch,	Same,	Land,	38	0	30	15	0	0	1	0	0	16	0	0
17	a	Terence & Patk. Cogan,	Same,	House, offices, and land,	–			–			0	5	0	0	5	0
–	b	Vacant,	Terence & Patk. Cogan,	House,	–			–			0	10	0	0	10	0
–	c	Vacant,	Same,	House,	–			–			0	15	0	4	15	0
18		Michael Brady,	C. T. Nesbit,	House, office, and land,	8	2	20	4	0	0	0	15	0	4	15	0
19	a	James Bennett,	Same,	House, offices, and land,	34	2	18	17	10	0	1	5	0	18	15	0
–	b	Margaret Gilroy,	James Bennett,	House,	–			–			0	10	0	0	10	0
–	c	Anne Timmon,	Same,	House,	–			–			0	5	0	0	5	0
–	d	Peter Lynch,	C. T. Nesbit,	Land,	0	0	20	0	1	0	–			0	1	0
–	e	Joseph Brady,	Same,	Land,	0	0	20	0	1	0	–			0	1	0
20		Anthony Brady,	Same,	House, offices, and land,	12	0	14	5	15	0	1	0	0	6	15	0
21		John Lynch,	Same,	House, offices, and land,	12	1	18	6	5	0	1	0	0	7	5	0
22		Edward Fitzsimons,	Same,	House, office, and land,	6	2	16	3	0	0	0	10	0	3	10	0
23	a	Michael Brady,	Same,	Herd's house and land,	14	3	13	7	10	0	0	10	0	8	0	0
–	b	Terence & Patk. Cogan,	Same,	Land,	0	1	24	0	5	0	–			0	5	0
24		Peter Brady,	Same,	Land,	7	0	31	3	0	0	–			3	0	0
25		John Brady,	Same,	Herd's house and land,	34	3	2	16	0	0	0	5	0	16	5	0
26		Patrick Brady,	Same,	House, offices, and land,	18	1	17	8	15	0	1	15	0	10	10	0
27		C. T. Nesbit,	In fee,	Land,	14	0	13	0	15	0	–			0	15	0

B

Valuation of Ireland, were published between 1848 and 1864. The Valuation is arranged by county, barony, poor law union, civil parish and townland, and lists every landholder and every householder in Ireland. Apart from townland address and householder's name, the particulars given are:

➤ name of the person from whom the property was leased ('immediate lessor');

➤ description of the property;

➤ acreage;

➤ valuation.

The only directly useful family information supplied is in areas where a surname was particularly common; the surveyors often adopted the Gaelic practice of using the father's first name to distinguish between individuals of the same name, so that 'John Reilly (James)' is the son of James, while 'John Reilly (Michael)' is the son of Michael. Copies of the Valuation are widely available in major libraries and record offices, both on microfiche and in their original published form. The dates of first publication will be found under the individual counties in Chapter 12.

The Valuation was never intended as a census substitute, and if the 1851 census had survived, it would have little genealogical significance. As things stand, however, it gives the only detailed guide to where in Ireland people lived in the mid-nineteenth century, and what property they possessed. In addition, because the Valuation entries were subsequently revised at regular intervals, it is often possible to trace living descendants of those originally listed by Griffith. (See 'Valuation Office Records' below.)

Indexes to Griffith's and Tithe Books

In the early 1960s the National Library undertook a project to index the surnames occurring in Griffith's Valuation and the Tithe Books, which produced the county-by-county series known as the 'Index of Surnames' or 'Householders Index'. This records the occurrence of households of a particular surname in each of the civil parishes of a county, giving the exact number of households in the case of Griffith's, as well as providing a summary of the total numbers in each barony of the county. Since it is not a true index, providing only an indication of the presence or absence of a surname in the Tithe Books, and the numbers of the surname in Griffith's, its usefulness is limited. For names which are relatively uncommon it can be invaluable, but is of little assistance for a county in which a particular surname is plentiful. It is most frequently used as a means of narrowing the number of parish records to be searched in a case where only the county of origin of an ancestor is known. The county volumes include outline maps of the civil parishes covered and a guide to the corresponding Catholic parishes. Full sets of the Index of Surnames can be found at the National Library, the

Surname			Barony
Fitzgerald	G2		Loughtee L.
Fitzgerald	G	T	Loughtee U.
Fitzgerald		T	Tullygarvey
Fitzgerald	G2	T	Clankee
Fitzgerald	G2		Clanmahon
Fitzmaurice	G		Tullyhunco
Fitzpatrick	G25	T	Tullyhaw
Fitzpatrick	G114	T	Loughtee L.
Fitzpatrick	G24	T	Tullyhunco
Fitzpatrick	G73	T	Loughtee U.
Fitzpatrick	G30	T	Tullygarvey
Fitzpatrick	G9	T	Clankee
Fitzpatrick	G33	T	Clanmahon
Fitzpatrick	G10	T	Castlerahan
Fitzsimmons		T	Tullyhunco
Fitzsimmons	G	T	Loughtee U.
Fitzsimmons	G	T	Clanmahon
Fitzsimon	G	T	Tullyhunco
Fitzsimon	G2	T	Loughtee U.
Fitzsimon	G7	T	Tullygarvey
Fitzsimon	G	T	Clankee
Fitzsimon	G		Clanmahon
Fitizsimon	G5	T	Castlerahan
Fitzsimon	G39	T	Castlerahan
Fitzsimons	G	T	Tullyhaw
Fitzsimons	G6	T	Loughtee L.
Fitzsimons	G12	T	Loughtee U.
Fitzsimons	G8	T	Tullygarvey
Fitzsimons	G7	T	Clankee
Fitzsimons	G14	T	Clanmahon
Fitzsimons	G6	T	Castlerahan
Flack		T	Tullyhunco
Flack	G2	T	Tullygarvey
Flack	G3	T	Clankee
Flaherty		T	Loughtee L.
Flanagan	G14	T	Tullyhaw
Flanagan	G3	T	Loughtee L.
Flanagan	G		Tullyhunco
Flanagan	G10	T	Loughtee U.
Flanagan	G	T	Tullygarvey
Flanagan	G4	T	Clankee
Flanagan	G3	T	Clanmahon
Flanagan	G14	T	Castlerahan
Flanigan	G2	T	Tullyhaw
Flanigan	G		Loughtee L.
Flanigan		T	Loughtee U.
Flannagan	G		Loughtee L.
Flannery	G		Loughtee U.
Fleming	G		Tullyhaw
Fleming	G	T	Loughtee L.
Fleming	G3	T	Tullyhunco
Fleming	G8	T	Loughtee U.
Fleming	G	T	Tullygarvey
Fleming	G	T	Clankee
Fleming	G9	T	Clanmahon
Fleming	G7	T	Castlerahan
Fletcher	G		Loughtee U.
Fleuker	G	T	Clankee
Flewker	G2	T	Clankee
Flinn		T	Clankee
Flinn	G	T	Clanmahon
Flood	G	T	Tullyhaw

Surname			Barony
Flood	G21	T	Loughtee U.
Flood	G18	T	Tullygarvey
Flood	G4	T	Clankee
Flood	G14	T	Clanmahon
Flood	G29	T	Castlerahan
Floody	G3	T	Tullygarvey
Floyd	G2	T	Loughtee U.
Flynn	G13	T	Tullyhaw
Flynn	G6	T	Loughtee L.
Flynn	G		Tullyhunco
Flynn	G3	T	Loughtee U.
Flynn		T	Tullygarvey
Flynn	G		Clankee
Flynn	G9	T	Clanmahon
Flynn	G20	T	Castlerahan
Foghlan	G		Tullyhaw
Folbus		T	Tullyhunco
Foley	G2		Tullygarvey
Follett	G		Loughtee U.
Fonor		T	Castlerahan
Forbes	G	T	Tullyhunco
Forbes	G	T	Clankee
Ford	G		Tullyhaw
Ford	G		Loughtee U.
Ford	G2	T	Tullygarvey
Ford	G		Clankee
Forde	G	T	Tullyhaw
Foreman	G6	T	Clankee
Forest			Loughtee U.
Forster		T	Loughtee U.
Forster	G10	T	Clanmahon
Forsyth	G3	T	Castlerahan
Foraythe	G3	T	Clanmahon
Fosqua		T	Tullygarvey
Foster	G	T	Tullyhaw
Foster	G6	T	Loughtee U.
Foster	G5		Tullygarvey
Foster	G9	T	Clanmahon
Foster	G3	T	Castlerahan
Fotton		T	Tullygarvey
Pottrell	G		Clankee
Fox	G2	T	Tullyhaw
Fox	G2	T	Tullyhunco
Fox		T	Loughtee U.
Fox	G4	T	Tullygarvey
Fox	G15	T	Clankee
Fox	G2	T	Clanmahon
Fox	G36	T	Castlerahan
Foy	G3	T	Loughtee L.
Foy	G2	T	Loughtee U.
Foy	G26	T	Tullygarvey
Foy	G5	T	Clankee
Foy	G	T	Clanmahon
Foy		T	Castlerahan
Foyragh		T	Tullygarvey
Frances	G	T	Clankee
Francey	G3		Clankee
Francis		T	Loughtee L.
Fraser	G3	T	Tullyhaw
Frazer	G		Tullyhaw
Frazer	G		Loughtee U.
Frazor		T	Tullyhunco

National Archives, the Public Record Office of Northern Ireland, and the Genealogical Office.

In recent years a number of full-name indexes to Griffith's have been produced on microfiche by All-Ireland Heritage and Andrew Morris, both in the US. These list alphabetically all the householders in the Valuation, and show the townland and civil parish in which the entry is recorded. For the moment, the following areas have been covered: Counties Cork, Fermanagh, Limerick, Tipperary, Waterford; the cities of Belfast, Cork and Dublin (All-Ireland Heritage); and Counties Mayo and Wicklow (Andrew Morris). As aids to locating individual families in these counties at the time of the Valuation, these are invaluable. However, they are not widely available as yet. The National Archives has copies of the indexes for Cork City and county, Dublin City, and Co. Fermanagh, while the National Library has copies of those for Counties Mayo and Wicklow.

VALUATION OFFICE RECORDS

The Valuation Office, set up to carry out the original Primary Valuation, is still in existence and has two related sets of records which are potentially valuable. The first of these are the notebooks used by the original Valuation surveyors, consisting of 'field books', 'house books' and 'tenure books'. All three record a map reference for the holdings they deal with, as in the published Valuation. The field books then record information on the size and quality of the holding, the house books record the occupiers' names and the measurements of any buildings on their holdings, and the tenure books give the annual rent paid and the legal basis on which the holding is occupied, whether by lease or at will. The tenure books also give the year of any lease, useful to know before searching estate papers or the Registry of Deeds. As well as containing information such as this, which does not appear in the published Valuation, the valuers' notebooks can also be useful in documenting any changes in occupation between the initial survey and the published results, for instance if a family emigrated in the years immediately before publication, since they pre-date the final publication itself by several years. Unfortunately, they are not extant for all areas. The National Archives now houses those which survive for the Republic of Ireland. Those covering Northern Ireland are now to be found in the Public Record Office of Northern Ireland.

The Valuation Office itself, at 6 Ely Place, Dublin 2, contains the second set of useful records. These are the 'Cancelled Land Books' and 'Current Land Books', giving details of all changes in the holdings, from the time of the Primary Valuation up to the present day. Any variations in the size or status of the holding, the names of the occupier or lessor, or the valuation itself, are given in the revisions carried out every few years. The Books can be very useful in pin-pointing a possible date of death or emigration, or in

CASTLERAHAN PARISH. CASTLERAHAN BARONY, OLDCASTLE UNION,

CO. CAVAN 32.

Griffith's Valuation Year 1856 - Tithe Applotment Book Year 1831.

Anderson	G		Cunningham	G2	T	Hanly	G2	T
Armstrong	G	T	Curran	G		Hanna	G	
			Cusack	G		Hanley		T
Balfe	G					Hartley		T
Barclay		T	Daly	G2	T	Haulton		T
Barry	G		Darcy		T	Hawthorn	G5	T
Bartley	G2	T	Darling	G		Haynes	G	
Bates	G		Dempsey	G		Heeny	G2	T
Bell	G		Dolan	G6	T	Heevy	G4	T
Bennett	G3	T	Donnelly	G2	T	Henesy	G	
Blackstock		T T	Dowland		T	Henway		T
Booker	G	T	Downs	G		Hourigan	G4	T
Boyd	G		Duffy	G3	T	Hughes	G3	
Boyers		T	Duigan	G		Humphries		T
Boylan	G4	T	Duignan	G2	T	Hunter	G3	T
Brady	G42	T				Hyland		T
Bray	G3	T	Evans	G2	T			
Brennan	G	T				Irwin	G2	
Briody	G		Fagan	G6	T			
Brookes	G		Farelly	G	T	James		T
Brown	G		Farrell	G9	T	Johnston	G	
Browne	G		Farrelly	G15	T			
Buchanan	G	T	Finigan	G	T	Kavanagh	G	
Byres	G6		Finn		T	Keane	G	T
			Finnegan	G2	T	Keelan	G	
Caffrey	G13	T	Fitzpatrick	G3	T	Kellett	G2	
Cahill	G4	T	Fitzsimon	G9	T	Kelly	G2	
Caldwell	G3	T	Fitzsimons	G	T	Kennedy	G3	T
Callaghan	G3		Fleming	G2		Kenny	G	
Carey	G		Flood	G5	T	Keoghan	G	T
Carolin		T	Flynn	G3	T	Kerr	G	
Carr	G		Foster	G2	T	Kiernan	G	T
Carroll	G		Fox	G6		Kilrien		T T
Cartan	G		Freeland	G	T	Kilroy		T
Clarekin	G2	T				Kimmins		T
Clarke	G5	T	Gaffney	G2	T	King	G3	
Cobey		T	Geghren		T			
Cochrane	G		Gelaher	G		Leeson	G	
Cogan	G12		Galligan		T	Leightel	G3	
Colerigg	G2	T	Gavan	G	T	Little		T
Colgan	G4	T	Gaynor	G6	T	Lord	G	
Colingg	G		Geoghegan	G2		Lougheed	G	
Comerford		T	Gibney	G3	T	Loughlin		T
Conaghty	G		Gibson	G	T	Love	G2	T
Condon		T	Gill	G		Lyddy	G	T
Connell	G4	T	Gillick	G	T	Lynch	G51	T
Connor	G	T	Gilroy	G				
Conway	G3		Glannon		T	McCabe	G13	T
Cooke	G	T	Goff		T	McCahill	G	T
Cooney	G		Gormley	G		McCormack	G	
Coote	G5	T	Grattan		T	McCutchion		T
Corrigan	G2	T	Graveny		T	McDermott	G	
Cosgrave	G	T	Gray		T	McDonald	G5	T
Coyle	G	T	Griffin		T	McDonnell	G	
Crawly	G	T	Griffith	G	T	McDowell	G2	
Cronin	G3	T				McEnermy		T
Cullen	G9	T	Halpin	G3	T	McEnroe	G14	T
						McEvoy	G	T

identifying a living relative. A large majority of those who were in occupation of a holding by the 1890s, when the Land Acts began to subsidise the purchase of the land by its tenant-farmers, have descendants or relatives still living in the same area. The Cancelled Land Books for Northern Ireland are now in the Public Record Office of Northern Ireland.

ESTATE RECORDS

In the eighteenth and nineteenth centuries the vast majority of the Irish population lived as small tenant-farmers on large estates owned for the most part by English or Anglo-Irish landlords. The administration of these estates inevitably produced large quantities of records—maps, tenants' lists, rentals, account books, lease books etc. Over the course of the twentieth century, as the estates have been broken up and sold off, many collections of these records have found their way into public repositories, and constitute a largely unexplored source of genealogical information.

There are, however, good reasons for their being unexplored. First, it was quite rare for a large landowner to have individual rental or lease agreements with the huge numbers of small tenants on his land. Instead, he would let a significant area to a middleman, who would then sublet to others, who might in turn rent out parts to the smallest tenants. It is very rare for estate records to document the smallest landholders, since most of these had no right of tenure in any case, being simply tenants 'at will'.

A related problem is the question of access. The estate records in the two major Dublin repositories, the National Archives and the National Library, are not catalogued in detail. The only comprehensive guide is given in Richard Hayes' 'Manuscript Sources for the Study of Irish Civilization' and its supplements, copies of which can be found in the National Library and National Archives. This catalogues the records by landlord's name and by county, with entries such as 'NL MS. 3185. Rent Roll of Lord Cremorne's estate in Co. Armagh, 1797'. Hayes gives no further details of the areas of the county covered, and it can be difficult to ascertain from the Tithe Books or Griffith's just who the landlord was; Griffith's only supplies the name of the immediate lessor. The holdings of the Public Record Office of Northern Ireland present similar problems, with access depending on a knowledge of the landlord's name. In addition, it should be added that many of the collections in the National Library have still not been catalogued at all, and thus remain completely inaccessible.

The largest single collection in the National Archives is the Landed Estate Court records, also known as the Encumbered Estate Courts, which are not catalogued in Hayes. The Court was set up to facilitate the sale of estates whose owners could not invest enough to make them productive, and between 1849 and 1857 oversaw the sale of more than 3,000 Irish estates. Its records contain many rentals and maps drawn up for the sales, but are so close in time to Griffith's as to make them of limited use except in very particular circumstances. Once again the principal problem of access is in identifying the relevant landlord, since they too are catalogued by landlord's name.

There are a number of ways to overcome, or partially overcome, this obstacle. With common sense, it is often possible to identify the landlord by examining Griffith's for the surrounding areas—the largest lessor is the likeliest candidate. If the immediate lessor in Griffith's is not the landlord, but a middleman, then it can be useful to try to find this middleman's own holding or residence and see who he was leasing from. Two publications may also be of value. O. H. Hussey de Burgh's *The Landowners of Ireland* provides a guide to the major landowners, the size of their holdings, and where in the country they were situated. *Landowners in Ireland: Return of owners of land of one acre and upwards . . .,* (London: 1876) is comprehensive to a fault, and is organised more awkwardly, alphabetically within county.

Despite all the problems, research in estate records can be very rewarding, especially for the period before the major nineteenth-century surveys. To take one example, the rent rolls of the estate of Charles O'Hara in Counties Sligo and Leitrim, which date from *c*.1775, record a large number of leases to smaller tenants, and supply the lives named in the leases, often specifying family relationships. It must be emphasised, however, that information of this quality is rare; the majority of the rentals and tenants' lists surviving only give details of major tenants.

A more detailed guide to the dates, areas covered, and class of tenants recorded in the estate papers of the National Library and National Archives is in the process of preparation by the Genealogical Office. To date, Counties Cork, Leitrim, Galway, Mayo, Roscommon and Sligo have been covered, and a brief outline of the results will be found in Chapter 12 under these counties.

PART 2

Other Sources

5

Wills

1. THE NATURE OF THE RECORDS

Wills have always been an extremely important source of genealogical information on the property-owning classes, in Ireland as elsewhere. They provide a clear picture of a family at a particular point in time, and can often supply enough details of a much larger network of relationships—cousins, nephews, in-laws and others—to produce quite a substantial family tree. Apart from their genealogical significance, wills can also evoke vividly the long-vanished way of life of those whose final wishes they record.

INFORMATION SUPPLIED
The minimum information to be found in a will is:
➤ the name, address and occupation of the testator;
➤ the names of the beneficiaries;
➤ the name(s) of the executor(s);
➤ the names of the witnesses;
➤ the date the will was made;
➤ the date of probate of the will.
Specific properties are usually, though not always, mentioned. The two dates, that of the will itself and of its probate, give a period during which the testator died. Up to the nineteenth century most wills were made close to the date of death, and witnesses were normally related to the person making the

will. As well as the minimum information, of course, many wills also contain much more, including at times addresses and occupations of beneficiaries, witnesses and executors, and details of family relationships, quarrels as well as affection.

Testamentary Authority before 1857

Before 1857 the Church of Ireland, as the Established Church, had charge of all testamentary affairs. Consistorial Courts in each diocese were responsible for granting probate, that is, legally authenticating a will and conferring on the executors the power to administer the estate. The Courts also had the power to issue letters of administration to the next of kin or the main creditor on the estates of those who died intestate. Each Court was responsible for wills and administrations in its own diocese. However, when the estate included property worth more than £5 in another diocese, responsibility for the will or administration passed to the Prerogative Court under the authority of the Archbishop of Armagh.

Consistorial Wills and Administrations

The wills and administration records of the Consistorial Courts were held locally in each diocese up to the abolition of the testamentary authority of the Church of Ireland in 1857. After that date the Public Record Office began the slow process of collecting the original records and transcribing them into Will and Grant Books. The Office then indexed the wills and Administration Bonds, the sureties which the administrators had to produce as a guarantee that the estate would be properly administered. None of the Consistorial Courts had records of all the wills or administrations they had dealt with. Very little earlier than the seventeenth century emerged, and the majority of the Courts appear to have had serious gaps before the mid-eighteenth century.

All the original wills and administrations in the Public Record Office were destroyed in 1922, along with almost all the Will and Grant Books into which they had been transcribed. The only exceptions are the Will Books for Down (1850–58) and Connor (1818–20, 1853–58), and the Grant Books for Cashel (1840–45), Derry and Raphoe (1818–21), and Ossory (1848–58).

The indexes to wills and administration bonds were not destroyed, although a number were badly damaged. These are available in the reading room of the National Archives. The wills indexes are alphabetical and normally give the testator's address and the year of probate, as well as occasionally specifying his occupation. The administration bonds indexes are not fully alphabetical, being arranged year by year under the initial letter of the surname of the deceased. They give the year of the bond, the full name and usually the address of the deceased, and sometimes his occupation. Some of the wills indexes have been published and details of these will be found at the end of this chapter.

Prerogative Wills and Administrations

To recap: an estate was dealt with by the Prerogative Court, rather than a Consistorial Court, if it covered property worth more than £5 in a second diocese. In general, then, Prerogative wills and administrations tend to cover the wealthier classes, merchants with dealings in more than one area, and those who lived close to diocesan borders. Up to 1816 the Prerogative Court was not housed in a single place, with hearings generally held in the residence of the presiding judge. From 1816 on, the King's Inns building in Henrietta St provided a permanent home. For this reason the records of the Court before 1816 cannot be taken as complete. After 1857 all these records were transferred to the Public Record Office, where the original wills and grants of administration were transcribed into Prerogative Will and Grant Books, and indexed. The indexes survived 1922, but all the original wills and grants, and almost all the Will and Grant Books were destroyed. Details of those Books which survived will be found at the end of this chapter.

The loss of the original Prerogative wills is mitigated to a large extent by the project carried out in the early decades of the nineteenth century by Sir William Betham, Ulster King of Arms. As well as preparing the first index of testators, up to 1810, he also made abstracts of the family information contained in almost all the wills before 1800. The original notebooks in which he recorded the information are now in the National Archives, and the Genealogical Office has his Sketch Pedigrees based on these abstracts and including later additions and amendments. The Public Record Office of Northern Ireland has a copy of the Genealogical Office series, without the additions and amendments, made by a successor of Betham's, Sir John Burke. Betham also made a large number of abstracts from Prerogative Grants up to 1802, the original notebooks for which are also in the National Archives. The Genealogical Office transcript copy (GO 257–260) is fully alphabetical, unlike the notebooks.

The first index to Prerogative wills, up to 1810, was published in 1897 by Sir Arthur Vicars, Burke's successor as Ulster King of Arms, and can be used as a guide to Betham's abstracts and Sketch Pedigrees with the proviso that wills from the decade 1800–1810 are not covered by Betham. The manuscript index for the period from 1811 to 1857 is in the National Archives reading room. As with the consistorial administration bonds indexes, the Prerogative Grants indexes are not fully alphabetical, being arranged year by year under the initial letter of the surname of the deceased.

Testamentary Authority after 1857

The Probate Act of 1857 did away with the testamentary authority of the Church of Ireland. Instead of the Consistorial Courts and the Prerogative Court, power to grant probate and issue letters of administration was vested in a Principal Registry in Dublin and eleven District Registries. Rules similar to those governing the geographical jurisdiction of the ecclesiastical courts applied, with the Principal Registry taking the place of the Prerogative Court, as well as covering Dublin and a large area around it. Transcripts of the wills proved and administrations granted were made in the District Registries, and the originals forwarded to the Principal Registry. Almost all the records of the Principal Registry were destroyed in 1922. The few surviving Will and Grant Books are detailed below. The Will Book transcripts made by the District Registries survived, however. The records of those Districts covering areas now in the Republic—Ballina, Cavan, Cork, Kilkenny, Limerick, Mullingar, Tuam and Waterford—are in the National Archives. For districts now in Northern Ireland—Armagh, Belfast and Londonderry— the Will Books are in the Public Record Office of Northern Ireland.

Fortunately, from 1858 a new system of indexing and organising wills and administrations had been devised. A printed, alphabetically ordered 'Calendar of Wills and Administrations' was produced for every year, and copies of all these have survived. For each will or administration, these record:
➢ the name, address and occupation of the deceased person;
➢ the place and date of death;
➢ the value of the estate;
➢ the name and address of the person or persons to whom probate or administration was granted.
In many cases the relationship of the executor is also specified. This means that despite the loss of so much original post-1857 testamentary material, some information at least is available on all wills or administrations from this period. Very often much that is of genealogical value can be gleaned from the Calendars, including such information as exact dates of death, places of residence and indications of economic status. A consolidated index covers the period between 1858 and 1877, making it unnecessary to search each yearly Calendar. The Calendars are on open access in the National Archives reading room.

Abstracts and Transcripts

As well as the original Consistorial and Prerogative wills and grants, and the transcripts made of them in the Will and Grant Books, a wide range of other sources exists, particularly for material before 1857. The most important of these is the collection of the National Archives itself, gathered after 1922 in

270 WILLS AND ADMINISTRATIONS. 1871.

HORGAN Daniel.

[191]   Effects under £200.

20 March.   Letters of Administration of the personal estate of Daniel Horgan late of Great George's-street **Cork** Builder deceased who died 21 February 1870 at same place were granted at **Cork** to Michael Joseph Horgan of the South Mall in said City Solicitor the Nephew of said deceased for the benefit of Catherine Horgan Widow John Horgan the Reverend David Horgan Ellen Gillman Mary Daly and Margaret Horgan only next of kin of said deceased.

HORNE Christopher.

[67]   Effects under £100.

7 March.   Letters of Administration of the personal estate of Christopher Horne late of Ballinasloe County **Galway** Gentleman a Widower deceased who died 21 March 1867 at same place were granted at the **Principal Registry** to Patrick Horne of Ballinasloe aforesaid M.D. the only Brother of said deceased.

HORNER Isabella.

[17]   Effects under £100.

29 April.   Letters of Administration of the personal estate of Isabella Horner late of Rahaghy County **Tyrone** Widow deceased who died 13 April 1871 at same place were granted at **Armagh** to James Horner of Rahaghy (Aughnacloy) aforesaid Farmer the Son and one of the next of kin of said deceased.

HORNIDGE John Isaiah.

[79]   Effects under £450.

8 June.   Letters of Administration (with the Will annexed) of the personal estate of John Isaiah Hornidge late of the South Dublin Union Workhouse **Dublin** Master of said Workhouse a Widower deceased who died 22 April 1871 at same place were granted at the **Principal Registry** to James Seymour Longstaff of Stephen's-green Dublin Merchant and William Thomas Orpin of George's-terrace George's-avenue Blackrock County Dublin Accountant the Guardians during minority only of the Daughter and only next of kin of deceased.

HOUSTON Eliza.

[337]   Effects under £200.

22 September.   Letters of Administration of the personal estate of Eliza Houston late of

an attempt to replace some at least of what had been lost. As well as original wills from private legal records and individual families, this ever-expanding collection also includes pre-1922 researchers' abstracts and transcripts. It is covered by a card index in the reading room, which also gives details of those wills and grants in the surviving pre-1857 Will and Grant Books. Separate card indexes cover the Thrift, Jennings and Crossley collections of abstracts, and the records of Charitable Donations and Bequests. The Public Record Office of Northern Ireland has made similar efforts, and the copies it holds are indexed in the Pre-1858 Wills Index, part of the Subject Index in the Public Search Room.

INLAND REVENUE RECORDS
The Inland Revenue in London kept a series of Annual Indexes to Irish Will Registers and Indexes to Irish Administration Registers from 1828 to 1879 which are now in the National Archives. These give the name and address of both the deceased and the executor or administrator. As well as the Indexes, the Archives also holds a set of the actual Inland Revenue Irish Will Registers and Irish Administration Registers for the years 1828–39, complete, apart from the Wills Register covering January to June 1834. The Will Registers are not exact transcripts of the original wills, but supply a good deal of detailed information including the precise date of death, the principal beneficiaries and legacies, and a brief inventory of the estate. The Administration Registers are less informative, but still include details of the date of death, the administrator and the estate.

LAND COMMISSION RECORDS
Under the provisions of the Land Purchase Acts, which subsidised the purchase of smallholdings by the tenants who occupied them, it was necessary for those wishing to sell to produce evidence of their ownership to the Irish Land Commission. As a result, over ten thousand wills were deposited with the Commission, the majority from the nineteenth century, but many earlier. The National Library holds a card index to the testators. The original documents are currently in the process of being transferred to the National Archives.

THE REGISTRY OF DEEDS
The registration of wills was normally carried out because of a legal problem anticipated by the executor(s) in the provisions—almost certainly the exclusion of parties who would feel they had some rights over the estate. Because of this, wills at the Registry cannot be taken as providing a complete picture of the family. Abstracts of all wills registered from 1708, the date of the foundation of the Registry, to 1832, were published in three volumes by the Irish Manuscripts Commission between 1954 and 1986. These are available on open shelves at the National Library and National Archives. Although the

abstracts record and index all the persons named, testators, beneficiaries and witnesses, they do not show the original provisions of the wills. These can be found in the original memorials in the Registry.

THE GENEALOGICAL OFFICE
Most of the will abstracts held by the Genealogical Office are covered by the Office's own index, GO MS. 429, which was published in *Analecta Hibernica*, No. 17, 1949 (NL Ir. 941 a 10). The manuscript index has since been added to, but is still not entirely comprehensive, excluding all the Betham material and many of the collections relating to individual families. A guide to the major collections is included in the reference guide at the end of this chapter.

OTHER SOURCES
There are many other collections of will abstracts and transcripts in such public repositories as the National Library, the Representative Church Body Library, the Royal Irish Academy, the Public Record Office of Northern Ireland and Trinity College Library. There are no separate indexes to these testamentary collections. Where a significant group of abstracts or transcripts exists, this is noted in the reference guide which follows.

2. A REFERENCE GUIDE

What follows is an attempt to provide a series of check-lists and guides to the various testamentary sources. Because of the changes in testamentary juris-diction in 1858, it is divided into two sections, dealing with records before and after that date. Section 1, Pre-1858, includes (1) a general check-list of surviving indexes; (2) a list of surviving Will and Grant Books; (3) a list of major collections of abstracts and transcripts, divided into (i) general collections, (ii) those relating to particular surnames, and (iii) those relating to particular diocesan jurisdictions; (4) a detailed list of surviving consistorial wills and administrations indexes, both published and in the National Archives. Section 2, Post-1858, covers (1) the yearly calendars; and (2) original wills and transcripts.

Section I. pre-1858

1. GENERAL INDEXES
1. Card Indexes, National Archives search room.
2. Pre-1858 Wills Index, PRONI reading room.
3. Indexes to Consistorial Wills and Administrations, diocese by diocese (see below for details).
4. Indexes to Prerogative Wills.

(a) Sir Arthur Vicars, *Index to the Prerogative Wills of Ireland, 1536–1810* (1897);
(b) MS. Index, 1811–1858, National Archives search room.
5. Index to Prerogative Grants, National Archives search room.
6. Index to Wills in the Records of the Land Commission, National Library.

2. SURVIVING WILL AND GRANT BOOKS
1. Prerogative Will Books: 1664–84, 1706–8 (A–W), 1726–28 (A–W), 1728–29 (A–W), 1777 (A–L), 1813 (K–Z), 1834 (A–E), National Archives, included in card index.
2. Prerogative Administrations: Grants 1684–88, 1748–51, 1839; Day Books, 1784–88, National Archives.
3. Consistorial Will Books: Connor (1818–1820, 1853–1858); Down (1850–1858), National Archives.
4. Consistorial Grant Books: Cashel (1840–1845); Derry and Raphoe (1812–1821); Ossory (1848–1858); National Archives.

3. ABSTRACTS AND TRANSCRIPTS
(i): *General Collections*
1. Betham abstracts from Prerogative Wills, to *c.*1800, National Archives (notebooks); Genealogical Office and Public Record Office of Northern Ireland (Sketch Pedigrees), (see Vicars above).
2. Betham abstracts from Prerogative Administrations, to *c.*1800, National Archives (notebooks); Genealogical Office (alphabetical listing).
3. Indexes to Irish Will Registers, 1828–79 (Inland Revenue), National Archives (see Testamentary Catalogue).
4. Irish Will Registers, 1828–1839 (Inland Revenue), National Archives (see Testamentary Catalogue).
5. Indexes to Irish Administration Registers, 1828–79 (Inland Revenue), National Archives (see Testamentary Catalogue).
6. Irish Administration Registers, 1828–1839 (Inland Revenue), National Archives (see Testamentary Catalogue).
7. Index to Will Abstracts at the Genealogical Office, *Analecta Hibernica*, 17; GO MS. 429.
8. P. B. Phair and E. Ellis, *Abstracts of Wills at the Registry of Deeds* (1708–1832), IMC, 1954–88.
9. Abstracts of wills of Irish testators registered at the Prerogative Court of Canterbury, 1639–98, NL MS. 1397.
10. Abstracts of miscellaneous eighteenth-century wills made by the Protestant clergy and their families, Representative Church Body Library (for the years 1828–39, see also NL MS. 2599).
11. Leslie Collection, 981 wills, NL MS. 1774, see also NL Pos. 799.
12. Ainsley Will Abstracts, GO 535 and 631.

13. Wilson Collection, NL Pos. 1990.
14. Welply Collection: 1,500 wills, 100 administrations, Representative Church Body Library, indexed in *The Irish Genealogist*, 1985/86.
15. Richey Collection, NL MSS. 8315-16.
16. Upton Collection, Royal Irish Academy, also NL Pos. 1997, principally families in Co. Westmeath, with some from Counties Cavan and Longford.
17. MacSwiney Papers, Royal Irish Academy, mainly Counties Cork and Kerry.
18. Westropp Manuscripts, Royal Irish Academy, mainly Counties Clare and Limerick.

(ii) *By Surname*

Burke	GO MS. 707.
Butler	Wallace Clare, *The Testamentary Records of the Butler Family*, 1932, NL Ir. 9292 b 11.
Dawson	Almost all eighteenth-century Dawson wills, NL MS. 5644/5.
Domville	NL MSS. 9384-86.
Drought	Crossley Abstracts, National Archives, also GO 417/8.
Gordon	GO MS. 702, Abstracts of most Irish Gordon wills.
Griffith	NL MS. 8392.
Greene	See National Archives Card Index.
Hamilton	Co. Down, PRONI T.702A.
Hill	GO MS. 691-92.
Kelly	GO MS. 415.
Manley	NL D.7075-86, the Manley family of Dublin and Offaly.
Mathews	Prerogative wills and administrations, PRONI T.681.
O'Loghlen	Co. Clare, NL Pos. 2543.
Skerrett	*The Irish Ancestor*, Vol. 5, No. 2, 1975.
Young	NL Pos. 1276.

(iii) *By Diocese*

A word of warning is necessary: the identification of a collection of abstracts or transcripts under a particular diocese does *not* necessarily mean that all the wills it covers belong to that diocese. In the case of the larger collections especially, it is just not possible to be absolutely precise about the areas covered.

Armagh

Four Wills of old English merchants of Drogheda, 1654-1717, JCLAS Vol. XX, 2, 1982

Alphabetical list of the prerogative wills of residents of Co. Louth up to 1810, NL, MS. 7314.

Index to wills of Dundalk residents, JCLAS, Vol. X, No. 2, 113-15, 1942.

Cashel and Emly
White, J. D., 'Extracts from original wills, formerly in the Consistorial Office, Cashel, later moved to Waterford Probate Court', *Kilkenny and South of Ire. Arch. Soc. Jnl.*, Ser. 2, Vol. 2, Pt 2, 1859; Vol. IV, 1862.

Clogher
Swanzy Collection, National Archives, T.1746 (1C–53–16); copies also at the Genealogical Office (GO 420, indexed in 429), and Representative Church Body Library; abstracts from Clogher and Kilmore Will Books, Marriage License Bonds, Administrations, militia lists; principal names include Beatty, Nixon, Armstrong, Young, Veitch, Jackson, Mee, Noble and Fiddes.

Clonfert
GO 707: Numerous abstracts, mainly relating to wills mentioning Burke families.

Cloyne
Welply Abstracts (4 volumes), Representative Church Body Library, indexed in *The Irish Genealogist*, 1985/1986.
Index to Will Abstracts at the Genealogical Office, *Analecta Hibernica*, 17; GO MS. 429.

Connor
Connor Will Book, 1818–20, 1853–58, National Archives.
Stewart-Kennedy notebooks, Will Abstracts, many from Down and Connor; principal families include Stewart, Clarke, Cunningham, Kennedy and Wade, Trinity College Library and PRONI; see also NL Pos. 4066.

Cork and Ross
Welply Abstracts (4 volumes), Representative Church Body Library, indexed in *The Irish Genealogist*, 1985/1986.
Caulfield transcripts, mainly sixteenth century, Representative Church Body Library; see also *Cork Hist. and Arch. Soc. Jnl*, 1903/1904.
Notes from wills of Cork Diocese, 1660–1700, NA M. 2760.

Derry
Amy Young, *300 Years in Inishowen* (NL Ir. 9292 y 1), contains 46 Donegal wills.

Down
Down Will Book, 1850–58, National Archives.
Stewart-Kennedy notebooks, Will Abstracts, many from Down and Connor; principal families include Stewart, Clarke, Cunningham, Kennedy and Wade, Trinity College Library and PRONI.

Dublin and Glendalough
Lane-Poole papers, NL MS. 5359 (abstracts).
Abstracts of wills proved in Dublin diocesan court, 1560–1710, A–E only, GO MS. 290.

Elphin
Wills and Deeds from Co. Sligo, 1605–32, NL. MS. 2164.

Kildare
Betham Collection, National Archives, Abstracts of almost all Kildare wills
    up to 1827; also NL Pos. 1784–85.

Killaloe and Kilfenora
O' Loghlen wills from Co. Clare, NL Pos. 2543.
Wills and Administrations from Counties Clare and Limerick, Westropp
    manuscript volume, 3A 39, Royal Irish Academy.

Kilmore
Swanzy Collection, National Archives, T.1746 (1C–53–16); copies also at the
    Genealogical Office (GO 420, indexed in 429), and Representative Church
    Body Library; Abstracts from Clogher and Kilmore Will Books, Marriage
    Licence Bonds, Administrations, militia lists; principal names include
    Beatty, Nixon, Armstrong, Young, Veitch, Jackon, Mee, Noble and Fiddes.

Leighlin
Carrigan Collection, NL. Pos. 903 (952 wills, mainly Ossory and Leighlin),
    indexed in *The Irish Genealogist*, 1970.
Abstracts from Ossory and Leighlin Admons, *The Irish Genealogist*, 1972.

Limerick
Hayes, R., 'Some Old Limerick Wills', *North Munster Antiquarian Journal*, Vol.
    I, 163–8, Vol. II, 71–5.
Wills and Administrations from Counties Clare and Limerick; Westropp
    manuscript volume, 3A 39, Royal Irish Academy.

Meath
Alphabetical list of the prerogative wills of residents of Co. Louth up to 1810,
    NL. MS. 7314.
Rice, G., 'Extracts from Meath priests' wills, 1658–1782', *Riocht na Midhe*, Vol.
    IV, No. 1, 68–71, 1967.

Ossory
Carrigan Collection, NL. Pos. 903 (952 wills, mainly Ossory and Leighlin),
    indexed in *The Irish Genealogist*, 1970.
Abstracts from Ossory and Leighlin Admons, *The Irish Genealogist*, 1972.
T. U. Sadleir, Abstracts from Ossory Admons, 1738–1884, NA 1A–37–33.
Calendar of Administrations, Ossory, NA T.7425.
GO 683–6, Walsh-Kelly notebooks. Will abstracts, mainly from Ossory.

Raphoe
Amy Young, *300 Years in Inishowen* (NL Ir. 9292 y 1). Contains 46 Donegal
    wills.

Tuam
GO 707, numerous abstracts, mainly relating to wills mentioning Burke families, 1784–1820.

Waterford and Lismore
Wills relating to Waterford, *Decies* (Journal of the Old Waterford Society), 16, 17, 19, 20, 22, 23 (NL Ir. 9414 d 5).
Jennings Collection, National Archives and *Decies* (above); 166 Waterford Wills and Administrations, NL D.9248–9413.

4. CONSISTORIAL WILLS AND ADMINISTRATION BONDS INDEXES, PUBLISHED AND IN THE NATIONAL ARCHIVES

Abbreviations

IA	*The Irish Ancestor* (NL Ir. 9205 1 3)
JCHAS	*Journal of the Cork Historical and Archaeological Society* (NL Ir. 794105 c 1)
JKAS	*Journal of the Kildare Archaeological Society* (NL Ir. 794106 k 2)
O'K.	Albert Casey (ed.) *O'Kief, Coshe Mang etc.* (NL Ir. 94145 c 12)
Ph.	Phillimore publication, open access, NA and NL
RDKPRI	Report of the Deputy Keeper of Public Records of Ireland

	Wills	*Admon Bonds*
Ardagh		
	1695–1858 (also IA, 1970)	1697–1850
Ardfert and Aghadoe		
	1690–1858 (Ph. 1690–1800; O'K. Vol. 5, 1690–1858)	1782–1858 (O'K. Vol. 5, 1782–1858)
Armagh		
	1666–1837 (A–L), 1677–1858 (M–Y), Drogheda District, 1691–1846	
Cashel and Emly		
	1618–1858 (Ph. 1618–1800)	1644–1858
Clogher		
	1661–1858	1660–1858

Clonfert

1663–1857   1771–1857
(IA, 1970)   (IA, 1970)

Cloyne

1621–1858   1630–1857
(Ph. 1621–1800;   (O'K. Vol. 6)
O'K. Vol. 8,
1547–1858)

Connor

1680–1846 (A–L),   1636–1858
1636–1857 (M–Y)

Cork and Ross

1548–1858   1612–1858
(Ph. & O'K. Vol. 8,   (O.K. Vol. 5)
1584–1800; JCHAS
1895–8: 1548–1833)

Derry

1612–1858   1698–1857
(Ph. 1612–1858)

Down

1646–1858   1635–1858

Dromore

1678–1858, with   1742–1858, with
Newry & Mourne,   Newry & Mourne,
1727–1858 (Ph.)   1811–45 (IA, 1969,
                                   Newry & Mourne)

Dublin and Glendalough

1536–1858   1636–1858
(RDKPRI Nos   (RDKPRI Nos
26 & 30)   26 & 30)

Elphin

1650–1858 (fragments)   1726–1857

Ferns

1601–1858 (fragments), 1765–1833
1603–1838 (F–V),
1615–1842 (unproved,
W only. Ph. 1601–1800)

Kildare

1661–1858   1770–1848
(Ph. 1661–1800;   (JKAS, 1907,
JKAS 1905: 1661–1858)   1770–1858)

Killala and Achonry

1756–1831 (fragments)   1779–1858
                                   (IA, 1975)

Killaloe and Kilfenora

1653–1858 (fragments)   1779–1858
(Ph. 1653–1800)   (IA, 1975)

Kilmore

1682–1858 (damaged)   1728–1858

Leighlin

1642–1858   1694–1845
(Ph. 1642–1800)   (IA, 1972)

Limerick

1615–1858   1789–1858
(Ph. 1615–1800)

Meath

1572–1858 (fragments),   1663–1857
partial transcript, 1635–1838,
NA 1A 42 167

Ossory

1536–1858 (fragments)   1660–1857
(Ph. 1536–1800)

Raphoe

1684–1858 (damaged)   1684–1858
(Ph.)

Tuam

1648–1858 (damaged)   1692–1857

Waterford and Lismore

1648–1858 (damaged)   1661–1857
(Ph. 1648–1800)

Section II. post-1858

1. YEARLY CALENDARS OF WILLS AND ADMINISTRATIONS, 1858 TO DATE
Provide: name, address and occupation of the deceased; place and exact date
of death; names and addresses of grantees of probate or administration, and
relationship; exact date of probate; value of the estate.

These are on open access in the search room of the National Archives
and the Public Record Office of Northern Ireland. The consolidated index,
1858–1877, is only in the National Archives.

2. ORIGINAL WILLS OR TRANSCRIPTS
(a) Card Index, National Archives search room
(b) Surviving Will and Grant Books in the National Archives, as follows:
    (i) Principal Registry Wills, 1874, G–M
       Principal Registry Wills, 1878, A–Z
       Principal Registry Wills, 1891, G–M
       Principal Registry Wills, 1896, A–F
       Principal Registry Wills, Dublin District, 1869, G–M
       Principal Registry Wills, Dublin District, 1891, M–P
       Principal Registry Wills, Dublin District, 1901, A–F
    (ii) Principal Registry Grants, 1878, 1883, 1891, 1893
    (iii) District Registry Will Books:
       Ballina, 1865 to date
       Cavan, 1858–1909
       Cork, 1858–1932
       Kilkenny, 1858–1911
       Limerick, 1858–1899
       Mullingar, 1858–1901
       Tuam, 1858–1929
       Waterford, 1858–1902.
(c) District Registry Will Books in the Public Record Office of Northern
    Ireland:
       Armagh, 1858–1900 (MIC 15C)
       Belfast, 1858–1900 (MIC 15C)
       Londonderry, 1858–1900 (MIC 15C).

6

The Genealogical Office

The Genealogical Office is the successor to the office of Ulster King of Arms, also known simply as 'The Office of Arms', which was created in 1552 when Edward VI designated Bartholomew Butler, the chief heraldic authority in Ireland, with the title of 'Ulster'. The reasons for the choice of 'Ulster' rather than 'Ireland' remain somewhat unclear; it seems likely that the older title of 'Ireland King of Arms' was already in use amongst the heralds at the College of Arms in London. Whatever the reason, Ulster King of Arms acquired full jurisdiction over arms in Ireland and retained it for almost four hundred years until 1943, when the Office was renamed the Genealogical Office, and Ulster became 'Chief Herald of Ireland', with substantially the same powers as his predecessor.

At the outset, the authority of Ulster was limited to those areas of the country under English authority; heraldry, as a feudal practice, was in any case quite alien to Gaelic culture. Up to the end of the seventeenth century, the functions of the Office remained purely heraldic, ascertaining and recording what arms were in use, and by what right families used them. From the late seventeenth century, Ulster began to acquire other duties, as an officer of the crown intimately linked to the government. These duties were largely ceremonial, deciding and arranging precedence on state occasions, as well as introducing new peers to the Irish House of Lords, and recording peerage successions. In essence these two areas, the heraldic and the ceremonial, remained the principal functions of the Office over the succeeding three centuries, with Ulster becoming registrar of the chivalric Order of St Patrick instituted in 1783, and continuing to have responsibility for the ceremonial aspects of state occasions at the court of the viceroy.

The functioning of the Office depended to an inordinate degree on the personal qualities of Ulster, and an unfortunate number of the holders of the position in the eighteenth century especially appear to have regarded it as a sinecure, paying little attention to the keeping of records and treating the manuscript collection as their personal property. It was only with the arrival of Sir William Betham in the early nineteenth century that the business of the Office was put on a sound footing, and serious attention paid to the collection and care of manuscripts. As a consequence, although a number of the official records are much earlier, the vast majority of the Office's holdings do not pre-date the nineteenth century.

In the course of carrying out its heraldic functions, the Office inevitably acquired a large amount of material of genealogical interest, since the right to bear arms is strictly hereditary. None the less, the new title given to the Office in 1943, 'The Genealogical Office', was somewhat inaccurate. Its principal function continues to be heraldic, the granting and confirmation of official achievements to individuals and corporate bodies. Up to the 1980s the Office also carried out commissioned research into family history. This service has been discontinued. In its place, the Office now has a Consultation Service which supplies detailed guidance on how to carry out research on individual families.

GENEALOGICAL OFFICE RECORDS

Manuscripts

The manuscripts of the Genealogical Office are numbered in a single series from 1 to 822. They are, however, of a very mixed nature, reflections of the Office's changing functions over the centuries, and are best dealt with in categories based on those functions. The following account divides them into (1) Official Records, (2) Administrative Records and Reference Works, and (3) Research Material.

(1) OFFICIAL RECORDS

A number of sets of manuscripts are direct products of the official functions of the Office and may be termed official records. On the heraldic side, the principal records are the Visitations (GO 47–9), the Funeral Entries (GO 64–79), the official grants and confirmations of arms (GO 103–111g), and the Registered Pedigrees (GO 156–182). In addition to these, four other manuscript groups reflect duties which Ulster's Office acquired over the centuries. These are the Lords Entries (GO 183–188), Royal Warrants for Changes of Name (GO 26 and 149–154A), Baronets Records (GO 112–4), and Gaelic Chieftains (GO 610 and 627).

The Visitations were an attempt to carry out in Ireland heraldic visitations along the lines of those which the College of Arms had been using in England for almost a century to control the bearing of arms. The results were meagre, confined to areas close to Dublin, and almost certainly incomplete even for those areas. The following places were covered: Dublin and parts of Co. Louth, 1568–70; Drogheda and Ardee, 1570; Swords, 1572; Cork, 1574; Limerick, 1574; Dublin City, 1607; Dublin county, 1610; and Wexford, 1610. They are indexed in GO 117.

The Funeral Entries, covering the period 1588 to 1691, make up some of the deficiencies of the Visitations. Their aim was to record the name, wife and issue of deceased nobility and gentry, along with their arms. In addition, many of the Entries include very beautiful illustrations of the arms and armorial devices used at the funeral, as well as notes on the ordering of the funeral processions and ceremonies. An index to the Entries is found in GO 386.

One of the later effects of the lack of visitations was to make it difficult for Ulster to verify from his own records that a particular family had a right to its arms. This gave rise to the practice, peculiar to Ireland, of issuing 'confirmations' of arms, which were taken as official registrations, and were dependent on an applicant being able to show that the arms in question had been in use in his family for three generations or one hundred years. The records of these confirmations and of actual grants of arms are found in GO 103–111g, dating from 1698 and still current. Earlier grants and confirmations are scattered through the manuscript collection; a complete index to all arms officially recorded in the Office is to be found in GO 422–3. Hayes' 'Manuscript Sources for the Study of Irish Civilization' reproduces this, and includes a summary of any genealogical information.

Since the right to bear arms is hereditary, the authentication of arms required the collection of a large amount of genealogical material. This is undoubtedly the origin of the Registered Pedigrees, GO 156–182, but the series very quickly acquired a life of its own, and the majority of entries are now purely genealogical. It is particularly important for the collection of eighteenth-century pedigrees of Irish émigrés to France, produced in response to their need to prove membership of the nobility; admission to such a position carried very substantial privileges, and the proofs required included the signature of Ulster. The series continues up to the present and is indexed in GO 469, as well as Hayes' 'Manuscript Sources'.

Partly as a result of difficulties concerning the status of lords who had supported James II, from 1698 one of Ulster's duties became the keeping of an official list of Irish peers, 'Ulster's Roll'. In theory all those entitled to sit in the Irish House of Lords, whether by creation of a new peerage or by succession, were obliged to inform Ulster before they could be officially introduced to the House. In practice the vast bulk of information collected relates to successions, with the heirs supplying the date of death and place of burial, arms, marriages and issue. The series covers the period from 1698 to 1939, and is indexed in GO 470.

In order to regulate the assumption of arms and titles, it became necessary after 1784 to obtain a warrant from the King for a change of name and
arms. From 1795 the Irish House of Lords made it obligatory to register such
a warrant in Ulster's Office. The result is the manuscript series known
officially as 'Royal Warrants for changes of name and licences for changes of
name'. Most of the nineteenth-century changes came about as a result of
wills, with an inheritance made conditional on a change of name. Hayes'
'Manuscript Sources' indexes the series.

A similar need to regulate the improper assumption of titles produced the
Baronet's records, GO 112–14. A royal warrant of 1789 for 'correcting and
preventing abuses in the order of baronets' made registration of their arms
and pedigrees with Ulster obligatory. The volumes are indexed in GO 470.

The records of Gaelic Chieftains in GO 610 and 627 are the consequence
of a revival instituted in the 1940s by Dr Edward MacLysaght, the first Chief
Herald of Ireland. He attempted to trace the senior lineal descendants in the
male line of the last recorded Gaelic 'Chief of the Name', who was then
officially designated as the contemporary holder of the title. The practice has
met with mixed success, since the collapse of Gaelic culture in the seventeenth century left an enormous gulf to be bridged, and the chieftainships
were not in any case originally passed on by primogeniture, but by election
within the extended kin-group. None the less, more than twenty chiefs have
been designated, and the records of the research which went into establishing
their right to the title are extremely interesting.

(2) Administrative records and reference works
Many of the documents, now part of the general manuscript series, simply
derive from the paperwork necessary to run an office. These include cash
books, receipts, Ulster's Diaries, letter books, day books, and records of fees
due for the various functions carried out by Ulster. Of these, the most
interesting from a genealogical point of view are the letter books (GO
361–78), copies of all letters sent out from the Office between 1789 and 1853,
and the Betham letters (GO 580–604), a collection of the letters received by
Sir William Betham between c.1810 and 1830, and purchased by the
Genealogical Office in 1943. The former are indexed volume by volume.
The latter are of more potential value. The only index, however, comes in
the original catalogue of the sale of the letters, dated 1936, a copy of which
is to be found at the Office, though not numbered among the manuscripts.
The catalogue lists the letters alphabetically by addresser, and a supple-
mentary surnames index provides a guide to the families dealt with. Another
eight volumes of the series, unindexed, are to be found in the National
Archives (M.744–51).

As well as documents produced in the day-to-day running of the Office,
a large number of manuscripts also relate to the ceremonial functions

performed by Ulster. These include official orders relating to changes of insignia, papers dealing with precedence and protocol, records of official functions at the vice-regal court, and the records of the Order of St Patrick. There is little of genealogical interest in these.

In the course of their heraldic and genealogical work, Ulster and his officers accumulated over the years a large series of manuscripts for use as reference works. These include manuscript armories, ordinaries of arms, treatises on heraldry and precedence, a series of English Visitations, and blazons of arms of English and Scottish peers. The bulk of the material is heraldic, but there is a good deal of incidental genealogical information, particularly in the seventeenth-century ordinaries of arms.

(3) RESEARCH MATERIAL

The most useful manuscripts in the Genealogical Office collection are those acquired and created to provide sources for genealogical research. The policy, begun in the early nineteenth century by Sir William Betham and continued by all his successors, has produced a wide range of material, much of it based on records which were destroyed in the Public Record Office in 1922. It may be divided into three broad categories: (i) Betham's own compilations; (ii) the collections of later genealogists; and (iii) other records. The sheer diversity of these documents makes a complete account impractical here; what follows is a broad outline.

The greatest single work produced by Betham is the collection of abstracts of family information from prerogative wills. These are divided into a number of series: GO 223–226 ('Old Series', Vols I–IV) covers wills before 1700; GO 227–254 ('New Series', Vols 1–31) covers wills from 1700 to c.1800. The series are roughly alphabetical, with each volume containing its own index. Sir Arthur Vicars' *Index to the Prerogative Wills of Ireland 1536–1810* provides a guide to wills covered. Many of the sketch pedigrees include later amendments and additions from other sources. GO 255–6 index all the marriage alliances recorded in the wills. Another series, GO 203–14 ('Will Pedigrees', Vols I–XII) represents an unfinished attempt to rearrange all these sketch pedigrees into strictly alphabetical order. Betham also produced a large number of sketch pedigrees based on other sources, collected as 'Ancient Anglo-Irish Families', Vols I–VI (GO 215–19), 'Milesian Families', Vols I–III (GO 220–22), and the '1st series', Vols I–XVI (GO 261–76) and '2nd series', Vols I–VII (GO 292–8). All these are indexed in GO 470.

As well as the sketch pedigrees and the letters (covered above under 'Administrative Records'), there are two other sources in the collection which owe their origin to Betham. The first of these, genealogical and historical excerpts from the plea rolls and patent rolls from Henry III to Edward VI (GO 189–93), constitute the single most important source of information on Anglo-Norman genealogy in Ireland. Betham's transcript of Roger O'Ferrall's

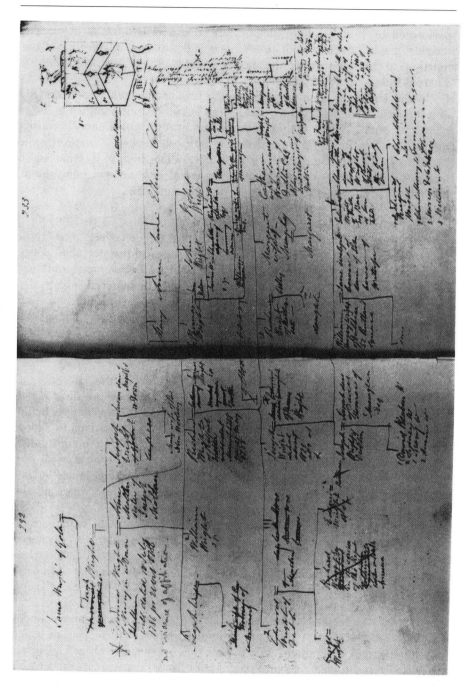

'Linea Antiqua', a collation of earlier genealogies compiled in 1709, is the Office's most extensive work on Gaelic, as opposed to Anglo-Irish genealogy. This copy (in three volumes, GO 145–7, with an index to the complete work in 147) also contains Betham's interpolations and additions, unfortunately unsourced. It records the arms of many of the Gaelic families covered, without giving any authority for them, and is the source of most of the arms illustrated in Dr Edward MacLysaght's *Irish Families*.

Pedigrees and research notes produced by later amateur and professional genealogists make up a large part of the Office's manuscript collection. Among those who have contributed to these are Sir Edmund Bewley, Denis O'Callaghan Fisher, Tenison Groves, Alfred Moloney, T. U. Sadleir, Rev. H. B. Swanzy and many others. For the most part, their records concern either particular groups of families or particular geographical areas. Some of these have their own indexes, some are covered by GO 470 and 117, others have will abstracts only indexed in GO 429. The numerical listing at the end of this chapter provides a guide. As well as these, some of the results of Ulster's Office's own research in the late nineteenth and early twentieth century are classed as manuscripts, GO 800–822. These constitute no more than a fraction of the total research information produced by the Office. They are indexed in Hayes' 'Manuscript Sources'.

A final class of records consists of extremely diverse documents, having only their potential genealogical usefulness in common. It includes such items as freeholders' lists from different counties; extracts from parish registers; transcripts of the Dublin City roll of freemen, of returns from the 1766 census, of city directories from various periods; and much more. More detailed information will be found in the list at the end of this chapter.

Archives

As well as the manuscripts series, now closed, the Genealogical Office also has extremely extensive archive records of the commissioned research it carried out up to the 1980s. For the closing decades of the nineteenth century and the early decades of the twentieth century, these records are still largely concerned with the Anglo-Irish. Manuscripts 800–822 cover perhaps 5 per cent of this material. The remainder is sorted in roughly alphabetical order in boxes along one whole wall of the Genealogical Office strong-room. It is to be hoped that the Office can acquire the resources to sort and index it soon, since it contains a great deal of very valuable information.

After the creation of the Genealogical Office in 1943, the focus of the commissioned research shifted, with most of the work now carried out on behalf of the descendants of emigrants to Australia and North America. There are over 20,000 research files giving details of the results of this research. A continuing project to index the families concerned has so far covered over 6,000 of these; the results are on computer at the Office.

RESEARCH IN GENEALOGICAL OFFICE MANUSCRIPTS

The biggest single obstacle to research in GO manuscripts is the lack of a single, comprehensive index. Many attempts have been made over the centuries of the Office's existence to produce such an index; the result has been a proliferation of partial indexes, each covering some of the collection, none covering it all. These are dealt with below. In addition, the policy used in the creation of manuscripts appears to have become somewhat inconsistent from the 1940s. Before then only the earliest and most heterogeneous manuscripts had been numbered in a single series, with each of the other groups simply having its own volume numbers, 'Lords Entries Vol. II' or 'Registered Pedigrees Vol. 12', for example. The laudable attempt to produce a consistent numbering system, starting at GO 1 and moving through the collection, seems to have given rise to the piecemeal addition of material which was more properly the preserve of the National Library. The subsequent transfers to the Library, and renumbering of remaining material, produced a virtual collapse of the system in the upper numbers. No manuscripts exist for many of the numbers between 600 and 800. The numerical list of manuscripts at the end of this chapter reflects the current situation, with titles no longer in the Office given in brackets.

Indexes

GO 59: This is a detailed calendar of manuscripts 1–58, particularly useful since many of these consist of very early heterogeneous material bound together for preservation.

GO 115: Indexes the following: Arms, A–C; Grants and Confirmations, A and B; Visitations; British Families; Funeral Entries; Registered Pedigrees, Vols 1–10. Only the Visitations (GO 47–9) and British Families (GO 44–6) are not indexed more fully elsewhere.

GO 116: An unfinished index.

GO 117: Duplicates much of the material indexed in GO 422, GO 470 and Hayes' 'Manuscript Sources'. Only the following are not covered elsewhere: Antrim Families (GO 213); Fisher MSS. (GO 280–85); Irish Arms at the College of Heralds (GO 37); Irish Coats of Arms (Fota) (GO 526); Heraldic Sketches (GO 125); Betham Letter Books (GO 362–78); Ecclesiastical Visitations (GO 198–9); Reynell MSS. (GO 445).

GO 148: Index to 'Linea Antiqua'. The version at the end of GO 147, 'Linea Antiqua', Vol. III, is more complete.

GO 255–6: Index to Alliances in Prerogative Wills (Betham).

GO 386: Index to the Funeral Entries.

GO 422–3: Index to arms registered at the Office.

GO 429: Eustace Index to Will Abstracts at the Genealogical Office. The published version in *Analecta Hibernica*, Vol. 17, is less extensive than the manuscript copy.

GO 469: Index to Registered Pedigrees. This appears to be less complete than the version included in Hayes' 'Manuscript Sources'. Attached to it is a typescript copy of the index to the Genealogical Office collection of pedigree rolls.

GO 470: Index to Unregistered Pedigrees. This is the single most useful index in the Office, covering the Lords Entries, the Betham pedigrees and many of the genealogists' pedigree collections. It is divided into three separate parts and gives the descriptive titles in use before the adoption of the single GO numbering system. The flyleaf lists the manuscripts covered.

GO 476: Numerical listing of GO manuscripts, dating from the 1950s, and now inaccurate for the higher numbers.

See also Hayes' 'Manuscript Sources for the Study of Irish Civilization'. This indexes the following: Registered Pedigrees, GO 800–822, Fisher MSS. (GO 280–85).

Access

The question of access to Genealogical Office manuscripts has long been somewhat vexed. The official policy of the Office is that the entire collection is to be microfilmed, and will eventually only be available to the public in that form. For the moment, only the most valuable manuscripts are on National Library microfilm, as follows:

MSS. NL Pos. 8286	GO 47, 48, 49, 64, 65
MSS. NL Pos. 8287	GO 66, 67, 68, 69
MSS. NL Pos. 8288	GO 70, 71, 72, 73
MSS. NL Pos. 8289	GO 74, 75, 76, 77, 78
MSS. NL Pos. 8290	GO 79, 103, 104, 105, 106
MSS. NL Pos. 8290A	GO 93, 94, 95
MSS. NL Pos. 8291	GO 107, 108, 109
MSS. NL Pos. 8292	GO 110, 111, 111A to p. 95
MSS. NL Pos. 8293	GO 111A from p. 96, 111B, 111C
MSS. NL Pos. 8294	GO 111D, 111E, 111F
MS. NL Pos. 8295	GO 112
MS. NL Pos. 8295A	GO 113
MS. NL Pos. 8295B	GO 141
MSS. NL Pos. 8296	GO 145, 146, 147 to p. 42
MSS. NL Pos. 8297	GO 147 from p. 43, 148, 149, 150 to p. 319
MSS. NL Pos. 8298	GO 150 from p. 319, 151, 152
MSS. NL Pos. 8299	GO 153, 154
MSS. NL Pos. 8300	GO 154A, 155, 156, 157, 158, 159 to p. 109

MSS. NL Pos. 8301	GO 159 from p. 110, 160, 161, 162, 163, 164
MSS. NL Pos. 8302	GO 165, 166, 167, 168
MSS. NL Pos. 8303	GO 169, 170
MSS. NL Pos. 8304	GO 171, 172, 173
MSS. NL Pos. 8305	GO 174, 175
MS. NL Pos. 8306	GO 176
MSS. NL Pos. 8307	GO 177, 178
MSS. NL Pos. 8308	GO 179, 180
MSS. NL Pos. 8309	GO 181, 182
MSS. NL Pos. 8310	GO 182A, 183, 184
MSS. NL Pos. 8311	GO 185, 186, 187
MSS. NL Pos. 8312	GO 188

For other manuscripts, access is through the National Library Manuscript reading room at 2 Kildare St, and is at the discretion of the Chief Herald.

GENEALOGICAL OFFICE MANUSCRIPTS

The following is a numerical list of Genealogical Office manuscripts, from 1 to 822. In the upper numbers especially, a significant proportion of the items have been moved. Where this is the case, the title is given in brackets and also, where possible, the destination of the manuscript.

GO MS.	Title	Index
1	Case of Precedence, List of Peers, 1634–89	
2	Royal Arms	
3	Letters, Vol. 1, Genealogical Scraps	
4	Exemption from Taxes etc.	
	List of Baronets etc.	
	Authority for Fees	
5	Funeral Arms temp. Preston, Ulster,	
	Commissions for Visitations	
6	Forms of Processions etc.	
7	Treatise on Heraldry, 1347	
8	Fees of Office, Precedence, Royal Pedigrees,	
	Order of Dignities, Irish Parliament	
9	Treatise on Nobility, Pedigrees of Ancient Baronies	
10	Ulster's Diaries, 1698–1800 (numbered 10A)	Own Index
11	Ulster's Diaries, 1800–1837 (numbered 11A)	Own Index
12	Synopsis of Heraldry and Treatise on Funerals	
13	Honours conferred in Ireland	
14	Fees of Office, Vol. 1, History of Ulster's Office	
15	*Monumenta Eblana*	
16	Miscellaneous Pedigrees and Letters	

218	Ancient Anglo-Irish Families, Vol. IV, P–W	470
219	Ancient Anglo-Irish Families, Vol. V, A–W	470
220	Milesian Families, Vol. I, A–D	470
221	Milesian Families, Vol. II, B–M	470
222	Milesian Families, Vol. III, B–T	470
223	Wills, Old Series, Vol. I, Browne, Fitzgerald, Hamilton, Stewart, Walker, White, Wilson	See Vicars
224–6	Wills, Old Series (pre–1700), Vols II–IV, A–Y	See Vicars
227–54	Wills, New Series, Vols 1–26, A–Z	See Vicars
255–6	Index to Alliances in Perogative Wills, Vol I, A–L, Vol. II, M–Z	See Vicars
257–60	Prerogative Administrations Intestate, Vols 1–4	Own Index
261–76	Betham Sketch Pedigrees; 1st Series, Vols I–XVI	470
277	Betham Peerage	
278	Ball	470
279	Stephens, Wexford Pedigrees; Calendar of Dublin Wills	470
280–5	Fisher MSS., Vols 1–6	Surnames in 117, Wills in 429
286	Fisher, TCD Matriculations, 1637–1730	Own Index
287	High Sheriffs of Counties	
288	Fisher, King's Inns Admissions, 1607–1771	
289	Fisher, Abstracts of Deeds and Wills, 1	Wills in 429
290	Fisher, Abstracts of Deeds and Wills, 2	Wills in 429
291	Index to Fisher MSS.	
292–8	Betham Sketch Pedigrees, 2nd Series, Vols I–VII	470
299	Proclamations and Ceremonials	
300	Ulster Office (misc.)	
301	Bath, now in National Library	
302	Funeral Processions (from Add. MSS. 1829, British Museum)	
303	Gentleman Ushers Book, 1842–64	
304	Funeral Viscount Nelson	
305	Bath	
306	Statutes of the Garter	
307	Order of the Bath (now at National Library)	
308	Order of St Patrick (Receipts etc.)	
309	Precedents of Receptions	
310	Order of St Patrick, Official Designs	
311	Gentleman Ushers Book, 1820–85	
312	Order of St Patrick, Installation papers (Betham)	
313	Order of St Patrick	
314	Knights Dubbed, Ulster's Rolls	

384	Donovan MS.	470
385	Bewley MS.	470
386	Index to Funeral Entries	
387	Knights dubbed in England	
388	Peers of Ireland, Ulster's Office Papers	
389–400	Davis MSS. Vols 9–20	Wills in 429
401	Copy of 295	
402	Fisher, Admissions to King's Inns, 1607–1771	
403	Royal Levees, 1821, 1824, 1849	
404	Davis MSS. Vol. I	470
405	Davis MSS. Vol. II	470
406	Carmichael MS.	470
407	Representative Peers, election lists	
408	Bewley family of Cumberland	
409–10	Warburton's *Lexicon Armorum*	
411	Arms of Foreign Royalties etc.	
412	Barry	470
413	Holland (tricks of arms)	Own Index
414	West	
415	Kelly, Wills	Wills in 429
416	Crossle	Own Index; Wills in 429
417–18	Drought	Wills in 429
419	Kemmis	
420	Swanzy Will Abstracts	Wills in 429
421	Prerogative Marriage Licences, see 605–7	
422	Arms Register I	
423	Arms Register II	
424–27a	Sadleir Will Abstracts, Vols 1, 2, 3, 4, 4a	Wills in 429
428	Plunkett, Bantry Account Book, 1825	
429	Eustace Index of Will Abstracts at GO	
430	1766 Religious Census Returns (photostat)	
431	'Extra Fisher'	
432–5	Irwin MSS.	Wills in 429
435a	Irwin MSS. Bulteel and other families	Wills in 429
436–41	Irwin MSS.	Wills in 429
442	Freeholders, Meath, Donegal, Fermanagh, Roscommon, Tipperary	
443	Freeholders, Clare, Kilkenny, Queen's, Westmeath, Armagh Poll Book, 1753	
444	Freeholders, Longford	
445–6a	Reynell MSS.	Own Index, partly in 117

447	Chester Refugees, 1688/9	
448	Newgate	
449	Burtchaell	
450	Molony and allied families	Wills in 429
451	Molony MS. Pedigrees etc. principally families of Blood, Blout, Brereton	Wills in 429
452	Molony MS. Abstracts from the *General Advertiser* and *Limerick Gazette*, 1804–20	Alphabetical order
453–55	Molony MS. Abstracts from the *Clare Journal* and *Ennis Chronicle*, 1778–1810	Alphabetical Order
456	Molony MSS. Misc. Pedigrees etc.	Wills in 429
457	Molony MSS. Misc. Pedigrees etc.	Wills in 429
458	Molony MSS. Misc. Pedigrees etc.	Wills in 429
459	Molony MSS. Misc. Pedigrees etc.	Wills in 429
460	Molony MSS. Pedigrees etc. principally families of Brew, Adams, Chartres	Wills in 429
461	Molony MSS. Will abstracts etc., family of Chartres	Wills in 429
462	Pedigree of Chartres	
463	Molony MSS. Notes on the families of Adams, Chartres, Tymens and England of Co. Clare	Wills in 429
464	Molony MSS. Misc. Pedigrees etc.	Wills in 429
465	Notes on the Molony family	Wills in 429
466	Molony MSS. Miscellaneous	
467	Pedigree of O'Donnellan	
468	Traill	470
469	Index of Registered Pedigrees	
470	Index of Unregistered Pedigrees	
471	Cavanagh and allied families	Own Index; Wills in 429
472	Calendar of Wills, Down Diocese	
473–5	Dublin Consistorial Marriage Licences	
476	List of MSS. at the GO	
477	Search Book	
478/9	Now 111e and 111f	
480	Bewley family of Cumberland	
481	List of Claims, 1701	
482	Athenry Peerage Letters, 1821–5	
483	Fisher Marriage Licences (see 144a)	
484	Smyly and allied families	
485	O'Brien Pedigrees	
486	Ulster's Office Form Book	
487	Abstracts from Charitable Wills	429

488	Kelly of Clare	
489	Delafield of Dublin	
490–93	Roll of Freemen, Dublin City	
494	Concordatum Pedigrees (Sadleir), 1817–21	Not indexed
495	Castleknock Parish Register	
496	Crossly's *Peerage*	
497	Patent of precedency	
498	Montgomery Pedigree	
499	Loftus Pedigree	
500	Burke–Ryan genealogy	
501	Walsh, Kelly and allied families	
502	(Betham Draft Book, now NL MS. 496)	
503	Donegan family	
504	Genealogy of family of Burgo French	
505	Pedigrees of Walker and allied families	
506	Stafford family history	
507	Loss of the Irish Crown Jewels	
508	Coachmakers' blazons of arms	
509	Alphabet of Irish and English Arms	
510	1642 Field Officers	
511	Arms of Protestant Bishops of Ireland	
512	Bewley Notebooks (Box)	Wills in 429
513	Precedents	
514	Ash, Co. Derry, *c.*1736	
515	Berkely Peerage, Pedigree, Correspondence and Notes	
516	Pedigree of O'Mangan, 1709	
517	O'Hanlon of Orior, Co. Armagh	
518	Delamere Notes	
519	Shaw and Joyce Pedigrees, Gun notes	
520–22	Blake and Butler Families of Tipperary and Clare	
523	Welply I, Chancery Bills, 1630–1785, mainly Chinnery and Phair families	
524	Welply II, Exchequer Bills, 1675–1810, mainly Chinnery family	
525	Eustace Miscellany	Own Index
526	Fota MS. (photostat), Irish Coats	Own Index
527	MacLysaght Miscellany	Own Index
528–34	Transcripts of Wills from the Society Of Genealogists, London	429
535	Ainsworth Wills	Alphabetical order
536	Religious Census Returns, 1766, I	
537	Religious Census Returns, 1766, II	
538	Hearth Money Rolls, Armagh, Donegal, 1664/5	

578   Parish Register Extracts
579   Army List, Ireland, 1746
580–604 Betham Letters, Vols 1–25
604a   Sherwood catalogue and Index to Betham letters
605–7   Prerogative Marriage Licences, 1630–1858, A–Z
608   Militia List, 1761
609   Irish Stockholders, 1779
610   Gaelic Chief's Authenticated Pedigrees, I
611   Lodge family
612–17   Index to Ossory, Ferns and Leighlin, Marriage
            Licence Bonds, 1691–1845
618   Ossory Administration Bonds, 1660–1857
619   Ware, Bishops
620   Miscellaneous Rentals
621   Photostats, Taylor papers, Hegarty Papers, Inscriptions
            from St Bede's R.C. Church, New South Wales
622   Ainsworth Miscellany
623   Limerick Freeholders, 1816–25
624   Frost, Co. Clare families   Own Index
625   *Bozzetti d'arme*   Own Index
626   Directory, Enniskillen, Ballyshannon, Donegal, 1839
627   Register of Gaelic Chiefs
628   Sadleir, Miscellaneous Pedigrees   470
628a   Sadleir, Order of Malta
629   O'Kelly Pedigrees
630   Miscellaneous Pedigrees (1908–1943)   Own Index
631   Ainsworth Wills, II   Not in 429
632   O'Malley
633   Delafield and Butler families
634   (O'Reilly Pedigrees)
635   Warren and allied families
636   Privy Councillors of Ireland
637   Forbes Genealogy
638   Nagle, White, Meekins, Madden, Vereker and
            Prendergast Pedigrees
639   Dillon Patents
640   (Betham Pedigrees, now in NL)
641   (Killaloe Catholic Parish Register Listing)
642   Kilkenny College and its masters
643   Material for Names Map
644   (*Stemmata Wyckhamiana*, NL)
645   Nangle (de Angulo) Pedigree
646   (Copies of GO Visitations, GO 46–8)

701	C. of I. Parish Register extracts, Ballingarry, Co. Limerick; Whitechurch, Co Wexford; Eyrecourt, Co. Galway; St Patrick's, Dublin	
702	Gordon MS. (Crossle)	
702a	Gordon MS. (Crossle), newspaper cuttings	
703	(–)	
704	Carroll Wills	
705	(List of Priests and Sureties, now NL MS. 5318)	
706	Glenville Crests	
707	Extracts from Tuam, Clonfert and Kilmacduagh, C. of I. Diocesan Records	
708	Kilkenny Pedigrees (from Burtchaell)	
709	(Grants, Q, now 111G)	
710	(Parish register listing)	
711	Memoir of the Butlers of Ormond	
712	(Book of Arms, now NL MS. 472)	
713	Irwin, Max, Butler, Crofts, McConnell, Herden	
714–38	Loose Pedigrees, A–W	470
739	(Now GO 496)	
740	(Johnston)	
741	(–)	
742	Miscellaneous Pedigrees and Notes, Edwards and allied families	
743	(Herbert Pedigrees)	
744	(Fitzgerald of Derrineel)	
745	(Notes for Irish Memorials Association)	
746	Kennedy, Scotland and Ireland, 1550–1820	
747	(Bewley Miscellany)	
748	(–)	
749–50	(Knights Dubbed, 1590–1800)	
751	(Sketches of Arms)	
752	Admissions to freedom of Dublin, 1468	
753	(Now GO 517)	
754	(Now GO 514)	
755	(Verner Family)	
756	(Now GO 513)	
757	(Now GO 503)	
758	(Now GO 499)	
759	(Now GO 509)	
760	Miscellany, Brownrigg and Ronson	
761	(Now GO 519)	
762	(Now GO 698)	
763	(Now GO 500)	

764   (Now GO 511)
765   Grainger and allied families
766   (Now GO 519)
767   (Now GO 504)
768   (Now GO 502)
769   (Now GO 508)
770   (Now GO 505)
771   (Now GO 517)
772   (Now GO 497)
773   (Now GO 506)
774   Royal Warrants in Changes of Name
775   (McWillan Pedigrees)
776   (Now GO 516)
777   Braddyl papers
778   (Montgomery Pedigree)
779–787 (Chevalier O'Gorman papers, now in NL)
788   (Register of Foreign Arms)
789   (Now GO 515)
790   (Photostat and Burgess Books)
791   (Extracts from Registered Pedigrees)
792   Pedigree and notes re Bushe
793   Lt Col O'Hea
794   Lodge Family Histories
795   (–)
796   (–)
797   (Hyde of Co. Cork)
798   History of the Hickeys
799   (–)
800–22 Loose Pedigrees, Searches, Correspondence   Hayes

7

Emigration

For the descendants of emigrants from Ireland wishing to trace their ancestors, it is a natural impulse to try first of all to identify emigration records in Ireland. Unfortunately, no centralised records of emigration exist. For North America in particular, when ships' passenger lists were kept, most appear to have been deposited at the port of arrival rather than departure; in general the authorities were more concerned with recording those entering a country than those leaving. The most comprehensive records for the US, therefore, are the Customs Passenger Lists, dating from 1820, and the Immigration Passenger Lists, from 1883, both in the National Archives in Washington. Unfortunately, the earlier lists are not very informative, giving only the country of origin of the emigrant. They have been collected by the US National Archives for the most important immigrant ports, Boston, New York, Baltimore and Philadelphia, as well as Mobile, New Bedford and New Orleans. Microfilm copies of the lists for New York and Boston are available at the National Library of Ireland. A full reference is given in the lists later in this chapter. No index to these is available in Ireland, making them very difficult to use if a relatively precise date of arrival is not known.

As well as these, however, there are many less comprehensive lists, published and unpublished, which record intending and actual emigrants and ships' passengers to North America. A number of attempts have been made to systematise access to these. The most important are the *Passenger and Immigration Lists Index* (3 vols), ed. P. William Filby and Mary K. Meyer, Gale, Detroit, 1981 (NL: RR 387, p 7), a consolidated index to a wide variety of lists relating to North American immigration from all over the world, and *The Famine Immigrants* (7 vols, indexed), Baltimore, the Genealogical Publishing Company, 1988 (NL Ir. 942 g 12), which records more than half a million Irish arrivals in New York between 1846 and 1851. Even these, however, cover only a fraction of the material of potential value. The listings further on in this chapter organise most of the available materials chronologically, to allow easy reference.

For Australia and New Zealand the situation is somewhat better. Because of the distance, very few emigrants could afford the journey themselves, and most, whether assisted free settlers or transported convicts, are therefore quite well documented. Transportation from Ireland, or for crimes committed in Ireland, lasted from 1791 to 1853, ending some fifteen years earlier than transportation from England. The only mass transportation later than 1853 was of sixty-three Fenians who were sent to Western Australia in 1868, aboard the last convict ship from England to Australia. The records of the Chief Secretary's Office, which had responsibility for the penal system, are the major Irish source of information on transportees. Not all the relevant records have survived, particularly for the period before 1836, but what does exist can provide a wealth of information. The records were formerly housed in the State Paper Office in Dublin Castle, which is now part of the National Archives and is situated at Bishop St, Dublin 8. The principal classes of relevant records are as follows:

1. PRISONERS' PETITIONS AND CASES, 1788–1836
These consist of petitions to the Lord Lieutenant for commutation or remission of sentence, and record the crime, trial, sentence, place of origin and family circumstances.

2. STATE PRISONERS' PETITIONS
These specifically concern those arrested for participation in the 1798 Rebellion, and record the same information as the main series of petitions.

3. CONVICT REFERENCE FILES FROM 1836
These continue the earlier petitions series and may include a wide range of additional material.

4. TRANSPORTATION REGISTERS FROM 1836
These record all the names of those sentenced to death or transportation, giving the name, age, date and county of trial, crime and sentence. Other details, including the name of the transport ship or the place of detention are sometimes also given.

5. MALE CONVICT REGISTER, 1842–47
In addition to the information supplied by the Transportation Registers, this volume also gives physical descriptions.

6. REGISTER OF CONVICTS ON CONVICT SHIPS, 1851–53
This gives the names, dates and counties of trial of those transported to Van Dieman's Land and Western Australia for the period covered.

7. FREE SETTLERS' PAPERS, 1828–52

After serving a minimum of four years, a male convict had the right to request a free passage for his wife and family. The Papers contain lists of those making such a request, along with transportation details and the name and address of the wife. A number of petitions from husbands and wives, and prisoners' letters, are also included.

To celebrate the Australian Bicentenary of 1988, all these records were microfilmed, and a computerised database of the surnames they contain was created. Copies of the microfilms and the database were presented to the Australian Government and can now be found in many state archives. The National Archives in Bishop St also retains copies, and the database in particular can save a great deal of time and effort. It supplies enough details from the originals to identify the relevant record.

For obvious reasons, the records relating to free settlers are more scattered and less easily researched. The single most useful source for early settlers, also invaluable for convicts, is the 1828 census of New South Wales, published by the Library of Australian History in 1980. Although the precise place of origin is not recorded, the details include age, occupation, marital status, and household. For later settlers, the University of Woolongong in Australia has produced on microfiche a complete index and transcript of all information concerning immigrants of Irish origin recorded on ships' passenger lists between 1848 and 1867. The Genealogical Office has a copy of this. The later lists in particular are extremely useful, often recording the exact place of origin as well as parents' names.

Other than these, the principal records likely to be of relevance are in the Colonial Office Papers of the United Kingdom Public Record Office at Kew, class reference CO 201. This class contains a wide variety of records, including petitions for assisted passages, emigrants' lists, records of emigrants on board ship, petitions from settlers for financial assistance, and much else. A number of these have been published in David T. Hawkings' *Bound for Australia* (Sussex: Phillimore and Co. 1987).

The remainder of this chapter is an attempt to present a systematic guide to emigration records of potential genealogical interest. It is divided into (1) passenger and emigrant lists in chronological order, and (2) published works on emigration. The latter is further subdivided into works dealing with (a) North America in general, (b) localities in North America, (c) the 'Scotch-Irish' in North America, (d) Australia and New Zealand, (e) France, (f) South Africa, (g) Argentina, and (h) the West Indies.

1. PASSENGER AND EMIGRANT LISTS
(IN CHRONOLOGICAL ORDER)

From: –   To: North America
Date: 1538–1825
Reference: H. Lancour and Wolfe, *A Bibliography of Ships' Passenger Lists*, London,
1963

From: –   To: America
Date: 17th–19th centuries
Reference: *Passenger and Immigration Lists Index* (3 vols), ed. P. William Filby
and Mary K. Meyer, Gale, Detroit, 1981, NL, RR 387, p 7

From: –   To: New England
Date: –
Reference: M. Tepper, *Passengers to America* (a consolidation of ships' passenger
lists from the New England Historical and Genealogical Register), Baltimore,
1977, NL 387, p 6

From: Britain   To: North America
Date: 1600–1700
Reference: J. C. Hotten, *Original Lists of Persons emigrating to America, 1600–1700*,
London, 1874 [reprint, 1968]

From: Britain and Ireland   To: America and West Indies
Date: 1727–31
Reference: 'Agreements to Serve in America and the West Indies', D.
Galenson, *The Genealogist's Magazine*, Vol. 19, No. 2

From: Ireland   To: America
Date: 1735–54
Reference: Lockhart, A., *Emigration Ireland to North America, 1660–1775*, New
York, 1976, Ir. 973 l 5 (indentured servants 1749–50, Felons 1735–54)

From: Kilkenny   To: Newfoundland
Date: 1750–1844
Reference: 'Inistiogue emigrants in Newfoundland', in Whelan, K. and
Nolan, W. (ed.), *Kilkenny History and Society*, Dublin, 1990, 345–405

From: Larne   To: Charleston, South Carolina
Date: 1773
Reference: Dickson, R. J., *Ulster Emigration to Colonial America, 1718–75*, London,
1976

From: Newry/Warrenpoint   To: New York and Philadelphia
Date: 1791–92
Reference: PRONI T.711/1

From: Ireland   To: Philadelphia
Date: 1800–1819
Reference: M. Tepper, *Passenger Arrivals at Philadelphia Port 1800–1819*, Baltimore, 1986, Ir. 970, p 12

From: Belfast, Dublin, Limerick, Londonderry, Newry, Sligo   To: US
Date: 1803, 1804
Reference: D. F. Begley, *Handbook on Irish Genealogy*, Dublin, 1984 (6th ed.) 101–110, 115

From: Ulster   To: US
Date: June 1804 to March 1806
Reference: PRONI T521/1, indexed in Report of the Deputy Keeper of Public Records (Northern Ireland), 1929

From: Ireland   To: America
Date: 1803–6
Reference: NL Pos. 993, PRONI T.3262

From: Newry   To: US
Date: 1803–31
Reference: Trainor, Brian, 'Sources for the Identification of Emigrants from Ireland to North America in the 19th Century', *Ulster Historical and Genealogical Guild Newsletter*, Vol. 1, Nos 2 and 3 (1979), Ir. 9292 u 3

From: Ireland   To: US
Date: 1811–17
Reference: *Passengers from Ireland*, Baltimore, 1980 (from 'The Shamrock'), see also D. F. Begley, *Handbook on Irish Genealogy*, Dublin, 1984 (6th ed.), 110–117

From: Londonderry   To: US
Date: 1815–16
Reference: PRONI T.2964 (add.)

From: Counties Carlow and Wexford   To: Canada
Date: 1817
Reference: K. Whelan and W. Nolan (ed.), *Wexford: History and Society*, Dublin, Geography Publications, 1987

From: –   To: New York
Date: 1820–65
Reference: Passenger arrivals lists, New York port, unindexed, NL Pos.
3919–4580, see National Library, Hayes Catalogue, for details of dates

From: –   To: Baltimore
Date: 1820–34
Reference: M. Tepper, *Passenger Arrivals at the Port of Baltimore*, Baltimore, 1982

From: Ireland   To: US
Date: 1821
Reference: *Irish Genealogical Helper*, No. 6, Jan. 1976, Ir. 9291 i 3

From: (not given)   To: New York (Arrivals)
Date: 1820–65
Reference: NL Pos. 3919–4520 (see Hayes Catalogue for details)

From: (not given)   To: Boston (Arrivals)
Date: 1820–64
Reference: NL Pos. 5896–959 (see Hayes Catalogue for details)

From: Ireland   To: Boston
Date: 1820–39
Reference: NL Special list, No. 200

From: –   To: US
Date: 1821–23
Reference: *Passengers Arriving in the U.S., 1821–1823*, NL 3251 u 1

From: Ireland   To: US
Date: 1822
Reference: *Irish-American Genealogist*, 1978, Ir. 9291 i 3

From: Londonderry   To: US
Date: 1826–90
Reference: PRONI D.2892

From: Co. Londonderry (parishes of Aghadowey, Balteagh, Bovevagh,
Coleraine, Dunboe, Drumachose, Limavady, Magilligan, Tamlaghfinlagan)
To: US
Date: 1833–34
Reference: See S. Martin, *Historical Gleanings from Co. Derry*, Dublin, 1955, Ir.
94112 m 2, also D. F. Begley, *Handbook on Irish Genealogy*, Dublin, 1984 (6th
ed.), 117–120

From: Counties Antrim and Derry   To: US
Date: 1833–39
Reference: Mitchell, Brian, *Irish Emigration Lists 1833–39*, Baltimore, Genealogical Publishing Company, 1989; PRONI MIC.6

From: Newry   To: St John's, New Brunswick
Date: 7 April 1834
Reference: Murphy, Peter, *Together in Exile*, Nova Scotia, 1991, 272–7

From: Londonderry   To: Philadelphia
Date: 1836–71
Reference: PRONI MF 14

From: Liverpool (Irish passengers)   To: Philadelphia
Date: 1840
Reference: PRONI T.2746

From: Limerick   To: North America
Date: 1841
Reference: *North Munster Antiquarian Journal*, Vol. XXIII, 1981

From: Shillelagh, Co. Wicklow (Coolattin estate)   To: US
Date: 1842–44
Reference: NL MS. 18, 429

From: Ireland   To: US
Date: 1846–51
Reference: *The Famine Immigrants* (7 vols, indexed), Ir. 942 g 12

From: Londonderry   To: America
Date: 1847–71
Reference: Brian Mitchell (ed.), *Irish Passenger Lists 1847–1871*, Baltimore, Genealogical Publishing Co. 1988

From: Coolattin (see above)   To: Quebec
Date: 1848
Reference: Ni MS. 18, 524, see also *West Wicklow Historical Society Journal*, No. 1

From: Ahascragh, Co. Galway, and Castlemaine, Co. Kerry   To: –
Date: 1848–52
Reference: *Analecta Hibernica*, Vol. 22, 1960

From: Ireland   To: Australia
Date: 1848–50
Reference: 'Barefoot and Pregnant? Female Orphans who emigrated from
Irish workhouses to Australia', 'Familia', *Ulster Genealogical Review*, Vol. II, No.
3, 1987

From: Londonderry   To: Philadelphia, St John, Quebec
Date: 1850–65
Reference: PRONI MF 13

From: Co. Galway (parishes of Kilchreest, Killigolen, Killinane, Killora,
Kilthomas and Isserkelly)   To: US and Australia
Date: *c*.1852–59
Reference: GO MS. 622

From: Liverpool (Irish Passengers)   To: US
Date: Oct.–Dec. 1853
Reference: R. ffolliott, *The Irish Ancestor*, 1975, 6–10

From: Queenstown (Cobh)   To: US
Date: May–June 1884
Reference: NL MS. 20616

From: Armagh, Derry, Donegal, Louth, Tyrone   To: (not given)
Date: 1890–1921
Reference: PRONI P.648(9) (Members of Girls' Friendly Society)

2. PUBLISHED WORKS ON EMIGRATION

(A) NORTH AMERICA, GENERAL

Bradley, A. K., *History of the Irish in America*, Chartwell, 1986, Ir. 942 b 19
Coldham, P. W., *The Complete Book of Emigrants, 1607–60* [. . .], Baltimore, 1987
Concannon and Cull, *Irish-American Who's Who*, Ir. 942 i 13
Davin, N. F., *The Irishman in Canada*, Shannon 1968, Ir. 971 d 1
Dickson, R., *Emigration to Colonial America 1775*, Ir. 3252 d 3
Donohoe, H., *The Irish Catholic Benevolent Union*, Ir. 973 d 6
Doyle, D., *Ireland, Irishmen, and Revolutionary America*, Dublin, 1981, Ir. 942 d 12
Doyle and Edwards (ed.), *America and Ireland 1776–1976*, London, 1980, Ir. 973 a 5
Elliott, B. S., *Irish Migrants in the Canadas* (Irish Protestants from Co. Tipperary
    especially), McGill, 1988
Friendly Sons of St Patrick,1771–1892, Ir. 973 c 1
Fromers, V., 'Irish Emigrants to Canada in Sussex Archives, 1839–47', *The
    Irish Ancestor*, 1974, 31–42
Hartigan, J., *The Irish in the American Revolution*, Washington, 1908, Ir. 973 h 8

Holder (ed.), *Emigrants from Britain to American Plantations, 1600–1700*, 9291 w 1
The Irish-American Genealogist, 1973–, Ir. 9291 i 3
Journal of the American-Irish Historical Society, Ir. 973 a 1
Knowles, Charles, *The Petition to Governor Shute in 1718: Scotch-Irish Pioneers in Ulster and America*, Ir. 973614
Leeson, F, 'Irish Emigrants to Canada, 1839–47', from the Wyndham estates in Counties Clare (especially), Limerick and Tipperary
Linden, *Irish Schoolmasters in the American Colonies, 1640–1775*, Ir. 942 r 9
Lockhart, A., *Emigration: Ireland to North America, 1660–1775*, New York, 1976, Ir. 973 l 5
Maguire, *The Irish in America*, New York, 1868, Ir. 973 m 3
Mannion, J. J., *Irish Settlements in Eastern Canada*, Toronto, 1974, Ir. 971 m 11
McGee, *Irish Settlers in North America*, New York, 1852, Ir. 970 m 1
Meagher, T. J., *From Paddy to Studs*, Westport, 1986, Ir. 942 f 8
Meyer (?), Early Irish Emigrants to America, 1803, 1806, *The Recorder*, June 1926, 973 r 1
Miller, K. A., *Exiles and Emigrants*, Oxford, 1985, Ir. 942 m 26
Mitchell, Brian, *Irish Emigration Lists 1833–39*, Baltimore, Genealogical Publishing Company, 1989 (Counties Antrim and Derry)
O'Brien, M. J., *A Hidden Phase of American History*, Baltimore, 1973 (Irishmen in the American Revolution), Ir. 9733 o 25
O'Brien, M. J., *Irish Settlers in America*, a consolidation of articles from the *Journal of the American-Irish Society*, Genealogical Publishing Company, Baltimore, 1979, Ir. 942 o 23
O'Driscoll, R. and Reynolds L. (ed.), *The Untold Story: the Irish in Canada*, Toronto, 1988 (2 vols)
Potter, G., *To the Golden Door*, Boston, 1960, Ir. 973 p 4
Reynolds, F., *Ireland's Important and Heroic Part . . .* (Irish in the American Revolution), Chicago, n.d., Ir. 973 r 3
Ridges, J. T., *Erin's Sons in America* (The AOH), New York, 1986, Ir. 973 r 7
Roberts, E. F., *Ireland in America*, London, 1931, Ir. 973 r 2
Shannon, W. V., *The American Irish*, New York, 1963, Ir. 973 s 3
Trainor, Brian, 'Sources for the Identification of Emigrants from Ireland to North America in the 19th Century', *Ulster Historical and Genealogical Guild Newsletter*, Vol. 1, Nos 2 and 3 (1979), Ir. 9292 u 3
Werkin, E., *Enter the Irish-American*, New York, 1976, Ir. 973 w 9
White, J., *Sketches from America*, London, 1870, Ir. 942 w 7
Wittke, C., *The Irish in America*, Baton Rouge, 1956, Ir. 973 w 2

(B) LOCALITIES IN NORTH AMERICA
Adams, E. and O'Keeffe, B. B., *Catholic Trails West: The Founding Catholic Families of Pennsylvania* (Vol. 1, St Joseph's Church, Philadelphia), Baltimore, Genealogical Publishing Company, 1988

Akenson, D. H., *The Irish in Ontario*, McGill, 1985, Ir. 971 a 8

Bannon, T., *Pioneer Irish in Onondaga*, London, 1911, Ir. 971 b 2

Burchell, R. A., *San Francisco Irish, 1848–1880*, Manchester University Press, 1979, Ir. 973 b 12

Callahan, *Irish-Americans and their Communities of Cleveland*

Clark, D., *The Irish Relations* (Irish-Americans in Philadelphia), New Jersey, 1982, Ir. 973 c 26

Clark, D., *The Irish in Philadelphia*, Philadelphia, 1973, Ir. 973 c 11

Cullen, J. B., *Story of the Irish in Boston*, Boston, 1893, Ir. 973 c 8

Cushing, J., *Irish Emigration to St John, New Brunswick, 1847*, St John, 1979, Ir. 942 c 16

Donovan, G. F., *The Irish in Massachusetts, 1620–1775*, St Louis, 1931, Ir. 9744 d 2

Fanning, C. (ed.), *Mr Dooley and the Chicago Irish*, New York, 1976, Ir. 973 d 10

Flannery, J. B., *The Irish Texans*, San Antonio, 1980, Ir. 973 f 4

Funchion, M. F., *The Irish in Chicago*, Chicago, 1987, Ir. 970 i 15

Funchion, M. F., *Chicago's Irish Nationalists 1881–1890*, New York, 1976, Ir. 973 f 1

Gearon, M. M., *Irish Settlers in Gardner, Massachusetts*, Gardner, 1932, Ir. 9744 g 1

Guerin, T., *The Gael in New France*, Montreal, 1946, Ir. 971 g 4

'Irish Settlers in early Delaware', *Pennsylvania History*, April 1947, Ir. 973 p 2

Kilkenny, J. F., 'The Irish of Morrow County, Oregon', *Historical Quarterly*, June 1968, Ir. 942 p 6

MacDonald, *History of the Irish in Wisconsin in the Nineteenth Century*, Washington, 1954, Ir. 973 m 9

Mackenzie, A. A., *The Irish in Cape Breton*, Cape Breton, 1979, Ir. 942 m 20

Mahony, M. E., *The Irish in Western Pennsylvania*, Pittsburgh, 1977, Ir. 973 m 16

New England Irish Guide 1987, Ir. 973 n 6

Niehaus, E. F., *The Irish in New Orleans 1800–1860*, Baton Rouge, 1965, Ir. 973 n 3

Oberster, W. H., *Texas Irish Empresarios and Their Colonies*, Austin, 1953, Ir. 973 o 10

O'Brien, M. J., *Pioneer Irish in New England*, New York, 1937, Ir. 974 o 6

O'Brien, M. J., *In Old New York: Irish Dead in Trinity and St Paul's Churchyards*, New York, 1928, Ir. 973 o 8

O'Brien, M. J., 'Grantees of Land in Virginia', *Journal of the American Irish Historical Society*, 13, 1913–14, 973 a 1

O'Gallagher, M., *St Patrick's and St Brigid's, Quebec*, Quebec, 1981, Ir. 942 o 29

Prendergast, T. F., *Forgotten Pioneers: Irish Leaders in Early California*, San Francisco, 1942, Ir. 942 p 13

Punch, T. M., *Some Sons of Erin in Nova Scotia*, Halifax, 1980, Ir. 971 p 10

Quigly, H., *The Irish Race in California and on the Pacific Coast*, San Francisco, 1878, Ir. 973 q 1

Redmond, P. M., *Irish Life in Rural Quebec*, Duquesne, 1983, Ir. 942 r 6

Ryan, D. P., *Beyond the Ballot Box: Boston Irish 1845–1917*, London, 1983, Ir. 973 r 4

Stewart, H. L., *The Irish in Nova Scotia*, Kentville, 1950, Ir. 971 s 2

Toner, P. M., *New Ireland Remembered: historical essays on the Irish in New Brunswick*, New Brunswick, 1988

Vinyard, J., *The Irish on the Urban Frontier* (Irish in Detroit 1850–1880), New York, 1976, Ir. 973 v 1

Williams, H. A., *History of the Hibernian Society of Baltimore 1803–1951*, Baltimore, 1951, Ir. 942 w 1

(C) SCOTCH-IRISH IN NORTH AMERICA

Bolton, C. K., *Scotch-Irish Pioneers*, Baltimore, 1967, Ir. 973 b 5

Cummings, H. M., *Scots Breed* (Scotch-Irish in Pennsylvania), Pittsburgh, 1964, Ir. 942 c 17

Dickson, R. J., *Ulster Emigration to Colonial America, 1718–75*, London, 1976

Dunaway, W., *Scotch-Irish of Colonial Pennsylvania*, Genealogical Publishing Company, Baltimore, 1985, Ir. 974 d 16

Glasgow, M., *Scotch-Irish in Northern Ireland and the American Colonies*, New York, 1936, Ir. 973 g 16

Marshall, W. F., *Ulster Sails West*, Ir. 973 m 5

Scotch-Irish Heritage Festival, Winthrop, 1981, Ir. 942 s 15

Shaw, J., *The Scotch-Irish in History*, Springfield, 1899, Ir. 942 s 13

Stone, F., *Scots and Scotch-Irish in Connecticut*, Univ. of Connecticut, 1978, Ir. 929 p 5

The Ulster-American Connection, New University of Ulster, 1976, Ir. 942 u 3

Wood, S. G., *Ulster Scots and Blandford Scouts* (Ulster Irish in Massachusetts), Mass, 1928, Ir. 973 w 1

(D) AUSTRALIA AND NEW ZEALAND

Cleary, P. J. S., *Australia's Debt to Ireland's Nation-builders*, Sydney, 1933, Ir. 994 c 6

Coffey and Morgan, *Irish Families in Australia and New Zealand 1788–1979* (4 vols, biographical dictionary), Melbourne, 1979, Ir. 942 c 14

Curry, C. H., *The Irish at Eureka*, Sydney, 1954, Ir. 993 c 7

Hawkings, David T., *Bound for Australia*, Sussex, Phillimore and Co., 1987

Hogan, J., *The Irish in Australia*, Melbourne, 1888, Ir. 994o

Hughes, Robert, *The Fatal Shore*, London, 1988

Kiernan, C. (ed.), *Australia and Ireland, 1788–1988*, Dublin, 1986, Ir. 942 a 9

Kiernan, T. J., *The Irish in Australia*, Dublin, 1954, Ir. 994 k 1

McDonagh and Mandle, *Ireland and Irish-Australians*, Sydney, 1982, Ir. 942 i 12

O' Farrell, P., *The Irish in Australia*, New South Wales, 1987, Ir. 942 o 29

Robinson, P., *The Hitch and Brood of Time: Australians 1788–1828*, Oxford, 1985, Ir. 993 r 5

Robson, L. L., *The Convict Settlers of Australia*, Melbourne, 1965
The Ulster Link (Magazine of the Northern Irish in Australia and New
   Zealand), Ir. 994 u 1

(E) FRANCE
Griffin, G., *The Wild Geese* (pen portraits), Ir. 920041 g 5
Hayes, R., *Ireland and Irishmen in the French Revolution*, Dublin, Ir. 94404 h 1
Hayes, R., *Irish Swordsmen of France*, Dublin, Ir. 94404 h 3
Hayes, R., *Biographical Dictionary of Irishmen in France*, Dublin 1949, Ir. 9440 h 16
Hayes, R., *Old Irish Links with France*, Dublin, Ir. 944 h 11
Lee, G. A., *Irish Chevaliers in the Service of France*, Ir. 340 l 3
Mathorez, J., 'Les irlandais nobles ou notables à Nantes aux XVIIe et
   XVIIIe siècles', Ir. 941 p 20
O'Callaghan, J. C., *History of the Irish Brigades*, Ir. 944 o 13
O'Connell, M. J., *The Last Colonel of the Irish Brigade* (Count O'Connell,
   1745–1833)
Hennessy, M., *The Wild Geese*, London, 1973, Ir. 942 h 10
Jones, P., *The Irish Brigade*, London, 1981, Ir. 942 j 3
Swords, L., *Irish-French Connections 1578–1978*, Paris, 1978, Ir. 942 i 6
Terry, James, *Pedigrees and Papers*, Ir. 9292 t 7

(F) SOUTH AFRICA
Dickson, G. D., *Irish Settlers to the Cape (1820)*, Cape Town, 1973, Ir. 968 d 7
The Irish in South Africa, 1920–1921, Ir. 968 i 2

(G) ARGENTINA
Coghlan, Eduardo, *Los Irlandeses en la Argentina*, Buenos Aires, 1987
Murray, *The Irish in Argentina*, Ir. 982 m 8

(H) WEST INDIES
'Documents relating to the Irish in the West Indies, with accounts of Irish
   Settlements, 1612–1752', *Analecta Hibernica*, Vol. 4, 140–286
Oliver, Vere L., *Caribbeana: Miscellaneous Papers Relating to the History, Topography,
   Genealogy and Antiquities of the British West Indies* (5 vols), London, 1912, NL
   9729 o 1
Oliver, Vere L., *The History of the Island of Antigua* (3 vols), London, 1894-9
Oliver, Vere L., *Monumental Inscriptions of the British West Indies*, London, 1904

8

The Registry of Deeds

1. SCOPE OF THE RECORDS

Since research in the Registry of Deeds can be very laborious and time-consuming, it is prudent to be aware of the limitations of its records before starting work there. The Registry was set up by the Irish Parliament in 1708 to assist in regularising the massive transfer of land ownership from the Catholic Anglo-Norman and Gaelic populations to the Protestant Anglo-Irish which had taken place over the preceding century. The registration of deeds was not obligatory; the function of the Registry was simply to provide evidence of legal title in the event of a dispute. These two facts, the voluntary nature of registration and the general aim of copperfastening the Cromwellian and Williamite confiscations, determine the nature of the records held by the Registry. The overwhelming majority deal with property-owning members of the Church of Ireland, and a disproportionate number of these relate to transactions which carried some risk of legal dispute. In other words, the deeds registered are generally of interest only for a minority of the population and constitute only a fraction of the total number of property transactions carried out in the country.

The implications of these facts are worth spelling out in detail. Over the most useful period of the Registry's records, the non-Catholic population of Ireland constituted, at most, 20 per cent of the total. The majority of these were dissenting Presbyterians largely concentrated in the north, and suffering restrictions on their property rights similar to those imposed on Catholics; very few deeds made by dissenting Protestants are registered. Of the remaining non-Catholics, the majority were small farmers, tradesmen or artisans, usually in a position of economic dependence on those with whom they might have property transactions, and thus in no position to dispute the terms of a deed. The records of the Registry therefore cover only a minority of the non-Catholic minority. There are exceptions of course—large landlords who made and registered great numbers of leases with their smaller tenants, marriage settlements between families of relatively modest means, the business transactions of the small Catholic merchant classes, the registration of the holdings of the few surviving Catholic landowners after the relaxation of the Penal Laws in the 1780s—but these remain very definitely exceptions. And for the vast bulk of the population, the Catholic tenant farmers, the possibility of a deed having been registered can almost certainly be discounted, since they owned nothing and had almost no legal rights to the property they rented.

A further limit to the scope of the records is the scant use made of the Registry before the middle of the eighteenth century. It was only from about the 1750s that registration became even relatively widespread, and its major genealogical usefulness is for the century or so from then until the 1850s, when it is generally superseded by other sources.

With these limitations in mind, it should now be said that, for those who made and registered deeds, the records of the Registry can often provide superb information. The propensity to register deeds appears to have run in families, and a single document can name two or three generations, as well as leading back to a chain of related records which give a picture of the family's evolving fortunes and the network of its collateral relationships.

2. REGISTRATION

Registration worked in the following way. After a deed had been signed and witnessed, one of the parties to it had a copy known as a 'memorial' made, signed it and had it witnessed by two people, at least one of whom had been a witness to the original. The memorial was then sworn before a Justice of the Peace as a faithful copy of the original and sent to the Registry. Here it was transcribed into a large manuscript volume and indexed. The original memorial was retained and stored, and these are all still preserved in the vaults of the Registry. For research purposes, however, the large manuscript volumes containing the transcripts of the memorials are used. Registration of a deed normally took place fairly soon after its execution, within a month or two in most cases, though delays of up to two years are quite common. If the gap between the execution and the registration of a deed is much more, this may be significant; it indicates an impending need for one of the parties to the deed or their heirs to be able to show legal proof of its execution. The most common reason for such a need would have been the death of one of the parties.

3. THE INDEXES

The indexing system used by the Registry is complicated and only partial. There are two sets of indexes, one by grantor's name (i.e. the name of the party disposing of the asset), and one by the name of the townland in which the property was situated. The Grantors' Index is fully alphabetical, and is divided into a number of sets covering different initial letters and periods. Between 1708 and 1833 the Grantors' Index records only the name of the grantor, the surname of the first grantee, along with the volume, and page and deed number. No indication is given of the location of the property concerned, an omission which can make a search for references to a family with a common surname very cumbersome indeed. After 1833 the Index is more comprehensive, showing the county in which the property was situated. In general, the Index is remarkably accurate, but there are some mistakes, particularly in the volume and page references. In such a case, the deed number can be used to trace the transcript; several transcribers worked simultaneously on different volumes, and the volume numbers were sometimes transposed. If, for example, Volume 380 is not the correct reference, Volumes 378–382 may contain the transcript. Within each volume the transcripts are numerically consecutive.

The Lands Index is subdivided by county, and within each county is roughly alphabetical, with townland names grouped together under their initial letter. This means that a search for deeds relating to, say, Ballyboy, Co. Roscommon, involves a search through all the references to Co. Roscommon townlands which start with 'B'. The information given in the Index is brief, recording only the surnames of two of the parties, as well as the volume, page and deed numbers. As with the Grantors' Index, the Index is divided into a number of sets covering different periods. After 1828 the Index further subdivides the townlands into baronies, making research a good deal more efficient. Along with the county volumes, there are separate indexes for corporation towns and cities. The subdivisions within these are somewhat eccentric, particularly in the case of Dublin, making it necessary to search even more widely than in the rural indexes. It should be pointed out that the Registry does not make it possible to trace the history of all the transactions in which a property was involved, since, inevitably, some of the deeds recording the transactions have not been registered.

In general, of the Registry's two sets of indexes, the Grantors' Index is the most genealogically useful, since it is strictly alphabetical and lists transactions by person rather than by property. The single greatest lack in the Registry is of an index to the grantees. The social range covered, given the distribution of wealth in the country, could be enhanced greatly by the production of such an index. Microfilm copies of both the Lands Index and the Grantors' Index, amounting to more than 400 reels, are available at the

National Library. Volume 1 of Margaret Falley's *Irish and Scotch-Irish Ancestral Research*, available on open shelves in the Library reading room, gives a complete breakdown of the locations and microfilm numbers of the indexes up to 1850 (pp 71–90). The Public Record Office of Northern Ireland also has a microfilm copy of the indexes, as well as of the memorial books themselves.

4. NATURE OF THE RECORDS

The archaic and legalistic terminology used in deeds can often make it extremely difficult to work out what precisely the parties to a deed intended it to do. This is particularly true in cases where earlier agreements are referred to but not recited in full. However, from a genealogical point of view, the precise nature of the transaction recorded is not always vital, and with a little practice it becomes relatively easy to pare the document down to the essentials of dates, placenames and personal names. It should be kept in mind that *all* personal names—buyers, sellers, trustees, mortgagees, witnesses—may be important and should be noted. None the less, there are numerous cases in which the nature of the deed is of interest, and in any case some advance knowledge will speed up the process of interpretation. What follows, therefore, is an attempt to clarify some of the less familiar terms, and to describe the most common or useful documents likely to be encountered.

The most important part of most deeds, the opening, follows an almost invariable pattern. After the phrase 'A memorial of', indicating that the transcript is of a copy rather than the original, the following are stated: (1) the nature of the deed; (2) the date on which the original was made; and (3) the names of the parties to the deed. It must be remembered that a number of people could constitute a single party for the purposes of a legal transaction. A typical opening would then be:

> A memorial of an indented deed of agreement dated October 13th 1793 between John O'Hara of Oak Park, Co. Meath, farmer, and George O'Hara of Balltown, Co. Meath, farmer, his eldest son of the first part, William Coakley of Navan, Co. Meath, merchant, of the second part, and Christopher French of Navan, gentleman, of the third part, in which . . .

Very often it is necessary to read no more than this to know that a deed is not relevant; if, for example, the research is on the O'Haras of Sligo, it is clear at a glance that the above document has no direct relevance. As happens so often in genealogy, however, the significance of information in a deed may only become clear retrospectively, in the light of something uncovered later. When carrying out a search for a particular family, therefore, it is a good idea to note briefly the important points in all deeds examined—names, addresses and occupations—whether or not they seem immediately relevant, so that if it subsequently emerges, for example, that the O'Haras of Sligo and Meath are related, the relevant deeds can be readily identified again.

Categorising the kinds of deeds which appear in the Registry can be difficult, since many of them are not what they appear to be. The most common misleading description in the opening of the memorial is the 'deed of lease and release', which may in fact be a conveyance or sale, a mortgage, a marriage settlement or a rent charge. 'Lease and Release' was a legal device whereby the obligation to record a conveyance publicly could be avoided; it was not obligatory to record a transaction to a tenant or lessee already in occupation, and it was not obligatory to record a lease for one year only. Accordingly, a lease for one year was first granted, and then the true transaction, conveyance, mortgage, marriage settlement or other, was carried out. It remained popular as a method of conveyance until 1845, when the *Statute of Uses* which made it possible was repealed.

Despite the difficulties created by such disguises as the 'lease and release', the underlying transactions do fall into a number of broad classes:

1. LEASES

By far the most common of the records in the Registry, leases could run for any term between 1 and 999 years, or could depend on the lives of a number of persons named in the document, or could be a mixture of the two, lasting, for example, three lives or sixty years, whichever was longer. Only leases for more than three years could be registered. The most genealogically useful information in leases is to be found in the lives they mention. The choice of lives generally rested with the lessee or grantee, and in most cases those chosen were related. Often the names and ages of the grantee's children can appear, extremely valuable for families in the eighteenth century. Leases for 900 years, or for lives renewable in perpetuity, which were much more common in Ireland than elsewhere, amounted to a permanent transfer of the property, although the grantor remained the nominal owner. As might be imagined, such leases provided a rich basis for legal disputes.

2. MARRIAGE SETTLEMENTS

Any form of pre-nuptial property agreement between the families of the prospective bride and groom was known as a 'marriage settlement', or 'marriage articles'. A variety of transactions can therefore be classed in this way. What they have in common is their aim to provide security, in particular to the women; since married women could hold no property in their own right, it was common practice for the dowry to be granted to trustees, rather than directly to the future husband, which allowed her some degree of independence. Commonly, also, the family of the prospective husband, or the husband himself, granted an annuity out of the income of his land to the future wife and children if he should pre-decease them. The information given in settlements varies, but in general it should include at a minimum the names, addresses and occupations of the bride, groom and bride's father. In addition, other relatives—brothers, uncles, etc.—also put in an appearance. For obvious reasons, therefore, marriage settlements are among the most useful of the records to be found in the Registry. The period for which they were most commonly registered appears to have been the three decades from 1790 to 1820. In searching the Grantors' Indexes for them, it should be remembered that they are not always indicated as such, and that the formal grantor may be a member of either family, making it necessary to search under both surnames.

3. MORTGAGES
In the eighteenth and nineteenth centuries, these were very commonly used as a form of investment on the one hand, and as a way of raising short-term cash on the other. They do not generally provide a great deal of family information, but since they were an endless source of legal disputes, they form a disproportionate number of the deeds registered. It was quite common for mortgages to be passed on to third or fourth parties, each hoping to make money, and the resulting deeds can be very complicated.

4. BILLS OF DISCOVERY
Under the Penal Laws, Catholics were not allowed to possess more than a very limited amount of land, and a Protestant who discovered a Catholic in possession of more than this amount could file a Bill of Discovery to claim it. In practice, most Bills appear to have been filed by Protestant friends of Catholic landowners to pre-empt hostile Discovery, and as a means of allowing them to remain in effective possession. Registered Bills are not common, but they are extremely interesting, both genealogically and historically.

5. WILLS
Only those wills likely to be contested legally, in other words those which omitted someone, almost certainly a family member who might have a legitimate claim, would have been registered. Abstracts of the personal and geographical information in all the wills registered between 1708 and 1832 have been published in P. B. Phair and E. Ellis (ed.), *Abstracts of Wills at The Registry of Deeds* (3 vols), Irish Manuscripts Commission, 1954–88. The full provisions of the wills are only to be found in the original memorials.

6. RENT CHARGES
These were annual payments of a fixed sum payable out of the revenue from nominated lands. They were used to provide for family members in straitened circumstances, or to pay off debts or mortgages in instalments. Once made, they could be transferred to others, and were valuable assets in their own

right. Depending on the terms, they can provide useful insights into family relationships and family fortunes.

Other miscellaneous classes of deed also appear. As outlined above, the only common feature is that they record a property transaction of some description; any family information they may contain is a matter of luck

More than most other repositories, research in the Registry of Deeds provides a very vivid sense of the past. The sack-covered, cumbersome transcript volumes, dusty and yellowing, smell of accumulated time, of lives long finished. It is a place to be approached in a spirit of patient exploration.

9

Newspapers

Newspapers are one of the most enjoyable and most difficult of genealogical sources. Faced with so much of the everyday particularity of the past, it is virtually impossible to confine oneself to biographical data; again and again research is sidetracked by simple curiosity. In addition to this, the endemic imprecision of family information means that it is almost always necessary to search a wide range of dates. A sustained search for genealogical information in original newspapers is, as a result, extremely time-consuming. If the efficient use of research time is a priority, newspapers are certainly not the place to start.

With this proviso in mind, it must be added that the destruction of so many Irish records in 1922 gives a disproportionate importance to Irish newspapers, and that when newspapers do produce information, it can be extremely rich. Event are reported virtually as they happen, within a few weeks at most, and the reports have an authority and accuracy which is hard to match, even making all necessary allowances for journalistic errors. Nor is it now any longer always necessary to search the original papers themselves, as we shall see.

1. INFORMATION GIVEN

There are two principal formats in which useful information appears, biographical notices and, in the early papers, advertisements. Up to the 1850s, the former consist largely of marriage announcements and obituaries; birth announcements tend to be sparse, relate only to the wealthiest classes, and often give no more than the father's name, taking the form, 'on the 12th, the lady of George Gratton Esq., of a son'. After the mid-nineteenth century, the number of birth notices rises sharply, but they remain relatively uninformative.

Marriage announcements contain a much broader range of information, from the bare minimum of the names of the two parties, to comprehensive accounts of the addresses, occupations and fathers' names. In the majority of cases, the name of the bride's father and his address are supplied, in a form such as 'married on Tuesday last Michael Thomson Esq. to Miss Neville eldest daughter of James Neville of Bandon Esq.' For many eighteenth-century marriages, a newspaper announcement may be the only surviving record, particularly where the relevant Church of Ireland register has not survived.

Obituaries are by far the most numerous newspaper announcements, and cover a much broader social spectrum than either births or marriages. Again, the kind of information given can vary widely, from the barest 'died at Tullamore Mr Michael Cusack' to the most elaborate, giving occupation, exact age and family relationships: 'died at the house of her uncle Mr Patrick Swan in George's St in the 35th year of her age Mrs Burgess, relict of Henry Burgess Esq., late of Limerick'. Precision such as this is rare, however; most announcements confine themselves to name, address, occupation and place of death. Because of the paucity of Catholic burial records, newspaper obituaries are the most comprehensive surviving records of the deaths of the majority of the Catholic middle classes. From about the 1840s, the number of both obituaries and marriage announcements rose sharply; unfortunately these events are by then usually more easily traceable in parish or civil records.

Advertisements, in the early newspapers especially, were more often paid announcements than true advertisements in the modern sense, and an extraordinary variety of information can be gleaned from them. The most useful types are as follows:

(I) ELOPEMENTS
A husband would announce that his wife had absconded, and disclaim all responsibility for any debts she might contract. Usually his address and her maiden surname are given.

(II) BUSINESS ANNOUNCEMENTS
The most useful are those which record the place and nature of the business, which announce a change of address or ownership for the business, or which record the succession of a son to a business after his father's death.

(III) BANKRUPTCIES
These generally request creditors to gather at a specified time and place, and can be useful in narrowing the focus of a search for relevant transactions in the Registry of Deeds.

As well as advertisements and biographical notices, of course, newspapers also reported the news of the day, concentrating on the details of court cases with particular relish. For an ancestor who was a convict, these hold great interest, since much of the evidence was reported verbatim, and may provide vital clues for further research. However, uncovering the relevant report depends very much on knowing the date of conviction with some degree of accuracy, as well as the area in which the trial is likely to have taken place.

2. PERSONS COVERED

Apart from reports of trials, genealogical information to be found in newspapers relates to fairly well-defined social groups. First, then as now, the doings of the nobility were of general interest, and their births, marriages and deaths are extensively covered. Next in terms of coverage are the merchant and professional classes of the towns in which the newspapers were published. These would include barristers and solicitors, doctors, masters of schools, military officers and clergy, as well as the more prosperous business people. It should be remembered that, from about the 1770s, this would include the growing Catholic merchant class. Next are the farming gentry from the surrounding areas. After them come the less well-off traders, traceable largely through advertisements. Finally, the provincial papers also cover the inhabitants of neighbouring towns in these same classes, albeit sparsely at times. *No* information is to be found concerning anyone at or below middle-farmer level, the great bulk of the population, in other words. This remains true even from the third and fourth decades of the nineteenth century, when the number of announcements rose markedly and the social classes covered broadened somewhat.

3. DATES AND AREAS

The earliest Irish newspapers were published in Dublin at the end of the seventeenth century. It was not until the mid-eighteenth century, however, that they became widespread and began to carry information of genealogical value. The period of their prime usefulness is from about this time, *c.*1750, to around the mid-nineteenth century, when other sources become more accessible and thorough. Obviously not all areas of the country were equally well served, particularly at the start of this period. Publications tended to be concentrated in particular regions, as follows:

(i) DUBLIN

The most important eighteenth-century publications were the *Dublin Evening Post*, started in 1719, *Faulkner's Dublin Journal*, from 1725, the *Freeman's Journal*, from 1763, and the *Dublin Hibernian Journal*, from 1771. As well as carrying plentiful marriage and obituary notices relating to Dublin and surrounding areas from about the mid-century, these papers also reproduced notices which had first appeared in provincial papers, something which should be kept in mind in cases where the original local newspapers have not survived. From the early nineteenth century a great proliferation of publications began to appear; unfortunately the custom of publishing family notices fell into disuse in the first decades of the century, and did not resume until well into the 1820s.

(II) CORK

After Dublin, Cork was the area of the country best served by newspapers, with many publications following the lead of the *Corke Journal* which began in 1753. As well as publishing notices relating specifically to Cork City and county, these papers also carried much of interest for other Munster counties, notably Kerry, and, like the Dublin papers, republished notices relating to Munster which had originally appeared in other publications. An index exists to newspaper biographical notices relating to Counties Cork and Kerry between 1756 and 1827, details of which will be found below.

(III) LIMERICK/CLARE

There was a great deal of overlap between the earliest Clare newspapers, the *Clare Journal* from 1787, and the *Ennis Chronicle* from 1788, and those of Limerick, where the first publications were the *Munster Journal* (1749) and the *Limerick Chronicle*. As well as Clare and Limerick, both groups of papers had extensive coverage of Co. Tipperary, and in the case of the Limerick publications, this coverage also extended to Kerry and Galway. The Molony series of manuscripts in the Genealogical Office (see Chapter 6) includes extensive abstracts from the Clare papers. Details of a more accessible and far-ranging set of abstracts will be found below.

(IV) CARLOW/KILKENNY

This area was covered by a single publication, *Finn's Leinster Journal*, which began in 1768. Although the advertisements are useful, early biographical notices are sparse. The earliest have been published in *The Irish Genealogist* (1987/88).

(V) WATERFORD

The earliest newspapers here were the *Waterford Chronicle* (1770), the *Waterford Herald* (1791), and the *Waterford Mirror* (1804). Few of the earliest issues appear to have survived. For surviving issues before 1800, *The Irish Genealogist* has published the biographical notices (1974, and 1976–80 incl.). Notices to 1821 are included with the abstracts for Clare/Limerick.

(VI) BELFAST AND ULSTER

The single most important newspaper in this area was the *Belfast Newsletter* which began publication in 1737. It had a wider geographical range than any of the Dublin papers, covering virtually all of east Ulster. Outside Belfast the most significant publications were the *Londonderry Journal*, from 1772, which also covered a good area of Donegal and Tyrone, and the *Newry Journal* and *Strabane Journal*, of which very few, if any, early issues survive.

4. LOCATIONS

The best single repository for Irish newspapers is the British Library. After 1826 the Library was obliged to hold a copy of all Irish publications, and from that date its collection is virtually complete. It also has an extensive, though patchy, collection before that date. Within Ireland the largest collection is held by the National Library, though this is by no means comprehensive. Many unique copies are held in local libraries and other repositories. No complete guide to dates and locations exists as yet. A census of the dates and locations of all surviving early Irish newspapers has recently been carried out jointly by the National Library and the British Library, however, and it is to be hoped that this will be published in the near future. For areas now in Northern Ireland, the Public Record Office of Northern Ireland has published a complete guide, *Northern Ireland Newspapers: Checklist with Locations*.

5. INDEXES

A number of indexes exist to the biographical material found in newspapers, which can greatly lighten the burden of research. Those dealing with single publications are as follows:

(i)   National Library index to the *Freeman's Journal* from 1763 to 1771;

(ii)   National Library index to marriages and deaths in *Pue's Occurrences* and the *Dublin Gazette*, 1730–1740, NL MS. 3197;

(iii) Henry Farrar's *Biographical Notices in Walker's Hibernian Magazine 1772–1812* (1889);

(iv)   Card indexes to the biographical notices in the *Hibernian Chronicle* (1771–1802), and the *Cork Mercantile Chronicle* (1803–1818), held by the Irish Genealogical Research Society in London;

(v)   Index to biographical material in the *Belfast Newsletter* (1737–1800— unfortunately in chronological rather than alphabetical order), held by the Linen Hall Library in Belfast.

As well as these, Volume 6 of Albert Casey's *O'Kief, Coshe Mang etc.* reprints the biographical notices from the *Kerry Evening Post* from 1828 to 1864, and these are included in the general index at the back of the volume. More useful than any of these, however, are two extraordinary works produced by Rosemary ffolliott, her 'Index to Biographical Notices Collected from Newspapers, Principally Relating to Cork and Kerry, 1756–1827', and 'Index to Biographical Notices in the Newspapers of Limerick, Ennis, Clonmel and Waterford, 1758–1821'. Both are in fact much more than simple indexes, transcribing and ordering alphabetically all the notices they record. Some idea of their scope can be gleaned simply by listing the newspapers they cover.

The former includes biographical notices relating to Cork and Kerry from the surviving issues of the following Cork papers: the *Cork Advertiser*, the *Cork Chronicle*, the *Cork Evening Post*, the *Cork Gazette*, the *Corke Journal*, the *Cork Mercantile Chronicle*, the *Cork Morning Intelligence*, the *Southern Reporter*, *The Constitution*, the *Hibernian Chronicle* and the *Volunteer Journal*. As well as these, it also records all notices relating to Cork and Kerry in *Finn's Leinster Journal*, the *Dublin Gazette*, the *Dublin Hibernian Journal*, *Faulkner's Dublin Journal*, the *Freeman's Journal*, the *Magazine of Magazines*, the *Limerick Chronicle* and the *Waterford Mirror*. The latter index extracts and indexes the biographical notices from the *Clonmel Herald*, the *Clonmel Gazette*, the *Clonmel Advertiser*, the *Ennis Chronicle*, the *Clare Journal*, the *Limerick Evening Post*, the *Limerick Gazette*, the *Limerick Chronicle*, the *Munster Journal*, the *Waterford Chronicle* and the *Waterford Mirror*. In addition, a number of eighteenth-century Dublin newspapers are included: the *Freeman's Journal*, *Faulkners' Dublin Journal*, the *Dublin Hibernian Journal* and the *Hibernian Chronicle*, and all notices for the areas covered by the above publications extracted, as well as notices relating to other Munster counties, and to Counties Galway, Mayo, Roscommon, Leitrim, Longford and King's (Offaly). Between the two works, then, virtually all the surviving eighteenth-century notices for the southern half of the country are extracted, along with a large proportion of notices up to 1821/1827, and most of the entries relating to Connacht, south Leinster and Munster which were picked up and reprinted by the Dublin papers. All in all, the two compilations constitute a magnificent work of scholarship. Unfortunately, neither is as widely available as it should be. The National Library and Cork City Library hold manuscript copies of the Cork and Kerry index (NL MSS. 19172–5). Limerick Archives (see Chapter 15 under 'The Irish Genealogical Project') has a copy of the more extensive Limerick, Ennis, Clonmel and Waterford index. The Genealogical Office has microfiche copies of both. Unfortunately these are not directly accessible to the public.

10

Directories

For those areas and classes which they cover, Irish directories are an excellent source, often supplying information not readily available elsewhere. Their most obvious and practical use is to find out where precisely in the larger towns a family lived, but for members of the gentry, and the professional, merchant and trading classes, they can show much more, providing indirect evidence of reversals of fortune or growing prosperity, of death and emigration. In many cases directory entries are the only precise indication of occupation. The only classes totally excluded from all directories are, once again, the most disadvantaged, small tenant farmers, landless labourers and servants. Virtually all classes other than these are at least partly included, in some of the nineteenth-century directories in particular. One point to be kept in mind when using any directory is that every entry is at least six months out of date by the time of publication. The account which follows divides directories into 1. Dublin Directories, 2. Country-wide Directories, and 3. Provincial Directories, supplying in each case the dates, locations and information included, followed, in the first two categories, by a chronological check-list.

1. DUBLIN DIRECTORIES

The Gentleman's and Citizen's Almanack, produced by John Watson, began publication in Dublin in 1736, and continued until 1844. However, the first true trade directories in Ireland were those published by Peter Wilson for Dublin City, starting in 1751 and continuing until 1837, with a break from 1754 to 1759. From the outset, these were considered as supplements to Watson's *Almanack* and were regularly bound with it. In 1787 the two publications were put together with the *English Court Registry*, and, until it ceased publication in 1837, the whole was known as *The Treble Almanack*.

Initially the information supplied in Wilson's *Directory* consisted purely of alphabetical lists of merchants and traders, supplying name, address and occupation. In the early years these were quite scanty, but grew steadily over the decades from less than a thousand names in the 1752 edition to almost five thousand in 1816. As well as merchants and traders, the last decades of the eighteenth century also saw the inclusion of separate lists of those who might now be termed 'The Establishment'—officers of the city guilds and of Trinity College, state officials, those involved in the administration of medicine and the law, Church of Ireland clergy etc. The range of people covered expanded markedly if a little eccentrically, in the early nineteenth century. The most permanent addition was a new section added in 1815 which covered the nobility and gentry. As well as this, a number of other listings of potential use to readers were added, though some appear only intermittently. Persons covered by these lists include pawnbrokers, bankers, apothecaries, police, dentists, physicians, militia officers and ships' captains.

The most significant difference between the *Treble Almanack* and Pettigrew and Oulton's *Dublin Almanac and General Register of Ireland*, which began annual publication in 1834, is the inclusion in the latter of a street-by-street listing, initially only of the inhabitants of Dublin proper, but enlarged year by year to encompass the suburbs. From 1835 this listing was supplemented by an alphabetical list of the individuals recorded. In theory at least, the combination of the two listings should now make it possible to track the movements of individuals around the city, an important feature since changes of address were much more frequent in the nineteenth century, when the common practice was to rent rather than purchase. Unfortunately, in practice the alphabetical list is much less comprehensive than the street list.

Pettigrew and Oulton also extended even further the range of persons covered. The officers of virtually every Dublin institution, club and society, as well as clergy of all denominations, are included. Another significant difference from the earlier *Treble Almanack* which should be kept in mind is the extension of the coverage outside the Dublin area. Under the rubric 'Official Authorities of Counties and Towns' Pettigrew and Oulton record the names of many of the rural gentry and more prosperous inhabitants of the large towns in their guise as local administrators. This is particularly useful for areas which were not served by a local directory, or for which none has survived. Similarly the officials of many of the better-known institutions and societies in the larger country towns are also recorded, as well as the more important provincial clergy.

The successor to Pettigrew and Oulton was Alexander Thom with his *Irish Almanac and Official Directory* which began in 1844 and has continued publication up to the present. As the name implies, it continued the extension of coverage outside Dublin. To take one year as an example, the 1870 edition includes, as well as the alphabetical and street listings for Dublin, alphabetical lists of the following for the entire country: army officers; attorneys, solicitors and barristers; bankers; Catholic, Church of Ireland and Presbyterian clergy;

coast guard officers; doctors; MPs; magistrates; members of the Irish Privy Council; navy and Marine officers; officers of counties and towns; and peers. Although Thom's is generally regarded as a Dublin directory, its usefulness goes well beyond Dublin.

As well as these annual directories, Dublin was also included in the country-wide publications of Pigot and Slater issued at intervals during the nineteenth century. The only significant difference is the arrangement of the individuals listed under their trades, making it possible to identify all those engaged in the same occupation, important at a time when many occupations were handed down from one generation to the next. These directories are dealt with more fully below.

Check-list

1751–1837   Wilson' *Directory*, from 1787 issued as part of *The Treble Almanack*.

1834–49   Pettigrew and Oulton's *Dublin Almanac and General Register of Ireland*.

from 1844   Thom's *Irish Almanac and Official Directory*, see also Pigot's and Slater's country-wide *Directories* from 1820.

The most comprehensive collections are held by the National Library and the National Archives. Copies can be requested directly at the reading room counter in both repositories without a call number.

2. COUNTRY-WIDE DIRECTORIES

Until the productions of Pigot and Co. in the early nineteenth century, very little exists which covers the entire country. Although not true directories in the sense of the Dublin publications, four works may be used in a similar way, at least as far as the country gentry are concerned. The earliest of these is George Taylor and Andrew Skinner's *Road Maps of Ireland* (1778), which prints maps of the principal routes from Dublin to the country towns, including the major country houses and the surnames of their occupants, with an alphabetical index to these surnames. The aim of William Wilson's *The Post-Chaise Companion* (1786) is similar, providing a discursive description of what might be seen on various journeys through the countryside. These descriptions include the names of the country houses and, again, their owners' surnames. There is no index. The next publications were the two editions, in 1812 and 1814, of Ambrose Leet's *Directory*. This contains an alphabetical listing of placenames—towns, villages, country houses, town-lands, in an arbitrary mix—showing the county, the nearest post town, and, in the case of the houses, the full name of the occupant. These names are then themselves indexed at the back of the volume.

1 N.—Bessborough-avenue.
Of North-strand-road.

1 Boyd, Mrs.	8l.
2 Flanagan, Mr. Thomas	
3 Freest, Mr. Patrick,	9l.
4 M'Carthy, Mr. Patk. J. G.P.O.	7l.
5 Hutchin, Mrs.	7l.
6 Purcell, Mr. Thomas,	10l.
7 Conroy, Mr. John,	10l.
8 Hatchell, Geo. master mariner,	8l.
9 Harbron, Mr. Wm. J.	9l.
10 Bell, Mr. Peter,	9l.
11 Keane, Alphons., photographer, and 94 North-strand,	9l.
12 Byrne, Mr. Joseph,	8l.
13 Goulding, Daniel, carpenter,	7l.
14 O'Kelly, Mr. Alexander,	7l.
15 Curtis, Mrs.	8l
16 O'Callaghan, Mrs.	8l.

Link Line

19 Frazer, Mr. James,	7l.
20 Reynolds, Mr. Thomas,	6l.
21 Robinson, Mr. Charles,	6l.
22 Armstrong, Mr. Andrew,	6l.

Link Line.

24 Wren, Mr. James,	6l.
25 Carroll, Mr. Patrick,	7l.
26 Byrne, Mr. Patrick,	7l.
27 M'Cauley, Mr. Peter,	7l.
28 Gregan, Mr. Hugh,	

Drumcondra Link Line Railway

32 Tomlinson, Mr. William,	12l.
33 Halliday, Mr. Thomas,	9l.
34 Grimes, James, engineer,	9l.
35 Wilcocks, Mr. Joseph,	9l.
36 Dillon, Mr. Andrew,	9l.
37 Lacy, Mr. James,	9l.
38 Scott, Mr. William,	9l.
39 Lambert, Mr. Thomas	7l.
40 Mooney, Mr. Mathew,	7l.
41 Hayden, Mr. John,	7l.
42 Smith, Mrs.	7l.
43 Hendry, Mr. William,	7l.
44 Sweny, Mr. Herbert Sidney,	7l.
45 Tuites, Mr. R.	7l.
46 Griffith, John,	7l.
47 Homan, Mr. Thomas,	4l. 10s.
48 Kennedy, Mrs.	4l. 10s.
49 Murphy, Mrs.,	6l.
50 Holmes, Mr. William,	6l.
51 Langan, Mr. John	

Bethesda-place.
Upper Dorset-street.
Three small cottages

3 S.—Bishop-street.

22½ Dunne, J. fishmonger,	7l.
23 Tenements,	16l.
24 Hayden, Mrs. board & lodging,	16l.

here Redmond's-hill & Peter's-row inters.

25 Kelly, James, grocer, wine and spirit dealer, & 13 Peter's-row,	58l.
26, 27, 27A, 28 to 39 Jacob, W. R. & Co. (limited)	
40, 41 & 42 Tonge and Taggart, *South City* foundry and iron works,	37l., 17l.
43 to 45 Tenements,	14l. to 17l.
46 Jacob, W. R. and Co. (limited) stores,	17l.

..........here Bishop-court intersects........

47 to 49 Tenements,	20l. 9l.
50 Jacob, W. R. and Co. stores,	30l.
51 Tenements,	26l.
52 & 53 Tenements,	21l., 24l.
54 & 55 Tenements,	17l., 16l.
56 Leigh, P. provision merchant,	21l.

Black-street.
Infirmary-road.
Twenty small houses — Artizan's Dwellings company.

3 N.—Blackhall-parade.
From Blackhall-street to King-street, Nth.
P. St. Paul.—Arran-quay W.

1 Bourke, Mr. James,	9l.
2 Duffy, Mrs. lodgings,	9l.
3 Murphy, Mrs. M.	13l.
4 & 5 Condron, J. horseshoer and farrier,	8l.
6 & 7 Chew T. C. & Co. wool merchants, with 55 and 56 Queen-street, and 27 Island-street	
8 Dardis, Mr. M.	17l.
9 Clarke, Joseph, watch maker,	14l.
10 Tenements,	14l.
11 Duignan, Mrs.	14l.

3 N.—Blackhall-place.
From Ellis's-quay to Stoneybatter.
P. St. Paul.—Arran-quay W.

KING's, OR BLUE COAT HOSPITAL—George R. Armstrong, esq. agent and registrar; Rev. T. P. Richards, M.A. chaplain & head master

1 and 2 Menton, Denis, dairy, and 17 King-street, north,	59l.
3 and 4 Losty, Mr. M. J.	30l. 34l.
5 Young, Mr. William	
6 and 7 Paul and Vincent, farming implement manufs. millwrights, and iron founders, chemical ma-	

30 McKeever, Mr. J.	
34 Dixon, Mrs.	
35 King, Mrs. M.	
36 Kirk, Mr. B.	
37 Muldoon, Mr. T.	
38 Behan, Mr. P.	
39 Donovan, Mr. Henry,	
40 *Dublin Prison Gate Mission Laundry* workroom, and dormitories— J. C. Wilkinson, secretary.	

3 N.—Blackhall-street
From Queen-street to Blackhall pl.
P. St. Paul.—Arran-quay W.

1 Gorman, Mrs.	
2 Hopkins, Mr. Robert,	
........here Blackhall-parade intersects	
3 Gordon, Samuel, wholesale manufacturer,	
4 *The National Hotel*—John W. proprietor,	
5 Baird, Mrs.	
6 Clancy, Mrs. Mary,	
„ Doyle, Mr. T. M.	
„ Montgomery, Mr. James	
7 Dillon, Mr. John,	
8 Lemass, Mr. Joseph,	
9 Nurses' Training Institute Miss Tierney Superintendent	
10 Mooney, Mrs.	
11 and 12 Ruins,	
13 Keogh, Mrs. J.	
14 Vacant,	
15 Tenements,	
........here Blackhall-place intersects	
16 to 18 Fitzgerald, P. corn and stores,	10l.
19 & 20 Hickey & Co. stores office	
21 & 22 *Cairn's Memorial Home*,	
23 Correll, Mr. J.	
24 Doran, Mr. C. J.	
25 Leahy, Mr. W. J.	
26 Doheney, Mr. Joseph	
27 Eivers & Rispin, cattle salesmen	
„ Curtis, T. H. forage contractor	
28 Ralph, Mrs.,	
29 Hickey, Paul,& Co. cattle salesmen, corn, hay, and wool factors	
30 Scott, Mr. John F.	
31 Byrne, Mr. P. J.	
32 Coble, Mrs.	

3 S.—Blackpitts
From New-row, South, to Green *P. St. Nicholas Without, east side* *Luke, west.—Merchants'-quay* *LETTER BOX, opp.*

The earliest country-wide directory covering more than the gentry was Pigot's *Commercial Directory of Ireland* published in 1820. This goes through the towns of Ireland alphabetically, supplying the names of nobility and gentry living in or close to the town, and arranging the traders of each town according to their trade. Pigot published a subsequent edition in 1824, and his successors, Slater's, issued expanded versions in 1846, 1856, 1870, 1881 and 1894; These followed the same basic format, dividing the country into four provinces, and then dealing with towns and villages alphabetically within each province. With each edition the scope of the directory was steadily enlarged, including ever more towns and villages. 'Guide to Irish Directories', Chapter 4 of *Irish Genealogy: A Record Finder* (Dublin: Heraldic Artists, 1981) includes a detailed county-by-county listing of the towns and villages covered by each edition. Otherwise, the most important differences between the various editions are as follows:

1824. This includes a country-wide alphabetical index to all the clergy, gentry and nobility listed in the entries for individual towns, omitted in subsequent issues.

1846. This includes the names of schoolteachers for the towns treated, a practice continued in following editions.

1881. This supplies the names of the principal farmers near each of the towns treated, giving the relevant parish. This feature was continued in the 1894 edition.

From 1824 separate alphabetical listings are given for the clergy, gentry and nobility of Dublin and most of the larger urban centres.

The best single collection of these directories is in the National Library, where most of the early editions have now been transferred to microfiche.

Check-list

1778   George Taylor and Andrew Skinner, *Road Maps of Ireland* (reprint IUP, 1969) NL Ir. 9141 t 1
1786   William Wilson's *The Post-Chaise Companion*, NL J 9141 w 13
1812   Ambrose Leet, *A List of [. . .] noted places*, NL Ir. 9141 l 10
1814   Ambrose Leet, *A Directory to the Market Towns, Villages, Gentlemen's Seats and other noted places in Ireland*, NL Ir. 9141 l 10
1820   J. Pigot, *Commercial Directory of Ireland*, NL Ir. 9141 c 25.
1824   J. Pigot, *City of Dublin and Hibernian Provincial Directory*, NL Ir. 9141 p 75
1846   Slater's *National Commercial Directory of Ireland*, NL Ir. 9141 s 30
1856   Slater's *Royal National Commercial Directory of Ireland*

1870   Slater's *Royal National Commercial Directory of Ireland*
1881   Slater's *Royal National Commercial Directory of Ireland*
1894   Slater's *Royal National Commercial Directory of Ireland*
        See also Dublin directories from 1834

3. PROVINCIAL DIRECTORIES

John Ferrar's *Directory of Limerick*, published in 1769, was the first directory to
deal specifically with a provincial town, and the practice spread throughout
Munster in the remaining decades of the eighteenth century, with Cork
particularly well covered. In the nineteenth century, local directories were
produced in abundance, especially in areas with a strong commercial identity
such as Belfast and the north-east, and, again, Munster. The quality and
coverage of these varies widely, from the street-by-street listings in Martin's
1839 *Belfast Directory* to the barest of commercial lists. A guide to the principal
local directories is included in the county source lists in Chapter 12. These
lists cannot, however, be regarded as complete; many small, local publications,
especially from the first half of the nineteenth century, are now quite rare,
with only one or two surviving copies. Locating these can be extremely
difficult. Some guides are:

James Carty, *National Library of Ireland Bibliography of Irish History 1870–1911*,
        Dublin, 1940.
Edward Evans, *Historical and Bibliographical Account of Almanacks, Directories etc. in
        Ireland from the Sixteenth Century*, Dublin, 1897.
M. E. Keen, *A Bibliography of Trade Directories of the British Isles in the Victoria and
        Albert Museum*, London, 1979.

PART 3

A Reference Guide

11

Occupations

Apothecaries
(a) GO MS. 648, Apothecaries, apprentices, journeymen and prosecutions, 1791–1829
(b) List of Licensed Apothecaries of Ireland 1872, NL Ir. 61501 i 1
(c) Admissions to the guilds of Dublin, 1792–1837, Reports from Committees, *Parliamentary Papers*, 1837, Vol. 11 (ii)
(d) NL Report on Private Collections, No. 208
(e) Records of Apothecaries Hall, Dublin, 1747–1833, NL Pos. 929

Artists
(a) *Artists of Ireland* (1796), Williams, NL Ir. 9275 w 3
(b) *Royal Hibernian Academy Exhibitors, 1826–1875*, NL Ir. 921 r 2
(c) *The Artists of Ireland*, Ann Crookshank and Knight of Glin, NL Ir. 750 c 2

Army/Militia
(a) GO MS. 608. 1761, Militia Lists for Counties Cork, Derry, Donegal, Down, Dublin, Kerry, Limerick, Louth, Monaghan, Roscommon, Tyrone, Wicklow
(b) GO MS. 579, Army Lists 1746–1772 (Athlone, Bandon, Cork, Drogheda, Dublin, Galway, Gort, Thurles, Tullamore)
(c) *Ireland's Memorial Records* (Biographical notes on soldiers in Irish regiments who died in World War I), NL Ir. 355942 i 3; see also GRO death records, 1914–1918 (separate listing)

(d) British Army records: (i) War Office records at the Public Record Office, Kew; Regimental records; Muster Rolls; Casualties; Widows; Soldiers' Documents (pensioners); Registers of Royal Hospital, Kilmainham, and Chelsea Hospital (Royal Hospital records also on microfilm at National Archives)

(e) Births, Marriages and Deaths of army personnel, 1796–1880; General Register Office, St Catherine's House, London

(f) Some published works:

Officers of the district corps of Ireland, 1797, King, NL Ir. 355 a 10

Officers (. . .) upon the establishment of Ireland, NL P 91

General and Field Officers 1740, Mullan, NL 355942 l 4

General and Field Officers 1755, Mullan, NL LO

General and Field Officers 1759, Mullan, NL LO

The Irish Army under King James, Thorpe, NL P 11 and P 12

English Army Lists, Dalton, NL 355942 d 2

Army Lists, Annual, Quarterly

A Bibliography of Regimental Histories of the British Army, A. S. White, NL 355942 w 13

In Search of Army Ancestry, G. Hamilton Edwards, Phillimore, 1977

ATTORNEYS AND BARRISTERS

(a) *King's Inns Admission Papers 1723–1867*, Phair and Sadlier, IMC, 1986, NL Ir. 340 k 1

(b) Dublin Directories, from the late eighteenth century

BAKERS

(a) Admissions to the guilds of Dublin, 1792–1837, Reports from Committees, *Parliamentary Papers*, 1837, Vol. 11 (ii)

(b) Freemen's Rolls of the City of Dublin, 1468–1485 and 1575–1774 in (i) GO 490–93 (Thrift Abstracts), (ii) Dublin City Archives (Original Registers), (iii) NL MSS. 76–9

BARBERS AND SURGEONS

(a) Admissions to the guilds of Dublin, 1792–1837, Reports from Committees, *Parliamentary Papers*, 1837, Vol. 11 (ii)

(b) Freemen's Rolls of the City of Dublin, 1468–1485 and 1575–1774 in (i) GO 490–93 (Thrift Abstracts), and (ii) Dublin City Archives (Original Registers)

BOOKSELLERS

(a) *Dictionary of Printers and Booksellers, 1668–1775*, E. R. McC. Dix, NL 6551 b 1, 6551 b 4

(b) *Notes On Dublin Printers in the Seventeenth Century*, T. P. C. Kirkpatrick, NL Ir. 65510941 k 1

(c) See also under 'Dix' in NL Author Catalogue for various provincial
     centres
(d) *Irish Booksellers and English Authors*, R. C. Cole, Dublin, 1954

BOARD OF ORDNANCE EMPLOYEES
(Mainly concerned with the upkeep of fortifications and harbours, with
some of the principal locations being Buncrana, Enniskillen, Ballincollig,
Cobh, Spike Island), *The Irish Genealogist*, 1985, NL Ir. 9291 i 2

BRICKLAYERS
Records of the Bricklayers and Stonemasons Guild from 1830, NA Acc.
1097

CARPENTERS, MILLERS, MASONS, PLUMBERS
(a) Admissions to the guilds of Dublin, 1792–1837, Reports from Committees,
     Parliamentary Papers, 1837, Vol. 11 (ii)
(b) Freemen's Rolls of the City of Dublin, 1468–1485 and 1575–1774 in (i)
     GO 490–93 (Thrift Abstracts), (ii) Dublin City Archives (Original Registers),
     and (iii) NL MSS. 76–9

CLERGYMEN
(1) Catholic
(a) *Maynooth Students, 1795–1895*, Hamill, NL Ir. 37841 h 15
(b) Priests Lists (by diocese), 1735–1835, NL MS. 1548
(c) List of Priests and Sureties, 1705, NL MS. 5318

(2) Church of Ireland
(a) List of regular clergy in Ireland, by county, with place of birth, order
     and residence, 1824, *Archivium Hibernicum*, Vol. 3, 49–86
(b) Biographical Succession Lists
(i) *By diocese*
     Ardfert and Aghadoe. Canon J. B. Leslie, NL Ir. 274146 l 2
     Armagh. Canon Leslie, NL Ir. 27411 l 4
     Cashel and Emly. John Seymour
     Connor. NL MS. 1773 (Leslie manuscript)
     Cork, Cloyne and Ross. William Meade
     Cork and Ross. W. Maziere Brady, *Records of Cork and Ross*
     Derry. Canon Leslie, NL Ir. 27411 l 7
     Down. Canon Leslie
     Dromore. H. B. Swanzy, NL Ir. 27411 s 2
     Dublin. NL MS. 1771 (Leslie manuscript)
     Clogher. Canon Leslie, NL Ir. 27411 l 3
     Ferns. Canon Leslie, NL Ir. 27413 l 3

Leighlin. NL MS. 1772 (Leslie manuscript)
Ossory. Canon Leslie, NL Ir. 27413 l 5
Raphoe. Canon Leslie, NL Ir. 27413 l 8
Ross. Charles Webster
Waterford and Lismore. William Remison
Fasti Hibernicae (Vols 1–5), Henry Cotton, NL Ir. 2741002 c 5
Fasti of St Patrick's, Dublin, H. J. Lawlor

(ii) Unpublished material on all clergy not covered above in Representative Church Body Library. See also NL MSS. 1775–6 (Leslie manuscript)

(c) NL MS. 2674, Pedigrees and families of Church of Ireland clergymen, from the seventeenth to the nineteenth century

(d) Fothergill, Gerald, *A List of Emigrant Ministers to America, 1690–1811*, London, 1904

(e) Church of Ireland Directories, as follows:
  1814 *Ecclesiastical Registry*, Samuel Percy Lea
  1817 *Irish Ecclesiastical Register*
  1818 *Irish Ecclesiastical Register*
  1824 *Irish Ecclesiastical Register*
  1827 *Irish Ecclesiastical Register*
  1830 *Ecclesiastical Register*, John C. Erck
  1841 *The Churchman's Almanack and Irish Ecclesiastical Register*, John Medlicott Burns
  1842 *Irish Ecclesiastical Directory*
  1843 *The Irish Clergy List*, John Medlicott Burns
  1858 *Clerical Directory of Ireland*, Samuel B. Oldham
  1862 to date, annually, *Church of Ireland Directory*

(3) Methodist

(a) *Minutes of the Methodist Conference*, 1757 to date, NL Ir. 287 m 4

(b) Published works:
Crookshank, C. H., *History of Methodism in Ireland, 1740–1860* (3 vols), Belfast, 1885–8; [Vol. 4 (1860–1960), H. Lee Cole, Belfast, 1961] NL Ir. 287 c 2
Cole, H. L., *History of Methodism in Dublin*, NL I 287 c 4
Gallagher, W., *Preachers of Methodism*, Belfast, 1965, NL Ir. 287 g 1
Smith, W., *History of Methodism in Ireland*, Dublin, 1830, J 2871, NL Ir. 2871 s 2

(4) Presbyterian

(a) Names of Presbyterian Clergymen and their congregations in Counties Antrim, Armagh, Down, Donegal, Fermanagh, Tyrone, Cork, Dublin, King's, Louth, Westmeath and Mayo, 1837, *New Plan for Education in Ireland 1838*, Part 1 (27, 28) 200–205

(b) Published Works:
Ferguson, Rev. S., *Brief Biographical Notices of some Irish Covenanting Ministers* (1897) [particularly eighteenth century], NL Ir. 285 f 1
History of Congregations, NL Ir. 285 h 8
Irwin, C. H., *A History of Presbyterians in Dublin and the South and West of Ireland*, 1890, NL Ir. 285 i 1
Latimer, W. T., *History of the Irish Presbyterians*, Belfast, 1902, NL Ir. 285 l 1 (early ministers especially)
McComb's Presbyterian Almanack, NL Ir. 285 m 1
Marshall W. F., *Ulster Sails West* (including Ulster Presbyterian ministers in America, 1680–1820), NL Ir. 973 m 5
McConnell, J., *Fasti of the Irish Presbyterian Church*, Belfast, 1938, NL Ir. 285 m 14
Reid, James Seiton, *History of the Presbyterian Church*, London, 1853, NL Ir. 285 r 1
Smith and McIntyre, *Belfast Almanack 1837*
Stewart, Rev. David, *The Seceders in Ireland, With Annals of Their Congregations*, Belfast, 1950
Witherow, Thomas, *Historical and Literary Memorials of Presbyterianism in Ireland*, Belfast, 1879
(c) Belfast Directories, *Martins's*, 1835–42, NL Ir. 9141111 [*sic*] m 4; from 1852, NL Ir. 91411 b 3

CLOCKMAKERS
(a) National Museum MS. List of Watch and Clockmakers in Ireland, 1687–1844, NL Pos. 204
(b) 'A List of Irish Watch- and Clockmakers', Geraldine Fennell, NL Ir. 681 f 10

COAST GUARD
See *Navy*

CONVICTS
(a) *Parliamentary Papers* Vol. 22 (1824): Convictions, 1814–23, Limerick City Assizes and Quarter sessions; All persons committed for trial under the Insurrection Act, 1823–24 in Counties Clare, Cork, Kerry, Kildare, Kilkenny, King's, Limerick and Tipperary
(b) Records of the State Paper Office, Prisoners' Petitions, see Chapter 7, 'Emigration'.
(c) Prosecutions at Spring Assizes, 1842–43, *Parliamentary Papers*, 1843, Vol. 50, (619) 34 ff.
(d) Original Prison Registers from *c.*1845 for individual prisons, in many cases giving details of prisoners' families; unindexed, in chronological order. National Archives

COOKS AND VINTNERS
(a) Admissions to the guilds of Dublin, 1792–1837, Reports from Committees, *Parliamentary Papers*, 1837, Vol. 11 (ii)
(b) Freemen's Rolls of the City of Dublin, 1468–1485 and 1575–1774 in (i) GO 490–93 (Thrift Abstracts), (ii) Dublin City Archives (Original Registers), and (iii) NL MSS. 76–9

DOCTORS
(a) Index to Biographical File of Irish Medics, T. P. C. Kirkpatrick, NL Library Office
(b) See under Kirkpatrick in NL Author Catalogue
(c) Local and Dublin Directories from the late eighteenth century
(d) Medical Directories: 1846, Croly, NL Ir. 6107 c 3; 1852–1860 (intermittent), NL Ir. 6107 i 2; from 1872 annually, NL Ir. 6107 i 2
(e) Addison, *Glasow University Graduates*
(f) Doolin, W., *Dublin's Surgeon Anatomists*, NL Ir. 610 p 4

GOLDSMITHS
(a) GO 665, Dublin Goldsmiths, 1675–1810
(b) *Journal of the Cork Hist. and Arch. Soc.* Ser. 2, Vol. VIII, 1902

LINEN WORKERS/WEAVERS
(a) Workers and Manufacturers in Linen, in *The Stephenson Reports*, 1755–84, NL Ir. 6551, Dublin
(b) 1796 Linen Board premiums for growing flax, NL Ir. 633411 i 7
(c) 1796 Spinning-wheel premium entitlement lists (64 per cent Ulster); All-Ireland Heritage microfiche index, National Archives

MEMBERS OF PARLIAMENT
NL MSS. 184 and 2098. See also local history source-lists under the relevant county

MERCHANTS
(a) Admissions to the guilds of Dublin, 1792–1837, Reports from Committees, *Parliamentary Papers*, 1837, Vol. 11 (ii)
(b) Freemen's Rolls of the City of Dublin, 1468–1485 and 1575–1774 in (i) GO 490–93 (Thrift Abstracts), (ii) Dublin City Archives (Original Registers), and (iii) NL MSS. 76–9
(c) See also local directories under county source lists

NAVY
(a) *The Navy List*, 1814, 1819, 1827–79, 1885 *et seq.*, NL 35905 Top floor [*sic*] (Seniority and disposition lists of all commissioned officers, masters,

pursers, surgeons, chaplains, yard officers, coast guards, revenue cruisers, packets)

(b) Records of the Public Record Office, Kew. See *Naval Records for Genealogists*, N. A. M. Rodger, HMSO, 1984

(c) *A Naval Biographical Dictionary (1849)*, W. R. O'Byrne, NL 9235 0 1

POLICEMEN

(a) RIC records, National Archives (Mf)

(b) Dublin Metropolitan Police records, National Archives and Garda Archives, Phoenix Park

(c) Annual RIC Directories from 1840, NL Ir. 3522 r 8

POST OFFICE EMPLOYEES

Pre-1922 records of the Post Office in the Public Record Office of Northern Ireland, Belfast

PRINTERS

(a) *Dictionary of Printers and Booksellers*, 1668–1775, E. R. McC. Dix, 6551 b 1, 6551 b 4

(b) *Notes on Dublin Printers in the Seventeenth Century*, T. P. C. Kirkpatrick, NL Ir. 65510941 k 1

(c) See also under 'Dix' in NL Author Catalogue for various provincial centres

PRISON WARDERS

Index to Registered Papers, State Paper Office (Original applications available)

PUBLICANS

Excise Licences in premises valued under £10, 1832–1838; Reports from Committees, *Parliamentary Papers*, 1837–38, Vol. 13 (2), 558–601 and 602–607

RAILWAY WORKERS

(a) (1870s to 1950s) Irish Transport Genealogical Archives, Irish Railway Record Society, Heuston Station, Dublin (open Tues. 8–10 p.m., by appointment with archivist)

(b) *Records of the Irish Transport Genealogical Museum*, Joseph Lecky

SEAMEN

(a) 'In Pursuit of Seafaring Ancestors', Frank Murphy, *Decies* 16, NL Ir. 9414 d 5

(b) Agreements and Crew Lists series in Public Record Office, Kew

(c) Cox, N. G., 'The Records of the Registrar-General of Shipping and Seamen', *Maritime History*, Vol. 2, 1972

SILVERSMITHS
(a) Assay Office, registrations of goldsmiths and silversmiths from 1637, see
    (b) below
(b) NL Pos. 6851 (1637–1702)
         Pos. 6785 (1704–1855, with some gaps)
         Pos. 6782 Freemen, 1637–1779
         Pos. 6784, 6788, 6851, Apprentices
(c) NA M. 465, Notes and pamphlets relating to goldsmiths and silversmiths
    in Cork, Dublin and Galway

SMITHS
(a) Admissions to the guilds of Dublin, 1792–1837, Reports from Committees,
    Parliamentary Papers, 1837, Vol. 11 (ii)
(b) Freemen's Rolls of the City of Dublin, 1468–1485 and 1575–1774 in (i)
    GO 490–93 (Thrift Abstracts), (ii) Dublin City Archives (Original
    Registers), and (iii) NL MSS. 76–9

STONEMASONS
    See *Bricklayers* above

TEACHERS
(a) List of all parochial schools in Ireland, including names of teachers and
    other details, 1824. Irish Education Enquiry, 1826, 2nd Report. (2 vols),
    NL Ir. 372 i 6. Indexed in 'Schoolmasters and mistresses in Ireland',
    Dingfelder, NL Ir. 372 d 38
(b) National School Records, National Archives (National Teachers' salary
    books from 1831)
(c) Published Works:
    Akenson, D. H., *The Irish Education Experiment*, London, 1970
    Brenan, *1775–1835: Schools of Kildare and Leighlin*, NL Ir. 37094135 b 4
    Corcoran, T. S., 'Some lists of catholic lay teachers and their illegal
    schools in the later Penal times', NL Ir. 370941 c 12
    ffolliott, R., 'Some schoolmasters in the diocese of Killaloe, 1808', *North
    Munster Antiquarian Journal*, Vol. XI, 1968
    Linden, *Irish school-masters in the American colonies*, NL Ir. 942 l 9
    Teachers of Cashel and Emly, 1750–60, *Catholic Bulletin*, Vol. XXIX,
    784–8

WATCHMAKERS
    See *Clockmakers*

WEAVERS
    See *Linen-workers*

12

County Source Lists

The source lists included here are intended primarily as working research tools, with references as specific as possible, and very little explanation of the records given. An outline of some of the categories used is thus necessary here.

CENSUS RETURNS AND SUBSTITUTES

Where no indication of the nature of the record is given, a description should be found in Chapter 2, 'Census Returns'. Griffith's Valuation and the Tithe Books are dealt with in Chapter 4, 'Land Records'. Locations are given in the text for all records mentioned, with, if possible, exact reference numbers. National Library call-numbers for published works should be found in the Local History or Local Journal sections.

LOCAL HISTORY

The bibliographies given are by no means exhaustive, and the works cited vary enormously in their usefulness. A large proportion of the entries also give the National Library call-number, but the absence of such a number does not mean that the work in question is not in the library.

LOCAL JOURNALS

The journals noted are those originating in, or covering part of, the particular county. Where possible, National Library call-numbers are given. The absence of the number means that the journal started publication relatively recently and, at the time of writing, had not yet been assigned a number.

GRAVESTONE INSCRIPTIONS

Many of the largest collections of indexed transcripts of gravestone inscriptions are now held by local heritage centres. For counties where this is the case, the name of the relevant centre is supplied. Further details will be found in Chapter 15, 'Services'. This section does not cover the transcripts published in the *Journal of the Association for the Preservation of the Memorials of the Dead*, since the records are not treated in a geographically consistent way. None the less, over the forty-seven years of its existence between 1888 and 1934, the *Journal* published a huge volume of inscriptions, many of which have since been destroyed. A composite index to surnames and places for the first twenty years of publication was published in 1910; the remaining volumes have their own indexes. The references to the IGRS collection in the Genealogical Office give the number of entries recorded in each graveyard. Again, National Library call-numbers for the local history journals or local histories will be found in the sections dealing specifically with the journals and histories.

ESTATE RECORDS

With the exception of Counties Cork, Galway, Leitrim, Mayo, Roscommon and Sligo, which include a summary of relevant catalogued records in the National Archives and National Library, the references given here cover only a fraction of the material of potential genealogical interest. A more detailed account of the nature of these records is given at the end of Chapter 4, 'Land Records'.

PLACENAMES

The only references given here are to works referring specifically to the relevant counties. Material of more general application for the entire island is as follows:

Townlands Indexes
Produced on the basis of the returns of the 1851, 1871 and 1901 censuses, these list all the townlands in the country in strict alphabetical order.

Addenda to the 1841 Census
Also known as the 1841 Townlands Index, this is also based on the census returns, but organises townlands on a different basis. They are grouped alphabetically within civil parishes, which are then grouped alphabetically within baronies, which are grouped by county. The organisation is very

useful in tracking down variant townland spellings; once it is known that a particular townland is to be found in a particular area, but the later Townlands Indexes do not record it, the general area can be searched in the 1841 Addenda for names which are close enough to be possible variants. (NL Ir. 310 c 1)

TOWNLANDS IN POOR-LAW UNIONS

Produced by the Office of the Registrar-General for use by local registration officers, this lists townlands in each Registration District, or Poor-Law Union (see Chapter 1, 'Civil Records'). It is useful in attempting to identify place-names given in civil records. (NL Ir. 9141 b 35)

TOPOGRAPHICAL DICTIONARY OF IRELAND, SAMUEL LEWIS, 1837

This goes through civil parishes in alphabetical order, giving a brief history, an economic and social description, and the names and residences of the 'principal inhabitants'. It also records the corresponding Catholic parish and the locations of Presbyterian congregations. The accompanying *Atlas* is useful in determining the precise relative positions of the parishes.

Other works of general interest include Yann Goblet's *Index to Townlands in the Civil Survey (1654–56)* (Irish Manuscripts Commission, 1954); *Locations of Churches in the Irish Provinces* (Church of Jesus Christ of Latter-day Saints, 1978), NL Ir. 7265 i 8; *The Parliamentary Gazetteer of Ireland* (1846), NL Ir. 9141 p 30.

CO. ANTRIM

Census returns and substitutes

1630	Muster Roll of Ulster. Armagh Co. Library, NL Pos. 206; PRONI D.1759/3C/1
1642	Muster Roll, PRONI T.8726/2
1659	Pender's 'Census', NL I 6551, Dublin
1666	Hearth Money Roll, NL Pos. 207
1666	Subsidy Roll, PRONI T.3022/4/1
1669	Hearth Money Roll, PRONI T.307 and NL MS. 9584
1740	Protestant Householders in the parishes of: Aghoghill, Armoy, Ballintoy, Ballymena, Ballymoney, Bellewillen, Billy, Clogh, Drumaul, Dunkegan, Dunluce, Finvoy, Kilraghtis, Loghall, Manybrooks, Rasharkin, Rathlin, Ramoan, GO 559, PRONI T.808/15258
1766	Aghoghill parish. RCB Library, NL MS. 4173, NA M.2476(1); Ballintoy parish. GO 536, NL MS. 4173; also PRONI T.808/15264
1776	'Deputy Court Cheque Book' (votes cast), PRONI D.1364/L/1
1779	Map of Glenarm, including tenants' names, *The Glynns*, No. 9, 1981
1796	Catholic migrants from Ulster to Mayo. See Mayo
1799–1800	Militia Pay Lists and Muster Rolls, PRONI T.1115/1A and B
1821	Government census, various fragments. Thrift Abstracts, NA
1820s/30s	Tithe Books
1832–37	Belfast Poll Book, PRONI D.2472
1833–39	Emigrants from Co. Antrim. Brian Mitchell, *Irish Emigration Lists 1833–39*, Baltimore, 1989
1837	Valuation of towns returning MPs (occupants and property values). Lisburn. *Parliamentary Papers*, 1837, Reports from Committees, Vol. II (i), Appendix G
1837	Marksmen (illiterate voters) in parliamentary boroughs: Belfast. *Parliamentary Papers*, 1837, Reports from Committees, Vol. II (i), Appendix A
1851	Aghoghill (Craigs townland only), Aghagallon (townlands of Montiaghs to Tiscallon), Agahalee, Ballinderry, Ballymoney (Garryduff townland only), Barnacastle, Drumkeeran, Dunaghy, Grange of Killyglen, Killead (Ardmore to Carnagliss townlands only), Kilwaughter, Larne, Rasharkin (Killydonnelly to Tehorney townland only), Tickmacreevan, NA and PRONI MIC. 5A/11–26
1855	Belfast Register of Electors, PRONI BELF5/1/1/1–2

1856/7	Voters' Lists. NL ILB 324
1861/2	Griffith's Valuation, Belfast—Alphabetical index to householders (All-Ireland Heritage)
1871	Creggan Upper, *Archivium Hibernicum*, Vol. 3
1876	Belfast Register of Electors, PRONI BELF5/1/1/1–2
1901	Census
1911	Census

Local history

Antrim Co. Library: subject catalogue of books and other material relating to Co. Antrim (1969), NL Ir. 941 p 43

Atkinson, E. D., *Dromore, an Ulster Diocese*, Dundalk, 1925

Ballymena: *Old Ballymena: a history of Ballymena during the 1798 Rebellion*, The Ballymena Observer, 1857, repub. 1938

Barr, W. N., *The oldest register of Derryaghy, Co. Antrim 1696–1772*, NL Ir. 9293 b 3

Bassett, G. H., *The Book of Antrim*, 1888

Benn, George, *A History of the Town of Belfast*, London, 1877–80

Bennett, T. J. G., *North Antrim Families*, Scotland, 1974

Boyd, H. A., *A History of the Church of Ireland in Ramoan Parish*, 1930

Carmody, Rev. W. P., *Lisburn Cathedral and its Past Rectors*, 1926

St John Clarke, H. J., *Thirty centuries in south-east Antrim: the Parish of Coole or Carnmoney*, Belfast, 1938, NL Ir. 27411 c 3

Ewart, L. M., *Handbook to the dioceses of Down, Connor and Dromore*.

'Notes on the ancient deeds of Carrickfergus', *R. Soc. Antiq.*, NL Ir. J. 1893

Hill, George, *The MacDonnells of Antrim*, Belfast, 1877

Joy, Henry, *Historical Collections relative to the town of Belfast*, Belfast, 1817

Lee, Rev. W. H. A., *St Colmanell, Aghoghill: A History of its Parish*, 1865

McSkimin, Samuel, *The History and Antiquities of the Town of Carrickfergus 1318–1839*, Belfast, 1909

Marshall, Rev. H. C., *The Parish of Lambeg*, 1933

Millin, S. S., *Sidelights on Belfast History*, 1932

O'Laverty, Rev. James, *An Historical Account of the Dioceses of Down and Connor*, 4 vols, Dublin, 1878–89

Owen, D. J., *History of Belfast*, Belfast, 1921, NL Ir. 94111 o 1

'Presbyterians in Glenarm', *The Glynns*, Vol. 9, 1981

Reeves, William, *Ecclesiastical Antiquities of Down, Connor and Dromore*, 1847

Robinson, Philip, *Irish Historic Towns Atlas: Carrickfergus*, Dublin, Royal Irish Academy, 1988

Shaw, William, *Cullybackey, the Story of an Ulster Village*, 1913

Shearman, H., *Ulster*, London, 1949 (incl. bibliographies), NL Ir. 91422 s 3

Young, Robert M., *Historical Notices of Old Belfast and its Vicinity*, 1896

Young, Robert M., *The Town Book of the Corporation of Belfast, 1613–1816*, 1892

Local journals

The Glynns: Journal of the Glens of Antrim Historical Society, NL Ir. 94111 9 2
Down and Connor Historical Society Magazine, NL Ir. 94115 [*sic*]
Lisburn Historical Society Journal, NL Ir. 94111 l 3
East Belfast Historical Society Journal, NL Ir. 94115 e 3

Directories

1819	Thomas Bradshaw, *General Directory of Newry, Armagh, Dungannon, Portadown, Tandragee, Lurgan, Waringstown, Banbridge, Warrenpoint, Rostrevor, Kilkeel and Rathfryland*
1820	J. Pigot, *Commercial Directory of Ireland* (Antrim, Belfast, Lisburn)
1820	Joseph Smyth, *Directory of Belfast and its Vicinity*
1820	*Belfast Almanack*
1824	Pigot and Co., *City of Dublin and Hibernian Provincial Directory*, NL Ir. 9141 p 75
1835	William Matier, *Belfast Directory*
1839	Matthew Martin, *Belfast Directory*, issued also 1841 and 1842
1846	Slater's *National Commercial Directory of Ireland*
1850	James A. Henderson, *Belfast Directory*
1852	James A. Henderson, *Belfast and Province of Ulster Directory*, issued also in 1854, 1856, 1858, 1861, 1863, 1865, 1868, 1870, 1877, 1880, 1884, 1887, 1890, 1894, 1900
1856	Slater's *Royal National Commercial Directory of Ireland*
1860	Hugh Adair, *Belfast Directory*
1865	R. Wynne, *Business Directory of Belfast*
1870	Slater's *Directory of Ireland*
1881	Slater's *Royal National Commercial Directory of Ireland*
1887	*Derry Almanac* (Portrush only)
1888	G. H. Bassett, *The Book of Antrim*
1894	Slater's *Royal Commercial Directory of Ireland*

Gravestone inscriptions

Ardclinis: *The Glynns*, Vol. IV, 1976
Ballycarley N.S. Presbyterian: *Gravestone Inscriptions, Co. Antrim*, Vol. 2
Ballygarvan R.C.: *Gravestone Inscriptions, Co. Antrim*, Vol. 2
Ballykeel: *Gravestone Inscriptions Co. Down*, Vol. I, George Rutherford, 1977
Ballyvallagh: *Gravestone Inscriptions Co. Antrim*, Vol. 2
Bunamargy: IGRS Collection, GO
Culfeightrin: *The Irish Ancestor*, Vol. II, No. 2, 1970
Glynn: *Gravestone Inscriptions Co. Down*, Vol. II, George Rutherford

Islandmagee: *Gravestone Inscriptions Co. Down*, Vol. II, George Rutherford
Killycrappin: *The Glynns*, Vol. V, 1977
Kilmore: *The Glynns*, Vol. IV, 1976
Kilroot: *Gravestone Inscriptions Co. Down*, Vol. II, George Rutherford
Lambeg: *Inscriptions on Tombstones in Lambeg Churchyard*, William Cassidy
Lisburn Cathedral: *Lisburn Cathedral and its Past Rectors*, W. P. Carmody, 1926
Magheragall: *Family Links*, Vol. 1, Nos 2 and 3, 1981
Raloo C. of I., Pres., N.S. Pres.: *Gravestone Inscriptions Co. Antrim*, Vol. 2
Templecorran: *Gravestone Inscriptions Co. Down*, Vol. II, George Rutherford

Estate records

Hereford estate, nineteenth century, *Lisburn Historical Society Journal*, No. 1, 1978.

Placenames

Townland maps, Londonderry Inner City Trust
Placenames of Co. Antrim: Tickmacreevan, *The Glynns*, Vol. 10, 1982; Ardclinis, *The Glynns*, Vol. 11, 1983; Parish of Skerry, *The Glynns*, Vol. 12, 1984; Parish of Lough Guile, *The Glynns*, Vol. 13, 1985; Armoy, *The Glynns*, Vol. 14, 1986; Carncastle and Killyglen, *The Glynns*, Vol. 15, 1987

CO. ARMAGH

Census returns and substitutes

1630	Muster Roll of Ulster, Armagh Co. Library, NL Pos. 206
1634	Subsidy roll, NA M.2471, 2475
1654–56	Civil Survey, NL Ir. 31041 c 4
1659	Pender's 'Census', NL I 6551 Dublin
1661	Books of Survey and Distribution, PRONI T.370/A and D.1854/1/8
1664	Hearth Money Roll, *Archivium Hibernicum*, 1936, also NL MS. 9856 (typed and indexed) and PRONI T.604
1689	Protestants attainted by James II, PRONI T.808/14985
1737	Tithe-payers, Drumcree, NL I 920041 p 1
1738	Freeholders, Armagh Co. Library, NL Pos. 206

1740	Protestant householders: Creggan, Mullaghbrack, Loughgall, Derrynoose, Shankill, Lurgan, Tynan parishes. NA 1A 46 100; GO 539; PRONI T.808/15258
c.1750	Volunteers and yeomanry of Markethill and district. See 'Cornascreeb' in NL Author catalogue
1753	Poll Book. GO MS. 443; NA M.4878; PRONI T.808/14936
1766	Creggan parish. GO 537; NA Parl. Ret. 657, PRONI
1770	Armagh City householders, NL MS. 7370 and PRONI T.808/14977
1793–1908	Armagh Militia Records, Armagh Co. Library, NL Pos. 1014
1796	Catholic migrants from Ulster to Mayo. See Mayo. Also 'Petition of Armagh migrants in the Westport area', *Cathair na Mart*, Vol. 2, No. 1 (Appendix)
1796	Spinning-Wheel Premium Lists. Microfiche index in National Archives, comprising, in the case of Co. Armagh, over 4,000 names
1799–1800	Militia Pay Lists and Muster Rolls, PRONI T.1115/2A–C
1813–20	Armagh Freeholders, NL Ir. 94116 a 1, Ir. 352 p 2; PRONI ARM 5/2/1–17
1820s/30s	Tithe Books
1821–31	Freeholders, PRONI T.862
1821	Government census, Kilmore parish, PRONI T.450. Various fragments. Thrift Abstracts, NA
1830–65	Methodist Records, Newry circuit, *Seanchas Ardmhacha*, 1977, Vol. 7, No. 2
1834–37	Valuation of Armagh town (heads of households), *Parliamentary Papers, 1837*, Reports from Committees, Vol. II (1), Appendix G
1837	Marksmen (i.e. illiterate voters), Armagh Borough, *Parliamentary Papers*, 1837, Reports from Committees, Vol. II (1), Appendix A
1839	Valuation of Co. Armagh, Armagh Co. Library, NL Pos. 99
1839	Freeholders, PRONI T.808/14961
1851	Freeholders, PRONI T.808/14927
1851	Government census. Various fragments, Thrift Abstracts, NA
1864	Griffith's Valuation
1864(?)	Tynan parish. See Marshall, NL I 94116
1901	Census
1911	Census

Local history

Armagh Road Presbyterian Church, Portadown (1868–1968), NL Ir. 2741 p 25
Armagh Royal School: Prizes and prizemen, 1854, NL P 439
'Balleer School: Copy-book of letters, 1827–29', NL Ir. 300 p 106

Donaldson, John, *A Historical and Statistical Account of the Barony of Upper Fews*
Ewart, L. M., *Handbook to the dioceses of Down, Connor and Dromore*
Galogly, John, *The History of St Patrick's Parish, Armagh*, 1880
Gwynn, A., *The medieval province of Armagh*, Dundalk, 1946, NL Ir. 27411 g 1
Historical sketches of various parishes, NL Ir. 27411 l 4 and 5
Hogg, Rev. M. B., *Keady Parish: A Short History of its Church and People*, 1928
Hughes, Thomas, *The History of Tynan Parish*, 1910
Marshall, J. J., *The History of Charlemont Fort and Borough . . .*, 1921
Mullaghbrack from the tithe-payers list of 1834, NL I 920041 p 1
Nelsen, S., *History of the Parish of Creggan in Counties Armagh and Louth from 1611 to 1840*, 1974, NL Ir. 941 p 43
Patterson, T., 'The Armagh Manor Court Rolls, 1625–27 and incidental notes on 17th century sources for Irish surnames in Co. Armagh', *Seanchas Ardmhacha*, 1957, 295–322
Shearman, H., *Ulster*, London, 1949 (incl. bibliographies), NL Ir. 91422 s 3
Stewart, James, *Historical Memoirs of the City of Armagh*, ed. Ambrose Coleman, Dublin, 1900
Swayne, John, *The register of John Swayne, Archbishop of Armagh, and Primate of Ireland, 1418–39*

Local journals

Craigavon Historical Society Review (from 1973)
Mullaghbawn Historical and Folk-Lore Society, NL Ir. 800 p 50
Seanchas Ardmhacha (Journal of the Armagh Diocesan Historical Society), NL Ir. 27411 s 4
Seanchas Dhroim Mor (Journal of the Dromore Diocesan Historical Society), NL Ir. 94115 s 3

Directories

1819   Thomas Bradshaw, *General Directory of Newry, Armagh, Dungannon, Portadown, Tandragee, Lurgan, Waringstown, Banbridge, Warrenpoint, Rostrevor, Kilkeel and Rathfryland*
1820   J. Pigot, *Commercial Directory of Ireland* (Antrim, Belfast, Lisburn)
1824   Pigot and Co., *City of Dublin and Hibernian Provincial Directory*, NL Ir. 9141 p 75
1841   Mathew Martin, *Belfast Directory*, issued also in 1842
1846   Slater's *National Commercial Directory of Ireland*
1852   James A. Henderson, *Belfast and Province of Ulster Directory*, issued also in 1854, 1856, 1858, 1861, 1863, 1865, 1868, 1870, 1877, 1880, 1884, 1887, 1890, 1894, 1900
1856   Slater's *Royal National Commercial Directory of Ireland*

1865   R. Wynne, *Business Directory of Belfast*
1870   Slater's *Directory of Ireland*
1881   Slater's R*oyal National Commercial Directory of Ireland*
1883   S. Farrell, *County Armagh Directory and Almanac*
1888   G. H. Bassett, *The Book of Armagh*
1894   Slater's *Royal Commercial Directory of Ireland*

Gravestone inscriptions

Creggan: *Seanchas Ardmhacha*, Vol. VI, 1976
Sandy Hill, Armagh City: *Seanchas Ardmhacha*, 1985
    Irish World (26 Market Square, Dungannon, Co. Tyrone, BT70 1AB)
have transcribed and computerised the inscriptions of more than 300 graveyards in the six counties of Northern Ireland, principally in the four western
counties of Armagh, Derry, Fermanagh and Tyrone.

Estate records

Brownlow estate rentals, Co. Armagh, 1636, 1659, 1667–77, Armagh Co.
    Library, NL Pos. 207.
Richard Johnstone: rentals, Counties Armagh, Down and Monaghan,
    1731, Armagh Co. Library, NL Pos. 1014.

Placenames

Townland maps, Londonderry Inner City Trust

CO. CARLOW

Census returns and substitutes

1641   Book of Survey and Distribution, NL MS. 971
1659   Pender's 'Census', I 6551, Dublin
1767   'Co. Carlow Freeholders', *The Irish Genealogist*, 1980
1798   Persons who Suffered Losses in the 1798 Rebellion, NL I 94107
1820s/30s Tithe Books
1832–37   Voters registered in Carlow Borough, NL, *Parliamentary Papers*,
            1837, Reports from Committees, Vol. II (2), 193–96

1837   Marksmen (illiterate voters) in parliamentary boroughs: Carlow,
             NL, *Parliamentary Papers*, 1837, Reports from Committees, Vol. II
             (i), Appendix A
1852/3   Griffith's Valuation, microfiche index (All-Ireland Heritage)
1901   Census
1911   Census

Local history

Brennan, M., *Schools of Kildare and Leighlin, 1775–1835*
Brophy, M., *Carlow Past and Present*, NL Ir. 94138 b 1
Carlow Parliamentary Roll, 1872 NL Ir. 94138 m 1
Coleman, James, 'Bibliography of the counties Carlow, Kilkenny and
    Wicklow', *Waterford and S–E of Ire. Arch. Soc. Jnl*, 11, 1907–8, 126–33, NL
    Ir. 794105 w 1
Coyle, James, *The Antiquities of Leighlin*
Hore, H. J., *The Social State of the Southern and Eastern Counties of Ireland in the
    Sixteenth Century*, 1870
O'Toole (ed.), *The Parish of Ballon, Co. Carlow*, 1933, NL Ir. 94138 o 3
Ryan, J., *The history and antiquities of the County Carlow*, Dublin, 1833, NL Ir.
    94138 r 1

Local journals

Carloviana, NL Ir. 94138 c 2
The Carlovian (1958), NL Ir. 92 p 88
Carlow Past and Present

Directories

1788   Richard Lucas, *General Directory of the Kingdom of Ireland*, NL Pos. 3729
1820   J. Pigot, *Commercial Directory of Ireland*
1824   Pigot and Co., *City of Dublin and Hibernian Provincial Directory*, NL Ir.
             9141 p 75
1839   T. Shearman, *New Commercial Directory for the Cities of Waterford and
             Kilkenny, Towns of Clonmel, Carrick-on-Suir, New Ross and Carlow*
1846   Slater's *National Commercial Directory of Ireland*
1856   Slater's *Royal National Commercial Directory of Ireland*
1870   Slater's *Directory of Ireland*
1881   Slater's *Royal National Commercial Directory of Ireland*
1894   Slater's *Royal Commercial Directory of Ireland*

Gravestone inscriptions

Ballycopagan New Cemetery: *Co. Carlow Tombstone Inscriptions*, Vol. 2, Ir. 9295
   c 3
Ballymurphy: *Co. Carlow Tombstone Inscriptions*, Vol. 3, Ir. 9295 c 3
Borris: *Co. Carlow Tombstone Inscriptions*, Vol. 2, Ir. 9295 c 3
Cloonegoose: *Co. Carlow Tombstone Inscriptions*, Vol. 2, Ir. 9295 c 3
Dunleckny: Andrew Morris (microfiche)
Kilcullen: *Co. Carlow Tombstone Inscriptions*, Vol. 3, Ir. 9295 c 3
Killedmond: *Co. Carlow Tombstone Inscriptions*, Vol. 3, Ir. 9295 c 3
Kiltennel: *Co. Carlow Tombstone Inscriptions*, Vol. 2
Linkardstown: IGRS Collection, GO
Rathanna: *Co. Carlow Tombstone Inscriptions*, Vol. 3, Ir. 9295 c 3
St Michael's: *Co. Carlow Tombstone Inscriptions*, Vol. 1, Ir. 9295 c 3
St Mullin's: *Co. Carlow Tombstone Inscriptions*, Vol. 1, Ir. 9295 c 3

Placenames

O'Toole, Edward, *The Place-names of Co. Carlow*, Ir. 94138 o 3

CO. CAVAN

Census returns and substitutes

1612–13	'Survey of Undertakers Planted in Co. Cavan', *Historical Manuscripts Commission Report*, 4, (Hastings MSS.) 1947, 159–82
1630	Muster Roll, *Breifny*, 1977/8, also NL Pos. 206
1664	Hearth Money Roll, parishes of Killeshandra, Kildallan, Killenagh, Templeport, Tomregan, PRONI
1703–4	Tenants of Robert Craigies, Co. Cavan (parishes of Kildallon and Killeshandra), *The Irish Ancestor*, 1978
1761	Poll Book, PRONI
1766	Protestants in parishes of Kinawley, Lavey, Lurgan, Munterconnaught, RCB Library, GO MS. 536/7, NA m 2476 (e)
1796	Catholic migrants from Ulster to Mayo. See Mayo
1802	Protestants in Enniskeen parish, *The Irish Ancestor*, 1973
1813–21	Freeholders, Co. Cavan, NL Ir. 94119 c 2
1814	Youthful Protestants in the parishes of Drung and Larah, *The Irish Ancestor*, 1978

1821	Parishes of Annageliffe, Ballymacue, Castlerahan, Castleterra, Crosserlough, Denn, Drumlumman, Drung, Kilbride, Kilmore, Kinawley, Larah, Lavey, Lurgan, Mullagh, Munterconnaught, National Archives
1833	Arms registered with the Clerk of the Peace, April, ILB 04 p 12 (over 1,500 names)
1820s/30s	Tithe Books
1841	Killeshandra parish (part). Also, some certified copies of census returns for use in claims for old age pensions. National Archives
c.1850	'List of inhabitants of Castlerahan barony', with Killinkere parish registers, NL Pos. 5349
1851	Certified copies of census returns for use in claims for old age pensions. National Archives
1856/7	Griffith's Valuation
1901	Census
1911	Census

Local history

Cavan County Library, *Guide to Local Studies Dept.*, NL Ir. 0179 p 6
Cavan Freeholders since 1813, NL Ir. 94119 c 2
Cullen, S., 'Sources for Cavan Local History', in *Breifny*, 1977–78
Cullen, S., *Sources for Cavan Local History*, 1965, NL Ir. 941 p 66
Cunningham, T. P., *The Ecclesiastical History of Larah Parish*, 1984, NL Ir. 27412 c 2
Healy, John, *History of the Diocese of Meath*, 2 vols, Dublin, 1908
MacNamee, James J., *History of the Diocese of Ardagh*, Dublin, 1954
McNiffe, L., 'A Short History of the Barony of Rosclogher, 1840–60', *Breifny*, 1983–84
Monahan, Rev. J., *Records Relating to the Diocese of Armagh and Clonmacnoise*, 1886
O'Connell, Philip, *The Diocese of Kilmore: its History and Antiquities*, Dublin, 1937
Shearman, H., *Ulster*, London, 1949 (incl. bibliographies), NL Ir. 91422 s 3
Smyth, T. S., *A civic history of the town of Cavan*, Cavan, 1934, Ir. 94119 s 1
'Sources of Information on the Antiquities and history of Cavan and Leitrim: Suggestions', *Breifny*, 1920–22

Local journals

Breifne, NL Ir. 94119 b 2
Breifny Antiquarian Society Journal (1920–33), NL Ir. 794106 b 1
Ardagh and Clonmacnoise Historical Society Journal (1926–51), NL Ir. 794105
The Drumlin, a Journal of Cavan, Leitrim and Monaghan, NL Ir. 05 d 345
Heart of Breifny, NL Ir. 94119 h 1

Directories

1820   J. Pigot, *Commercial Directory of Ireland*
1824   Pigot and Co., *City of Dublin and Hibernian Provincial Directory*, NL Ir. 9141 P 75
1852   James A. Henderson, *Belfast and Province of Ulster Directory*, issued also in 1854, 1856, 1858, 1861, 1863, 1865, 1868, 1870, 1877, 1880, 1884, 1887, 1890, 1894, 1900
1856   Slater's *Royal National Commercial Directory of Ireland*
1870   Slater's *Directory of Ireland*
1881   Slater's *Royal National Commercial Directory of Ireland*
1894   Slater's *Royal Commercial Directory of Ireland*

Gravestone inscriptions

Ballanagh (C. of I.): GO MS. 622, 107
Billis: GO MS. 622, 182
Callowhill: *Breifne*, 1982/3
Castlerahan: *Breifne*, 1925/6
Cavan: *Breifne*, 1986
Cloone (St Michael's): *Seanchas Ardmhacha*, Vol. 10, No. 1, 1980/81, 63–84
Crosserlough: *Breifne*, 1976 and IGRS Collection, GO
Denn: *Breifne*, 1924
Darver: *Breifne*, 1922
Drumlane: *Breifne*, 1979
Kildrumfertan: *Breifne*, 1965
Lavey: GO MS. 622, 181
Lurgan: *Breifne*, 1961
Magherintemple: *Breifne*, 1963
Munterconnaught: *Breifne*, 1927/8
Templeport: *Breifne*, 1971

Estate records

1771 survey of the estates of Alexander Sanderson, NL.
Settings of Lord Headford's Cavan estates, 1831 (including a list of tenants' names by townland), NL MS. 25394.

Placenames

Parishes, baronies and denominations in each parish, alphabetical, NL JP 2168
Townland maps, Londonderry Inner City Trust

CO. CLARE

Census returns and substitutes

1641	Book of Survey and Distribution, Irish Manuscripts Commission, 1947. Also NL MS. 963
1659	Pender's 'Census', NL I 6551, Dublin
1745	Voters, TCD MS. 2059
1821	Ennis (part), see pre-1901 census catalogue, National Archives
1820s/30s	Tithe Books
1829	Freeholders, NL P.5556
1837	Marksmen (illiterate voters) in parliamentary boroughs: Ennis. NL, *Parliamentary Papers*, 1837, Reports from Committees, Vol. II (i), Appendix A
1850	Deaths in Kilrush and Ennistymon workhouses, hospitals, infirmaries, 25/3/1850–25/3/1851. NL, Accounts and Papers, *Parliamentary Papers*, 1851, Vol. 49, (484) 1–47
1855	Griffith's Valuation
1866	Kilfenora, NL Pos. 2440
1901	Census
1911	Census

Local history

Clancy, J., *Short History of the Parish of Killanena or Upper Feakle*, NL Ir. 941 p 27

Clancy, J., 'Gleanings in 17th century Kilrush', *North Munster Antiq. Jnl*, No. 3, 1942–43

Coleman, J., 'Limerick and Clare Bibliography', *Limerick Field Club Jnl*, No. 3, 1907

Dwyer, Philip, *The Diocese of Killaloe, from the Reformation to the Close of the Eighteenth Century*, Dublin, 1878

Enright, F., 'Pre-famine Reform and Emigration on the Wyndham Estate in Clare', *The Other Clare*, 1984

Fahey, J., *The History and Antiquities of the Diocese of Kilmacduagh*, Dublin, 1893

Frost, James, *The history and topography of Co. Clare from the earliest times to the beginning of the eighteenth century*, Dublin, 1893, NL Ir. 94143 f 3

Hayes-McCoy, G. A., *Index to 'The Compossicion Booke of Connoght, 1585'*, Irish Manuscripts Commission, Dublin, 1945

O'Mahoney, C., 'Emigration from Kilrush Workhouse, 1848–1859', *The Other Clare*, 1983

Westropp Manuscripts, Royal Irish Academy, Will abstracts mainly from Counties Clare and Limerick

White, Rev. P., *History of Clare and the Dalcassian Clans of Tipperary, Limerick and Galway*, Dublin, 1893

Local journals

The Other Clare (Journal of the Shannon Archaeological and Historical Society). NL Ir.
9141 p 71
North Munster Antiquarian Society Journal. NL Ir. 794105 n 1 (Index 1897–1919,
NL Ir. 7941 n 1)
Dál gCais. NL Ir. 94143 d 5

Directories

1788   Richard Lucas, *General Directory of the Kingdom of Ireland*, NL Pos. 3729
1820   J. Pigot, *Commercial Directory of Ireland*
1824   Pigot and Co., *City of Dublin and Hibernian Provincial Directory*, NL Ir.
       9141 p 75
1842   *A Directory of Kilkee*, NL Ir. 61312 h 1
1846   Slater's *National Commercial Directory of Ireland*
1856   Slater's *Royal National Commercial Directory of Ireland*
1866   George H. Bassett, *Directory of the City and County of Limerick and of the
       principal Towns in Counties Tipperary and Clare*, NL Ir. 914144 b 5
1870   Slater's *Directory of Ireland*
1881   Slater's *Royal National Commercial Directory of Ireland*
1886   Francis Guy, *Postal Directory of Munster*, NL Ir. 91414 g 8
1893   Francis Guy, *Postal Directory of Munster*
1894   Slater's *Royal Commercial Directory of Ireland*

Gravestone inscriptions

Ballyalla (Ennis): GO MS. 622, 79/80
Ballyvaughan: IGRS Collection, 5, GO
Cloony South: IGRS Collection, 12, GO
Coad: IGRS Collection, 32, GO
Corofin, St Catherine's: IGRS Collection, 24, GO
Kilcorcoran: IGRS Collection, 41, GO
Kildeema: IGRS Collection, 30, GO
Kilfarboy: IGRS Collection, 56, GO
Kilfenora (ex. Cathedral): IGRS Collection, 48, GO
Killaloe Cathedral: *Year Book of St Flannan's Cathedral*
Killaspuglonane: IGRS Collection, 12, GO
Killenagh: IGRS Collection, 7, GO
Killernan: IGRS Collection, 95, GO
Killinaboy: IGRS Collection, 28, GO
Kilmacrehy: IGRS Collection, 50, GO

Kilmurry Ibrickane: IGRS Collection, 28, GO
Kilrush (C. of I.): IGRS Collection, 27, GO
Kilshanny: IGRS Collection, 30, GO
Kiltenantlea (Dooass): IGRS Collection, 19, GO
Kilvoidane: IGRS Collection, 15, GO
Memorials of the Dead in West Clare (Cantwell), *The Other Clare*, 1983
Milltown Malbay (C. of I.): IGRS Collection, 18, GO
Noughaval: IGRS Collection, 22, GO
Rath: IGRS Collection, 17, GO

Estate records

Note on the Leconfield estate papers at the National Archives, Accession No.
   1074 (Vandeleur leases, Kilrush, 1816–1929, Lord Leconfield rentals,
   1846–1917, including comments on age, health, poverty, etc.), *North
   Munster Antiquarian Journal*, Vol. XXIII, 1981.
Roxton estate rentals, Inchiquin barony, Co. Clare, 1834, NA MS. 5764.
O'Callaghan-Westropp estate rentals, barony of Tulla Upper, NL MS. 867.
19th Century, Inchiquin Papers, NL MSS. 14, 355 ff. (Dromoland especially).

Placenames

Frost, J., 'Townland Names of Co. Clare', *Limerick Field Journal*, Vols 1 and 2,
   1897–1904, NL Ir. 794105 l 1
Townland maps, Londonderry Inner City Trust

CO. CORK

Census returns and substitutes

1641	Survey of Houses in Cork City, listing tenants and possessors, National Archives, Quit Rent Office Papers
1641	Book of Survey and Distribution (proprietors in 1641, grantees in 1666–68), NL MS. 966–7
1654	*Civil Survey*, Vol. VI, Parishes of Aghabulloge, Aghina, Aglish, Ballinaboy, Ballyvourney, Carnaway, Carrigrohanbeg, Clondrohid, Currykippane, Desertmore, Donoughmore, Drishane,

Garrycloyne, Granagh, Inchigeelagh, Inniscarra, Kilbonane, Kilcolman, Kilcorney, Kilmihil, Kilmurry, Kilnamartyra, Knockavilly, Mocloneigh, Macroom, Matehy, Moviddy, Templemichael, Whitechurch

1662–7 Subsidy rolls, Condons and Clangibbons baronies (extracts), NA M.4968. Also NA M.2636 (Grove-White Abstracts)

1700–1752 Freemen, Cork City. National Archives, M.4693

1753 Also later years. Householders St Nicholas parish, Cork City, C. of I. registers

1756–1827 Biographical notices from Cork and Kerry newspapers, arranged alphabetically, NL MSS. 19,172–5

1757 Able-bodied male Protestants, parishes of Brigown, Castletown Roche, Clonmeen, Farrihy, Glanworth, Kilshannig, Marshallstown, Roskeen, *An Anglo-Irish Miscellany*, M. D. Jephson, 1964

1766 Parishes of Aghabullog, Aghada, Ardagh and Clonpriest, Ballyhea, Carrigdownane, Castlelyons, Castlemartyr, Castletown Roche, Churchtown, Clenor, Clondrohid, Clondullane, Clonfert, Clonmee, Clonmult and Kilmahon, Cloyne and Ballintemple, Coole, Farrihy, Garrycloyne, Glanworth, Ightermurragh, Imphrick, Inniscarra and Matehy, Kildorrery, Killogrohanebeg, Kilnamartyra, Kilshannig, Kilworth and Macroney, Knockmourne and Ballynoe, Lisgoold and Ballykeary, Litter, Macroom, Magourney and Kilcolman, Mallow, Marshalstown, Middleton, Mourne Abbey, Nathlash and Carrigdownane, Ruskeen and Kilcummy, Templemolaga, Shandrum, Whitechurch and Grenagh, Youghal, NA 1A 41 67; Rathbarry, Ringrone, NA 1A 46 49; Dunbulloge, JCHAS Vol. 51; Kilmichael, JCHAS Vol. 26

1783 Freemen and freeholders, Cork City, NL P 2054

1793 Householders in the parish of St Anne's, Shandon, 1793, and of additional houses built up to 1853, JCHAS, Vol. 47, 87–111

1814 Jurors, Co. Cork, Grove-White Abstracts, NA M2637

1817 Freemen, Cork City, NL P722

1820s/30s Tithe Books

1830 Houseowners, St Mary's Shandon. JCHAS Vol. 49

1830–37 Registered householders, Cork City (alphabetical). NL, Reports from Committees, *Parliamentary Papers*, 1837/8, Vol. 13 (2), 554–7

1832–37 Voters, Cork City, NL, Reports from Committees, *Parliamentary Papers*, 1837/8, Vol. 13 (1), 320/1

1834–37 Valuation of Bandonbridge, Kinsale, Youghal towns, Houses valued over £5 (householders), NL, *Parliamentary Papers*, 1837, Reports from Committees, Vol. II (1), Appendix G

1834 Protestant parishioners in the Ballymodan part of Bandon, NL MS. 675

1834	Protestant families in Magourney parish. With C. of I. parish registers, NA M 5118
1837	Marksmen (i.e. illiterate voters), Bandonbridge, Kinsale, Youghal Boroughs. NL, *Parliamentary Papers* 1837, Reports from Committees, Vol. II (1), Appendix A
1837	Lists of waste and poor, Cork City parishes. NL, Reports from Committees, *Parliamentary Papers*, 1837/8, Vol. 13 (1), 324–34
1843–50	Records of Easter and Christmas dues paid in the parish of Ballyclogh, with name of parishioners, including children, NL Pos. 5717
1851	Parishes of Kilcrumper (part), Kilworth, Leitrim (part), Macrony (part), NA m. 4685
1851/3	Griffith's Valuation, Alphabetical index to householders (microfiche), National Archives
1901	Census
1911	Census

Local history

Ballydesmond emigration: see Quit Rent Papers, National Archives, see also *Analecta Hibernica*, Vol. 22

Barry, E., *Barrymore: the records of the Barrys of Co. Cork*, NL Ir. 9292 b 19

Bennett, G., *The history of Bandon and the principal towns of the West Riding of Cork*, Cork, 1869, NL Ir. 94145 b 1

Brady, W. Maziere, *Clerical and Parochial Records of Cork, Cloyne and Ross*, 3 vols, London, 1864

Casey, A. (ed.), *O'Kief Coshe Mang etc.*, NL Ir. 94145 c 12

Caulfield, R., *The register of the parish of Holy Trinity Cork, 1643–1668*, P 1079

Caulfield, R., *The Annals of St Fin Barres Cathedral*, Cork, 1870

Caulfield, R., The Pipe Roll of Cloyne, JCHAS, 1918

Caulfield, R. (ed.), *Council Book of the Corporation of Cork, 1609–43, 1690–1800*, Guildford, 1876

Caulfield, R. (ed.), *Council Book of the Corporation of Kinsale*, Guildford, 1879

Caulfield, R. (ed.), *Council Book of the Corporation of Youghal, 1610–1659, 1666–87, 1690–1800*, Guildford, 1878

Cole, Rev. J. H., *Church and Parish Records of the United Dioceses of Cork, Cloyne and Ross*, Cork, 1903 (Continuation of Brady—see above)

Collins, J. T., 'Co. Cork families 1630–35', JCHAS, No. 204, 1961

Cusack, Mary F., *A History of the City and County of Cork*, Dublin, 1875

Darling, John, *St Multose Church Kinsale*, Cork, 1895

Dennehy, The Ven. Archdeacon, *History of Queenstown*, Cork, 1923

Gibson, C. B., *The history of the county and city of Cork*, London, 1861, J 94145

Grove-White, Col James, *Historical and Topographical Notes etc. on Buttevant, Castletownroche, Doneraile, Mallow and places in their vicinity*, Cork, 1905–16

Grove-White, Col James, *History of Kilbryne Doneraile, Cork*, Cork, 1915
Grove-White Abstracts, National Archives, indexed extracts from the
    following Church of Ireland parish registers: Ballyclogh (NA M 2601);
    Ballyhooly (NA M 2602); Bridgetown and Kilcummer (NA M 2603);
    Buttevant (NA M 2604); Carrigleamleary (NA M 2605); Castlemagner
    (NA M 2606); Castletownroche (NA M 2607); Churchtown (NA M
    2609); Clenor (NA M 2610); Clonfert and Newmarket (NA M 2611);
    Clonmeen (NA M 2612); Doneraile (NA M 2613); Drishane (NA M
    2614); Dromtariffe (NA M 2615); Farahy (NA M 2616); Glanworth (NA
    M 2617); Kanturk (NA M 2618); Kilbolane (NA M 2619); Kilbrin (NA M
    2620); Kilshannig (NA M 2621); Holy Trinity (NA M 2608); Kilworth
    (NA M 2622); Lisgoold (NA M 2623); Litter (NA M 2624); Mallow (NA
    M 2625); Marshallstown (NA M 2626); Monanimy (NA M 2628);
    Mourne Abbey (NA M 2627); Rahan (NA M 2629); St Finbarr and SS
    Peter and Paul (NA M 2630); St Nathlash (NA M 2631); Shanrahan (NA
    M 2632); Tullylease (NA M 2633); Wallstown (NA M 2634)
Hartnett, P. J., *Cork City, its History and Antiquities*, 1943
Holland, Rev. W., *History of West Cork and the Diocese of Ross*, Skibbereen, 1949
Hore, H. J., *The Social State of the Southern and Eastern Counties of Ireland in the
    Sixteenth Century*, 1870
Jephson, M. D., *An Anglo-Irish Miscellany*, NL Ir. 9292 j 2
Maps of Kilmeen and Castleventry parishes, NL Ir. 94145 o 5
McLysaght, E., *The Kenmare Manuscripts*, Dublin, 1942
MacSwiney Papers, Royal Irish Academy. Historical notes and will abstracts,
    mainly from Counties Cork and Kerry
O'Murchadha, D., *Family Names of Co. Cork*, Dublin, 1985
O'Sullivan, Florence, *The History of Kinsale*, Dublin, 1916
Post Office Directory, 1844–45, J 914145
Quinlan, P., *Old Mitchelstown and the Kingston family*, Ir. 941 p 66
Reedy, Rev. Donal A., *The Diocese of Kerry*, Killarney
Smith, Charles, *The ancient ant present state of the county and city of Cork*, Dublin,
    1750 (see also JCHAS, 1893–94)
Tucky, Francis, *The County and City of Cork Remembered*
West, W., *Directory and picture of Cork, 1810*, J 914145
Windele, J., *Cork historical and descriptive notices . . . to the middle of the 19th century*,
    Cork, 1910, NL Ir. 94145 w 3
Windele MSS.: Information on Cork and Kerry families, including Coppinger,
    Cotter, Crosbie, O'Donovan, O'Keeffe, McCarthy, Sarsfield and others,
    NL Pos. 5479

Local journals

Cork Historical and Archaeological Society Journal, NL Ir. 794105 c 1
Bandon Historical Journal, NL Ir. 94145 b 12

Seanchas Chairbre, NL Ir. 94145 s 6
Seanchas Duthala (Duhallow magazine), NL Ir. 94145 s 3

Directories

1787   Richard Lucas, *Cork Directory*, JCHAS, 1967
1788   Richard Lucas, *General Directory of the Kingdom of Ireland*, NL Pos. 3729
1797   John Nixon, *Cork Almanack*
1809   Holden's *Triennal Directory*
1810   William West, *Directory of Cork*
1812   John Connor, *Cork Directory*
1817   John Connor, *Cork Directory*
1820   J. Pigot, *Commercial Directory of Ireland*
1824   Pigot and Co., *City of Dublin and Hibernian Provincial Directory*, NL Ir. 9141 p 75
1826   John Connor, *Cork Directory*
1828   John Connor, *Cork Directory*
1846   Slater's *National Commercial Directory of Ireland*
1856   Slater's *Royal National Commercial Directory of Ireland*
1870   Slater's *Directory of Ireland*
1875   Francis Guy, *Directory of the County and City of Cork*
1881   Slater's *Royal National Commercial Directory of Ireland*
1886   Francis Guy, *Postal Directory of Munster*, NL Ir. 91414 g 8
1889   Francis Guy, *City and County Cork Almanack and Directory*, issued annually from this date
1894   Slater's *Royal Commercial Directory of Ireland*

Gravestone inscriptions

Abbeystrewery (C. of I. interior): IGRS Collection, 30, GO
Adrigole (C. of I.): IGRS Collection, 4, GO
Aghinagh: JCHAS, No. 216, 1967
Aughadown (C. of I. interior): IGRS Collection, 15, GO
Ballyclogh: *O'Kief Coshe Mang etc.*, Vol. 8
Ballycurrany: JCHAS, No. 237, 1978
Ballymodan, St Peter's: Droichead na Banndan Community Cooperative Society Ltd, 1986
Ballyvourney: *O'Kief, Coshe Mang etc.*, Vol. 6
Bantry Abbey: IGRS Collection, 393, GO
Bantry: IGRS Collection, 77, GO
Bantry (St Finbarr's): IGRS Collection, 101, GO
Bere Island: IGRS Collection, 17, GO
Caheragh (C. of I.): IGRS Collection, 13, GO

Caheragh (Catholic): IGRS Collection, 4, GO
Carrigrohanebeg: JCHAS, No. 218, 1968
Catlemagner: *O'Kief, Coshe Mang etc.*, Vol. 6
Castletown Berehaven: IGRS Collection, 37, GO
Clondrohid: *O'Kief, Coshe Mang etc.*, Vol. 6
Clonfert: *O'Kief, Coshe Mang etc.*, Vol. 6
Clonmeen (Lyre and Banteer): *O'Kief, Coshe Mang etc.*, Vol. 7
Clonmult: JCHAS, No. 223/4/5, 1976/7
Cullen: *O'Kief, Coshe Mang etc.*, Vol. 6
Dangandonovan: JCHAS, No. 229, 1974
Desertmore: JCHAS, No. 219, 1969
Drishane: *O'Kief,Coshe Mang etc.*, Vol. 6
Dromagh: *O'Kief, Coshe Mang etc.*, Vol. 8
Dromtariffe: *O'Kief, Coshe Mang etc.*, Vol. 6
Drumlave: IGRS Collection, 1, GO
Dunderrow: JCHAS, No. 224, 1971
Fermoy (Military only): *The Irish Sword*, Nos 51/3, 1977/9
Inchigeela: *O'Kief, Coshe Mang etc.*, Vol. 6
Kilbrin: *O'Kief, Coshe Mang etc.*, Vol. 8
Kilbrogan: (Catholic and C. of I.) Droichead na Banndan Community Co-
    operative Society Ltd, 1986
Kilcaskan: IGRS Collection, 7, GO
Kilcatherine: IGRS Collection, 4, GO
Kilcoe (C. of I.): IGRS Collection, 2, GO,
Kilcoe (old): IGRS Collection, 6, GO
Kilcorney: *O'Kief, Coshe Mang etc.*, Vol. 7
Kilcrea Friary: JCHAS, No. 226, 1972
Kilcummin: *O'Kief, Coshe Mang etc.*, Vol. 6
Killaconenagh: IGRS Collection, 49, GO
Killeagh: JCHAS, No. 226, 1972
Kilnaglory: JCHAS, No. 220, 1969
Kilnamanagh: IGRS Collection, 5, GO
Kilnamartyra: *O'Kief, Coshe Mang etc.*, Vol. 6
Kilmeen: *O'Kief, Coshe Mang etc.*, Vol. 6
Lackeragh: IGRS Collection, 1, GO
Lisgoold: JCHAS, No. 237, 1978
Macloneigh: *O'Kief, Coshe Mang etc.*, Vol. 8
Macroom: *O'Kief, Coshe Mang etc.*, Vol. 8
Mallow: *O'Kief, Coshe Mang etc.*, Vol. 8
Molagga: *The Irish Genealogist*, 1955
Nohovaldaly: *O'Kief, Coshe Mang etc.*, Vol. 8
Rossmacown R.C.: IGRS Collection, 13, GO
St Finbarr's: *St Finbarr's Cathedral*, A. C. Robinson, 1897

Skibbereen R.C. Cathedral interior: IGRS Collection, 13, GO
Thornhill: IGRS Collection, 1, GO
Timoleague: GO MS. 622, 113
Tisxon: JCHAS, No. 222, 1970
Titeskin: JCHAS, No. 221, 1970
Tullylease: *O'Kief, Coshe Mang etc.*, Vol. 8
Youghal (Collegiate Church): *The Handbook for Youghal*, W. G. Field, 1896/
    1973

Estate records

LANDLORD

Lord **Arden**: NL MS. 8652, Rentals 1824–1830, all tenants, covering town-
    lands in the civil parishes of Bregoge, Buttevant, Catlemagner, Clonfert,
    Dromtarriff and Dungourney.

Earl of **Bantry**: NL MS. 3273, Rentals, 1829, all tenants, covering townlands
    in the civil parishes of Kilcaskan, Kilcatherine and Killaconenagh.

(**Barrymore** barony): 'Tenant Farmers on the Barrymore Estate', JCHAS
    Vol. 51, 31–40.

Bennett: Rental of the Bennett estate, 1770 (mainly Cork City and sur-
    rounding areas), NL Pos. 288.

Sir John **Benn-Walsh**: Donnelly, J. S., 'The journals of Sir John Benn-Walsh
    relating to the management of his Irish estates (1823–64)', *Journal of the
    Cork Hist. and Arch. Soc.*, Vol. LXXXI, 1975.

Bishop of Cork: NA M6087. Rentals 1807–1831, major tenants only,
    townlands in the civil parishes of Aghadown, Ardfield, Fanlobbus,
    Kilbrogan, Kilmocomoge, Kilsillagh, Ross, St Finbarr's, Skull.

Boyle/Cavendish: NL MSS. 6136–898. The Lismore Papers. Rentals,
    valuations, lease books, account books for the estates of the Earls of Cork
    and the Dukes of Devonshire, 1570–1870, generally covering only major
    tenants. A detailed listing is given in NL Special List 15, covering
    townlands in the civil parishes of Ahern, Ardagh, Ballymodan, Ballynoe,
    Brinny, Clonmult, Clonpriest, Ightermurragh, Kilbrogan, Killeagh, Kill-
    owen, Kinneigh, Knockmourne, Lismore, Mogeely, Murragh, St Finbarr's,
    Youghal.

Richard **Cox**: NA Gordon Presentation 214. Rentals 1839, major tenants only,
    townlands in the civil parishes of Aghinagh, Clondrohid, Desertserges,
    Fanlobbus, Kilcaskan, Kilmeen, Kilmichael, Kilnamartery, Macloneigh.

Earbery estates: NL MS. 7403, Rentals 1788–1815 (principally major tenants);
    NL MS. 5257, full tenants list, 1800; townlands in the civil parishes of
    Aghabulloge, Clondrohid, Donoghmore, Kilmurry.

Robert Hodges **Eyre**: NL MSS. 3273, 3274, Rentals, 1833 and 1835, of the
    Bere Island estate, all tenants, civil parish of Killaconenagh.

James **Graham**: NA M2329, Rentals *c*.1763, major tenants only, covering townlands in the civil parish of Killathy.

Rev. Edmund **Lombard**: NL MS. 2985, Rentals, 1795, major tenants only, covering townlands in the civil parishes of Kilmacdonagh and Kilshannig.

Newenham?: NL MS. 4123, Rentals *c*.1825, all tenants, covering townlands in the civil parishes of Kilcrumper, Kilworth, Leitrim, Macroney.

Richard **Neville**: NL MS. 3733, Rentals of lands in Counties Cork, Kildare and Waterford, principally major tenants, covering townlands in the civil parishes of Aglishdrinagh and Cooliney.

O'Murchadha, D., 'Diary of Gen. Richard O'Donovan, 1819–23', JCHAS, 1986 (Lands in West Cork).

Perceval, Lord Egmont: Rentals, 1688–1750, major tenants only, NL Pos. 1355 (1688), NL Pos. 4674 (1701–12, 1713–14), NL Pos. 4675 (1714–19), NL Pos. 4676 (1720–24, 1725–27), NL Pos. 4677 (1728–33), NL Pos. 4678 (1734–38), NL Pos. 4679 (1739–41, 1742–46), NL Pos. 4680 (1747–50), covering townlands in the civil parishes of Aglishdrinagh, Ballyclogh, Bregoge, Brigown, Britway, Buttevant, Castlemagner, Churchtown, Clonfert, Cullin, Dromtarriff, Hackmys, Imphrick, Kilbrin, Kilbrogan, Kilbroney, Kilcaskan, Kilgrogan, Kilmichael, Kilroe, Liscarroll, Rathbarry.

George **Putland**: NL MSS., 1814–1827, eleven rentals of land in Counties Cork, Carlow, Kilkenny, Tipperary and Wicklow, principally major tenants, covering townlands in the civil parishes of Garrycloyne, Matehy and Templeusque.

Thomas **Ronayne**: NL MS. 1721, Rentals 1755–1777, major tenants only, covering townlands in the civil parishes of Carrigaline, Clonmel, Killanully, Kilquane, Middleton and Templerobin.

Shuldam: NL MS. 3025, Estate map 1801–1803, with some tenants' names given, covering townlands in the civil parishes of Dreenagh, Fanlobbus, Iveleary and Kilmichael.

(No landlord given): NL MS. 13018, Rental *c*.1835–37, major tenants only, covering townlands in the civil parishes of Castlelyons, Gortroe, Knockmourne and Rathcormack.

(No landlord given): NL MS. 3273, Rentals 1821, covering all tenants, townlands in the civil parish of Kilmocomoge.

Placenames

Townland Maps, Londonderry Inner City Trust
'Placenames in the parish of Kilcaskan', M. MacCarthaigh, JCHAS, 1980

CO. DERRY

Census returns and substitutes

1618	Survey of Derry City and county, TCD MS. 864 (F.I.9.)
1620–22	Muster Roll, PRONI T.510/2
1628	*Houses and Families in Londonderry, 15 May 1628* (ed. R. G. S. King, 1936)
1630	Muster Roll of Ulster. Armagh Co. Museum, NL Pos. 206 and PRONI T.1759/3C/2
1654/6	Civil Survey, Vol. III. NL I 6551, Dublin
1659	Pender's 'Census', NL Ir. 31041 c 4
1661	Books of Survey and Distribution, PRONI D.1854/1/23 and T.370/C
1663	Hearth Money Roll, NL MS. 9584 and PRONI T.307
1740	Protestant Householders: Aghadowey, Anlow, Artrea, Arigall, Ballinderry, Ballynascreen, Ballyscullion, Balten, Banagher, Beleaghron, Belerashane, Belewillen, Boveva, Coleraine, Comber, Desart, Desartloin, Desertmartin, Drumachose, Dunboe, Dungiven, Faughanvale, Glendermot, Killcranaghen, Killowen, Killylagh, Kilrea, Lissan, Creely, Tamlaghtard, Tamlaght, Templemore, Termoneny. GO 539 and PRONI T.808/15258
1766	Artrea, Desertlin, Magherafelt, NA 1A 46 49; Boveagh, Comber, Drumachose, Inch, NA 1A 41 100; Protestants in Ballynascreen, Banagher, Dungiven, Leck; Desertmartin (all); RCB Library. Also PRONI T.808/15264–7
1796	Catholic migrants from Ulster to Mayo. See Mayo
1796	Spinning-Wheel Premium Lists. Microfiche index in National Archives. Names and parishes of those granted spinning-wheels by the government on the basis of areas planted with flax, comprising, in the case of Co. Londonderry, over 8,000 names
1797–1804	Yeomanry muster rolls, PRONI T.1021/3
1808–13	Freeholders lists, NA M.6199
1813	Freeholders (A–L), PRONI T.2123
1820s/30s	Tithe Books
1829	Census of Protestants, Chapel of the Woods parish, PRONI T.308
1832	Voters List, Londonderry City, PRONI T.1048/1–4
1831	Aghadowey, Aghanloo, Agivey, Arboe, Artrea, Ballinderry, Balteagh, Banagher, Ballyaughran, Ballymoney, Ballynascreen, Ballyrashane, Ballyscullion, Ballywillin, Boveagh, Clondermot, Coleraine, Cumber, Desertlyn, Derryloran, Desertmartin,

Desertoghill, Drumachose, Dunboe, Dungiven, Errigal, Faughan-vale, Kilcrea, Kilcunaghan, Killeagh, Killowen, Lissane, Maghera, Magherafelt, Macosquin, Tamlaght, Tamlaght Finlagan, Tam-laght O'Crilly, Tamlaghtard, Templemore, Termoneny, Kill-dollagh (Glendermot). National Archives and PRONI MIC5A/6–9

1833–39   Emigrants from Co. Londonderry, in Brian Mitchell, *Irish Emigration Lists, 1833–39*, Baltimore, 1989

1833/4   Emigrant lists, various parishes, Martin, *Historical Gleanings from Co. Derry*, NL Ir. 94112 m 5

1837   Aldermen, Burgesses and Freemen of Coleraine. *Parliamentary Papers*, 1837, Reports from Committees, Vol II (2), Appendix B

1837   Valuation of towns returning MPs (occupants and property values). *Parliamentary Papers*, 1837, Reports from Committees, Vol. II (i), Appendix G

1837   Marksmen (illiterate voters) in parliamentary boroughs: Londonderry and Coleraine. *Parliamentary Papers*, 1837, Reports from Committees, Vol. II (i), Appendix A

c.1840:   Freeholders Register, PRONI D.834/1
1858/9   Griffith's Valuation
1868   Voters List, Londonderry City, PRONI D.1935/6
1901   Census
1911   Census

Local history

Bernard, Nicholas (ed.), *The Whole Proceedings of the Siege of Drogheda* [&] *Londonderry*, Dublin, 1736

Boyle, E. M. F–G., *Records of the town of Limavady, 1609–1808*, Londonderry, 1912, NL Ir. 94112 b 2

Carson, W. R. H., *A bibliography of printed material relating to the county and county borough of Londonderry*, 1969, NL Ir. 914112 c 8

Colby, Col, *Ordnance Survey Memoir of the county of Londonderry*, Dublin, 1837

Ferguson, Rev. S., *Some items of Historic Interest about Waterside* (with tables of householders in Glendermot parish, 1663, 1740), Londonderry, 1902

Graham, Rev. John, *Derriana, a History of the Siege of Derry and the Defence of Enniskillen in 1688 and 1689, with Biographical Notes*, 1823, NL J94112

Henry, Samuel, *The Story of St Patrick's Church, Coleraine*, n.d.

Hughes, Sam, *City on the Foyle*, Londonderry, 1984

Innes R., *Natural History of Magiligan Parish in 1725*

Kernohan, J. W., *The County of Londonderry in Three Centuries*, Belfast, 1921

King, R. G. S., *A Particular of the houses and families in Londonderry, 15/5/1628*. NL Ir. 94112 l 1

Londonderry Voters list, 1868, NL JP 733
Martin, S., *Historical gleanings from Co. Derry*, Dublin 1955, NL Ir. 94112 m 5
Moody. T. W., *The Londonderry plantation. 1609–41*, Belfast 1939, NL Ir. 94112
    m 2
Mullen, Julia, *The Presbytery of Limavady*, Limavady, 1989
Mullen, T. H., *Ballyrashane*, 1969, NL Ir. 9292 m 33
Mullen, T H., *Ulster's Historic City, Derry, Londonderry*, Coleraine, 1986
Mullen, T. H., *Aghadowey*, NL Ir. 94112 m 8
Murray, Rev. Lawrence P., *History of the Parish of Creggan in the Seventeenth and
    Eighteenth Centuries*, Dundalk, 1940
O'Laverty, Rev. James, *An Historical Account of the Dioceses of Down and Connor*,
    4 vols, Dublin, 1878–89
Phillips, Sir Thomas, *Londonderry and the London Companies*, PRONI, Belfast,
    1928
Public Record Office of Northern Ireland, *A Register of Trees for Co.
    Londonderry, 1768–1911*, Belfast, 1984 (including names of tenant planters)
Simpson, Robert, *The Annals of Derry*, Londonderry, 1847
Witherow, Thomas, *Derry and Enniskillen, in the year 1689*, 1873, 1885
Witherow, Thomas (ed.), *A True Relation of the Twenty Week Siege . . .*, London,
    1649
Young, William R., *Fighters of Derry, their Deeds and Descendants*, 1932

Local journals

Benbradagh (Dungiven parish magazine)
Down and Connor Historical Society Magazine, NL Ir. 94115 [*sic*]
Clogher Record (Journal of the Clogher Diocesan Historical Society), NL Ir. 94114 c 2
Derriana (Journal of the Derry Diocesan Historical Society), NL Ir. 27411 d 4
South Derry Historical Society Journal, NL Ir. 914112 s 21

Directories

1820   J. Pigot, *Commercial Directory of Ireland*
1824   Pigot and Co., *City of Dublin and Hibernian Provincial Directory*, NL Ir.
        9141 p 75
1835   William Matier, *Belfast Directory*
1842   Mathew Martin, *Belfast Directory*
1846   Slater's *National Commercial Directory of Ireland*
1852   James A. Henderson, *Belfast and Province of Ulster Directory*, issued also
        in 1854, 1856, 1858, 1861, 1863, 1865, 1868, 1870, 1877, 1880, 1884,
        1887, 1890, 1894, 1900
1856   Slater's *Royal National Commercial Directory of Ireland*
1865   R. Wynne, *Business Directory of Belfast*

1870   Slater's *Directory of Ireland*
1881   Slater's *Royal National Commercial Directory of Ireland*
1887   *Derry Almanac*
1894   Slater's *Royal Commercial Directory of Ireland*

Estate records

Desertmartin Estate Rentals, *Derriana*, 1981–82.

Gravestone inscriptions

Ballinderry: *South Derry Historical Society Journal*, 1982/3
Derry City: Irish World (see below)
Eglish: *South Derry Historical Society Journal*, 1981/2
Magherafelt (Old): *South Derry Historical Society Journal*, 1980/81
Old Glendermot: (unpub.) National Archives, search room
    Irish World (26 Market Square, Dungannon, Co. Tyrone, BT70 1AB) have transcribed and computerised the inscriptions of more than 300 graveyards in the six counties of Northern Ireland, principally in the four western counties of Armagh, Derry, Fermanagh and Tyrone.

Placenames

Munn, A. M., *Note on the placenames (. . .) of Derry*, NL Ir. 92942 m 18
Townland maps, Londonderry Inner City Trust

CO. DONEGAL

Census returns and substitutes

1612–13   'Survey of Undertakers Planted in Co. Donegal', *Historical Manuscripts Commission Report*, 4 (Hastings MSS.), 1947, 159–82
1630   Muster Roll, *Donegal Annual*, Vol. X, No. 2. NL Pos. 206
1641   Book of Survey and Distribution, NL MS. 968
1654   Civil Survey, Vol. III, I 6551 Dublin
1659   Pender's 'Census', NL Ir. 31041 c 4
1665   Hearth Money Roll, GO 538, NL MS. 9583, PRONI T.307/D
1740   Protestant Householders: parishes of Clonmeny, Culdaff, Desertegney, Donagh, Fawne, Movill, Templemore. GO 539

1761–75   Freeholders NL P. 975; GO MS. 442; PRONI T.808/14999
1766   Donoghmore parish, NA m 207/8; Protestants in Leck, NA 1A 41 100
1770   Freeholders entitled to vote, NL MSS. 987–8
1782   Persons in Culdaff, *300 Years in Inishowen*, Amy Young
1796   Spinning-Wheel Premium Lists. Microfiche index in National Archives, comprising, in the case of Co. Donegal, over 14,000 names
1799   Protestant Householders, Templecrone parish, *The Irish Ancestor*, 1984
1802/3   Protestants in part of Culdaff parish, *300 Years in Inishowen*, Amy Young
1820s/30s Tithe Books
1857   Griffith's Valuation
1901   Census
1911   Census

Local history

Allingham, H., *Ballyshannon: its history and antiquities (with some account of the surrounding neighbourhood)*, Londonderry, 1879, NL Ir. 94113 a 1
Conaghan, Pat, *Bygones: New Horizons on the History of Killybegs*, Killybegs, 1989
Doherty, William J., *Inis-Owen and Tirconnel: being some account of the antiquities . . . of Donegal*, Dublin, 1895, NL Ir. 94113 d 1
Harkin, William, *Scenery and Antiquities of North West Donegal*, 1893
Hill, George, *Facts from Gweedore*, Dublin, 1854
Lucas, Leslie W., *Mevagh Down the Years*, Belfast, 1983
MacDonagh, J. C. T., 'Bibliography of Co. Donegal', *Donegal Hist. Soc. Jnl*, 1947–50, 217–30
Maguire, V. Rev. Canon, *The History of the Diocese of Raphoe*, 2 vols, Dublin
Shearman, H., *Ulster*, London, 1949 (incl. bibliographies), NL Ir. 91422 s 3
Swan, H. P., *The Book of Inishowen*, Buncrana, 1938
Young, Amy, *300 Years in Inishowen*, Belfast, 1929, NL Ir. 9292 y 1

Local journals

Donegal Annual, NL Ir. 94113 d 3
Journal of the Donegal Historical Society (1947–51), as above
Clogher Record (Journal of the Clogher Diocesan Historical Society), NL Ir. 94114 c 2
Derriana (Journal of the Derry Diocesan Historical Society), NL Ir. 27411 d 4

Directories

1824   Pigot and Co., *City of Dublin and Hibernian Provincial Directory*, NL Ir. 9141 P 75

1839   *Directory of the Towns of Sligo, Enniskillen, Ballyshannon Donegal, etc.*
1846   Slater's *National Commercial Directory of Ireland*
1854   James A. Henderson, *Belfast and Province of Ulster Directory*, issued also in 1856, 1858, 1861, 1863, 1865, 1868, 1870, 1877, 1880, 1884, 1887, 1890, 1894, 1900
1856   Slater's *Royal National Commercial Directory of Ireland*
1870   Slater's *Directory of Ireland*
1881   Slater's *Royal National Commercial Directory of Ireland*
1887   *Derry Almanac*, annually from this year
1894   Slater's *Royal Commercial Directory of Ireland*

Gravestone inscriptions

Assaroe Abbey: *Donegal Annual*, Vol. III, No. 3, 1957
Ballyshannon: *Donegal Annual*, Vol. XII, No. 2, 1978, see also Allingham (above: 'Local history')
Finner: *Where Erne and Drowes Meet the Sea*, P. O'Gallachair
Inver C. of I.: IGRS Collection, GO
Killaghtee: IGRS Collection, 31, GO
St Catherine's (old) Killybegs: IGRS Collection, GO
SS. Conal and Joseph: IGRS Collection, GO

Estate records

LANDLORD
Thomas **Connolly**, Henry **Bruen**, H. G. **Cooper**, Sarah E. **Connolly**, Sale of estates of with rentals, Parishes of Drumholme, Donegal, Bally-shannon, NL ILB 347 1 15.
William **Connolly**: Lives in leases on the Ballyshannon estate, 1718–58, NL MS. 5751, and *Donegal Annual*, No. 33, 1981 (1718–26).
A. **Murry-Stewart**: Rentals, 1842, 1845, including lands in the parishes of Killymard, Killybegs, Killaughtee, Kilcar, Innisgale, NL MS. 5465, 5466.
H. G. **Murry-Stewart**: Rentals, 1847–1859, including lands in the parishes of Killymard, Killybegs, Killaughtee, Kilcar, Innisgale, NL MSS. 5467–5476.

Placenames

Townland maps, Londonderry Inner City Trust

CO. DOWN

Census returns and substitutes

1630	Muster Roll of Ulster. Armagh Co. Library, NL Pos. 206, PRONI D.1759/3C/1
1642–43	Muster Roll, PRONI T.563/1
1642	Donaghadee Muster Roll, PRONI T.2736/1
1659	Pender's 'Census', NL Ir. 31041, c 4
1661	Books of Survey and Distribution, PRONI T.370/A and D.1854/1/18
1663	Subsidy Roll. NL Pos. 206; NA M.2745; PRONI T.307
1708	Householders in Downpatrick town, *The City of Downe*, R. E. Parkinson, NL Ir. 94115 p 1
1740	Protestant Householders (part), PRONI T.808/15258
1766	Kilbroney, Seapatrick, Inch, Shankill, NL MS. 4173
1777	Freeholders Register (also 1780–95), PRONI DOW 5/3/1 and 2
1789	'Deputy Court Cheque Book' (votes cast), PRONI D.654/A3/1B
c.1790	Lecale Barony freeholders, PRONI T.393/1
1796	Catholic migrants from Ulster to Mayo, see Mayo
1796	Spinning-Wheel Premium Lists. Microfiche index in National Archives, comprising, in the case of Co. Down, over 5,000 names
1798	Persons who Suffered Losses in the 1798 Rebellion. NL I 94107
1799–1800	Militia Pay Lists and Muster Rolls, PRONI T.1115/4A–C
1813–21	Freeholders, PRONI T.761/19
1815–46	Downpatrick electors, NL MS. 7235
1821	Various parishes, Thrift Abstracts, National Archives
1824	Freeholders, PRONI T.761/20
1820s/30s	Tithe Books
1832–37	Belfast Poll Book, PRONI D.2472
1837	Valuation of towns returning MPs (occupants and property values): Newry. *Parliamentary Papers*, 1837, Reports from Committees, Vol. II (i), Appendix G
1837	Marksmen (illiterate voters) in parliamentary boroughs: Newry, Downpatrick. *Parliamentary Papers*, 1837, Reports from Committees, Vol. II (i), Appendix A
1841–61	Religious censuses, parish of Scarva, RCBL MS. 65
1851	Various Parishes. Thrift Abstracts, National Archives
1851/61	Census of Presbyterian Parishioners of Loughinisland, *Family Links*, Vol. 1 Nos 5 and 7, 1982/83
1852	Poll Book (votes cast), incomplete, PRONI D.671/02/5–6
1855	Belfast Register of Electors, PRONI BELF5/1/1/1–2
1857	Poll Book (votes cast), incomplete, PRONI D.671/02/7–8

1863/4   Griffith's Valuation, Belfast—Alphabetical index to householders,
          All-Ireland Heritage microfiche, National Archives
1876   Belfast Register of Electors, PRONI BELF5/1/1/1–2
1901   Census
1911   Census

Local history

The Ards: a local history source list, NL Ir. 914115 p 15

Atkinson, Edward D., *An Ulster Parish: Being a History of Donaghcloney*, 1898
    (Waringstown, Co. Down)

Castlereagh: some local sources, NL Ir. 914115 p 15

Clandeboye: a reading guide, NL Ir. 914115 p 15

Cowan, J. Davison, *An Ancient Parish, Past and Present; being the Parish of
    Donaghmore, County Down*, London, 1914, NL Ir. 94115 c 1

Crossle, Francis, *Local Jottings of Newry Collected and Transcribed* (Vols 1–34),
    Newry, 1890–1910

Donaghadee: a local history list, NL Ir. 9411 s 12

Ewart, L. M., *Handbook to the dioceses of Down, Connor and Dromore*

Haddock, Josiah, *A Parish Miscellany, Donaghcloney*

Hamilton, William, *The Hamilton Manuscripts* (containing some account of the
    settlement of the territories of Upper Clandeboye, Great Ares and
    Dufferin . . . in the reigns of James I and Charles I), (ed. T. K. Lowry),
    Belfast 1867. NL Ir. 94115 h 1

Harris, Walter, *The Ancient and Present State of the County of Down*, Dublin, 1744,
    I 94115 h 2

Hill, Rev. George, *Montgomery Manuscripts, 1603–1706*, Belfast, 1869

Keenan, Padraic, *Historical Sketch of the Parish of Clonduff*, Newry, 1941

Killyleagh and Crossegar: a local history list, NL Ir. 914115 p 15

Knox, Alexander, *History of the County Down*, Dublin, 1875

Linn, Capt. Richard, *A history of Banbridge* (ed. W. S. Kerr), Belfast, 1935,
    (including Tullylish)

O'Laverty, Rev. James, *The History of the Parish of Hollywood*, n.d.

O'Laverty, Rev. James, *An Historical Account of the Dioceses of Down and Connor*,
    4 vols, Dublin, 1878–89

Parkinson, Edward, *The City of Down from its earliest days*, Belfast, 1928

Pilson, A., *Downpatrick and its Parish Church* (including lists of clergy and
    churchwardens), 1852. P 1938

Pooler, L. A., *Down and its Parishes*, 1907

Reside, S. W., *St Mary's Church, Newry: its History*, 1933

Shearman, H., *Ulster*, London, 1949 (incl. bibliographies), NL Ir. 91422 s 3

Smith, Charles, and Harris, Walter, *The ancient and present state of the county of
    Down*, Dublin, 1744, I 94115 h 2

Smith, K., Bangor Reading List, *Journal of the Bangor H.S.*
Stevenson, John, *Two Centuries of Life in Down, 1600–1800*, Belfast, 1920
Stewart, Rev. D., *Tullylish, Parish of: Historical Notes*

Local journals

Down and Connor Historical Society Magazine, NL Ir. 94115 [*sic*]
East Belfast Historical Society Journal (from 1981)
Journal of the Bangor Historical Society
Lecale Miscellany (from 1983)
Old Newry Journal (from 1977)
Saintfield Heritage
Seanchas Dhroim Mor (Journal of the Dromore Diocesan Historical Society), NL Ir.
  94115 s 3
Upper Ards Historical Society Journal, NL Ir. 94115 u 1

Directories

1819   Thomas Bradshaw, *General Directory of Newry, Armagh, Dungannon, Porta-
        down, Tandragee, Lurgan, Waringstown, Banbridge, Warrenpoint, Rostrevor,
        Kilkeel and Rathfryland*
1820   J. Pigot, *Commercial Directory of Ireland*
1820   Joseph Smyth, *Directory of Belfast and its Vicinity*
1824   Pigot and Co., *City of Dublin and Hibernian Provincial Directory*, NL Ir.
        9141 p 75
1841   Mathew Martin, *Belfast Directory*, issued also in 1842
1846   Slater's *National Commercial Directory of Ireland*
1852   James A. Henderson, *Belfast and Province of Ulster Directory*, issued also
        in 1854, 1856, 1858, 1861, 1863, 1865, 1868, 1870, 1877, 1880, 1884,
        1887, 1890, 1894, 1900
1856   Slater's *Royal National Commercial Directory of Ireland*
1865   R. Wynne, *Business Directory of Belfast*
1870   Slater's *Directory of Ireland*
1881   Slater's *Royal National Commercial Directory of Ireland*
1883   S. Farrell, *County Armagh Directory and Almanac*
1894   Slater's *Royal Commercial Directory of Ireland*

Gravestone inscriptions

Vols 1–19, R. S. J. Clarke, 1966–81, NL Ir. 9295 c 1

Aghlisnafin, Vol. 9
Annahilt, Vol. 18
Ardkeen, Vol. 13
Ardglass, Vol. 8
Ardquin, Vol. 13
Baileysmill, Vol. 2
Ballee, Vol. 8
Balligan, Vol. 14
Balloo, Vol. 17
Ballyblack, Vol. 12
Ballycarn, Vol. 3
Ballycopeland, Vol. 16
Ballycranbeg, Vol. 13
Ballycruttle, Vol. 8
Ballyculter, Vol. 8
Ballygalget, Vol. 13
Ballygowan, Vol. 5
Ballyhalbert, Vol. 15
Ballyhemlin, Vol. 14
Ballykinler, Vol. 9
Ballymacashin, Vol. 6
Ballymageogh, Vol. 10
Ballymartin, Vol. 10
Ballynahinch,Vol. 9
Ballyphilip, Vol 13
Ballytrastan, Vol. 13
Bangor, Vol. 17
Barr, *An Ancient Irish
    Parish*, J. D. Cowan
Blaris, Vol. 5
Boardmills, Vol. 2
Breda, Vol. 1
Bright, Vol. 8
Cargacreevy, Vol. 18
Carrowdore, Vol 14
Carryduff, Vols 1 and 18
Castlereagh, Vol. 1

Clandeboye, Vol. 17
Cloghy, Vol. 14
Clough, Vol. 9,
Comber, Vol. 5
Copeland Islands, Vol. 16
Donaghadee, Vol. 16
Donaghcloney, *An Ulster Parish*
    E. D. Atkinson
Donaghmore, *An Ancient Irish
    Parish*, J. D. Cowan
Downpatrick, Vol. 7
Dromara, Vol. 19
Dromore, Vol. 19
Drumaroad, Vol. 9
Drumbeg, Vol. 3
Drumbo, Vols 1, 4 and 18
Dundonald, Vol. 2
Dunsfort, Vol. 8
Edenderry, Vol. 3
Eglantine, Vol. 18
Gilnahirk, Vol. 18
Glasdrumman, Vol. 10
Glastry, Vol. 15
Glansha, Vol. 1
Greyabbey, Vol. 12
Groomsport, Vol. 17
Hillhall, Vol. 1
Hillsborough, Vol. 18
Holywood, Vol. 14
Inch, Vol. 7
Inishargy, Vol. 14
Kilcarn, Vol. 5
Kilclief, Vol. 8
Kilhorne, Vol. 10
Kilkeel, Vol. 10
Killarney, Vol. 2
Kilarsey, Vol. 6

Killinakin, Vol. 6
Killinchy, Vols 5 and 6
Killough, Vol. 8
Killybawn, Vol. 1
Killyleagh, Vols 6 and 7
Killysuggan, Vol. 5
Kilmegan, Vol. 9
Kilmood, Vol. 5
Kilmore, Vol. 3
Kilwarlin, Vol. 18
Kircubbin, Vol. 12
Knock, Vol. 4
Knockbreckan, Vols 1 and 18
Knockbreda, Vol. 2
Legacurry, Vol. 2
Lisbane, Vol. 13
Loughaghery, Vol. 18
Loughinisland, Vols 9 and 12
Magheradrool, Vols 9 and 12
Magherahamlet, Vol. 9
Magheralin, Vol. 19
Maze, Vol. 18
Millisle, Vol. 16

Moira, Vol. 18
Moneyrea, Vol. 1
Mourne, Vol. 10
Movilla, Vol. 11
Newtownards, Vol. 11
Old Court, Vol. 8
Portaferry, Vol. 13
Rademan, Vol. 3
Raffrey, Vol. 5
Rathmullen, Vol. 9
Ravara, Vol. 5
Saintfield, Vol. 3
Saul, Vols 7 and 8
Seaforde, Vol. 9
Slanes, Vol. 14
Tamlaght, Vol. 10
Templepatrick, Vol. 14
Tullymacnous, Vol. 6
Tullynakill, Vol. 1
Waringstown, *An Ulster Parish*,
   E. D. Atkinson
Whitechurch, Vol. 15

BELFAST INSCRIPTIONS
Christ Church, Vol. 1
Shankill, Vol. 1
Milltown, Vol. 2
Balmoral Friend's, Vol. 3

St George's, Vol. 1
Friar's Bush, Vol. 2
Balmoral, Vol. 3
Malone Presbyterian, Vol. 3

Placenames

Townland maps, Londonderry Inner City Trust

CO. DUBLIN

Census returns and substitutes

1568	Herald's Visitation of Dublin, GO 46; NL Pos. 957
1607	Herald's Visitation of Dublin City, GO 48; NL Pos. 8286
1610	Herald's Visitation of Dublin county, GO 48; NL Pos. 8286
1621	St John's parish cess lists, also for years 1640 and 1687, Appendix to Vol. I of the Parish Register Society, 1906
1634	Subsidy roll, NA M.2469
1641	Book of Survey and Distribution, NL MS. 964
1652	Inhabitants of the baronies of Newcastle and Uppercross, NA 1A 41 100
1654–56	Civil Survey, Vol. VII, Irish Manuscripts Commission
1659	Pender's 'Census'
1663–68	Subsidy roll for Co. Dublin, NA M.2468
1663	Hearth Money Roll for parts of Counties Dublin and Kildare, *Kildare Arch. Soc. Jnl*, Vol. X, 245
1664	Persons with 6 hearths or upwards, Dublin City, RDKPRO 57, 560
1667–1810	Assessments for the parish of St Bride's, TCD M.2063
1680–86	Index to an applotment book for Dublin City, NA M.4979
1680	Pipe water accounts, *The Irish Genealogist*, 1987
1696	Poll tax assessments for 1696 and 1699, NA M.2469
1711–1835	Annual Cess Applotment books of St Michan's parish, RCBL
1730–40	Index to marriages and deaths in *Pue's Occurrences* and *The Dublin Gazette*, NL MS. 3197
1756	Inhabitants of St Michael's parish, *The Irish Builder*, Vol. 33, 701/1
1763–71	Index to *Freeman's Journal*, Dublin, NL reading room counter
1766	Religious census, Parishes of Castleknock, Taney, Donnybrook, Crumlin, RCB Library, Crumlin; also in GO 537
1767	Freeholders, Dublin City, NA M.4910–2
1778–82	Catholic Merchants, Traders and Manufacturers of Dublin, *Reportorium Novum* 2 (2), 1960, 298–323
1791–1831	Register of children at Baggot St school (Incorporated Soc. for Promoting Protestant Schools), NL Pos. 2884
1791–1957	Register of Admissions to Pleasant's Female Orphan Asylum, including places of birth and families, NL MS. 1555. See also NL MSS. 1556 and 1558
1793–1810	Census of Protestants in Castleknock, GO 495
1798	List of persons who suffered loss of property in 1798, NL JLB 94107

1798–1836	Register of children at Santry school (Incorporated Soc. for Promoting Protestant Schools), NL Pos. 2884
1800–1816	Card index to biographical notices in *Faulkner's Dublin Journal*, NL
1805–39	Register of children at Kevin St school (Incorporated Soc. for Promoting Protestant Schools), NL Pos. 2884
1806	Voters Lists, by occupation, Dublin City, Ir. 94133 d 13
1820	Freemen voters, NL P 734
1821	Some extracts. Thrift Abstracts, National Archives
1820s/30s	Tithe Books
1830	Freeholders, Dublin City and county, NL MS. 11, 847
1831	Householders in St Bride's parish, NL P. 1994
1834/5	Returns of those liable for paving-tax. Inquiry into the impeachment of Alderman Richard Smith, State Paper Office
1835	Dublin City Parliamentary Election (Alphabetical list of voters with addresses and occupations), Ir. 94133 d 12
1835–37	Dublin county freeholders and leaseholders, NL MS. 9363
1840–1938	Admissions and Discharge registers for Dublin City workhouses (North and South Union), National Archives
1841	Voters Lists, Dublin City, Ir. 94133 d 15
1841	Some extracts. Thrift Abstracts, National Archives
1848/51	Griffith's Valuation. Alphabetical index to householders on microfiche in National Archives
1851	Index to heads of households, by street and parish, National Archives
1864	City of Dublin Voters List, by district and street, Ir. 94133 d 16
1865/6	Voters Lists, Dublin City, Ir. 94133 d 15
1878	Parliamentary Voters, South Dock Ward, NL ILB 324 d
1901	Census
1911	Census

Local history

Adams, B. N., *History and Description of Santry and Cloghran Parishes*, Dublin, 1883

Alphabetical list of the constituency of the University of Dublin, 1865, Ir. 37841 t 2 and 1832; JP 1375; also LO

Appleyard, D. S., *Green Fields Gone Forever*, Ir. 94133 a 5 (Coolock and Artane area)

Ball, F. E., *A history of the county of Dublin*, Dublin, 1902–20, Ir. 94133 b 1:

1. Monkstown, Kill-o'-the Grange, Dalkey, Killiney, Tully, Stillorgan, Kilmacud
2. Donnybrook, Booterstown, St Bartholomew, St Mark, Taney, St Peter, Rathfarnham

3. Tallaght, Cruagh, Whitechurch, Kilgobbin, Kiltiernan, Rathmichael, Old Connaught, Saggart, Rathcoole, Newcastle.
4. Clonsilla, Leixlip, Lucan, Aderrig, Kilmactalway, Kilbride, Kilmahuddrick, Esker, Palmerstown, Ballyfermot, Clondalkin, Drimnagh, Crumlin, St Catherine, St Nicholas Without, St James, St Jude, Chapelizod
5. Howth
6. Castleknock, Mulhuddert, Cloghran, Ward, St Margaret's, Finglas, Glasnevin, Grangegorman, St George, Clonturk

Blacker, Rev. Beaver H., *Sketches of the Parishes of Booterstown and Donnybrook*, 1860–74
Clarke, Mary, 'Sources for Genealogical Research in Dublin Corporation Archives', *The Irish Genealogist*, 1987
Craig, Maurice, *Dublin 1660–1800*, Dublin, 1952
Cullen, L. N., *Princes and Pirates: the Dublin Chamber of Commerce, 1783–1983*, Ir. 94133 c 17
Donnelly, N., Series of short histories of Dublin parishes, Ir. 27413 d 1
Donnelly, N., *State of RC Chapels in Dublin 1749*, I 2820941 p 10
Doolin, W., *Dublin's Surgeon Anatomists*, Ir. 610 p 4
Dublin in Books: A reading list from the stock of Dublin Public Libraries (1982), Ir. 01 p 9
See Dublin under 'Municipal Council' (in NL Author Catalogue) for reports of various corporation meetings, lists of freemen, aldermen, bailiffs etc.
Gilbert, Sir John T., *A History of the City of Dublin*, Dublin, 1854–59
Gilbert Library: Dublin and Irish Collections, Ir. 02 p 50
Harris, Walter, *The History and Antiquities of the City of Dublin*, Dublin, 1776
Harrison, W., *Dublin Houses/or Memorable Dublin Houses, 1890*, Ir. 94133 h 5
Kingston, Rev. John, *The Parish of Fairview*: 'Including the present parishes of Corpus Christi, Glasnevin, Larkhill, Marino, and Donnycarney', Dundalk, 1953
Lawler, Hugh J., *The Fasti of St Patrick's, Dublin*, 1930
Le Fanu, T. P., *The Huguenot Churches of Dublin and their Ministries* (1905), P. 2274
MacGiolla Phadraig, Brian, *History of Terenure*, Dublin, 1954
MacSorley, Catherine M., *The Story of Our parish: St Peter's Dublin*, Dublin, 1917
Maxwell, Constantia, *Dublin under the Georges, 1714–1830*, London, 1956, Ir. 94133 h 5
McCready, C. T., *Dublin street names, dated and explained*, Dublin, 1892 (including bibliography), Ir. 92941 m 1 (and LO)
Monks, W., *Lusk, a Short History*, Ir. 9141 p 85
O'Driscoll, J., *Cnucha: a history of Castleknock and district*, Ir. 94133 o 9
Shepherd, E., *Behind the Scenes: the story of Whitechurch district*, Ir. 94133 s 8
St Peter's Parochial Male and Female Boarding Schools, Sunday, Daily and Infant Schools: Reports 1850–60, P. 439
Stephen's Green Club, list of members, 1882, Ir. 367 s 12

Warburton, John, Whitlow, James, and Walsh, Robert, *History of the City of Dublin*, London, 1818

Local journals

Dublin Historical Record (Journal of the Old Dublin Society), Ir. 94133 d 23
Reportorium Novum: Dublin diocesan historical record, Ir. 27413 r 3

Directories

1751   Peter Wilson, 'An Alphabetical List of the Names and Places of Abode of the Merchants and Traders of the City of Dublin', issued annually as part of *The Treble Almanack*, from 1755 to 1837

1820   J. Pigot, *Commercial Directory of Ireland*

1824   Pigot and Co., *City of Dublin and Hibernian Provincial Directory*, NL Ir. 9141 p 75

1834   Pettigrew and Oulton, *Dublin Almanack and General Register of Ireland*, issued annually from 1834 to 1849

1844   Alexander Thom, *Irish Almanack and Official Directory*, issued annually from 1844

1846   Slater's *National Commercial Directory of Ireland*

1856   Slater's *Royal National Commercial Directory of Ireland*

1870   Slater's *Directory of Ireland*

1881   Slater's *Royal National Commercial Directory of Ireland*

1894   Slater's *Royal Commercial Directory of Ireland*

Gravestone inscriptions

Abbotstown (Castleknock): IGRS Collection, 29, GO. Also GO MS. 622, 89

Baldoyle, old: IGRS Collection, 3, GO

Chapelizod: *The Irish Genealogist*, Vol. V, No. 4, 1977

Cloghran: *History and Description of Santry and Cloghran Parishes*, B. W. Adams, 1883

Clondalkin (Kilmahuddrick): IGRS, Dublin City and County Gravestone Inscriptions, Vol. 2 (unpub.), NA Search Room and GO

Clondalkin (Mount St Joseph): IGRS Dublin City and County Gravestone Inscriptions, Vol. 2 (unpub.), NA Search Room and GO

Cloghran, south: IGRS Collection, 11, GO

Dalkey: *The Irish Genealogist*, Vol. V, No. 2, 1975

Dublin City: Christ Church, *Inscriptions on the monuments (. . .) in Christ Church (. . .)*, John Finlayson, 1878

    Crumlin: *The Irish Genealogist*, Vol. 7, No. 3, 1988

    Goldenbridge: IGRS Dublin City and County Gravestone Inscriptions, Vol. 1 (unpub.), NA Search Room and GO

Huguenot cemetery, Merrion Row, 1693: IGRS Dublin City and County Gravestone Inscriptions, Vol. 2 (unpub.), NA Search Room and GO; Parkinson, Dublin Family History Society, 1988

Jewish Graveyard, Fairview Strand: IGRS Collection, 137, GO

Merrion: IGRS Dublin City and County Gravestone Inscriptions, Vol. 2 (unpub.), NA Search Room and GO

St Andrew's (coffin plates): *The Irish Genealogist*, Vol. V, No. 1, 1974

St Andrew's (interior): IGRS Collection, 50, GO

St Catherine's, S. Murphy, Divelina, 1987

St James' (C. of I.): (unpub.), National Archives Search Room

St Matthew's (C. of I.), Ringsend: IGRS Dublin City and County Gravestone Inscriptions, Vol. 2 (unpub.), NA Search Room and GO

SS. Michael and John (coffin plates): *The Irish Genealogist*, Vol. V, No. 3, 1976

St Paul's (C. of I.): JRSAI, Vol. CIV, 1974

St Paul's (C. of I. graveyard): IGRS Collection, 6,

Kilbarrack: IGRS Collection, 38, GO

Kilbride (Baldonnell): IGRS, Dublin City and County Gravestone Inscriptions, Vol. 2 (unpub.), NA Search Room and GO

Killiney (old churchyard): *The Irish Genealogist*, Vol. IV, No. 6, 1973

Kill o' the Grange: *The Irish Genealogist*, Vol. IV, No. 5, 1972

Kilmactalway (Castle Bagot, Baldonnell): IGRS Dublin City and County Gravestone Inscriptions, Vol. 2 (unpub.), NA Search Room and GO

Kilternan (C. of I. interior): IGRS Collection, 18, GO

Kilternan (old): IGRS Dublin City and County Gravestone Inscriptions, Vol. 2 (unpub.), NA Search Room and GO

Leixlip: *The Irish Genealogist*, Vol. IV, No. 2, 1969

Lucan: *The Irish Genealogist*, Vol. V, No. 6, 1976

Lucan (Esker old): IGRS Dublin City and County Gravestone Inscriptions, Vol. 2 (unpub.), NA Search Room and GO

Lucan (St Mary's): IGRS Dublin City and County Gravestone Inscriptions, Vol. 2 (unpub.), NA Search Room and GO

Monkstown: *The Irish Genealogist*, Vol. IV, Nos 3 and 4, 1970/1

Mulhuddert: GO MS. 622, 96

Newcastle (C. of I.): IGRS Dublin City and County Gravestone Inscriptions, Vol. 2 (unpub.), NA Search Room and GO

Newcastle (Loughtown Lr): IGRS Dublin City and County Gravestone Inscriptions, Vol. 2 (unpub.), NA Search Room and GO

Newcastle (R.C.): IGRS Dublin City and County Gravestone Inscriptions, Vol. 2, (Unpub.), NA Search Room and GO

Old Connaught: IGRS Collection, 54, GO

Palmerstown: *The Irish Genealogist*, Vol. V, No. 8, 1978

Portmarnock old: IGRS Collection, 81, GO

Portmarnock (C. of I.): IGRS Collection, GO
Rathcoole: IGRS Dublin City and County Gravestone Inscriptions, Vol. 2
    (unpub.), NA Search Room and GO
Rathfarnham: *The Irish Genealogist*, 1987
Rathmichael: IGRS Collection, 31, GO
St Doolough's, Balgriffin: IGRS Collection, 48, GO
Santry: *History and Description of Santry and Cloghran Parishes*, B. W. Adams, 1883
Tallaght: *The Irish Genealogist*, Vol. IV, No. 1, 1968
Taney: *The Parish of Taney*, F. E. Ball, 1895
Tully: IGRS Collection, 50, GO
Whitechurch: *The Irish Genealogist*, 1990

Estate records

Claremorris estate rental, Galway, Mayo, Dublin, 1833, NL.

Placenames

Placenames of Dublin, The O'Rahilly, Ir. 92942 o 2
Parish Guide to the Archdiocese of Dublin (1958) Ir. 27413 d 3

CO. FERMANAGH

Census returns and substitutes

1612–13	'Survey of Undertakers Planted in Co. Fermanagh', *Historical Manuscripts Commission Report*, 4 (Hastings MSS.), 1947, 159–82
1630	Muster Roll, PRONI T.808/15164
1631	Muster Roll, *History of Enniskillen*, W. C. Trimble
1659	Pender's 'Census', Ir. 31041 c 4
1661	Books of Survey and Distribution, PRONI T.370/B and D.1854/1/20
1662	Subsidy roll (Enniskillen), NL MS. 9583; PRONI T.808/15068
1665	Hearth Money Roll, NL MS. 9583, *Clogher Record*, 1957; PRONI T.808/15066
1747	Poll Book (votes cast), PRONI T.808/15063
1766	Boho, Derryvullen, Devenish, Kinawley, Rossory, NA m. 2476 (d)

1770	Freeholders, GO 443, NL MS. 787–8
1788	Poll Book (votes cast), PRONI T.808/15075, T.543, T.1385
1794–99	Militia Pay Lists and Muster Rolls, PRONI T.1115/5A–C
1796	Catholic migrants from Ulster to Mayo. See Mayo
1796–1802	Freeholders, PRONI D.1096/90
1797	Yeomanry Muster Rolls, PRONI T.1021/3
1821	Parishes of Aghalurcher (part) and Derryvullen, NA and PRONI
1820s/30s	Tithe Books
1832	Enniskillen registered voters. Reports from Committees, *Parliamentary Papers*, 1837–38, Vol. 13 (2), 554–7
1837	Freeholders. Reports from Committees, *Parliamentary Papers*, 1837–38, Vol. 11 (1), (39) 7–21
1841	Certified copies of census returns for use in claims for old age pensions. National Archives and PRONI
1851	Townland of Clonee, parish of Drumkeeran. Certified copies of census returns for use in claims for old age pensions, National Archives
c.1861	Protestant inhabitants of Boho parish, NA T.3723
1862	Griffith's Valuation. Alphabetical index to householders, on microfiche, National Archives
1901	Census
1911	Census

Local history

Belmore, Earl of, *Parliamentary Memoirs of Fermanagh and Tyrone, 1613–1885*, Dublin, 1887

Bradshaw, W. H., *Enniskillen Long Ago: an Historic Sketch of the Parish . . .*, 1878

Dundas, W. H., *Enniskillen parish and town*, 1913, Dundalk, Ir. 94118 d 2

Graham, Rev. John, *Derriana, a History of the Siege of Derry and the Defence of Enniskillen in 1688 and 1689, with Biographical Notes*, 1823

King, Sir Charles (ed.), *Henry's 'Upper Lough Erne in 1739'*, Dublin, 1892

MacKenna, J. E., *Devenish, its history, antiquities and traditions*, 1897

Martin, S., *Historical gleanings from Co. Derry (and some from Fermanagh)*, Dublin, 1955, Ir. 94112 m 5

O'Connell, Philip, *The Diocese of Kilmore: its History and Antiquities*, Dublin, 1937

Shearman, H., *Ulster*, London, 1949 (incl. bibliographies), Ir. 91422 s 3

Steele, W. B., *The parish of Devenish*, 1937

Trimble, W., *The history of Enniskillen*, Vols I–III, Enniskillen, 1921, Ir. 94118 t 1

Directories

1824	Pigot and Co., *City of Dublin and Hibernian Provincial Directory*, NL Ir. 9141 p 75

1839   *Directory of the Towns of Sligo, Enniskillen, Ballyshannon, Donegal, etc.*
1846   Slater's *National Commercial Directory of Ireland*
1852   James A. Henderson, *Belfast and Province of Ulster Directory*, issued also
        in 1854, 1856, 1858, 1861, 1863, 1865, 1868, 1870, 1877, 1880, 1884,
        1887, 1890, 1894, 1900
1856   Slater's *Royal National Commercial Directory of Ireland*
1870   Slater's *Directory of Ireland*
1881   Slater's *Royal National Commercial Directory of Ireland*
1887   *Derry Almanac*, annually from this year
1894   Slater's *Royal Commercial Directory of Ireland*

Local journals

Clogher Record (Journal of the Clogher Diocesan Historical Society), Ir. 94114 c 2

Gravestone inscriptions

Aghalurcher: *Clogher Record*, Vol. II, No. 2, 1958
Aghavea: *Clogher Record*, Vol. IV, Nos 1 and 2, 1960/1
Devenish: St Molaise's and Devenish Abbey: *Devenish, its History, Antiquities,
    and Traditions*, J. E. MacKenna, F. E. Bigger, 1897
Donagh: *Clogher Record*, Vol. 1, No. 3, 1955
Drumully: *Clogher Record*, Vol. 1, No. 2, 1954
Enniskillen: *Enniskillen Parish and Town*, W. H. Dundas, 1913
Galoon: *Clogher Record*, Vol. X, No. 2, 1980
Holywell: *Clogher Record*, Vol. II, No. 1, 1957
Kinawley: *Clogher Record*, Vol. I, No. 4 1956
Monea: *The Parish of Devenish*, W. B. Steele, 1937
Templenafrin: *Clogher Record*, Vol. II, No. 1, 1957
Tullymageeran: *Clogher Record*, Vol. II, No. 3, 1959

Irish World (26 Market Square, Dungannon, Co. Tyrone, BT70 1AB) have
transcribed and computerised the inscriptions of more than 300 graveyards in
the six counties of Northern Ireland, principally in the four western counties of
Armagh, Derry, Fermanagh and Tyrone.

Placenames

Townland maps, Londonderry Inner City Trust

CO. GALWAY

Census returns and substitutes

1640	Irish Papist Proprietors, Galway Town. In Hardiman (see 'Local History' below), Appendix 7
1641	Book of Survey and Distribution NL MS. 969
1657	English Protestant Proprietors, Galway town. In Hardiman (see 'Local History' below)
1727	A Galway election list, JGHAS 1976
1749	Parishes of Ahascra, Athleague, Ballynakill, Drimatemple, Dunamon, Kilbegnet, Killian, Killosolan. NA 1A 36 1
1791	Survey of Loughrea town (occupiers). JGHAS,Vol. 23 No. 3
1794	Catholic Freemen of Galway town, JGHAS Vol. 9, No. 1
1798	List of those who suffered loss in 1798 Rebellion. NL JLB 94107
1806–10	Catholic householders, Killalaghten. In the Catholic parish registers of Killalaghten. NL Pos. 2431
1820s/30s	Tithe Book
1821	Parishes of Aran, Athenry, Kilcomeen, Kiltallagh, Killimore, Kilconickny, Kilreekill. National Archives. Also Loughrea (fragments) GO Ms 622, 53 ff.
1827	Protestants in Aughrim parish. NA M 5359
1829–58	Rentals of the estate of Sir George Shee, in and around Dunmore; National Archives, M.3105–3120.
1834	List of parishioners, Kinvara and Killina; NL Pos 2442.
1836	Freeholders, Co. Galway; *The Galway Advertiser*, March 1836.
1837	Valuation of towns returning M.P.s (occupants and property values): Galway. *Parliamentary Papers*, 1837, Reports from Committees, Vol II (i), Appendix G
1841	Loughrea census fragments; National Archives. M 1502 & GO MS. 622, 53 ff.
1848–52	Ahascra assisted passages, *Anecta Hibernica*, Vol 22, 1960
1850–59	Emigrants to Australia and the US from the parish of Kilcreast, with some from the parishes of Killigolen, Killinane, Killora, Rilthomas and Isserkelly, GO MS. 622
1851	Loughrea census fragments; National Archives, M 150
1855	Griffith's Valuation
1901	Census
1911	Census

Local history

Berry, J. F. *The Story of St Nicholas' Church, Galway*, 1912. Ir 7265 b 5
Cooney, D. L. *Methodism in Galway*, 1978, Ir. 200 p 14

D'Alton, E. *History of the Arch-diocese of Tuam*, Dublin 1928, Ir. 27412 d 1
Egan, Patrick K. *The parish of Ballinasloe its history from the earliest times to the present day*, Dublin, 1960
Fahey, J., *The History and Antiquities of the Diocese of Kilmacduagh*, Dublin, 1893
Goaley, M., *History of Annaghdown*, Ir. 274 p 31
Hardiman, James, *History of the town county of Galway . . . to 1820*, Galway, 1958, I 94124 h 1
Hayes-McCoy, G. A., *Index to 'The Compossicion Booke of Connoght, 1585'*, Irish Manuscripts Commission, Dublin, 1945
Irish Countrywomen's Association, *Portrait of a Parish: Ballynakill, Connemara*
Kavanagh, M., *A Bibliography of the Co. Galway*, 1965. Ir. RR 01524
Knox, H. T., *Notes on the Early History of the Diocese of Tuam Killala and Achony*, Dublin, 1904
MacLochlainn, T., *A Historical Survey of the Parish of Ahascra, Caltra & Castleblakeney*, 1979. Ir. 9141 p 79
MacLochlainn, T., *The Parish of Aughrim & Kilconnell*, 1980, Ir. 94124 m 4
MacLochlainn, T., *The Parish of Lawrencetown & Kiltormer*, 1981, Ir. 94124 m 5
Naughton, M., *The History of St Francis' Parish, Galway*, 1984, Ir. 27412 n 1
O'Neill, T. P., *The Tribes & Other Galway Families, 1484–1984*, Ir. 927, p 5
O'Sullivan, M. D., *Old Galway: the history of a Norman colony in Ireland*, Cambridge, 1942, Ir 94124 o 4
Robinson, Tim, *Connemara*, Roundstone, 1990.

Local journals

Journal of the Galway Historical and Archaeological Society. Ir. 794105 g 1

Directories

1820   J. Pigot, *Commercial Directory of Ireland*
1824   Pigot & Co., *City of Dublin and Hibernian Provincial Directory*, NL Ir 9141 p 75
1846   Slater's *National Commercial Directory of Ireland*
1856   Slater's *Royal National Commercial Directory of Ireland*
1870   Slater's *Directory of Ireland*
1881   Slater's *Royal National Commercial Directory of Ireland*
1894   Slater's *Royal Commercial Director of Ireland*

Gravestone inscriptions

Claregalway: IGRS Collection, 172, GO
Clontuskert: IGRS Collection, GO
Cregg: IGRS Collection, 70, GO

Drumacoo: IGRS Collection, GO
Kilmacduagh: *The Irish Ancestor*, Vol. VII, No. 1, 1975
Tumnahulla: IGRS Collection, 2, GO

Estate records

LANDLORD

Bellew estate wages book, 1679–1775, NL MS. 9200.

Col John **Browne**: NL Pos. 940, Account of the sales of the estates of Col. John Browne in Counties Galway and Mayo, compiled in 1778, giving names of major tenants and purchasers 1698–1704, and those occupying the estates in 1778, covering townlands in the civil parishes of Ballynakill, Cong, Kilcummin, Killannin, Omey, Ross.

Lord **Clanmorris**: NL MS. 3279, Estate rental, 1833, all tenants, covering townlands in the civil parish of Claregalway.

Dillon, Barons Clonbrock: NL MS. 19501, tenants' ledger 1801–06, indexed; NL MSS. 19585–19608 (24 vols), rentals and accounts, 1827–1840, all tenants; NL MSS. 22008, 22009, maps of the Co. Galway estates, with full valuation of all tenants' holdings; NL MSS. 19609–19616, rentals and accounts, 1840–44, all tenants; covering townlands in the civil parishes of Ahascragh, Aughrim, Fohanagh, Kilcoona, Killaan, Killallaghtan, Killosolan, Kilteskil.

Francis Blake **Knox**: NL MS. 3077, Rental, 1845–66, covering townlands in the civil parishes of Annaghdown, Kilmacduagh, Kilmoylan.

French family: NL MS. 4920, rent ledger, Monivea estate, 1767–77, major tenants only; NL MS. 4929, estate accounts and wages book, 1811/12, all tenants, with index; NL MS. 4930, accounts and wages book, 1830–33, Covering townlands in the civil parishes of Abbeyknockmoy, Athenry, Cargin, Claregalway, Monivea, Moylough, Oranmore.

Lieut Edward **Hodson**: NL MS. 2356, Rent rolls and tenants' accounts, 1797–1824, indexes. Covering townlands in the civil parish of Kiltormer.

Richard **St George** Mansergh St George: NL Pos. 5483, (a) Rental of Headford town (all tenants), (b) estate rentals (major tenants only), both 1775, covering townlands in the civil parishes of Cargin, Donaghpatrick, Kilcoona, Kilkilvery, Killursa.

George **Shee**: NA M3105–3120, yearly rentals of the estate in and around Dunmore, 1837–1859, all tenants, covering townlands in the civil parishes of Addergoole, Boyounagh, Clonbern, Dunmore.

Trench: NL MS. 2577, Estate rental, 1840–50. Covering townlands in the civil parishes of Ballymacaward, Kilbeacanty, Killaan, Killimordaly.

Theobold **Wolfe**: NL MS. 3876, estate maps with names of major tenants, 1760, indexed. Covering townlands in the civil parishes of Kilmallinoge and Tiranascragh.

(No Landlord Given): NL 21 g 76 (14) and 21 g 76 (26). Maps of Cloonfane
   and Carogher townlands in Dunmore parish, with tenants' names, mid-
   nineteenth century.
(No Landlord Given): NL MS. 4633, survey of occupiers, townlands of
   Ballinasoora, Streamsfort, Fortlands, Woodlands, parish of Killimordaly.
   1851.
(No Landlord Given): NL MSS. 2277–2280, Rentals, 1854–85, townlands of
   Ballyargadaun, Leitrim More, Kylebrack, Knockash, in the civil parishes
   of Leitrim and Kilteskil.

Placenames

Townland maps. Londonderry Inner City Trust

CO. KERRY

Census returns and substitutes

1586	Survey of the estates of the Earl of Desmond, recording lease-holders, NA M.5037
1641	Book of Survey and Distribution, NL MS. 970
1654	Civil Survey, Vol. IV, Dysert, Killury, Rathroe, I 6551 Dublin
1659	Pender's 'Census', Ir. 31041 c 4
1756–1827	'Biographical notices from Cork and Kerry newspapers, arranged alphabetically', NL MSS. 19,172–5
1799	Petition of 300 prominent Catholics of Co. Kerry, *The Dublin Evening Post*, 9 June 1799
1821	Some extracts, Tralee and Annagh, Thrift Abstracts, National Archives
1821	Parish of Kilcummin. Royal Irish Academy, McSwiney papers, parcel f, no. 3
1820s/30s	Tithe Books
1834–35	Householders, parishes of Dunquin, Dunurlin, Ferriter, Killem-lagh, Kilmalkedar, Kilquane, Marhin, Prior, JKAHS, 1974–75
1835	Tralee Voters, JKAHS, No. 19, 1986
1847–51	Assisted passages, Castlemaine estate, Kiltallagh parish, *Analecta Hibernica*, No. 22, 1960

1852   Griffith's Valuation
1901   Census, indexed in Jeremiah King's *County Kerry, Past and Present*,
          1931, NL I 94146
1911   Census

Local history

Allman, J., *Causeway, location, lore and legend*, Naas, 1983
Harrington, T. J., *Discovering Kerry*, Dublin, 1976
Brady, W. Maziere, *The McGellycuddy Papers*, London, 1867
Casey, A. (ed.), *O'Kief, Coshe Mang etc.* Ir. 94145 c 12
Cusack M. F., *History of the kingdom of Kerry*, London, 1871
Denny, H., *A Handbook of Co. Kerry Family History etc.*, 1923, Ir. 9291 d 1
Donovan, T. M., *A Popular History of East Kerry*, 1931
Finuge Heritage Society, *A span across time: Finuge, a folk history*
Hickson, Mary, *Selections from Old Kerry Records, Historical and Genealogical*,
          London, 1872–74
Keane, L., *Knocknagoshel: then and now*, Kerry County Library, 1985
King, J., *County Kerry, Past and Present*, 1931 I 94146
Lansdowne, H., *Glanarought and the Petty-Fitzmaurices*, 1937, Ir. 94146 l 1
McLysaght, E., *The Kenmare Manuscripts*, Dublin, 1942
McMoran, R., *Tralee, a short history and guide to Tralee and environs*, 1980
MacSwiney Papers, Royal Irish Academy. Historical notes and will abstracts,
          mainly from Counties Cork and Kerry
Mould, D. C. Pochin, *Valentia: portrait of an island*, Dublin, 1978
O'Connor, T., *Ardfert in Times Past*, Tralee, 1990
Reedy, Rev. Donal A., *The Diocese of Kerry*, Killarney
Smith, Charles, *The Ancient and Present State of the County of Kerry*, Dublin, 1756
Windele MSS. Information on Cork and Kerry families, including Cop-
          pinger, Cotter, Crosbie, O'Donovan, O'Keeffe, McCarthy, Sarsfield and
          others. NL Pos. 5479. See also Casey, A. (ed.), *O'Kief, Coshe Mang etc.* (NL
          Ir. 94145 c 12), Vol. 7

Local journals

Journal of the Kerry Archaeological Historical Society, Ir. 794105 k 1
Kerry Archaeological Magazine (1908–20), reference as above
Kenmare Literary and Historical Society Journal

Directories

1824   Pigot and Co., *City of Dublin and Hibernian Provincial Directory*, NL Ir.
          9141 p 75

1846   Slater's *National Commercial Directory of Ireland*
1856   Slater's *Royal National Commercial Directory of Ireland*
1870   Slater's *Directory of Ireland*
1881   Slater's *Royal National Commercial Directory of Ireland*
1886   Francis Guy, *Postal Directory of Munster*, NL Ir. 91414 g 8
1893   Francis Guy, *Directory of Munster*
1894   Slater's *Royal Commercial Directory of Ireland*

Gravestone inscriptions

Aghadoe: *O'Kief Coshe Mang etc.*, Vol. 6
Aghavallin (C. of I.): Kerry Genealogical Society (see below)
Aglish: *O'Kief, Coshe Mang etc.*, Vol. 6
Ardfert: *O'Kief, Coshe Mang etc.*, Vol. 8
Ballymacelligot: *O'Kief, Coshe Mang etc.*, Vol. 8
Caherciveen (Killevanoge): IGRS Collection, 57, GO
Caherciveen (Marian Place): IGRS Collection, 5, GO
Castleisland: *O'Kief, Coshe Mang etc.*, Vol. 6
Clogherbrien: *O'Kief, Coshe Mang etc.*, Vol. 8
Currans: *O'Kief, Coshe Mang etc.*, Vol. 6
Duagh: Finuge Heritage Society (see below)
Dysert: *O'Kief, Coshe Mang etc.*, Vol. 6
Finuge: Finuge Heritage Society (see below)
Galey: Finuge Heritage Society (see below)
Kilcummin: *O'Kief, Coshe Mang etc.*, Vol. 6
Killarney and Muckross Abbey: *O'Kief, Coshe Mang etc.*, Vol. 6
Kilnanare: *O'Kief, Coshe Mang etc.*, Vol. 6
Killeentierna: *O'Kief, Coshe Mang etc.*, Vol. 6
Killorglin: *O'Kief, Coshe Mang etc.*, Vol. 8
Lislaughtin Abbey (Aghavallin): Kerry Genealogical Society (see below)
Murher: Kerry Genealogical Society (see below)
Nohoval: *O'Kief, Coshe Mang etc.*, Vol. 8
O'Brennan: *O'Kief, Coshe Mang etc.*, Vol. 8
Raheenyhooig: (Dingle) IGRS Collection, 49, GO
Rathmore: *O'Kief, Coshe Mang etc.*, Vol. 6
Tralee: *O'Kief, Coshe Mang etc.*, Vol. 8
Finuge Heritage Society: Teach Siamsa, Finuge House, Co. Kerry
Kerry Genealogical Society, 119/120 Rock St, Tralee, Co. Kerry

Estate records

LANDLORD
Browne, Earls of Kenmare: assorted rentals, maps and estate accounts for
    areas around Kenmare and in the barony of Dunekerron, from 1620 to

1864 in McLysaght, E., *The Kenmare Manuscripts*, Dublin, 1942. See also *O'Kief, Coshe Mang etc*, Vols 6, 7, 9.

The Orpen estates: G. Lyne, 'Land Tenure in Tuosist and Kenmare', [1696–1775], *Kerry Arch. and Hist. Soc. Jnl*, 1976/78/79.

Thomas Sandes. Rental of the estate, 1792–1828, covering parts of the parishes of Aghavallin, Kinaughtin, Murher, NL MS. 1792.

Placenames

Townland Maps, Londonderry Inner City Trust

CO. KILDARE

Census returns and substitutes

1641	Book of Survey and Distribution. NL MS. 971. Also JKAS, Vol. X, 1922–8
1654	Civil Survey, Vol. VIII. I 6551 Dublin
1659	Pender's 'Census', Ir. 31041 c 4
1663	Hearth Money Roll (partial), JKAS, Vol. 10, No. 5, Vol. 11, No. 1
1775–1835	*Schools of Kildare and Leighlin*, Brennan, Ir. 37094135 b 4
1798	List of those who suffered loss in 1798 Rebellion. NL JLB 94107
1820s/30s	Tithe Books
1831	Kilcullen, Protestant returns. Nineteenth century census returns, National Archives
1837	Registered Voters, NL MS. 1398
1840	Castledermot and Moone, NL Pos. 3511
1851	Griffith's Valuation
1901	Census
1911	Census

Local history

Andrews J. H., *Irish Historic Towns Atlas: Kildare*, Dublin, Royal Irish Academy, 1986

Carville, Geraldine, *Monasterevin, Valley of Roses*, Moore Abbey, 1989

Comerford, Erv. M., *Collections relating to Kildare and Leighlin*, 1883

Costello, Con, *Looking Back, Aspects of History, Co. Kildare*, Naas, 1988
Costello, Con, *Kildare: Saints, Soldiers and Horses*, Naas, 1991
Doohan, Tony, *A History of Cellbridge*, n.d.
Dunlop, Robert, *Waters under the Bridge*, Brannockstown, 1988
Leadbeater, Mary, *The Annals of Ballitore*, London, 1862, Ir. 92 1 8
Kavanagh, M. V., *A Contribution towards a Bibliography of the Co. Kildare*, 1977, Ir.
    94135 k 1
Mac Suibhne, Peadar, *Rathangan*, 1975
Mulhall, Mary, *A History of Lucan*, Lucan, 1991
Naas Local History Group, *Nas na Riogh: . . . an illustrated history of Naas*, Naas,
    1990
Nelson, Gerald, *A History of Leixlip*, Kildare Co. Library, 1990
O Conchubhair, Seamus, *A History of Kilcock and Newtown*, 1987
O Muineog, Micheal, *Kilcock GAA, A History*, 1989
O'Sullivan, Peter, *Newcastle Lyons, A Parish of the Pale*, Dublin, Geography
    Publications, 1986
Paterson, J. (ed.), *Diocese of Meath and Kildare: an historical guide*, 1981. Ir. 941 p 75
Raymond, B., *The Story of Kilkenny, Kildare, Offaly and Leix*, 1931 I 9141 p 1
Reid, J. N. S., *Church of St Michael & All Angels, Clane*, 1983
'Some Authorities for Kildare County History', *Kildare Arch. Soc. Jnl*, No. 10,
    1922–28, 155–60

Local journals

Journal of the Co. Kildare Archaeological Society, Ir. 794106 k 2

Directories

1788   Richard Lucas, *General Directory of the Kingdom of Ireland*, NL Pos. 3729
1824   Pigot Co., *City of Dublin and Hibernian Provincial Directory*, NL Ir. 9141 p
       75
1846   Slater's *National Commercial Directory of Ireland*
1856   Slater's *Royal National Commercial Directory of Ireland*
1870   Slater's *Directory of Ireland*
1881   Slater's *Royal National Commercial Directory of Ireland*
1894   Slater's *Royal Commercial Directory of Ireland*

Gravestone inscriptions

Athy: GO MS. 622, 89
Ballyshannon (Kilcullen): GO MS. 622, 108
Barberstown: *Kildare Arch. Soc. Jnl*, 1977/8
Castledermot (C. of I.): IGRS Collection, 71/2, GO
Castledermot Friary: IGRS Collection, 2, GO

Castledermot (R.C.): IGRS Collection, 5, GO
Dunmanogue: IGRS Collection, 21, GO
Fontstown: GO MS. 622, 148/9
Harristown: GO MS. 622, 126/7
Killeen Cormac: IGRS Collection, 58/55, GO
Kilteel: *Kildare Arch. Soc. Jnl*, 1981/82
Knockbane: IGRS Collection, 2, GO
Knockpatrick: IGRS Collection, 57, GO
Ladychapel: IGRS Collection, 145, GO
Mageny: GO MS. 622, 108
Taghadoe: IGRS Collection, 12, GO
Timolin: IGRS Collection, 33, GO

Placenames

Townland Maps, Londonderry Inner City Trust

CO. KILKENNY

Census returns and substitutes

1641	Book of Survey and Distribution NL MS. 975
1654	Civil Survey, Vol. VI, Kilkenny City I 6551 Dublin
1659	Pender's 'Census'. NL Ir. 31041 c 4
1664	Hearth Money Rolls, parishes of Agherney, Aghavillar, Bellaghtobin, Belline, Burnchurch, Callan, Castleinch, Clone, Coolaghmore, Coolcashin, Danganmore, Derrinahinch, Dunkitt, Earlstown, Eyverk, Fartagh, Inishnagg and Stonecarthy, Jerpoint, Kells, Kilbeacon and Killahy, Kilcolm, Kilferagh, Kilkredy, Killamery, Killaloe, Killree, Kilmoganny, Kiltackaholme, Knocktopher and Kilkerchill, Muckalee and Lismatigue, Outrath, Ratbach, Rathpatrick, Tullaghanbrogue, Tullaghmaine, Urlingford. *The Irish Genealogist*, 1974–75
1684–1769	Registers of Kilkenny College, NL Pos. 4545
1702	Partial lists, St Mary's and St Canice's parishes Kilkenny City. NA 1A 55 83
1715	Protestant males between 16 and 60 in St John's parish, Kilkenny City, NA 1A 55 83

1750–1844	Inistiogue emigrants in Newfoundland, *Kilkenny History and Society*, ed. Whelan and Nolan, 345–405
1775	Landowners, GO 443
1785–1879	Kilkenny city deeds, *Old Kilkenny Review*, Vol. 2, No. 4
1797	Chief Catholic inhabitants, Parishes of Graiguenamanagh and Knocktopher, *The Irish Ancestor*, 1978
1809–19	Freeholders. NL MS. 14181
1811–58	Registers and Accounts of St Kieran's College, NL Pos. 973
1821	Extracts from the 1821 census, parishes of Aglish, Clonmore, Fiddown, Kilmacow, Polerone, Rathkyran, Whitechurch. GO 684 (Walsh-Kelly notebooks), also *The Irish Genealogist*, Vol. 5, 1978
1821	Parishes of Aglish and Portnascully, *The Irish Ancestor*, 1976; Extracts from Pollrone parish, *The Irish Genealogist*, 1977
1820s/30s	Tithe Books
1831	Extracts from the 1831 census, parishes of Aglish, Clonmore, Kilmacow, Polerone, Rathkyran, Tybroghney, GO 684 (Walsh-Kelly notebooks)
1841	Extracts from the 1841 census, parishes of Aglish and Rathkyran, GO 684 (Walsh-Kelly notebooks)
1841	Townlands of Aglish and Portnahully, parish of Aglish, *The Irish Ancestor*, 1977
1849/50	Griffith's Valuation
1851	Parish of Aglish, *The Irish Ancestor*, 1977. Also GO 684 (Walsh-Kelly notebooks)
1850s	Castlecomer assisted passages. See Hayes catalogue.
1901	Census
1911	Census

Local history

Alsworth, W.J., *History of Thomastown and District*, 1953, NL JP, 1996
Brennan, T. A., *A History of the Brennans of Idaugh in Co. Kilkenny*, 1979, NL Ir. 9292 b 45
Burtchaell, G., *MPs for the County and City of Kilkenny 1295–1888*, Dublin, 1888
Carrigan, Rev. William, *The History and Antiquities of the Diocese of Ossory*, 4 vols, Dublin, 1905
Coleman. James, 'Bibliography of the counties Carlow, Kilkenny and Wicklow,' *Waterford and S–E of Ire. Arch. Soc. Jnl*, 11, 1907–8, 126–33
Egan, P. M., *Illustrated Guide to the City and County of Kilkenny*, Ir. 914139 e 2
Fitzmaurice, S. A., 'Castleharris', *Old Kilkenny Review*, 1979
Healy, William, *History and antiquities of Kilkenny county and city*, Kilkenny, 1893, NL Ir. 94139 h 1

Hogan, John, *Kilkenny, the Ancient City of Ossory*, Kilkenny, 1884

Hore, H. J., *The Social State of the Southern and Eastern Counties of Ireland in the Sixteenth Century*, 1870

Kenealy, M., 'The Parish of Aharney and the Marum Family', *Old Kilkenny Review*, 1976

Kilkenny Corporation, *Catalogue of Deeds*, NL Ir. 94139 k 2

Nolan, W., *Fassidinin: Land, Settlement and Society in South-East Ireland, 1600–1850*, 1979, NL Ir. 94139 n 1

Phelan, M., 'Callan Doctors', *Old Kilkenny Review*, 1980

Prim, J. G. A., 'Documents connected with the city of Kilkenny militia in the 17th and 18th centuries', *Kilkenny and S–E Ire. Arch. Soc. Jnl*, 1854–55, 231–74

Raymond, B., *The Story of Kilkenny, Kildare, Offaly and Leix*, 1931 NL I 9141 p 1

Whelan K. and Nolan, W. (ed.), *Kilkenny History and Society*, Dublin, 1990

Local journals

Journal of the Butler Society

Old Kilkenny Review, NL Ir. 94139 o 3

Kilkenny and South-East of Ireland Archaeological Society Journal, J 7914 (to 1890), NL Ir. 794105 r 1 (after 1890), indexed, as *The Journal of the Royal Society of Antiquaries of Ireland*, in three parts, 1849–89, 1881–1910, 1911–1930, Ir. 794105 r 1

Transactions of the Ossory Archaeological Society, NL Ir. 794105 o 1

Deenside

Directories

1788   Richard Lucas, *General Directory of the Kingdom of Ireland*, NL Pos. 3729

1820   J. Pigot, *Commercial Directory of Ireland*

1824   Pigot and Co., *City of Dublin and Hibernian Provincial Directory*, NL Ir. 9141 p 75

1839   T. Shearman, *New Commercial Directory for the Cities of Waterford and Kilkenny, Towns of Clonmel, Carrick-on-Suir, New Ross and Carlow*

1846   Slater's *National Commercial Directory of Ireland*

1856   Slater's *Royal National Commercial Directory of Ireland*

1870   Slater's *Directory of Ireland*

1881   Slater's *Royal National Commercial Directory of Ireland*

1884   George H. Bassett, *Kilkenny City and County Guide and Directory*

1894   Slater's *Royal Commercial Directory of Ireland*

Gravestone inscriptions

Ballygurrim: IGRS Collection, 16, GO
Ballyreddin: IGRS Collection, 7, GO
Ballytarsny: IGRS Collection, 24, GO
Beal Borr (Annamult): IGRS Collection, 7, GO
Ben Fada(Radestown): IGXS Collection, 27, GO
Cappagh (Inistioge): GO MS. 622, 173
Castle Inch: IGRS Collection, 30, GO
Church Clara: IGRS Collection, 56, GO
Clashacrow: IGRS Collection, 10, GO
Clonmore: IGRS Collection, 30, GO
Danesfort: GO MS. 622, 147
Dunkitt: IGRS Collection, 113, GO
Dunmore old (Bleach Rd): IGRS Collection, 33, GO
Dysert (Castlecomer): IGRS Collection, 13, GO
Freynestown (Liscoffin): IGRS Collection, 18, GO
Freshford old: IGRS Collection, 148, GO
Gaulskill old: IGRS Collection, 39, GO
Gaulskill C. of I.: IGRS Collection, 11, GO
Grove (Tullaghanbrogue): IGRS Collection, 119, GO
Johnswell: IGRS Collection, 197, GO
Kells Priory: IGRS Collection, 16, GO
Kells (St Kieran's): IGRS Collection, 76, GO
Kilbeacon: IGRS Collection, 42, GO
Kilbride: IGRS Collection, 13, GO
Kilcolumb: IGRS Collection, 53, GO
Kilcready: IGRS Collection, 35, GO
Kilcurl: IGRS Collection, 5, GO
Kilfera (with Sheestown): IGRS Collection, 3, GO
Kilkenny (St Canice's Cathedral): *The History (. . .) of St Canice, Kilkenny*,
    James Graves and J. G. A. Prim, 1857
St Canice's Graveyard: IGRS Collection, 502, GO
St Canice's R.C.: IGRS Collection, 45, GO
St John's Priory: IGRS Collection, 116, GO
St John's (Dublin Rd): IGRS Collection, 611, GO
St Mary's, Kilkenny: *Old Kilkenny Review*, 1979/80/81
St Maul's, Green Bridge: IGRS Collection, 18, GO
St Patrick's Graveyard: IGRS Collection, 280, GO
Killahy: IGRS Collection, 13, GO
Killaspy: IGRS Collection, 3, GO
Kilmacow: IGRS Collection, 119, GO
Kilmodimoge (Bullock Hill): IGRS Collection, 6, GO

Kilree: IGRS Collection, 73, GO
Kilvinoge: IGRS Collection, 10, GO
Knocktoper: *Kilkenny Gravestone Inscriptions: 1, Knocktopher*, Kilkenny Archaeological
    Society, 1988
Maddoxtown: IGRS Collection, 60, GO
Muckalee: IGRS Collection, 23, GO
Outrath: IGRS Collection, 86, GO
Portnascully: IGRS Collection, 52, GO
Rathcoole: IGRS Collection, 22, GO
Sheepstown: IGRS Collection, 4, GO
Sheestown: See Kilfera
Stonecarty: IGRS Collection, 22, GO
Templemartin: IGRS Collection, 51, GO
Thornback: IGRS Collection, 137, GO
Three Castles: IGRS Collection, 66, GO
Tubrid Old: IGRS Collection, 3, GO
Tullamaine: IGRS Collection, 34, GO
Ullid: IGRS Collection, 15, GO

Placenames

O'Kelly, O., *The Placenames of the Co. Kilkenny*, 1985, Ir. 92942 o 15

CO. LAOIS

Census returns and substitutes

1641	Book of Survey and Distribution, NL MS. 972
1659	Pender's 'Census', NL Ir. 31041 c 4
1664	Hearth Money Roll, parishes of Killenny and Moyanna. National Archives, Thrift Abstracts 3737
1668–69	Hearth Money Roll baronies of Maryborough and Upper Ossory. National Archives, Thrift Abstracts 3738
1758–75	Freeholders, *Co. Kildare Archaeological Society Journal*, Vol VIII, 309–27
1766	Parish of Lea, RCB Library
1821	Mountrath. Nineteenth century census returns, National Archives

1820s/30s	Tithe Books
1832, 1840	Owners and occupiers, Lea parish; NL MS. 4723/4
1844	Register of Arms, Baronies of Upper Ossory, Maryborough, Cullenagh, 433 names
1847	Voters' List, NL ILB 04 P 12
1851/2	Griffith's Valuation
1901	Census
1911	Census

Local history

Abbeyleix, 1953, Ir. 94137 s 1

Carrigan, Rev. William, *The History and Antiquities of the Diocese of Ossory*, 4 vols, Dublin, 1905

Ledwich, Edward A., *A Statistical Account of the Parish of Aghaboe*, 1796

Members of Parliament for Laois and Offaly, 1801–1918, 1983, Ir. 328 m 6

O'Byrne, D., *History of Queen's County*, 1856, Ir. 94137 o 2

O'Hanlon, John and O'Leary, Edward, *History of the Queen's County*, Dublin, 1907–14, Ir. 94137 o 3

O'Shea and Feehan, *Aspects of Local History*, 1977, Ir. 941 p 36

Paterson, J. (ed.), *Diocese of Meath and Kildare: an historical guide*, 1981, Ir. 941 p 75

Raymond, B., *The Story of Kilkenny Kildare, Offaly and Leix*, 1931, I 9141 p 1

Local journals

Laois Heritage: bulletin of the Laois Heritage Society, Ir. 9413705 l 1

Directories

1788	Richard Lucas, *General Directory of the Kingdom of Ireland*, NL Pos. 3729
1824	Pigot and Co., *City of Dublin and Hibernian Provincial Directory*, NL Ir. 9141 p 75
1846	Slater's *National Commercial Directory of Ireland*
1856	Slater's *Royal National Commercial Directory of Ireland*
1870	Slater's *Directory of Ireland*
1881	Slater's *Royal National Commercial Directory of Ireland*
1894	Slater's *Royal Commercial Directory of Ireland*

CO. LEITRIM

Census returns and substitutes

1600–1868   Roll of all the gentlemen . . ., NL P 2179
1659   Pender's 'Census', NL Ir. 31041 c 4
1791   Freeholders, GO 665
1792   Protestants in the barony of Mohill, *The Irish Ancestor*, Vol. 16
            No. 1
1807   Freeholders, Mohill barony, NL MS. 9628
1820   Freeholders, NL MS. 3830
1821   Parish of Carrigallen, NL Pos. 4646
1820s/30s   Tithe Books
1851   Catholic Householders, Mohill Parish. Leitrim Heritage Centre,
            Ballinamore, Co. Leitrim
1852   Voters in Oughteragh, Cloonclare, Cloonlogher, *Breifne*, Vol. 5,
            No. 20
1856   Griffith's Valuation
1861   Catholic householders, Mohill parish. Leitrim Heritage Centre,
            Ballinamore, Co. Leitrim
1901   Census
1911   Census

Local history

Clancy and Forde, *Ballinalera Parish, Co. Leitrim: aspects of its history and traditions*,
    1980, NL Ir. 94121 c 2
Freeman,T.W., *The Town and District of Carrick-on-Shannon*, 1949, NL P. 1916
Hayes-McCoy, G. A., *Index to 'The Compossicion Books of Connoght, 1585'*, Irish
    Manuscripts Commission, Dublin, 1945
Kiltubbrid, 1984, NL Ir. 397 k 4
Logan, P. L., *Outeragh, My Native Parish*,1963, NL Ir. 941 p 74
'Sources of Information on the Antiquities and history of Cavan and Leitrim:
    Suggestions', *Breifny* 1920–22
MacNamee, James J., *History of the Diocese of Ardagh*, Dublin, 1954
Monahan, Rev. J., *Records Relating to the Diocese of Ardagh and Clonmacnoise*, 1886
O'Connell, Philip, *The Diocese of Kilmore: its History and Antiquities*, Dublin, 1937

Local journals

Ardagh and Clonmacnoise Historical Society Journal (1926–51), NL Ir. 794105
Breifne, Ir. 94119 b 2

Breifny Antiquarian Society Journal (1920–33), Ir. 794106 b 1
The Drumlin: a Journal of Cavan, Leitrim and Monaghan, Ir. 05 d 34

Gravestone inscriptions

Leitrim Heritage Centre, Ballinamore, Co. Leitrim, holds indexed transcripts
of gravestone inscriptions covering the entire county, comprising 85 Catholic churches and graveyards, 27 Church of Ireland, and 1 Presbyterian.

Directories

1824   Pigot and Co., *City of Dublin and Hibernian Provincial Directory*, NL Ir.
        9141 p 75
1846   Slater's *National Commercial Directory of Ireland*
1856   Slater's *Royal National Commercial Directory of Ireland*
1870   Slater's *Directory of Ireland*
1881   Slater's *Royal National Commercial Directory of Ireland*
1894   Slater's *Royal Commercial Directory of Ireland*

Estate records

LANDLORD

Earl of **Bessborough**: NA M3374; rental, 1805, major tenants only; NA
M3370, valuation of estate, 1813, all tenants; NA M3383, tenants with
leases, 1813; NA M3384, rental, 1813, all tenants; covering townlands in
the civil parishes of Fenagh and Kiltubbrid.

Clements: NL MSS. 3816–3827, rentals of the Woodford estate, 1812–1828,
all tenants, covering townlands in the civil parish of Carrigallen; NL
MSS. 12805–7, 3828, rental, 1812–1824 (with gaps) of Bohey townland in
Cloone civil parish.

Sir Humphrey **Crofton**: NL MS. 4531. Rental, March 1833, with tenants'
names in alphabetical order, covering townlands in the civil parishes of
Cloone, Kiltoghert, Mohill, Oughteragh.

William **Johnson**: NL MS. 9465, rental of the Drumkeeran estate, 1845–56,
all tenants, covering townlands in the civil parish of Inishmagrath.

King: NL MS. 4170, Rent roll and estate accounts, 1801–1818, major tenants
only, covering townlands in the civil parishes of Fenagh and Kiltubbrid.

Earl of **Leitrim**: NL MS. 12787; rental and accounts, 1837–42, all tenants;
NL MSS. 5728–33; rentals 1838–65, all tenants; NL MSS. 5803–5,
rentals, 1842–55, all tenants; NL MSS. 12810–12; rentals 1844–8, all
tenants; NL MSS. 179, 180; rentals 1844 and 1854, all tenants; covering
townlands in the civil parishes of Carrigallen, Cloone, Clooneclare,
Inishmagrath, Killasnet, Kiltoghert, Mohill.

Viscount **Necomen**: NA M2797, rental, 1822, mainly larger tenants, covering townlands in the civil parish of Drumlease.

Francis **O'Beirne**: NL MS. 8647 (14), rental, 1850, mainly large tenants, covering townlands in the civil parishes of Cloone, Drumlease, Kiltoghert.

Charles Manners **St George**: NL MSS. 4001–22, annual accounts and rentals. Covering townlands in the civil parish of Kiltoghert.

Nicholas Loftus **Tottenham**: NL MS. 9837, 26 maps, with major tenants only, covering townlands in the civil parishes of Clooneclare, Inishmagrath, Rossinver.

Ponsonby **Tottenham**: NL MS. 10162, printed rental, 1802, mainly larger tenants, covering townlands in the civil parishes of Clooneclare and Rossinver

Owen **Wynne**: NL MSS. 5780–2, rentals and expense books, 1737–68, major tenants only; NL MSS. 5830–31, rent ledgers 173853, 1768–73, major tenants only, indexed, NL MSS. 3311–31, a rental and two rent ledgers, yearly from 1798 to 1825, with all tenants; covering townlands in the civil parishes of Clooneclare, Cloonlogher, Killanummery, Killasnet, Rossinver.

Placenames

Townland maps, Londonderry Inner City Trust

CO. LIMERICK

Census returns and substitutes

1569	Freeholders, NL Pos. 1700
1570	Freeholders and Gentlemen in Co. Limerick, JNMAHS, 1964
1586	Survey of leaseholders on the Desmond estates, NA M.5037
1641	Book of Survey and Distribution, NL MS. 973
1654–56	Civil Survey, Vol. IV, NL I 6551 Dublin
1660	Rental of lands in Limerick City and County, NL MS. 9091
1664	Askeaton Hearth Money Rolls, *North Munster Archaeological and Historical Society Journal*, 1965
1673	Part of Limerick city (estates of the earls of Roscommon and Orrery) with occupiers' names and valuation, NL Pos. 792

1746–1836	Freemen, Limerick City, *North Munster Archaeological and Historical Society Journal*, 1944/5, NL Pos. 5526
1761	Limerick City Freeholders, NL MS. 16092; County freeholders, NL MS. 16093
1766	Abington, Cahircomey, Cahirelly, Carrigparson, Clonkeen, Kilkellane, Tuogh. NA 1A 46 49; Protestants in the parishes of Croagh, Kilscannel, Nantinan and Rathkeale, *The Irish Ancestor*, 1977
1776	Freeholders entitled to vote, NA M 1321–2
1776	Voters' List, NA M.4878
1793	'Two Lists of People Resident in the Area of Newcastle in 1793 and 1821', *The Irish Ancestor*, Vol. 16, No. 1 (1984)
1798	Rebel Prisoners in Limerick Jail, JNMAHS, Vol. 10 (1), 1966
1813	Chief inhabitants of the parishes of St Mary's and St John's, Limerick, *The Irish Ancestor*, Vol. 17 No. 2. (1985)
1816–28	Freeholders, GO 623
1821	Fragments for Kilfinane District, JNMAHS, 1975
1821	Some extracts. Thrift Abstracts, National Archives.
1821	'Two Lists of People Resident in the Area of Newcastle in 1793 and 1821', *The Irish Ancestor*, Vol. 16, No. 1 (1984)
1820s/30s	Tithe Books
1829	Limerick Freeholders, GO 623
1835	Parish of Templebredin, JNMAHS, 1975
1835–39	List of inhabitants of Limerick taking water (Waterworks accounts) NL Pos. 3451
1840	Freeholders, Barony of Coshlea, NL MS. 9452
1846	Survey of Households in connection with famine relief, Loughill, Foynes, Shanagolden areas, NL MS. 582
1851	Some extracts. Thrift Abstracts, National Archives
1851/2	Griffith's Valuation. Alphabetical index to householders, on microfiche, National Archives
1870	Rate Book for Clanwilliam barony, NA M 2434
1901	Census
1911	Census

Local history

Countess of Dunraven, *Memorials of Adare*, Oxford, 1865
Cromwellian Settlement of Co. Limerick, *Limerick Field Journal*, Vols 1–8, 1897–1908, NL Ir. 794205 l 1
Dowd, Rev. James, *Limerick and its Sieges*, Limerick, 1896
Dowd, Rev. James, *St Mary's Cathedral Limerick*, 1936
Dwyer, Philip, *The Diocese of Killaloe*, Dublin, 1878
Ferrar, John, *A History Of the City of Limerick*, Limerick, 1767

Ferrar, John, *The History of Limerick, Ecclesiastical, Civil and Military from the earliest records to the year 1787*, Limerick, 1787

Fitzgerald, P. and McGregor, J. J., *The history, topography and antiquities of the city and county of Limerick*, Dublin, 1826–27

Hamilton, G. F., *Records of Ballingarry*, Limerick, 1930, NL Ir. 94144 h 2

Hayes, R., *The German Colony in County Limerick*, Reprint, from *The North Munster Antiquarian Soc. Journal*, Limerick, 1937

Lee, Rev. Dr C., 'Statistics from Knockainy and Patrickswell parishes, 1819–1940'. *Journal of the Cork Historical and Archaeological Society*, Vol. 47, No. 165

Lenihan, Maurice, *Limerick, its history and antiquities*, Dublin 1866, NL Ir. 94144 l 1

MacCaffrey, James, *The Black Book of Limerick*, 1907

Meredyth, Francis, *Descriptive and Historic Guide, St Mary's Cathedral*, Limerick, 1887

Nash, Roisin, *A bibliography of Limerick*, Limerick, 1962

Seymour, St John D., *The Diocese of Emly*, Dublin, 1913

Westropp Manuscripts, Royal Irish Academy. Will abstracts mainly for Counties Clare and Limerick

White, Rev. P., *History of Clare and the Dalcassian Clans of Tipperary, Limerick and Galway*, Dublin, 1893

Local journals

North Munster Antiquarian Society Journal, NL Ir. 794105 n 1 (Index 1897–1919, Ir. 7941 n 1)

Old Limerick Journal, NL Ir. 94144 o 2

Limerick Field Journal, NL Ir. 794205 l 1

Lough Gur Historical Society Journal (from 1985)

Directories

1769	John Ferrar, *Directory of Limerick*
1788	Richard Lucas, *General Directory of the Kingdom of Ireland*, NL Pos. 3729
1809	Holden's *Triennial Directory*
1820	J. Pigot, *Commercial Directory of Ireland*
1824	Pigot and Co., *City of Dublin and Hibernian Provincial Directory*, NL Ir. 9141 p 75
1846	Slater's *National Commercial Directory of Ireland*
1856	Slater's *Royal National Commercial Directory of Ireland*
1866	George H. Bassett, *Directory of the City and County of Limerick and of the principal Towns in Counties Tipperary and Clare*, NL Ir. 914144 b 5
1870	Slater's *Directory of Ireland*
1879	George H. Bassett, *Limerick Directory*

1881   Slater's *Royal National Commercial Directory of Ireland*
1886   Francis Guy, *Postal Directory of Munster*, NL Ir. 91414 g 8
1893   Francis Guy, *Postal Directory of Munster*
1894   Slater's *Royal Commercial Directory of Ireland*

Gravestone inscriptions

Ardcanny: *The Irish Ancestor*, Vol. IX, No. 1, 1977
Ardpatrick: *Reflections (. . .) on Ardpatrick*, John Fleming, 1979
Askeaton: IGRS Collection, GO
Athlacca: *Dromin, Athlacca*, Mainchin Seoighe, 1978
Ballingarry: *Records of Ballingarry*, G. F. Hamilton, 1930
Bruree: *Bru Ri: the History of the Bruree District*, Mainchin Seoighe, 1973
Dromin: *Dromin, Athlacca*, Mainchin Seoighe, 1978
Grange: *The Irish Ancestor*, Vol. XII, 1980
Kilbehenny: *The Irish Genealogist*, Vol II, No. 11, 1954
Knockainey (Lough Gur): *Lough Gur Historical Society Journal*, No. 1 1985
Knockainey (Patrickswell): *Lough Gur Historical Society Journal*, No. 2 1986
Nantinan: *The Irish Ancestor*, Vol. XII, 1980
Plassey: GO MS. 622, 85
Rathkeale: *The Irish Ancestor*, Vol. XIV, No. 2, 1982
St Mary's Cathedral: *The Monuments of St Mary's*, M. J. Talbot, 1976
Stradbally: IGRS Collection, GO
Tankardstown: *Bru Ri: the History of the Bruree District*, Mainchin Seoighe, 1973

Estate records

'Description of the estate of John Sadleir in Limerick and Tipperary', JP 3439.

Placenames

Townland Maps, Londonderry Inner City Trust

CO. LONGFORD

Census returns and substitutes

1641   Book of Survey and Distribution, NL MS. 965

1659   Pender's 'Census', Ir. 31041 c 4

1729   Presbyterian exodus from Co. Longford, *Breifny*, 1977/8

1731   Protestants in the parish of Shrule, RCB Library

1747–1806 Freeholders, Registration book, NA M 2745

1766   Protestants in the parishes of Abbeylara and Russough, RCB Library, GO 537

*c.*1790   Freeholders NA M 2486–8, NL Pos. 1897

1795–1862 Charlton Marriage Certificates, NA 1A–42–163/4, indexed in Accessions, Vol. 37

1796   Spinning-Wheel Premium Lists, microfiche index in National Archives, comprising, in the case of Co. Longford, over 3,000 names

1800–1835 Freeholders, GO 444

1820s/30s Tithe Books

1828–36   Freeholders certificates, NA M.2781

1834   Granard, full census, in Catholic registers, NL Pos. 4237

1838   Householders, Mullinalaghta parish (Scrabby and Columbkill), *Teathbha*, Vol. 1, No. 3, 1973

1854   Griffith's Valuation

1901   Census, indexed in Leahy, David, *Co. Longford and its People*, Dublin, Flyleaf Press, 1990

1911   Census

Local history

Brady, G., *In Search of Longford Roots*, Offaly Historical Society, 1987, Ir. 94136 t 1

Butler, H. T. and H. E., *The Black Book of Edgeworthstown, 1585–1817*, 1927

Cobbe, D., *75 Years of the Longford Leader*, 1972, NL ILB 07

Devaney, O., *Killoe: History of a Co. Longford Parish*, 1981, Ir. 9413 d 1

Farrell, James P., *History of the county of Longford*, Dublin, 1891, Ir. 94131 f 2

Healy, John, *History of the Diocese of Meath*, 2 vols, Dublin, 1908

Leahy, David, *Co. Longford and its People*, Dublin, Flyleaf Press, 1990

Murtagh, H., *Irish Midland Studies*, 1980, Ir. 941 m 58

Stafford, R. W., *St Patrick's Church of Ireland, Granard: Notes of Genealogical and Historical Interest*, 1983, Ir. 914131 s 3

Local journals

Ardagh and Clonmacnoise Historical Society Journal (1926–51), Ir. 794105

Teathbha (Journal of the Longford Historical Society), Ir. 94131 t 1

Directories

1824 Pigot and Co., *City of Dublin and Hibernian Provincial Directory*, NL Ir. 9141 p 75
1846 Slater's *National Commercial Directory of Ireland*
1856 Slater's *Royal National Commercial Directory of Ireland*
1870 Slater's *Directory of Ireland*
1881 Slater's *Royal National Commercial Directory of Ireland*
1894 Slater's *Royal Commercial Directory of Ireland*

Estate records

Adair estate, Clonbroney parish, 1738–67, NL MS. 3859.
Aldborough estate rentals, 1846, NA M.2971.
Newcomen estates: maps of estates to be sold, 20 July 1827, NL Map Room.

Placenames

Townland Maps, Londonderry Inner City Trust
McGivney, J., *Place-names of the Co. Longford*, 1908, 92942

CO. LOUTH

Census returns and substitutes

1600 'Gentlemen of Co. Louth', JCLAS, Vol. 4, No. 4, 1919/20
1641 Book of Survey and Distribution, NL MS. 974
1659 Pender's 'Census', NL Ir. 31041 c 4
1663/4 Hearth Money Roll, JCLAS, Vol. 6, Nos 2 and 4; Vol. 7, No. 3
1666/7 Hearth Money Roll of Dunleer parish, *The Irish Genealogist*, 1969
1683 Louth brewers and retailers, JCLAS, Vol. 3, No. 3
1683 Drogheda merchants, JCLAS, Vol. 3, No. 3
1739–41 Corn census of Co. Louth, JCLAS, Vol. 11, No. 4, 254–86
1756 Commissions of Array, giving lists of Protestants who took the oath, NL Pos. 4011
1760 Ardee parish, *The Irish Genealogist*, 1961

1766	Ardee, Ballymakenny, Beaulieu, Carlingford, Charlestown, Clonkeehan, Darver, Drumiskin, Kildermock, Killeshiel, Louth, Mapestown, Phillipstown, Shanliss, Smarmore, Stickallen, Tallonstown, Termonfeckin. NA 1A 41 100; Creggan, NA 1A 46 49; also Nelson, *History of the Parish of Creggan* . . ., NL, Ir. 941 p 43
1782–92	Cess-payers, parishes of Cappagh, Drumcar, Dysert, Moylary, Monasterboice, JCLAS, Vol. 9, No. 1
1791	Landholders, Dromiskin parish, *History of Kilsaran* . . ., J. B. Leslie
1796	Spinning-Wheel Premium Lists, microfiche index in National Archives, comprising, in the case of Co. Louth, over 4,000 names
1798	Drogheda voters list, JCLAS, Vol. XX, 1984
1801	Tithe applotment, Stabannon and Roodstown parishes, *History of Kilsaran* . . ., J. B. Leslie
1802	Protestant parishioners of Carlingford, JCLAS, Vol. 16, No. 3
1802	Drogheda voters list, JCLAS, Vol. XX, 1984
1816	Grand Jurors, NL, Ir. 6551, Dundalk
1821	Freeholders, NL, Ir. 94132 1 3
1820s/30s	Tithe Books
1830–65	Methodist records, Newry Circuit, *Seanchas Ardmhacha*, Vol. 7, No. 2, 1977
1834	Tallonstown parish, JCLAS, Vol. 14
1837	Valuation of towns returning MPs (occupants and property values): Drogheda, Dundalk. *Parliamentary Papers*, 1837, Reports from Committees, Vol. II (i), Appendix G
1837	Marksmen (illiterate voters) in parliamentary boroughs: Drogheda, Dundalk. *Parliamentary Papers*, 1837, Reports from Committees, Vol. II (i), Appendix A
1852	Mosstown and Phillipstown, JCLAS, 1975
1852	Voting electors, NL MS. 1660
1854	Griffith's Valuation
1865	Parliamentary voters, P. 2491
1901	Census
1911	Census

Local history

Bernard, Nicholas (ed.), *The Whole Proceedings of the Siege of Drogheda* [&] *Londonderry*, Dublin, 1736

Conlon, L., *The Heritage of Collon*, 1984, NL, Ir. 94132 c 5

'Cromwellian and Restoration settlements in the parish of Dundalk', JCLAS, Vol. XIX, 1, 1977

D'Alton, John, *The history of Drogheda*, Dublin, 1844, Ir. 94132 d 1

D'Alton, John, *The history of Dundalk*, Dublin, 1864, NL, Ir. 94132 d 2

Duffner, P., *Drogheda: the Low Lane Church 1300–1979*, Ir. 94132 d 7
'Families at Mosstown and Phillipstown in 1852', JCLAS, Vol. XVIII, 3, 1975
Henderson's Post Office Directory of Meath and Louth, 1861
ICA, *A Local History Guide to Summerhill and Surrounding Areas*, NL, Ir. 94132 i 1
Keenan, Padraic, 'Clonallon Parish: its Annals and Antiquities', JCLAS, Vol.
    X
Kieron, J. S., *An Outline History of the Parish of St Mary's Abbey*, 1980, NL, Ir.
    91413 p 12
Leslie, J. B., *History of Kilsaran Union of Parishes*, 1908, NL, Ir. 94132 l 1
L'Estrange, G., *Notes and Jottings concerning the parish of Charlestown Union*, 1912,
    NL, Ir. 94132 l 2
'Methodist Baptismal Records of Co. Louth, 1829–1865', JCLAS, Vol.
    XVIII, 2, 1974
McCullen, J., *The Call of St Mary's*, 1984, NL, Ir. 27413 m 8
Murphy, Peter, *Together in Exile*, Nova Scotia, 1991 (Carlingford emigrants to
    St John's, New Brunswick)
Nelson, S., *History of the Parish of Creggan in Counties Armagh and Louth from 1611
    to 1840*, 1974, NL, Ir. 941 p 43
'Notes on the Volunteers, Militia and Yeomanry, and Orangemen of Co.
    Louth', JCLAS, Vol. XVIII, 4, 1976
'Old Title Deeds of Co. Louth, Dundalk, 1718–1856', JCLAS, Vol. XX, 1,
    1981
O'Neill, C. P., *History of Dromiskin*, 1984, NL, Ir. 94132 o 4
Paterson, J. (ed.), *Diocese of Meath and Kildare: an historical guide*, 1981, NL, Ir.
    941 p 75
Redmond, B., *The Story of Louth*, 1931, NL, Ir. 9141 p 1
Tempest, H. S., *Descriptive and Historical Guide to Dundalk and District*, 1916, NL,
    Ir. 94132 t 1
Witherow, Thomas, *The Boyne and the Aghrim*, 1879

Local journals

Clogher Record (Journal of the Clogher Diocesan Historical Society), NL, Ir. 94114 c 2
Co. Louth Archaeological and Historical Society Journal, NL, Ir. 794105 l 2
Journal of the Old Drogheda Society, NL, Ir. 94132 o 3

Directories

1820   J. Pigot, *Commercial Directory of Ireland*
1824   Pigot and Co., *City of Dublin and Hibernian Provincial Directory*, NL, Ir.
        9141 p 75
1830   McCabe's *Drogheda Directory*
1846   Slater's *National Commercial Directory of Ireland*

1856   Slater's *Royal National Commercial Directory of Ireland*
1870   Slater's *Directory of Ireland*
1881   Slater's *Royal National Commercial Directory of Ireland*
1886   George H. Bassett, *Louth County Guide and Directory*
1890   Tempest's *Almanack and Directory of Dundalk*, issued annually from this
       date
1894   Slater's *Royal Commercial Directory of Ireland*

Gravestone inscriptions

Ardee: *The Irish Genealogist*, Vol. III, No. 1, 1956
Ballymakenny: *Seanchas Ardmhacha*, 1983/4
Ballymascanlon: JCLAS, Vol. XVII, No. 4, 1972
Beaulieu: JCLAS, Vol. XX, No. 1
Carlingford: JCLAS, Vol. XIX, No. 2, 1978
Castlebellingham: *History of Kilsaran Union of Parishes in the Co. of Louth*, J. B.
    Leslie, 1908
Charlestown: *Notes and Jottings concerning the Parish of Charlestown Union*, G. W. C.
    L'Estrange, 1912
Clonkeen: *Notes and Jottings concerning the Parish of Charlestown Union*, G. W. C.
    L'Estrange, 1912
Clonmore: JCLAS, Vol. XX, No. 2
Dromiskin: *History of Kilsaran Union of Parishes in the Co. of Louth*, J. B. Leslie,
    1908
Faughart: *Tombstone Inscriptions from Fochart*, Dundalgan Press, 1968
Faughart (Urnai): *Urnai*, D. Mac Iomhair, Dundalk, 1969
Dunany and Salterstown: JCLAS, Vol. XX, No. 3 (1983)
Dysert, Grange, and Drumshallon: JCLAS, Vol. XIX, 3 (1979)
Kildemock: JCLAS, Vol. XIII, No. 1
Killanny: *Clogher Record*, Vol. VI, No. 1, 1966
Kilsaran: *History of Kilsaran Union of Parishes in the Co. of Louth*, J. B. Leslie, 1908
Manfieldstown: *History of Kilsaran Union of Parishes in the Co. of Louth*, J. B.
    Leslie, 1908
Mayne: JCLAS, Vol. XX, No. 4 (1984)
Newtownstalaban: JCLAS, Vol. XVII, No. 2, 1970
Rathdromin: JCLAS, Vol. XIX, No. 1, 1970
St Mary's 'Abbey', Louth: JCLAS, Vol. XIX, No. 4 (1980)
Seatown, Dundalk: *Tempest's Annual*, 1967, 1971/2
Stabannon: *History of Kilsaran Union of Parishes in the Co. of Louth*, J. B. Leslie,
    1908
Stagrennon: *Journal of the Old Drogheda Society*, 1977
Tullyallen: *Seanchas Ardmhacha*, Vol. VII, No. 2, 1977

Estate records

'Tenants of Omeath', 1865, JCLAS, Vol. XVII, 1, 1973.
'Details of the Anglesea estate papers in PRONI', JCLAS, Vol. XVII, 1, 1973 (see also JCLAS, XII, 2).
'Drumgooter: A tenant farm in the 18th and 19th Centuries (from a rent roll of the estate of Sir John Bellew)', JCLAS, Vol. XX, 4, 1984.
'Papers from the Roden estate, Clanbrassel estate map, 1785', JCLAS, Vol. XX, 1 1981.
Trench estate rentals, Drogheda, NL MS. 2576.

Placenames

Townland Maps, Londonderry Inner City trust
Townland Survey of Co. Louth—Newtownstalagan, JCLAS, Vol. XIX, No. 1 (1977)
Townland Survey of Co. Louth—Beaulieu, JCLAS, Vol. XIX, No. 4 (1980)
Townland Survey of Co. Louth—Mullacrew, JCLAS, Vol. XX, No. 1 (1980)

CO. MAYO

Census returns and substitutes

1600s	Mayo landowners in the seventeenth century, *R. Soc. Antiq. of Ire. Jnl*, 1962, 153–62
1783	Ballinrobe, *Analecta Hibernica*, Vol. 14
1785–1815	Westport Rent Rolls, *Cathair na Mart*, Vol. 2, No. 1, 1982
1796	Catholics Emigrating from Ulster to Mayo, *Seanchas Ardmhacha*, 1958, 17–50; see also 'Petition of Armagh migrants in the Westport area', *Cathair na Mart*, Vol. 2, No. 1 (Appendix)
1796	Spinning-Wheel Premium Lists, microfiche index in National Archives, comprising, in the case of Co. Mayo, over 5,000 names
1798	List of those who suffered loss in 1798 Rebellion, NL JLB 94107
1818	Tithe Collectors' account book, parishes of Kilfian and Moygownagh, NA M.6085
1820	Protestants in Killalla, NA MFCI 32

1820s/30s Tithe Books
1832 Protestants, Foxford, NL MS. 8295
1841 Some extracts, Newport. Thrift Abstracts, National Archives
1856/7 Griffith's Valuation
1901 Census
1911 Census

Local history

Achill, 15th report of the mission/report of Achill Orphan Refuges (1849), NL Ir. 266 a 8
Crossmolina Parish: An Historical Survey, NL Ir. 94123 c 5
Hayes-McCoy, G. A., *Index to 'The Compossicion Booke of Connoght, 1585'*, Irish Manuscripts Commission, Dublin, 1945, NL Ir. 9412 c 1
Hurley, Rev. Timothy, *St Patrick and the Parish of Kilkeeran*, Vol. 1
Knox, H. T., *Notes on the Early History of the Dioceses of Tuam, Killala and Achonry*, Dublin, 1904
Knox, H. T., *The history of Mayo to the close of the 16th century*, Dublin, 1908, NL Ir. 94123 k 2 (and LO)
McDonnell, T., *Diocese of Killala*, NL Ir. 94123 m 7
MacHale (ed.), *The Parishes in the Diocese of Killala*, NL Ir. 27414 m 6
O'Hara, B., *Killasser: a history*, 1981, Ir. 94123 o 6
O'Sullivan, W. (ed.), *The Strafford Inquisition of Co. Mayo*, NL Ir. 94123 o 4
St Muiredach's College, Ballina, Roll 1906–1979, NL Ir. 259 m 2/Ir. 37941 s 18

Local journals

Cathair na Mart (Journal of the Westport Historical Society), NL Ir. 94123 c 4
North Mayo Historical and Archaeological Journal, Ir. 94123 n 4

Directories

1824 Pigot and Co., *City of Dublin and Hibernian Provincial Directory*, NL Ir. 9141 p 75
1846 Slater's *National Commercial Directory of Ireland*
1856 Slater's *Royal National Commercial Directory of Ireland*
1870 Slater's *Directory of Ireland*
1881 Slater's *Royal National Commercial Directory of Ireland*
1894 Slater's *Royal Commercial Directory of Ireland*

Estate records

LANDLORD

Lord **Altamont**: NA M5788 (2), Rental of the Westport estate, 1787, principally major tenants. The section on Westport town is published in *Cathair na Mart*, Vol. 2, No. 1, along with a rent roll for the town from 1815; covering townlands in the civil parishes of Aghagower, Burriscarra, Burrishoole, Kilbelfad, Kilbride, Kilconduff, Kildacomoge, Kilfian, Killdeer, Kilmaclasser, Kilmeena, Moygownagh, Oughaval.

Earl of **Arran**: NL MS. 14087, leases on the Mayo estate, 1720–1869, mentioning lives in the leases; NL MS. 14086; valuation survey of the Mayo estates, 1850–52, all tenants; covering townlands in the civil parishes of Addergoole, Ardagh, Ballysakeery, Crossmolina, Kilbelfad, Kilcummin, Kilfian, Killala, Kilmoremoy.

Col John **Browne**: NL Pos. 940, account of the sales of the estates of Col John Browne in Counties Galway and Mayo, compiled in 1778, giving names of major tenants and purchasers, 1698–1704, and those occupying the estates in 1778, covering townlands in the civil parishes of Addergoole, Aghagower, Aglish, Ballintober, Ballyhean, Ballyovey, Ballysakeery, Breaghwy, Burrishoole, Cong, Crossmolina, Drum, Islandeady, Kilcommon, Kilgeever, Killeadan, Kilmaclasser, Kilmainemore, Kilmeena, Manulla, Moygownagh, Oughaval, Robeen, Tonaghty, Turlough.

Lord **Clanmorris**: NL MS. 3279, Rental, 1833, all tenants, covering townlands in the civil parishes of Kilcommon, Kilmainemore, Mayo, Robeen, Rosslee, Tonaghty, Toomour.

Domville: NL MS. 11816, Rentals, 1833–36, 1843, 1847, 1851, all tenants, covering townlands in the civil parishes of Killasser, Manulla, Robeen.

Francis Blake **Knox**: NL MS. 3077, Rental of the estates in Counties Galway, Mayo and Roscommon.

Henry **Knox**: NA 5630 (1), Rental, early nineteenth century, all tenants, covering townlands in the civil parishes of Crossmolina, Doonfeeny, Kilfian, Kilmoremoy.

Thomas **Medlicott**: NL MS. 5736 (3), Tithe Applotment Book, Achill; NL MSS. 5736 (2), 5821, Rent rolls, showing lives in leases, 1774, 1776, major tenants only; covering townlands in the civil parishes of Achill, Aghagower, Burrishoole, Kilcommon, Kilmeena, Kilmore.

Sir Neal **O'Donel**: NL MS. 5738 and 5744, leaseholders on the estates, 1775–1859, 1828, giving lives mentioned in leases, mainly major tenants; NL MS. 5736, Rental, 1788, major tenants only; NL MS. 5281, Rental, 1805, major tenants only; NL MS. 5743, Rental, 1810, major tenants only; NL MS. 5281, Rental, 1828, major tenants only; covering townlands in the civil parishes of Achill, Aghagower, Burrishoole, Cong, Kilcommon, Kilgeever, Kilmore, Kilmaclasser.

Sir Samuel **O'Malley**: NA M1457 (published in *Cathair na Mart*, Vol. 6, No. 1), valuation of the Mayo estates, 1845, all tenants, covering townlands in the civil parishes of Aglish, Kilgeever, Kilmeena.

Placenames

Townland maps, Londonderry Inner City Trust

CO. MEATH

Census returns and substitutes

1641	Book of Survey and Distribution, NL MS. 974
1654/6	Civil Survey, Vol. III, NL I 6551, Dublin
1659	Pender's 'Census', NL Ir. 31041 c 4
1766	Protestants in Ardbraccan, RCB Library, GO 537
1770	Freeholders, NL MS. 787–8
1781	Voters List, NA M.4878, 4910–12
1792	Hearth tax collectors account and collection books: parishes of Colp, Donore, Duleek, Kilshalvan, NL MS. 26735; Ardcath, Ardmulchan, Ballymagarvy, Brownstown, Clonalvy, Danestown, Fennor, Kentstown, Knockcommon, Rathfeigh, NL MS. 26736; Athlumney, Danestown, Dowdstown, Dunsany, Kilcarn, Killeen, Macetown, Mounttown, Tara, Trevet, NL MS. 26737; St Mary's Drogheda, NL MS. 26739
1793	Hearth tax collectors account and collection books; parishes of Ardagh, Dowth, Gernonstown, Killary, Mitchelstown, Siddan, Slane, Stackallen, NL MS. 26738
1795–1862	Charlton Marriage Certificates, NA 1A–42–163/4, indexed under men's names in Accessions, Vol. 37
1796	Spinning-Wheel Premium Lists, microfiche index in National Archives, comprising, in the case of Co. Meath, over 3,000 names
1797–1801	Athboy Tithe Valuations, NA MFCI 53, 54
1802–6	Protestants in the parishes of Agher, Ardagh, Clonard, Clongill, Drumconrath, Duleek, Emlagh, Julianstown, Kentstown, Kilbeg, Kilmainhamwood, Kilskyre, Laracor, Moynalty, Navan,

	Robertsown, Raddenstown, Rathcore, Rathkenny, Rathmolyon, Ratoath, Skryne, Staffordstown, Stamullen, Tara, Trevett, Templekeran, *The Irish Ancestor*, 1973
1813	Protestant children at Ardbraccan school, *The Irish Ancestor*, 1973
1821	Parishes of Ardbraccan, Ardsallagh, Balrathboyne, Bective, Churchtown, Clonmacduff, Donaghmore, Donaghpatrick, Kilcooly, Liscartan, Martry, Moymet, Navan, Newtownclonbun, Rathkenny, Rataine, Trim, Trimblestown, Tullaghanoge. National Archives
1820s/30s	Tithe Books
1833	Protestant Cess payers, parishes of Colpe and Kilshalvan
1835	Tubber parish, NL Pos. 1994
c.1850	Register of land occupiers, with particulars of land and families, in the Unions of Kells and Oldcastle, NL MS. 5774
1855	Griffith's Valuation
1865	Census of the town and parks of Kells, Headfort papers, NL MS. 25423
1866–73	Stamullen emigrants, with parish records, National Library
1871	Drumcondra and Loughbraclen, transcript in Catholic parish records
1901	Census
1911	Census

Local history

Brady, J., *A short history of the parishes of the diocese of Meath, 1867–1944*, Ir. 94132 b 2
Carty, Mary Rose, *History of Killeen Castle*, Dunsany, 1991
Cogan, J., *Ratoath*, Ir. 9141 p 84
Coogan, O., *Dunshaughlin, Culmullen and Knockmark*, 1988
D'Alton, John, *Antiquities of the County of Meath*, Dublin, 1833
French, Noel, *Trim Traces and Places*
French, Noel, *Navan by the Boyne*
French, Noel, *Athboy, a short history*
French, Noel (ed.), *Nobber, a step back in time*
French, Noel, *Tracing Your Ancestors in Co. Meath*
Healy, John, *History of the Diocese of Meath*, 2 vols, Dublin, 1908
Henderson's *Post Office Directory of Meath and Louth*, 1861, Ir. 914132 m 3
ICA: *A local history guide to the parish of Summerhill and its surrounding areas*, 1981, Ir. 941, p 75
Larkin, Wm, Map of County, 1812, see NL Map Room
Mooneystown Valuation Survey and Field Book, 1838, P 2011
O'Connell, Philip, *The Diocese of Kilmore: its History and Antiquities*, Dublin, 1937
Parish Guide to Meath (1968), Ir. 270 p 2

Paterson, J. (ed.), *Diocese of Meath and Kildare: an historical guide*, 1981, Ir. 941 p 75
Sims, A., *Irish Historic Towns Atlas: Kells*, Dublin, Royal Irish Academy, 1991

Local journals

Annala Dhamhliag, The annals of Duleek (from 1971), NL I 94132 a 1
Seanchas Ard Mhacha (Journal of the Armagh Diocesan Historical Society), NL Ir.
   27411 s 4
Riocht na Midhe (Records of the Meath Archaeological and Historical Society), NL Ir.
   94132 r 1

Directories

1824   Pigot and Co., *City of Dublin and Hibernian Provincial Directory*, NL Ir.
        9141 p 75
1846   Slater's *National Commercial Directory of Ireland*
1856   Slater's *Royal National Commercial Directory of Ireland*
1870   Slater's *Directory of Ireland*
1881   Slater's *Royal National Commercial Directory of Ireland*
1894   Slater's *Royal Commercial Directory of Ireland*

Gravestone inscriptions

Agher: *The Irish Ancestor*, Vol. X, No. 2, 1978
Ardmulchan: 'Monumental Inscriptions from some Graveyards in Co.
   Meath', N. French (unpub.), National Archives search room
Ardsallagh: 'Monumental Inscriptions from some Graveyards in Co. Meath',
   N. French (unpub.), National Archives search room
Arodstown: *Riocht na Midhe*, Vol. VI, No. 1, 1975
Athboy: *The Irish Ancestor*, Vol. XII, Nos 1 and 2, 1981
Athlumney: IGRS Collection, GO
Ballygarth: IGRS Collection, GO
Balfeaghan: IGRS Collection, 21, GO
Balsoon: *The Irish Ancestor*, Vol. VII, No. 2, 1976
Castlejordan: IGRS Collection, 89, GO
Castlekieran: IGRS Collection, 39, GO
Churchtown (Dunderry): IGRS Collection, 59, GO
Clady: IGRS Collection, GO
Clonabreany: *Riocht na Midhe*, Vol. VI, No. 2, 1976
Clonmacnuff: IGRS Collection, 70, GO
Cortown: IGRS Collection, 120, GO
Danestown: *Riocht na Midhe*, Vol. V, No. 4, 1974
Donaghmore: 'Monumental Inscriptions from some Graveyards in Co.
   Meath', N. French (unpub.), National Archives search room

Dowdstown: 'Monumental Inscriptions from some Graveyards in Co. Meath', N. French (unpub.), National Archives search room
Drumlargan: *The Irish Ancestor*, Vol. XII, Nos 1 and 2, 1980
Duleek: *The Irish Genealogist*, Vol. 3, No. 12, 1967
Dunboyne: *The Irish Ancestor*, Vol. XI, Nos 1 and 2, 1979
Dunboyne C. of I.: IGRS Collection, GO
Dunmoe: 'Monumental Inscriptions from some Graveyards in Co. Meath', N. French (unpub.), National Archives search room
Fore: IGRS Collection, GO
Gallow: IGRS Collection, 39, GO
Gernonstown: 'Monumental Inscriptions from some Graveyards in Co. Meath', N. French (unpub.), National Archives search room
Girly (C. of I. and Catholic): 'Monumental Inscriptions from some Graveyards in Co. Meath', N. French (unpub.), National Archives search room
Hermitage: 'Monumental Inscriptions from some Graveyards in Co. Meath', N. French (unpub.), National Archives search room
Hill of Ward: 'Monumental Inscriptions from some Graveyards in Co. Meath', N. French (unpub.), National Archives search room
Kells: *The Irish Genealogist*, Vol. III, No. 12, 1967
Kilcarn: 'Monumental Inscriptions from some Graveyards in Co. Meath', N. French (unpub.), National Archives search room
Kilbride: *Riocht na Midhe*, Vol. VI, No. 3, 1977
Kilcooly (Trim): IGRS Collection, 8, GO
Kildalkey: IGRS Collection, 117, GO
Kilaconnigan: IGRS Collection, 100, GO
Killeen: *Riocht na Midhe*, Vol. IV, No. 3, 1970
Kilmore: *Riocht na Midhe*, Vol. VI, No. 1, 1975
Loughcrew: *The Irish Ancestor*, Vol. IX, No. 2, 1977
Loughsallagh: IGRS Collection, 60, GO
Macetown: IGRS Collection, 7, GO
Maudlin (Trim): IGRS Collection, 3, GO
Moy: *The Irish Ancestor*, Vol. VI, No. 2, 1974
Moyagher: *The Irish Ancestor*, Vol. VIII, No. 1, 1976
Moymet: IGRS Collection, 54, GO
Navan (C. of I.): with Church records, NA Mf CI 45
Oldcastle: *Riocht na Midhe*, Vol. IV, No. 2, 1968
Rathfeigh: IGRS Collection, 42, GO
Rathkenny: 'Monumental Inscriptions from some Graveyards in Co. Meath', N. French (unpub.), National Archives search room
Rathmore: *The Irish Ancestor*, Vol. VII, No. 2, 1975
Ratoath: 'Monumental Inscriptions from some Graveyards in Co. Meath', N. French (unpub.), National Archives search room
Scurlogstown: IGRS Collection, 17, GO

Skryne: 'Monumental Inscriptions from some Graveyards in Co. Meath', N. French (unpub.), National Archives search room

Stackallen: 'Monumental Inscriptions from some Graveyards in Co. Meath', N. French (unpub.), National Archives search room

Trimblestown: 'Monumental Inscriptions from some Graveyards in Co. Meath', N. French (unpub.), National Archives search room

Tullyhanogue: 'Monumental Inscriptions from some Graveyards in Co. Meath', N. French (unpub.), National Archives search room

Tycroghan: IGRS Collection, 4, GO

Estate records

Balfour tenants, townlands of Belustran, Cloughmacow, Doe and Hurtle, 1838, JCLAS, Vol. 12, No. 3, 1951.

Newcomen estates, maps of estates to be sold, 20 July 1827, NL Map Room.

Reynell family rent books, 1834–48, NL MS. 5990.

William Barlow Smythe, Collinstown, Farm a/c book, NL MS. 7909.

Trench estate rentals, Drogheda, NL MS. 2576.

Tenants of the Wellesley estate at Dengen, Ballymaglossan, Moyare, Mornington and Trim, 1816, *Riocht na Midhe*, Vol. 4, No. 4, 1967.

Placenames

Townland Maps, Londonderry Inner City Trust

Walsh, P., *Some Place-names in Ancient Meath*, NL I 92941

CO. MONAGHAN

Census returns and substitutes

	Medieval Clones families, *Clogher Record*, 1959
1641	Book of Survey and Distribution, NL MS. 976
1659	Pender's 'Census', NL Ir. 31041 c 4
1663/5	Hearth Money Roll, *A History of Monaghan*, D. C. Rushe
1738	Some Clonea Inhabitants, *Clogher Record*, Vol. 2, No. 3, 1959
1777	Some Protestant Inhabitants of Carrickmacross, *Clogher Record*, Vol. 6, No. 1, 1966

1796   Catholic migrants from Ulster to Mayo, see Mayo
1796   Spinning-Wheel Premium Lists, microfiche index in National
            Archives, comprising, in the case of Co. Monaghan, over 6,000
            names
1821   Thrift Abstracts, see *Clogher Record*, 1991
1820s/30s   Tithe Books
1841   Some extracts. Thrift Abstracts, National Archives.
1843   Magistrates, landed proprietors, 'etc.', NL MS. 12, 767
1847   Castleblayney Poor Law Rate Book, *Clogher Record*, Vol. 5, No. 1,
            1963
1851   Some extracts. Thrift Abstracts, National Archives.
1858/60   Griffith's Valuation, All-Ireland Heritage microfiche index
1901   Census
1911   Census

Local history

Bell, Rev. J. Brian A., *A History of Garmany's Grove Presbyterian Church*, Armagh,
    1970
Carville, G., *Parish of Clontibret*, NL Ir. 941 p 74
Cotter, Canon J. B. D., *A Short History of Donagh Parish*, Enniskillen, 1966
Duffy J. (ed.), *A Clogher Record Album: a diocesan history*, NL Ir. 94114 c 3
Gilsenan, M., *Hills of Magheracloone 1884–1984*, 1985, NL Ir. 94117 g 1
Haslett, A. and Orr, Rev. S. L., *Historical Sketch of Ballyalbany Presbyterian
    Church*, Belfast, n.d.
Leslie, Seymour, *Of Glaslough in Oriel*, 1912
Livingstone, Peadar, *The Monaghan Story*, Enniskillen, 1980
Marshall, J., *History of the Town and District of Clogher, Co. Tyrone, parish of Errigal
    Keerogue, Tyrone and Errigal Truagh in the Co. of Monaghan*, 1930, NL I 94114
McCluskey, Seamus, *Emyvale Sweet Emyvale*, Monaghan, 1985
McKenna, J. E., *Parochial Records*, 2 vols, Enniskillen, 1920
McIvor, John, *Extracts from a Ballybay Scrapbook*, Monaghan, 1974
Monaghan Election Petition 1826, minutes of evidence, NL Ir. 32341 m 52
Monaghan Election Petition 1834, minutes of evidence, NL Ir. 32341 m 50
Mulligan, E. and McCloskey, B., *The Replay: A Parish History: Kilmore and
    Drumsnat*, Monaghan, 1984, NL Ir. 94117 m 10
Na Braithre Criostai Mhuineacháin, *Monaghan Memories*, Monaghan, 1984
O Mordha, P., *The Story of the G.A.A. in Currin and an outline of Parish History*,
    Monaghan, 1986
Rushe, Denis Carolan, *Historical Sketches of Monaghan*, Dundalk, 1895
Rushe, Denis Carolan, *Monaghan in the 18th century*, Dublin and Dundalk, 1916
Rushe, Denis Carolan, *History of Monaghan for two hundred years 1660–1860*,
    Dundalk, 1921

St Macartan's College 1840–1990, Monaghan, 1990
Shirley, Evelyn P., *The History of the County of Monaghan*, London, 1879
Shirley, Evelyn P., *Some Account of the Territory and Dominion of Farney*, London,
    n.d.
Shirley, Evelyn P., *Lough Fea*, 2 vols, London, 1859, 1869
Swanzy, C. E., *The MacKennas of Truagh*, 1977, NL Ir. 9292 s 20
Swanzy, H. B., *Parish of Clontibret, Co. Monaghan: Record of Vicars and Churchwardens
    from 1662–1924*, Newry, 1925
Watson, William, *Some Records of the Monaghan Regiment of Militia* [from 1793 to
    1871], Monaghan, 1871
Wilkinson, W. R., *Our Good School upon the Hill*, NL Ir. 372 w 10

Local journals

Clogher Record (Journal of the Clogher Diocesan Historical Society), NL Ir. 94114 c 2
The Drumlin, a Journal of Cavan, Leitrim and Monaghan, NL Ir. 05 d 34
Macalla (1976–1979)
Clann MacKenna Journal

Directories

1824   Pigot and Co., *City of Dublin and Hibernian Provincial Directory*, NL Ir.
        9141 p 75
1846   Slater's *National Commercial Directory of Ireland*
1852   James A. Henderson, *Belfast and Province of Ulster Directory*, issued also
        in 1854, 1856, 1858, 1861, 1863, 1865, 1868, 1870, 1877, 1880, 1884,
        1887, 1890, 1894, 1900
1856   Slater's *Royal National Commercial Directory of Ireland*
1865   R. Wynne, *Business Directory of Belfast*
1870   Slater's *Directory of Ireland*
1881   Slater's *Royal National Commercial Directory of Ireland*
1894   Slater's *Royal Commercial Directory of Ireland*
1897   *Gillespie's Co. Monaghan Directory and Almanac*

Gravestone inscriptions

Aghabog and Killeevan: *Clogher Record*, Vol. XI, No. 1
Cahans (Presbyterian): Monaghan Ancestral Research Group (see below)
Clontibret (Presbyterian): Monaghan Ancestral Research Group (see below)
Clontibret (C. of I.): Monaghan Ancestral Research Group (see below)
Clontibret: *Clogher Record*, Vol. VII, No. 2, 1974
Clones and Roslea: *Clogher Record*, 1982–84
Clones (St Tighernach's C. of I.): *Clogher Record*, Vol. XIII, No. 1, 1988

Coolshannagh, Monaghan: Monaghan Ancestral Research Group (see below)
Donagh: *Clogher Record*, Vol. II, No. 1, 1957
Drumsnat: *Clogher Record*, Vol. VI, No. 1, 1966
Drumswords (Killeevan Parish): *Clogher Record*, 1985
Edergole (Ematris): Monaghan Ancestral Research Group (see below)
Glaslough: *Clogher Record*, Vol. IX, No. 3, 1978
Killanny: *Clogher Record*, Vol. VI, No. 1, 1966
Killeevan and Aghabog: *Clogher Record*, 1982
Kilmore: *Clogher Record*, 1983 and 1985
Magheross: *Clogher Record*, Vol. V, No. 1, 1963
Mullandoy: *Clogher Record*, Vol. VI, No. 1, 1966
Old Errigal: *Clogher Record*, 1987
Rackwallace: *Clogher Record*, Vol. IV, No. 3, 1962
Tydavnet: *Clogher Record*, Vol. I, No. 1, 1954
Urbleshanny (Tydavnet): Monaghan Ancestral Research Group (see below)
Monaghan Ancestral Research Group, 6 Tully, Monaghan, Co. Monaghan

Estate records

LANDLORD
Anketell estate rentals, 1784–89, *Clogher Record*, Vol. XI, No. 3.
Balfour rentals of 1632 and 1636, *Clogher Record*, 1985.
James **Forster**: Five Rent Rolls, 1803–08, 1812–24, covering townlands in
     the parishes Aghabog, Killeevan, Tydavnet, Tyholland, Monaghan An-
     cestral Research Group.
Kane: Rentals, 1840–41; Account Books, 1842–44; Arrears, 1848, 1849, 1852;
     Rent Receipts, 1851–52; covering townlands in the parish of Tydavnet,
     Monaghan Ancestral Research Group.
Ker: Landholders, Newbliss, 1790–c.1830, Killeevan civil parish, *Clogher
     Record*, 1985.
Rossmore estate: Maps with tenants' names, c.1820–1852, Monaghan town
     and surrounding areas, Monaghan Ancestral Research Group.
Weymouth estate, Magheross: Survey, major tenants only, Monaghan
     Ancestral Research Group.
Wingfield estate: Rentals and arrears, 1852, county and town of Monaghan,
     Monaghan Ancestral Research Group.

NO LANDLORD GIVEN
Ballybay estate rentals, 1786, *Clogher Record*, Vol. XI, No. 1.
Castleblayney Rent Book, 1772, *Clogher Record*, Vol. X, No. 3.

Emy and Glaslough estates: Rent Roll, 1752–60, principally major tenants; civil parishes of Donagh and Errigal Truagh, Monaghan Ancestral Research Group.

Monaghan Manor and Lordship: Rent Roll, 1790, principally major tenants.

Placenames

Townland maps, Londonderry Inner City Trust

CO. OFFALY

Census returns and substitutes

1641	Book of Survey and Distribution, NL MS. 972
1659	Pender's 'Census', NL Ir. 31041 c 4
1766	Ballycommon, JKAS, Vol. VII, also GO 537
1770	Voters, NL MS. 2050
1802	Protestants in the parishes of Ballyboggan, Ballyboy, Castlejordan, Clonmacnoise, Drumcullin, Eglish, Gallen, Killoughey, Lynally, Rynagh, Tullamore, *The Irish Ancestor*, 1973
1821	Parishes of Aghacon, Birr, Ettagh, Kilcolman, Kinnitty, Letterluna, Roscomroe, Rocrea, Seirkieran, National Archives
1824	Catholic householders, Lusmagh parish, in Catholic registers
1830	Contributors to new Catholic church in Lusmagh, with Catholic registers
1820s/30s	Tithe Books
1840	Eglish and Drumcullin parishes, in Catholic registers of Eglish (NL Pos. 4175)
1852	Assisted passages from Kilconouse, Kinnitty parish, *Analecta Hibernica*, Vol. 22, 1960
1854	Griffith's Valuation
1901	Census
1911	Census

Local history

Byrne, M., *Durrow and its History*, NL Ir. 9141 p 71
Byrne, M., *Sources for Offaly History* (1977), NL Ir. 94136 b 1

Byrne, M., *Towards a History of Kilclonfert*, NL Ir. 94136 t 1
Byrne, M., *Tullamore Catholic parish: a Historical Survey*, NL r 27414 b 7
Feehan, J., *The Landscape of Slieve Bloom: a study of the natural and human heritage*, 1979, NL Ir. 91413 f 4
Ferbane Parish and its Churches, NL Ir. 91413 f 4
Finney, C. W., *Monasteroris Parish, 8th May 1778–8th May 1978*, NL Ir. 200 p 23
Gleeson, J., *History of the Ely O'Carroll Territory or Ancient Ormond*, 1915, NL Ir. 94142 g 1
Meehan, Patrick, *Members of Parliament for Laois and Offaly, 1801–1918*, 1983, NL Ir. 328 m 6
Paterson, J. (ed.), *Diocese of Meath and Kildare: an historical guide*, 1981, NL Ir. 941 p 75
Raymond, B., *The Story of Kilkenny, Kildare, Offaly and Leix*, 1931, NL I 9141 p 1

Local journals

Ardagh and Clonmacnoise Historical Society Journal (1926–51), Ir. 794105

Directories

1824   Pigot and Co., *City of Dublin and Hibernian Provincial Directory*, NL Ir. 9141 p 75
1846   Slater's *National Commercial Directory of Ireland*
1856   Slater's *Royal National Commercial Directory of Ireland*
1870   Slater's *Directory of Ireland*
1881   Slater's *Royal National Commercial Directory of Ireland*
1890   John Wright, *The King's Co. Directory* (reprinted as *Offaly 100 Years Ago*, Tullamore, 1989)
1894   Slater's *Royal Commercial Directory of Ireland*

Gravestone inscriptions

Cloonygowan (C. of I.): GO MS. 622, 182
Daingean, Offaly Historical Society Series, No. 4
Edenderry, Offaly Historical Society Series, No. 3
Kilclonfert: in Byrne, *Towards a History of Kilclonfert*, NL Ir. 94136 t 1
Kilmachonna, Offaly Historical Society Series, No. 2
Lusmagh, Offaly Historical Society Series, No. 2
Monasteroris, Offaly Historical Society Series, No. 3
Rahan: Offaly Historical Society Series, No. 1

Placenames

Townland Maps, Londonderry Inner City Trust

CO. ROSCOMMON

Census returns and substitutes

1659	Pender's 'Census', NL Ir. 31041 c 4
1749	Aughrim, Ardcarn, Ballintober, Ballynakill, Baslick, Boyle, Bumlin, Cam, Clontuskert, Cloocraff, Cloonfinlough, Cloony-gormican, Creeve, Drimatemple, Dunamon, Dysart, Estersnow, Elphin, Fuerty, Kilbride, Kilbryan, Kilcolagh, Kilcooley, Kilcorkey, Kilgefin, Kilglass, Kilkeevin, Killinvoy, Killuken, Kilumnod, Kilmacallen, Kilmacumsy, Kilmore, Kilronan, Kiltoom, Kiltrustan, Kilnamagh, Lisonuffy, Ogulla, Oran, Rahara, Roscommon, St John's Athlone, St Peter's Athlone, Shankill, Taghboy, Termonbarry, Tibohine, Tisrara, Tumna, NA 1A 36 1
1780	Freeholders, GO 442
1790–99	Freeholders, C. 30 lists, NL MS. 10130
1796	Spinning-Wheel Premium Lists: microfiche index in National Archives, comprising, in the case of Co. Roscommon, over 3,000 names
1813	Freeholders, NL ILB 324
1821	Some extracts. Thrift Abstracts, National Archives
1820s/30s	Tithe Books
1836	Voters list, NL Ir. 32341 r 20
1841	Some extracts. Thrift Abstracts, National Archives
1848	Male Catholic inhabitants of the parish of Boyle, NL Pos. 4692
1851	Some extracts. Thrift Abstracts, National Archives
1857/8	Griffith's Valuation
1901	Census
1911	Census

Local history

Athlone: Materials from printed sources relating to the history of Athlone and surrounding areas, 1699–1899, NL MSS. 1543–7, including an index volume

Beckett, Rev. M., *Facts and Fictions of Local History* (Kiltullagh district), 1929

Burke, Francis, *Lough Ce and its annals: North Roscommon and the diocese of Elphin in times of old*, Dublin, 1895, NL Ir. 27412 b 1

Hayes-McCoy, G. A., *Index to 'The Compossicion Booke of Connoght, 1585'*, Irish Manuscripts Commission, Dublin, 1945, NL Ir. 9412 c 1

Monaghan, Rev. J., *Records Relating to the Diocese of Ardagh and Clonmacnoise*, 1886

Knox, H. T., *Notes on the Early History of the Dioceses of Tuam, Killala and Achonry*, Dublin, 1904

Local journals

Ardagh and Clonmacnoise Historical Society Journal (1926–51), NL Ir. 794105

Directories

1824   Pigot and Co., *City of Dublin and Hibernian Provincial Directory*, NL Ir.
        9141 p 75
1846   Slater's *National Commercial Directory of Ireland*
1856   Slater's *Royal National Commercial Directory of Ireland*
1870   Slater's *Directory of Ireland*
1881   Slater's *Royal National Commercial Directory of Ireland*
1894   Slater's *Royal Commercial Directory of Ireland*

Gravestone inscriptions

Aughrim (old): Heritage and Genealogy Society (see below)*
Cam: IGRS Collection, 138, GO
Cloonfinlough: Heritage and Genealogy Society (see below)*
Dysert: IGRS Collection, 103, GO; also Heritage and Genealogy Society
    (see below)*
Elphin (C. of I. Cathedral): GO MS. 622, 151
Fuerty: Heritage and Genealogy Society (see below)*
Hill St (C. of I.): GO MS. 622, 168
Jamestown: GO MS. 622, 170
Kiltrustan: Heritage and Genealogy Society (see below)*
Kilverdin: Heritage and Genealogy Society (see below)*
Lisonuffy: Heritage and Genealogy Society (see below)*
Roscommon (C. of I.): Heritage and Genealogy Society (see below)*
Strokestown: Heritage and Genealogy Society (see below)*, also GO MS. 622,
    174 and 182
Taughmaconnell: IGRS Collection, 71, GO
Tisrara: IGRS Collection, 144, GO

* Co. Roscommon Heritage and Genealogy Society, the County Heritage Centre,
  Strokestown, Co. Roscommon

Estate records

LANDLORD
Frances **Boswell**: NL Pos. 4937, Rent ledger, *c.*1760–86, major tenants only,
    covering townlands in the civil parish of Kilronan.
John **Browne**: NL 16 1 14 (8), map of Carronaskeagh, Cloonfinlough parish,
    May 1811, with tenants' names.

Baron **Clonbrock**: NL MS. 19501, Tenants' ledger, 1801–06, indexed, covering townlands in the civil parish of Taughmaconnell.

Edward **Crofton**: NL MS. 19672, Rent roll, May 1778, major tenants only, covering townlands in the civil parishes of Baslick, Estersnow, Kilbryan, Kilgefin, Killinvoy, Killumod, Kilmeane, Kiltrustan, Ogulla.

Sir Humphrey **Crofton**: NL MS. 4531, Rental, March 1833, tenants' names alphabetically, covering townlands in the civil parish of Tumna.

Sir Thomas **Dundas**: NL MSS. 2787, 2788, Rentals, 1792, 1804, major tenants only, covering townlands in the civil parishes of Boyle, Estersnow, Kilnamanagh, Tumna.

Walker **Evans**: NL MS. 10152, Leases, c.1790, covering townlands in the civil parish of Creeve.

Gen'l (?) **Gunning**: NL MS. 10152, Rental, 1792, major tenants only, covering townlands in the civil parishes of Athleague, Fuerty, Kilcooley.

King: NL MS. 4170, Rent rolls and accounts, 1801–1818, major tenants only, covering townlands in the civil parishes of Creeve, Elphin, Kilmore.

Francis Blake **Knox**: NL MS. 3077, Rentals, 1845–66, covering townlands in the civil parishes of Cloonfinlough, Rahara.

Lord **Lorton**: NL MSS. 3104/5, Lease Books, 1740–1900, including many leases to small tenants, with lives mentioned in the leases, covering townlands in the civil parishes of Ardcarn, Aughrim, Boyle, Creeve, Elphin, Estersnow, Kilbryan, Kilnamanagh.

Charles Manners **St George**: NL MSS. 4001–22, Accounts and rentals (annual), 1842–46, 1850–55, 1861–71, covering townlands in the civil parishes of Ardcarn, Killukin, Killumod.

Rev. Rodney **Ormsby**: NL MS. 10152, Leases c.1803, Grange townland.

Pakenham-Mahon: NL MS. 10152, Rent roll, 1725, major tenants only; NL MS. 10152, rent roll, 1765–68, major tenants only; NL MS. 2597, rent ledger, 1795–1804, indexed; NL MSS. 5501–3, rent ledgers, 1803–1818, 1824–36, part indexed; NL MS. 9473, tenants of Maurice Mahon, c.1817; NL MS. 9471, rentals and accounts, 1846–54; covering townlands in the civil parishes of Bumlin, Cloonfinlough, Elphin, Kilgefin, Kilglass, Kilnamanagh, Kiltrustan, Lisonuffy, Shankill; also NL MS. 9472, rent ledger, 1840–48, Kilmacumsy parish.

Sandford: NL MS. 10152, Rental (major tenants only), 1718; NL MS. 10152, Leases, c.1750; NL MS. 10152, Lands to be settled on the marriage of Henry Sandford, with tenants' names, 1750; NL MSS. 4281–9, Annual Rentals, 1835–45; covering townlands in the civil parishes of Ballintober, Baslick, Kilkeevin, Boyle, Kiltullagh, Tibohine.

Thomas **Tenison**: NL MS. 5101, Rental and Accounts, 1836–40, covering townlands in the civil parishes of Ardcarn and Kilronan.

(No Landlord Given): NL MS. 24880, List of tenants, Moore parish, 1834.

Placenames

Townland maps, Londonderry Inner City Trust

CO. SLIGO

Census returns and substitutes

1632	Strafford survey, 1632, landed proprietors, clergy, tenants and others, alphabetical list
1659	Pender's 'Census', NL Ir. 31041 c 4
1664	Hearth Money Roll, Irish Manuscripts Commission, 1967
1749	Parishes of Aghanagh, Ahamlish, Ballynakill, Ballysumaghan, Drumcliff, Drumcolumb, Killadoon, Kilmacallan, Kilmactranny, Kilross, Shancough, Sligo, Tawnagh, NA 1A 36 1
1790	Voters' list, NL MS. 2169
1795	Freeholders, NL MS. 3136, 1796; NL MS. 2733
1798	Persons who Suffered Loss of Property in the Rebellion, NL JLB 94107
1820s/30s	Tithe Books
1832–37	Registered voters, Sligo borough, *Parliamentary Papers*, 1837, Reports from Committees, Vol. II (2)
1858	Griffith's Valuation
1901	Census
1911	Census

Local history

Farry, M., *Killoran and Coolaney: a local history*, 1985, NL Ir. 94122 f 1

Finn, J., *Gurteen, Co. Sligo, its history, antiquities and traditions*, 1981, NL Ir. 94122 p 1

Hayes-McCoy, G. A., *Index to 'The Compossicion Booke of Connoght, 1585'*, Irish Manuscripts Commission, Dublin, 1945, NL Ir. 9412 c 1

McDonagh, J. C., *History of Ballymote and the Parish of Emlaghfad*, 1936, NL Ir. 94122 m 1

McGuinn, J., *Curry*, 1984, NL Ir. 94122 m 8

McTernan, J. C., *Historic Sligo* ('a bibliographical introduction to the antiquities, history, maps and surveys, MSS., newspapers, historic families, and notable individuals of Co. Sligo'), 1965, NL Ir. 94122 m 4

O'Rourke, T., *History and Antiquities of the Parishes of Ballysadare and Kilvarnet*, 1878, NL I 94122 (including histories of the O'Haras, Coopers, Percevals and other families)

O'Rourke, T., *History of Sligo, town and county*, Dublin, 1889

Monahan, Rev. J., *Records Relating to the Diocese of Ardagh and Clonmacnoise*, 1886

Knox, H. T., *Notes on the Early History of the Dioceses of Tuam, Killala and Achonry*, Dublin, 1904

Petition by Sligo Protestants, 1813, NL P. 504

Wood-Martin, W. G., *History of Sligo* (3 vols), NL Ir. 94122 w 1

Wood-Martin, W. G., *Sligo and the Enniskilleners, from 1688–91*, Dublin, 1882

Local journals

Ardagh and Clonmacnoise Historical Society Journal (1926–51)

Directories

1820	J. Pigot, *Commercial Directory of Ireland*
1824	Pigot and Co., *City of Dublin and Hibernian Provincial Directory*, NL Ir. 9141 p 75
1839	*Directory of the Towns of Sligo, Enniskillen, Ballyshannon, Donegal, etc.*
1846	Slater's *National Commercial Directory of Ireland*
1856	Slater's *Royal National Commercial Directory of Ireland*
1870	Slater's *Directory of Ireland*
1881	Slater's *Royal National Commercial Directory of Ireland*
1889	*Sligo Independent County Directory*
1894	Slater's *Royal Commercial Directory of Ireland*

Gravestone inscriptions

Calry: IGRS Collection, GO

St John's, Sligo (C. of I.): *Church and Parish of St John*, Tyndall, Ir. 2741 p 20

Sligo Abbey: IGRS Collection, GO

The County Heritage Centre, Stephen St, Sligo, has transcribed and indexed the gravestone inscriptions for all but ten of the graveyards and churches in the county.

Estate records

LANDLORD

Francis **Boswell**: NL Pos. 4937, Rental, c.1760–1786, major tenants only, covering townlands in the civil parishes of Ahamlish, Drumrat.

Cooper family: NL MSS. 3050–3060, eleven volumes of rentals and rent ledgers, 1775–1872, major tenants only; NL MS. 3076, rental 1809/10, major tenants only; NL MSS. 9753–57, rentals and accounts, major tenants only; covering townlands in the civil parishes of Achonry, Ahamlish, Ballysadare, Ballysumaghan, Drumcolumb, Drumcliff, Killery, Killaspugbrone, Kilmacallan, Kilmorgan, Kilross, Tawnagh, Templeboy.

Sir Malby **Crofton**: NA M938X, rental, 1853, with all tenants; NA M940X, leases on the estate, including many small tenants, and mentioning lives in the leases; covering townlands in the civil parishes of Dromard, Templeboy.

Sir Thomas **Dundas**: NL MSS. 2787, 2788, rentals, 1792, 1804, major tenants only, covering townlands in the civil parishes of Aghanagh, Drumrat, Emlaghfad, Kilcolman, Kilfree, Kilglass, Kilmacallan, Kilmacteigue, Kilmactranny, Kilmoremoy, Kilshalvey, Skreen.

Lord **Lorton**: NL MSS. 3104, 3105, lease books, 1740–1900, including many leasees to small tenants, with lives mentioned in leases, covering townlands in the civil parishes of Aghanagh, Drumcolumb, Kilfree, Killaraght, Kilmacallan, Kilshalvey, Toomour.

Charles **O'Hara** the younger: NL Pos. 1923, Rent roll, c.1775, all tenants, giving lives named in leases, covering townlands in the civil parishes of Achonry, Ballysadare, Killoran, Kilvarnet.

The Earl of **Strafford** (and others): NL MS. 10223, estate rentals, 1682 and 1684, major tenants only (includes a large part of Sligo town), covering townlands in the civil parishes of Ahamlish, Ballysadare, Ballysumaghan, Calry, Cloonoghill, Dromard, Drumcliff, Kilfree, Killoran, Kilaspugbrone, Kilmacallan, Kilmacowen, Kilmacteigue, Kilross, St John's, Skreen, Templeboy, Toomour.

Owen **Wynne**: NL MSS. 5780–5782, rentals and expense books, 1737–68, major tenants only; NL MSS. 5830–1, rent ledgers, 1738–53, 1768–73, major tenants only, indexed; NL MSS. 3311–13, a rental and two rent ledgers, yearly from 1798 to 1825, with all tenants; covering townlands in the civil parishes of Ahamlish, Ballysadare, Calry, Drumcliff, Killoran, St John's, Tawnagh, Templeboy.

Placenames

Townland maps, Londonderry Inner City Trust

CO. TIPPERARY

Census returns and substitutes

1595	Freeholders, NL Pos. 1700
1635	Census of Newport and Birdhill, NL Pos. 1561
1641	Book of Survey and Distribution, NL MS. 977
1641–63	Proprietors of Fethard, *The Irish Genealogist*, Vol. 6, No. 1, 1980
1653	Name of soldiers and adventurers who received land in Co. Tipperary under the Cromwellian settlement, *The Cromwellian Settlement of Ireland*, John Prendergast, Dublin, 1922
1654	Civil Survey, Vols I and II, NL I 6551, Dublin
1659	Pender's 'Census', NL Ir. 31041 c 4
1666/7/8	Three Hearth Money Rolls, *Tipperary's Families*, T. Laffan (ed.), Dublin, 1911, NL Ir. 9292 l 11
1703	Minister's money account, Clonmel, *Analecta Hibernica*, 34
1750	Catholics in the parishes of Barnane, Bourney, Corbally, Killavanoge, Killea, Rathnaveoge, Roscrea, Templecree, Templetouhy, *The Irish Genealogist*, 1973
1766	Athassel, Ballintemple, Ballycahill, Ballygriffin, Boytonreth, Brickendown, Bruis, Clerihan, Clonbeg, Cloneen, Clonoulty, Clonbolloge, Clonpet, Colman, Cordangan, Corrogue, Cullen, Dangandargan, Drum, Dustrileague, Erry, Fethard, Gaile, Grean, Horeabbey, Killardry, Killbrugh, Killea, Kilconnel, Kilfeacle, Killavanoge, Knockgrafton, Killnerath, Kiltynan, Lattin, Magorban, Mealiffe, Newchapel, Pepperstown, Railstown, Rathcoole, Relickmurry, Redcity, Shronell, St John's Cashel, St Patricksrock, Solloghodmore, Templebeg, Templemore, Templeneiry, Templenoe, Tipperary, Toom, NA 1A 46 49; Ballingarry, Uskeane, GO 536
1776	Voters lists, NA M.4910–12, 4878; Freeholders, NA M.1321–2, GO 442
1799	Census of Carrick-on-Suir, NL Pos. 28
1813	Valuation of Roscrea, NA MFCI 3
1821	Clonmel, National Archives, m 242²
1821	Modreeny, extracts, GO MS. 572
1828	Clonmel, houses and occupiers, *Parliamentary Papers*, Reports from Committees, Vol. 11 (2), 1837
1820s/30s	Tithe Books
1832–37	Registered voters, Clonmel and Cashel boroughs, *Parliamentary Papers*, 1837, Reports from Committees, Vol. II (2)
1835	Parish of Templebredin, JNMAHS, 1975
1835	Newport and Birdhill, NL P. 1561

1837	Protestant parishioners, Clogheen union, 1837, 1877, 1880, *The Irish Ancestor*, Vol. 17, No. 1, 1985
1851	Griffith's Valuation, alphabetical index to householders, All-Ireland Heritage microfiche, National Archives
1901	Census
1911	Census

Local history

Atlas of the parishes of Cashel and Emly, 1970, ILB 94143 a 3

Burke, William P., *History of Clonmel*, Waterford, 1907, Ir. 94142 b 1

Callanan, M., *History of 4 Tipperary Septs—O'Kennedys, O'Dwyers, O'Mulryans, O'Meaghers*, 1933, Ir. 9292 c 16

Coffey, G., *Evicted Tipperary*, Ir. 330 p 22

Cotter, James, *Tipperary*, New York, 1929

Dwyer, Philip, *The Diocese of Killaloe*, Dublin, 1878

Feehan, J., *The Landscape of Slieve Bloom: a study of the natural and human heritage*, 1979, Ir. 91413 f 4

Fitzgerald, S., *Cappawhite and Doon*, Ir. 9141 p 43

Flynn, Paul, *The book of the Galtees and the golden vale: a border history of Tipperary, Limerick and Cork*, Dublin, 1926, Ir. 94142 f 2

Gleeson, J., *History of the Ely O'Carroll Territory or Ancient Ormond*, 1915, Ir. 94142 g 1

Gleeson, J., *Cashel of the Kings*, Dublin, 1927

Gorman (ed.), *Records of Moycarkey and Two-Mile-Borris*, 1955, Ir. 94142 g 4

Hayes, W. J., *Tipperary Remembers*, 1976, Ir. 914142 H 9

Hemphill, W. Despard, *Clonmel and the surrounding country*, 1860

Kenny, M., *Glankeen of Borrisoleigh: a Tipperary Parish*, 1944, Ir. 94142 k 2

McIlroy, M., *Gleanings from Garrymore* (Townland), n.d.

Neely, W. S., *Kilcooley: land and parish in Tipperary*, 1983, Ir. 94142 n 1

O'Dwyer, M. and L., *The Parish of Emly, its history and heritage*, Emly, 1987

Power, V. Rev. P., *Waterford and Lismore: A Compendious History of the Dioceses*, Cork, 1937

Pyke, D., *Parish Priests and Churches of St Mary's, Clonmel*, 1984, Ir. 274 p 40

Ryan, C. A., *Tipperary Artillery, 1793-1889*, 1890, Ir. 355942 t 1

Sheehan, E. H., *Nenagh and its Neighbourhood* (including many family records), n.d.

Watson, Col S. J., *A Dinner of Herbs: a history of Old St Mary's Church, Clonmel*, Clonmel, 1988

Whelan, K. and Nolan, W., *Tipperary: History and Society*, Dublin, 1985

White, James (ed.), *My Clonmel Scrap Book*, n.d.

White, Rev. P., *History of Clare and the Dalcassian Clans of Tipperary, Limerick and Galway*, Dublin, 1893

Local journals

North Munster Antiquarian Society Journal, NL Ir. 794105 n 1 (Index 1897–1919, Ir. 7941 n 1)
Eile (Journal of the Roscrea Heritage Society), Ir. 94142 e 1
Cois Deirge, Ir. 94142 c 4
Clonmel Historical and Archaeological Society Journal, Ir. 94142 c 2

Directories

1788	Richard Lucas, *General Directory of the Kingdom of Ireland*, NL Pos. 3729
1820	J. Pigot, *Commercial Directory of Ireland*
1824	Pigot and Co., *City of Dublin and Hibernian Provincial Directory*, NL Ir. 9141 p 75
1839	T. Shearman, *New Commercial Directory for the Cities of Waterford and Kilkenny, Towns of Clonmel, Carrick-on-Suir, New Ross and Carlow*
1846	Slater's *National Commercial Directory of Ireland*
1856	Slater's *Royal National Commercial Directory of Ireland*
1866	George H. Bassett, *Directory of the City and County of Limerick and of the principal Towns in the Counties of Tipperary and Clare*, NL Ir. 914144 b 5
1870	Slater's *Directory of Ireland*
1881	Slater's *Royal National Commercial Directory of Ireland*
1886	Francis Guy, *Postal Directory of Munster*, NL Ir. 91414 g 8
1889	George H. Bassett, *The Book of County Tipperary*
1894	Slater's *Royal Commercial Directory of Ireland*

Gravestone inscriptions

Ballyclerihan: IGRS Collection, 145, GO
Holy Cross (C. of I.): GO MS. 622, 176/7
Kilmore: *The Irish Genealogist*, Vol. II, No. 10, 1953
Kiltinane: GO MS. 622, 144
Knigh: National Archives, search room
Littleton: GO MS. 622, 171
Newchapel: IGRS Collection, 101, GO
Uskeane: *The Irish Genealogist*, Vol. III, No. 2, 1957

Estate records

Description of the estate of John Sadleir in Limerick and Tipperary, JP 3439.
Newcomen estates: maps of estates to be sold, 20 July 1827, NL, Map Room.

Placenames

Townland Maps, Londonderry Inner City Trust

CO. TYRONE

Census returns and substitutes

1612–13	'Survey of Undertakers Planted in Co. Tyrone', *Historical Manuscripts Commission Report*, 4 (Hastings MSS.), 1947, 159–82
1630	Muster Roll, NL Pos. 206, PRONI T.808/15164
1631	Muster Roll, PRONI T.934
1654/6	Civil Survey, Vol. III, NL I 6551, Dublin
1660	Poll Book, NL Pos. 206
1661	Books of Survey and Distribution, PRONI T.370/C and D.1854/1/23
1664	Hearth Money Roll, NL MSS. 9583/4; also *Clogher Record*, 1965, *Seanchas Ardmhacha*, 1960/61 and PRONI T.283 D/2
1665	Subsidy roll, 1665, 1668, NL Pos. 206; PRONI T.458/1
1666	Hearth Money Roll, PRONI T.307
1699	Protestants in the parishes of Drumragh, Badoney and Cappagh, GO Sources Box 6
1740	Protestants, Derryloran and Kildress, RCB Library, PRONI T.808/15258
1766	Aghalow, Artrea, Carnteel, Clonfeacle, Derryloran, Donaghendry, Errigal Keerogue, Kildress, NA 1A 46 49, PRONI T.808/15264–7
1795–98	Voters List, Dungannon barony, PRONI TYR5/3/1
1796	Catholic migrants from Ulster to Mayo, see Mayo
1796	Spinning-Wheel Premium Lists, microfiche index in National Archives, comprising, in the case of Co. Tyrone, over 11,000 names
1821	Some extracts, Aghaloo. Thrift Abstracts, National Archives
1820s/30s	Tithe Books
1834	Valuation of Dungannon, *Parliamentary Papers*, 1837, Reports from Committees, Vol. II (i), Appendix G
1834	Clonoe (Coalisland), NL Pos. 5579
1851	Griffith's Valuation
1901	Census
1911	Census

Local history

Ardtrea Parish Ordnance Survey Memoir, 1833–36, NL Ir. 914112 o 6

Belmore, Earl of, *Parliamentary Memoirs of Fermanagh and Tyrone, 1613–1885*, Dublin, 1887

Donnelly, T. P., *A History of the Parish of Ardstraw West and Castlederg*, 1978, NL Ir. 94114 d 6

Drumquin . . . *A Collection of Writings and Photographs of the Past*, NL Ir. 91411 p
    10
Duffy J. (ed.), *A Clogher Record Album: a diocesan history*, NL Ir. 94114 c 3
Hutchison, W. R., *Tyrone precinct: a history of the plantation settlement of Dungannon
    and Mountjoy to modern times*, Belfast, 1951
Johnson and Preston, *Methodism in Omagh* . . . *over two centuries*, NL Ir. 27411
    p 5
Marshall J., *History of the Town and District of Clogher, Co. Tyrone, parish of Errigal
    Keerogue, Tyrone, and Errigal Truagh in the Co. of Monaghan*, 1930, NL I 94114
Marshall, J., *Vestry Records of the Church of St. John, parish of Aghalow*
O'Daly B., 'Material for a history of the parish of Kilskeery', *Clogher Record*,
    1953/4/5
Rutherford, J., *Donagheady: Presbyterian Churches and Parish*, 1953, NL Ir. 285 r 7
Shearman, H., *Ulster*, London, 1949 (incl. bibliographies)
Tyrone Almanac and Directory, 1872, NL Ir. 914114 t 2

Local journals

Seanchas Ard Mhacha (Journal of the Armagh Diocesan Historical Society), NL Ir.
    27411 s 4
Clogher Record (Journal of the Clogher Diocesan Historical Society), NL Ir. 94114 c 2
Derriana (Journal of the Derry Diocesan Historical Society), NL Ir. 27411 d 4
Duchas Neill, Journal of the O'Neill Country Society (from 1987)

Directories

1819   Thomas Bradshaw, *General Directory of Newry, Armagh, Dungannon,
        Portadown, Tandragee, Lurgan, Waringstown, Banbridge, Warrenpoint, Rostrevor,
        Kilkeel and Rathfryland*
1820   J. Pigot, *Commercial Directory of Ireland*
1824   Pigot and Co., *City of Dublin and Hibernian Provincial Directory*, NL Ir.
        9141 p 75
1842   Matthew Martin, *Belfast Directory*
1846   Slater's *Directory*
1852   James A. Henderson, *Belfast and Province of Ulster Directory*, issued also
        in 1854, 1856, 1858, 1861, 1863, 1865, 1868, 1870, 1877, 1880, 1884,
        1887, 1890, 1894, 1900
1856   Slater's *Royal National Commercial Directory of Ireland*
1865   R. Wynne, *Business Directory of Belfast*
1870   Slater's *Directory of Ireland*
1881   Slater's *Royal National Commercial Directory of Ireland*
1887   *Derry Almanac*, annually from this year
1894   Slater's *Royal Commercial Directory of Ireland*

Gravestone inscriptions

Clogher: *Clogher Cathedral Graveyard*, John Johnstone, 1972
Donaghacavey: *Clogher Record*, Vol. VII, No. 2, 1970
Drumglass: *Seanchas Ardmhacha*, Vol. VII, No. 2, 1974
Kilskeery: *Clogher Record*, Vol. VIII, No. 1, 1973

Irish World (26 Market Square, Dungannon, Co. Tyrone, BT70 1AB) has transcribed and computerised the inscriptions of more than 300 grave-yards in the six counties of Northern Ireland, principally in the four western counties of Armagh, Derry, Fermanagh and Tyrone.

Placenames

Townland maps, Londonderry Inner City Trust

CO. WATERFORD

Census returns and substitutes

1542–1650	Freemen of Waterford, *The Irish Genealogist*, Vol. 5, No. 5, 1978
1641	Book of Survey and Distribution, NL MS. 970
1641	Houses and tenants, Waterford City, National Archives, Quit Rent Office Papers; also JCHAS, Vol. 51, 1946
1662	Subsidy Roll of Co. Waterford, *Analecta Hibernica*, Vol. 30
1663	Waterford City inhabitants, including occupations, JCHAS, Vol. 51
1664–66	*Civil Survey*, Vol. VI
1766	Killoteran, NA 1A 46 49
1772	Hearth Money Roll for parts of Co. Waterford, *Waterford and South-East of Ireland Archaeological and Historical Society Journal*, Vol. XV, 1912
1775	Gentry of Co. Waterford, *Jnl of the Waterford and S.E. Ire. Arch. Soc.*, Vol. 16, No. 2, 1913
1776	Killoteran parish, NA 1A 46 49
1777–96	Births, Marriages and Deaths from Waterford newspapers, *The Irish Genealogist*, 1973, 1980, 1982

1778	Inhabitants of Waterford City, *Freeman's Journal*, 29 Oct. 1778; 5 Nov. 1778
1792	Leading Catholics of Waterford, *The Irish Ancestor*, Vol. 8, No. 11
1807	Waterford City voters, *The Irish Ancestor*, Vol. 8, No. 11
1821	Townland of Callaghane, parish of Ballygunner, *Decies* 16; Extracts from Waterford City, *The Irish Genealogist*, 1968/9
1820s/30s	Tithe Books
1847	Principal fishermen, Ring. J. Alcock, *Facts from the Fisheries, 1847*
1848/51	Griffith's Valuation, alphabetical index to householders (All-Ireland Heritage)
1901	Census
1911	Census

Local history

Butler, M., *The Barony of Gaultiere*, n.d.

Charter of the Liberties of Waterford, including a list of mayors, sheriffs and bailiffs, 1377–1806, NL I 6551; Kilkenny Council Books of the Corporation of Waterford, 1662–1700, NL Ir. 94141 p 3

Cuffe, Major O. T., *Records of the Waterford Militia, 1584–1885*, (1885), NL 355942

Downey, Edmund, *The story of Waterford to the middle of the 18th century*, Waterford, 1914, NL Ir. 94141 d 1

Egan, P. M., *History, guide and directory of the city and county of Waterford*, Kilkenny, 1891, NL Ir. 94191

Fitzpatrick, Thomas, *Waterford during the Civil War, 1641–53*, 1912

Ochille, F., *The Holy City of Ardmore, Co. Waterford*, Youghal, n.d.

Pender, S., *Waterford merchants abroad*, Ir. 941 p 23

Power, Rev. Patrick, *History of the County of Waterford*, Waterford, 1933

Power V. Rev. P., *Waterford and Lismore: A Compendious History of the Dioceses*, Cork, 1937

Rent and arrears due to the corporation for 1792, NL P 3000

Ryland, R. H., *The history, topography and antiquities of the county and city of Waterford*, London, 1824, NL Ir. 9141 r 1

Smith, Charles, *The ancient and present state of the county and city of Waterford . . .*, Dublin, 1774, NL Ir. 94141 s 1

Waterford Historical Society Proceedings, newspaper cuttings relating to Waterford, in nine vols, NL ILB 94141

Directories

| 1788 | Richard Lucas, *General Directory of the Kingdom of Ireland*, NL Pos. 3729 |
| 1809 | Holden's *Triennial Directory* |

1820   J. Pigot, *Commercial Directory of Ireland*
1824   Pigot and Co., *City of Dublin and Hibernian Provincial Directory*, NL Ir.
        9141 p 75
1839   T. Shearman, *New Commercial Directory for the Cities of Waterford and
        Kilkenny, Towns of Clonmel, Carrick-on-Suir, New Ross and Carlow*
1839   T. S. Harvey, *Waterford Almanac and Directory*
1846   Slater's *National Commercial Directory of Ireland*
1856   Slater's *Royal National Commercial Directory of Ireland*
1866   T. S. Harvey, *Waterford Almanac and Directory*
1869   Newenham Harvey, *Waterford Almanac and Directory*
1870   Slater's *Directory of Ireland*
1873   *Illustrated Waterford Almanack and Directory*, NL Ir. 014141 w 15
1881   Slater's *Royal National Commercial Directory of Ireland*
1886   Francis Guy, *Postal Directory of Munster*, NL Ir. 91414 g 8
1893   Francis Guy, *Postal Directory of Munster*
1894   Slater's *Royal Commercial Directory of Ireland*

Local journals

Decies (Journal of the Old Waterford Society), NL Ir. 9414 d 5
Journal of the Waterford and South-East of Ireland Archaeological Society, NL Ir.
    794105 w 1

Gravestone inscriptions

Affane: *The Irish Genealogist*, Vol. II, No. 9, 1952
Ballygunner Old: IGRS Collection, 56, GO
Ballynakill House: IGRS Collection, 16, GO
Ballynakill C. of I.: IGRS Collection, 40, GO
Churchtown (Dysert): *Decies* 25, 1984
Clashmore: *The Irish Genealogist*, Vol. II, No. 8, 1950
Crook Old: IGRS Collection, 138, GO
Crook R.C.: IGRS Collection, 4, GO
Carbally: IGRS Collection, 153, GO
Drumcannon: IGRS Collection, 86, GO
Dunhill Old: IGRS Collection, 23, GO
Dunmore East C. of I.: IGRS Collection, 123, GO
Faha Chapel of Ease: *Decies* 17, 1981
Faithlegg: IGRS Collection, 166, GO
Fenough: IGRS Collection, 16, GO
Fiddown: GO MS. 622, 150
Guilcagh C. of I.: IGRS Collection, 11, GO
Islandikane: IGRS Collection, 9, GO

Kilbarry: IGRS Collection, 48, GO
Killea Old: IGRS Collection, 94, GO
Killotteran: IGRS Collection, 31, GO
Kill St Lawrence: IGRS Collection, 170, GO
Kilmedan: IGRS Collection, 122, GO
Knockeen: IGRS Collection, 6, GO
Lisnakill: IGRS Collection, 35, GO
Mothel: *Decies*, 38, 39
Newcastle: IGRS Collection, 38, GO
Passage: IGRS Collection, 1, GO
Portlaw C. of I.: IGRS Collection, 7, GO
Rathgormuck: *Decies*, 37
Rathmoylan: IGRS Collection, 10, GO
Reisk: IGRS Collection, 86, GO
Stradbally, *Decies*, Vol. XVI, 1981
Waterford, St Patrick's: *Catholic Record of Waterford and Lismore*, Rev. P. Power,
    1916
Whitechurch: *The Irish Ancestor*, Vol. V, No. 1, 1973

Estate records

Rent roll, 1564, NL MS. 9034.
'Tenants of Bellew properties in and adjoining Dungarvan in 1760', *Waterford and South-East of Ireland Archaeological and Historical Society Journal*, Vol. XIX, No. 4, 1911.
'Ballysagart estate, 1849', *Decies* 27, 1984.
'The estate of George Lane Fox' (1857, mainly Kilbarry parish), *Decies* 26, 1984.

Placenames

Townland Maps, Londonderry Inner City Trust
Power, P., *The Place-names of Decies* (1907)

CO. WESTMEATH

Census returns and substitutes

1641   Book of Survey and Distribution, NL MS. 965
1659   Pender's 'Census', NL Ir. 31041 c 4
1666   Hearth Money Roll of Mullingar, *Franciscan College Journal*, 1950
1761–88   Freeholders, NL MSS. 787/8
1763   Poll Book, GO 443
1802–3   Protestants in the parishes of Ballyloughloe, Castletown Delvin,
          Clonarney, Drumraney, Enniscoffey, Kilbridepass, Killalon,
          Kilcleagh, Killough, Killua, Killucan, Leney, Moylicar,
          Rathconnell, *The Irish Ancestor*, 1973
1820s/30s Tithe Books
1832   Voters, *The Irish Genealogist*, Vol. 5, Nos 2 and 6; Vol. 6, No. 1
          (1975, 1979, 1980)
1837   Marksmen (i.e. illiterate voters), Athlone Borough, *Parliamentary
          Papers*, 1837, Reports from Committees, Vol. II (1), Appendix A
1835   Tubber parish, NL Pos. 1994
1854   Griffith's Valuation
*c.*1855 Partial census of Streete parish, NL Pos. 4236
1901   Census
1911   Census

Local history

Athlone: Material from printed sources relating to the history of Athlone and
    surrounding areas, 1699–1899, NL MSS. 1543–7, including an index
    volume
Clarke, Desmond, 'Athlone, a bibliographical study', *An Leabhar*, No. 10,
    1952, 138–9
Clarke, M. V., *Register of the priory of the Blessed Virgin Mary at Tristernagh*, IMC,
    NL Ir. 271 c 22
Egan, O., *Tyrellspass, Past and Present*, 1986, NL Ir. 94131 e 1
Grand Jurors: genealogies of the grand jurors of Co. Westmeath, 1727–1853,
    NL Ir. 94131 g 1
Monahan, Rev. J., *Records Relating to the Diocese of Ardagh and Clonmacnoise*, 1886
Irish Midland Studies (1980), NL Ir. 941 m 58
Paterson, J. (ed.), *Diocese of Meath and Kildare: an historical guide*, 1981, NL Ir. 941
    p 75
Sheehan J., *Westmeath as others saw it . . . AD 900 to the present*, (1982), NL Ir.
    94131 s 5

Stokes, George T., *Athlone, the Shannon and Louth Ree*, Dublin and Athlone, 1897, NL Ir. 91413 s 1
Westmeath Local Studies: a guide to sources, NL Ir. 94131 k 1
Woods, James, *Annals of Westmeath*, Dublin, 1907, NL Ir. 94131 w 1
Upton Papers, Royal Irish Academy: Wills and Deeds mainly relating to Co. Westmeath, NL Pos. 1997

Local journals

Journal of the Old Athlone Society, NL Ir. 94131 o 1
Ardagh and Clonmacnoise Historical Society Journal (1926–51), NL Ir. 794105
Riocht na Midhe (Records of the Meath Archaeological and Historical Society), NL Ir. 94132 r 1

Directories

1820   J. Pigot, *Commercial Directory of Ireland*
1824   Pigot and Co., *City of Dublin and Hibernian Provincial Directory*, NL Ir. 9141 p 75
1846   Slater's *National Commercial Directory of Ireland*
1856   Slater's *Royal National Commercial Directory of Ireland*
1870   Slater's *Directory of Ireland*
1881   Slater's *Royal National Commercial Directory of Ireland*
1894   Slater's *Royal Commercial Directory of Ireland*

Gravestone inscriptions

Athlone: *Athlone Abbey Graveyard Inscriptions*, H. A. Ryan, Longford/Westmeath Joint Libraries Committee, 1987
St Mary's Church of Ireland, with parish registers, NL Pos. 5309
St Peter's Church of Ireland, with parish registers, NL Pos. 5309
Ballyloughloe (Mount Temple): *The Irish Ancestor*, Vol. IV, No. 2, 1972
Carrick (near Mullingar): GO MS. 622, 171
Castletown (Finea): GO MS. 622, 107
Fore: IGRS Collection, 27, GO
Kilcleagh: *Moate, Co. Westmeath, a history of the Town and District*, Liam Cox, 1981
Killua: 'Monumental Inscriptions from some Graveyards in Co. Meath', N. French (unpub.), National Archives search room
Kilomenaghan: *Moate, Co. Westmeath, a history of the Town and District*, Liam Cox, 1981
Moate: *Moate, Co. Westmeath, a history of the Town and District*, Liam Cox, 1981
Mullingar (C. of I.): Dun na Si Heritage Centre, Moate, Co. Westmeath
Stonehall (C. of I.): GO MS. 622, 183
Streete: *Riocht na Midhe*, Vol. IV, No. 3, 1969

Placenames

Walsh, Rev. Paul, *The Place-names of Westmeath*, Ir. 92942 w 1

CO. WEXFORD

Census returns and substitutes

1618	Herald's Visitation of Co. Wexford, GO 48, NL Pos. 8286
1641	Book of Survey and Distribution, NL MS. 975
1654/6	Civil Survey, Vol. IX, NL I 6551, Dublin
1659	Pender's 'Census', NL Ir. 31041 c 4
1665–1839	Free Burgesses of New Ross, *Proceedings of the Royal Society of Antiquaries of Ireland*, Ser. 5, Vol. 1, pt 1 (1890), 298–309
1766	Ballynaslaney, NA 1A 41 100; Protestants in Edermine, GO 537
1776	Freemen of Wexford, *The Irish Genealogist*, 1976
1789	Protestant householders in the parish of Ferns, *The Irish Ancestor*, Vol. 13, No. 2, 1981
1792	Some Protestant householders in the parishes of Ballycanew and Killtrisk, *The Irish Ancestor*, Vol. 13, No. 2, 1981
1798	Protestants murdered in the rebellion, Cantwell, *Memorials of the Dead, Co. Wexford*, Vol. 10, 432; NL Ir. 9295 c 2
1798	List of persons who suffered loss of property in 1798, NL JLB 94107
1820s/30s	Tithe Books
1853	Griffith's Valuation
1861	Catholics in Enniscorthy parish, in Catholic records
1867	Marshallstown, *The Irish Genealogist*, 1985
1901	Census
1911	Census

Local history

Coghlan, P. J., *A directory for the co. of Wexford . . . townlands, gentlemen's seats and noted places*, 1867, NL Ir. 914138

Doyle, Lynn, *Ballygullion, County Wexford*, 1945

Doyle, Martin, *Notes and Gleanings Relating to the County of Wexford*, Dublin, 1868

Flood, W. H. Grattan, *History of Enniscorthy, County Wexford*, n.d.

Griffiths, George, *The chronicles of the county of Wexford*, NL Ir. 94138 g 1

Hay, Edward, *History of the Insurrection of County Wexford in 1798*, Dublin, 1803

Hore, H. J., *The Social State of the Southern and Eastern Counties of Ireland in the Sixteenth Century*, 1870

Hore, P. H., *History of the town and county of Wexford*, London, 1900–11, 6 vols, NL Ir. 94138 h 2

Kirk, Francis J., *Some Notable Conversions in the Co. of Wexford*, (1901)

'Owners of Land of one acre and upwards, Co. Wexford', NL I 6551, Wexford

Shapland Carew Papers and Maps, IMC, NL Ir. 399041 c 5

Local journals

Journal of the Old Wexford Society, Ir. 94138 o 5

The Past (Journal of the Ui Cinsealaigh Historical Society), Ir. 941382 p 1

Directories

1788   Richard Lucas, *General Directory of the Kingdom of Ireland*, NL Pos. 3729

1820   J. Pigot, *Commercial Directory of Ireland*

1824   Pigot and Co., *City of Dublin and Hibernian Provincial Directory*, NL Ir. 9141 p 75

1839   T. Shearman, *New Commercial Directory for the Cities of Waterford and Kilkenny, Towns of Clonmel, Carrick-on-Suir, New Ross and Carlow*

1846   Slater's *National Commercial Directory of Ireland*

1856   Slater's *Royal National Commercial Directory of Ireland*

1870   Slater's *Directory of Ireland*

1872   George Griffith, *County Wexford Almanac*

1881   Slater's *Royal National Commercial Directory of Ireland*

1885   George H. Bassett, *Wexford County Guide and Directory*

1894   Slater's *Royal Commercial Directory of Ireland*

Gravestone inscriptions

Memorials of the Dead, Brian J. Cantwell, Co. Wexford (complete): Vols V to IX, Master Index, Vol. X, Ir. 9295 c 2 and National Archives search room

Estate records

Alcock estate tenants, Clonmore, 1820, NL MS. 10169.

Baron Farnham estate rent books for Bunclody, 1775–1820, NL MSS. 787–8.

Co. Wexford rent lists, eighteenth century, NL MS. 1782.
Shapland-Carew rent books, 1740–63, NA 1A 41 49; see also Local History.

CO. WICKLOW

Census returns and substitutes

1641	Book of Survey and Distribution, NL MS. 969
1669	Hearth Money Roll, GO 667; NA m 4909
1745	Poll Book, PRONI 2659
1766	Dunganstown, Rathdrum, Wicklow, Ballynaslaney (Protestants only), GO 537
1792–96	Valuation of Corn Tithes, Newcastle, Co. Wicklow, with tenants' names, NL MS. 3980
1798	List of persons who suffered loss of property in 1798, NL JLB 94107
1820s/30s	Tithe Books
1847–56	Index to the Coolattin estate emigration records, *Journal of the West Wicklow Historical Society*, No. 1, 1983/4
1852/3	Griffith's Valuation, microfiche Index, Andrew Morris
1901	Census
1911	Census

Local history

Black, A. and C., *Guide to Dublin and Co. Wicklow*, 1888
Coleman, James, 'Bibliography of the counties Carlow, Kilkenny and Wicklow', *Waterford and S–E of Ire. Arch. Soc. Jnl*, 11, 1907–8, 126–33
Scott, G. D., *The stones of Bray* (the barony of Rathdown), Dublin, 1913, Ir. 914133 b 2

Local journals

Journal of the West Wicklow Historical Society
Journal of the Old Bray Society
Arklow Historical Society Journal, Ir. 94134 a 1

Directories

1788   Richard Lucas, *General Directory of the Kingdom of Ireland*, NL Pos. 3729
1824   Pigot and Co., *City of Dublin and Hibernian Provincial Directory*, NL Ir.
        9141 p 75
1846   Slater's *National Commercial Directory of Ireland*
1856   Slater's *Royal National Commercial Directory of Ireland*
1870   Slater's *Directory of Ireland*
1881   Slater's *Royal National Commercial Directory of Ireland*
1894   Slater's *Royal Commercial Directory of Ireland*

Gravestone inscriptions

Memorials of the Dead, Brian J. Cantwell, Co. Wicklow (complete), Vols I to IV;
    Master Index, Vol. X, Ir. 9295 c 2 and National Archives search room

Placenames

Townland Maps, Londonderry Inner City Trust
Price, Liam, *The Place-names of Co. Wicklow*, Dublin 1945–58, Ir. 92942 p 3

13

Family Histories

What follows is a full listing of the Irish family history section ('Ir. 9292') of the National Library of Ireland. Part 1 consists of individual works given alphabetically under the principal family treated. No attempt has been made to standardise 'O' and 'Mc', and it may be necessary to check names with and without the prefix. Part 2 lists general works under the author's surname. Although it is probably the largest single collection of Irish family histories, the Ir. 9292 section is by no means comprehensive, and does not include all the material of potential genealogical interest in the Library. It consists of two principal categories, published and privately printed pedigrees and family histories from the nineteenth and early twentieth century, generally relating to the Anglo-Irish, and the results of genealogical research, often carried out by the descendants of emigrants to the US, either in typescript or privately printed. The quality of both categories varies enormously. Also included here are some only of the Library's manuscript holdings.

PART 1

A

Adams: Rev. B. W. Adams, *A genealogical history of the family of Adams of Cavan*, 1903, Ir. 9292 a 7

Alen: H. L. L. Denny, *An account of the family of Alen of St Wolstan's, Co. Kildare*, 1903, Ir. 9292 a 1

Allen: W. E. D. Allen, *David Allen: the history of a family firm, 1857-1957*, Ir. 9292 a 8

Amory: Gertrude Meredith, *The Descendants of Hugh Amory, 1605-1805*, 1901, Ir. 9292 a 2

Anderson: (1) A. L. B. Anderson, *The Andersons of Co. Kilkenny*, 1931, Ir. 9292 a 11

(2) J. G. T Anderson, *Family Descent of Andersons of Flush and Bawn, Sixmile-cross, Co. Antrim*, 1977, Ir. 9292 a 11

Andrews: John Burls (ed.), *9 Generations: a history of the Andrews family of Comber*, 1958, Ir. 9292 a 9

Anketell: *A Short History of the Family of Anketell . . . compiled by one of its members*, 1901, Ir. 9292 a 6

Archdale: Henry B. Archdale, *Memoirs of the Archdales with the descents of some allied families*, Enniskillen, 1925, Ir. 9292 a 3

Ash: Rev. T. Martin (ed.), *The Ash Mss of 1735*, 1890, Ir. 9292 a 4

Aylmers: Sir F. J. Aylmer, *The Aylmers of Ireland*, 1931, Ir. 9292 a 5

B

Bagenal: P. H. Bagenal, *Vicissitudes of an Anglo-Irish Family, 1530-1800*, 1925, Ir. 9292 b 1

Ball: Rev. W. Ball Wright, *Ball Family Records*, 1908, Ir. 9292 b 2

Barrington: Amy Barrington, *The Barringtons: a Family History*, 1917, Ir. 9292 b 20

Barry: (1) A. de Barry, *De L'origine des Bary d'Irlande*, 1900, Ir. 9292 b 13

(2) C. de Bary, *Étude sur l'histoire des Bary-Barry*, 1927, Ir. 9292 b 24

(3) Rev. F. Barry, *Barrymore: records of the Barrys of Co. Cork from the earliest times to the present*, 1902, Ir. 9292 b 19

Barton: F. B. Barton, *Some account of the family of Barton*, 1902, Ir. 9292 b 12

Beamish: C. T. M. Beamish, *A genealogical study of a family in Co. Cork and elsewhere*, Ir. 9292 b 23

Beck: J. W. Beck, *Beck of Ireland*, 1930, Ir. 9292 p 23 (3)

Bernard: *The Bernards of Kerry*, 1922, Ir. 9292 b 3

Bessborough: Earl of Bessborough, *Lady Bessborough and her family circle*, London, 1940, Ir. 9292 b 17

Bewley: Sir E. T. Bewley, *The Bewleys of Cumberland and their Irish descendants*, 1902, Ir. 9292 b 4

Bingham: (1) M. Bingham, *Peers and Plebs: two families in a changing world*, London, 1975, Ir. 9292 b 35

(2) R. E. McCalmont, *Memoirs of the Binghams*, London, 1915, Ir. 9292 b 21

Birch: M. E. Birch, *The Birch genealogy*, Canada, 1978, Ir. 9292 b 44

Blacker: L. C. M. Blacker, *History of the Family of Blacker of Carrickblacker in Ireland*, 1901, Ir. 9292 b 5

Blake: (1) Martin J. Blake, *An Account of the Blakes of Galway*, 1898, Ir. 9292 b 60

(2) Martin J. Blake, *Blake Family Record, 1300–1700*, 1902, 1905, Ir. 9292 b 6

Blayney: E. Rowley-Morris, *The family of Blayney . . .*, 1890, Ir. 9292 b 7

Boleyn: E. G. S. Reilly, *Historical anecdotes of the families of Boleyn, Carey, Mordaunt, Hamilton and Jocelyn . . .*, Newry, 1825, Ir. 9292 b 14

Bolton: C. K. Bolton, *Bolton families in Ireland*, 1937, Ir. 9292 b 15

Bourne: M. A. Strange, *The Bourne families of Ireland*, 1970, Ir. 9292 b 32

Bowen: Elizabeth Bowen, *Bowen's Court*, London, 1944, Ir. 9292 b 18
Boyle: E. M. F. G. Boyle, *Genealogical Memoranda relating to the family of Boyle of Limavady*, 1903, Ir. 9292 b 8
Braden: B. B. Peel, *In search of the Peels and the Bradens*, Edmonton, 1986, Ir. 9292 p 23 (4)
Braly: (1) D. Braly, *A history of the Bralys*, 1975, Ir. 9292 b 38
    (2) D. Braly, *The Bralys, a family of the old south and the wild west*, 1980, Ir. 9292 b 50
Brennan: T. A. Brennan, *A history of the Brennans of Idough, Co. Kilkenny*, New York, 1975, Ir. 9292 b 42, 45
Brett: C. E. B. Brett, *Long Shadows Cast Before*, Edinburgh, 1978, Ir. 9292 b 43
Bronte: J. Cannon, *The road to Haworth*, London, 1980, Ir. 9292 b 49
Brooke: R. F. Brooke, *The burning river*, Dublin, 1961, Ir. 9292 b 27
Browne: (1) J. More, *A tale of two houses*, Shrewsbury, 1978, Ir. 9292 b 47
    (2) D. Browne, *Westport House and the Brownes*, 1981, Ir. 9292 b 52
Bryan: G. and J. Latterell, *Genealogical information on the Bryan/O'Bryan and Fitzgerald families*, 1981, Ir. 9292 b 54
Bullock: J. W. Beck, *Bullock or Bullick of Northern Ireland*, 1931, Ir. 9292 b 16
Burke: (1) T. U. Sadleir, *The Burkes of Marble Hall*, n.d., Ir. 9292 b 10
    (2) E. Burke, *Burke People and Places*, Whitegate, 1984, Ir. 9292 b 55
Butler: (1) *Account of the Family of Butlers . . .*, 1716, Ir. 9292 b 11
    (2) 'Journal of the Butler Society', 1968–, Ir. 9292 b 28
    (3) W. Clare, *Testamentary Records of the Butler Family*, Peterborough, 1932, Ir. 9292 b 59
Byrne: Mrs D. Byrne, 'Byrne and Kelly Notes' (typescript), 1968, Ir. 9292 b 29

C

Cahalan: D. Cahalan, *Patrick Cahalan 1833–1915, and his relatives in Ireland and America*, Berkeley, 1980, Ir. 9292 c 27
Cairns: H. C. Lawlor, *A History of the Family of Cairnes or Cairns*, 1906, Ir. 9292 c 1
Caldwell: W. H. Greaves-Bagshawe, *The Caldwell family of Castle Caldwell, Co. Fermanagh*, Ir. 9292 c 24
Camac: Frank O. Fisher, *Memoirs of the Camacs of Co. Down*, 1897, Ir. 9292 c 2
Caraher: 'Caraher Family History Society Journal', 1980–, Ir. 9292 c 28
Carlisle: R. H. Crofton, *Ann Jane Carlisle and her descendants*, 1950, Ir. 9292 c 15
Carey: (1) E. G. S. Reilly, *Historical anecdotes of the families of Boleyn. Carey, Mordaunt, Hamilton, and Jocelyn . . .*, Newry, 1825, Ir. 9292 b 14
    (2) H. Rudnitzky, *The Careys*, Belfast, 1978, Ir. 9292 c 23
Carson: (1) J. Carson, *Short history of the Carson family*, Belfast, 1909, Ir. 9292 c 3
    (2) J. Carson, *The Carsons of Monanton, Ballybay, Co Monaghan*, Lisburn, 1931, Ir. 9292 c 31

Cartland: G. and J. B. Cartland, *The Irish Cartlands and Cartland Genealogy*, Tasmania, 1978, Ir. 9292 c 30

Caulfield: B. Connor, *Clan Cathmhaoil or Caulfield Family*, Dublin, 1808, Ir. 9292 c 4

Charley: Irene Charley, *The romance of the Charley family*, 1970, Ir. 9292 c 21

Chichester: A. and B. Chichester, *History of the family of Chichester*, London, 1808, Ir. 9292 c 18

Clancy: M. Clancy, *Clancy: a brief family history*, US, 1980, Ir. 9292 p 20 (1)

Clayton: J. Paul Ryalands, *Some account of the Clayton family of . . . Doneraile and Mallow*, Liverpool, 1880, Ir. 9292 r 6

Coffey: A. Cuffez, *Coffey Genealogy*, Vols 1 and 2, 1983, Ir. 9292 c 25, 29

Cole: R. L. Cole, *The Cole family of West Carbery*, Belfast, 1943, Ir. 9292 c 13

Coote: *Historical and genealogical records of the Coote family*, 1900, Ir. 9292 c 6

Copinger: W. A. Copinger, *History of the Coppingers or Copingers of Co. Cork*, 1882, Ir. 9292 c 7

Conway: S. T. McCarthy, *Three Kerry Families: Mahonys, Conways and Spotiswoods*, Folkestone, 1923, Ir. 9292 m 7

Corry: Earl of Belmore, *History of the Corry Family of Castlecoole*, 1891, Ir. 9292 c 8

Cox: John H. R. Cox, *Claim of J. H. R. Cox to the Baronetcy of Cox of Dunmanway, Co. Cork* (. . .), 1912–14, Ir. 9292 c 9

Crawford: Robert Crawford, *The Crawfords of Donegal and how they came there*, 1886, Ir. 9292 c 14

Crichton: J. H. Steele, *Genealogy of the Earls of Erne*, London, 1910, Ir. 9292 e 5

Crofton: H. T. Crofton, *Crofton Memoirs: Account of John Crofton of Ballymurray, Co. Roscommon*, 1911, Ir. 9292 c 10

Crozier: R. A. Foulke, *The Crozier family of Dublin and Prince Edward Island*, US, 1979, Ir. 9292 c 26

D

Darbyshire: J. Harris, *The Darbyshire Genealogy*, Knollwood, 1983, Ir. 9292 d 15

Denham: C. H. Denham, *Denhams of Dublin*, Dublin, 1936, Ir. 9292 D 4

Devereux: G. O'C. Redmond, *The family of Devereux of Ballymagir*, 1891, Ir. 9292 d 1

Dignam: H. M. Dignam, *A chronicle of the Dignam family of Ireland and Canada*, Toronto, 1962, Ir. 9292 d 8

Dillon: (1) G. D. F. Dillon, *Lineage of G. D. F. Dillon, gent.*, Ir. 9292 d 9

(2) *Pedigree of Dillon. Vicounts Dillon*, 1912, Ir. 9292 d 2

(3) J. J. Dillon, *Claim of the Dillon family of Proudston to the Great Chamberlainship of all England*, 1829, Ir. 9292 d 7

Dineen: R. V. Spear, *The descendants of Redmond Peter Fahey and Cecilia Haverty, and John Sweeney and Mary Dineen, 1810–1894*, US, 1984, Ir. 9292 s 21

Donnelly: R. Fajazakas, *The Donnelly Album*, Ir. 9292 d 10
Downshire: H. McCall, *The House of Downshire*, Belfast, 1881, Ir. 9292 d 3
Downey: L. C. Downey, *A history of the Protestant Downey families of Counties Sligo, Leitrim, Fermanagh and Donegal*, 1931, Ir. 9292 d 13
Ducey: A. C. Ducey, *A family lifeline*, Chicago, 1981, Ir. 9292 d 14
Dundon: T. J. Dundon, *The Dundon Family*, Wisconsin, 1977, Ir. 9292 d 12
Dunlevy: G. D. Kelley, *A genealogical history of the Dunlevy family*, 1901, Ir. 9292 d 5

E

Eager: F. J. Eager, *The Eager family of Co. Kerry*, 1860, Ir. 9292 e 1
Ebel: M. Bingham, *Peers and Plebs: two families in a changing world*, London, 1975, Ir. 9292 b 35
Echlin: J. R. Echlin, *Genealogical memoirs of the Echlin family*, 1881, Ir. 9292 e 2
Edgeworth: (1) Harriet J. Butler (ed.), *The Black Book of Edgeworthstown*, 1917, Ir. 9292 e 3
       (2) E. E. McDonald, *The American Edgeworths*, Virginia, 1970, Ir. 9292 e 9
Ellis: W. S. Ellis, *Notices of the Ellises of England, Scotland and Ireland*, 1881, Ir. 9292 e 7
Ellison: H. H. Ellison, *In Search of my Family*, Dublin, 1971, Ir. 9292 e 10
Ely: *Adam Loftus and the Ely Family*, n.d., Ir. 9292 l 17
Emmett: T. A. Emmett, *The Emmett Family*, 1898, Ir. 9292 e 4
Eyre: (1) A. S. Hartigan, *A short account of the Eyre family of Eyre Court*, 1899, Ir. 9292 e 6
       (2) I. Gantz, *Signpost to Eyrecourt*, Bath, 1975, Ir. 9292 e 11

F

Fahey: R. V. Spear, *The descendants of Redmond Peter Fahey and Cecilia Haverty, and John Sweeney and Mary Dineen, 1810–1894*, US, 1984, Ir. 9292 s 21
Farnham: *Farnham Descents from Henry III*, Cavan, 1860, Ir. 9292 f 14
Ferrall: R. B. Ferrall, *History of the Ferralls and their American Genealogy*, US, 1981, Ir. 9292 f 18
Filory: S. P. Filory, *Fragments of family history*, London, 1896, Ir. 9292 f 3
Finn: T. M. MacKenzie, *Dromana: Memoirs of an Irish Family*, 1916, Ir. 9292 f 1
Finnegan: C. Fitzgibbon, *Miss Finnegan's Fault*, Ir. 9292 f 8
Fitzgerald: (1) Marquis of Kildare, *Descents of the Earls of Kildare and their wives*, Dublin, 1866–69, Ir. 9292 f 13
       (2) M. Estouche, *Heirs and Graces: the claim to the dukedom of Leinster*, London, 1981, Ir. 9292 f 16
       (3) J. A. King, *The Irish lumberman-farmer: Fitzgeralds, Harrigans and others*, California, 1982, Ir. 9292 f 17
       (4) *The case of Charlotte Fitzgerald and the barony of Roscommon*, 1921, Ir. 9292 f 20

(5) S. Hayman (ed.), *Unpublished Geraldine Documents* (2 volumes), 1870–81, Ir. 9292 g 2

(6) J. A. Gaughan, *The Knights of Glin, a geraldine family*, Dublin, 1978, Ir. 9292 g 17

(7) H. J. Gerrard, *The Meath Geraldines*, 1964, Ir. 9292 p 7 (6)

Fitzwilliam: D. G. Holland, *The Fitzwilliam, O'Brien and Watson families: history and genealogy*, 1973, Ir. 9292 f 11

Fleetwood: Sir E. Bewley, *An Irish Branch of the Fleetwood Family*, 1908, Ir. 9292 f 2

Fleming: (1) L. T. Fleming, *Fleming and Reeves of Co. Cork*, 1975, Ir. 9292 p 12 (4)

(2) Sir William Betham, *History and genealogical memoir of the family of Fleming of Slane*, Dublin, 1829, Ir. 9292 f 10; Ir. 9292 9 7 (10)

Flood: C. R. Patterson, *Flood Family Triad*, US, 1982, Ir. 9292 p 22

Folliots: Sir E. Bewley, *The Folliots of Londonderry and Chester*, 1902, Ir. 9292 f 5

Forbes: John Forbes, *Memoirs of the Earls of Granard*, 1868, Ir. 9292 g 5

French: *Origin of the family of French in Connaught*, Tuam, 1928, Ir. 9292 f 6

French: Rev. H. B. Swanzy, *The Families of French of Belturbet and Nixon of Fermanagh and their Descendants*, 1908, Ir. 9292 f 15

Fulton: Sir T. Hope, *Memoirs of the Fultons of Lisburn*, 1903, Ir. 9292 f 7

G

Galbraith: C. L. House, *The Galbraiths and the Kootenays*, New York, 1969, Ir. 9292 g 26

Galwey: C. J. Bennett, *The Galweys of Lota*, 1909, Ir. 9292 g 1

Gillman: A. W. Gillman, *Searches into the History of the Gillman or Gilman Family . . . in Ireland*, 1895, Ir. 9292 g 3

Goodbody: (1) M. I. A. Goodbody, *The Goodbody Family of Ireland*, Halstead, 1979, Ir. 9292 g 20

(2) M. I. A. Goodbody, *Goodbodys of Clara*, 1965, Ir. 9292 g 12

Gormley: V. R. and T. M. Spear, *Descendants of Bernard Gormley in New Brunswick*, California, 1982, Ir. 9292 g 25

Gowan: J. H. B. Gowan, *The genealogy of the Clan Gowan* (2 volumes), Bucks, 1978, Ir. 9292 g 19

Grace: Sheffield Grace, *Memoirs of the Family of Grace*, 1823, Ir. 9292 g 4

Grady: J. L. Grady, *From Ireland . . .*, 1984, Ir. 9292 g 24

Graves: H. H. G. MacDonnell, *Some Notes on the Graves family*, Dublin, 1889, Ir. 9292 g 18

Green: H. B. Swanzy and T. G. Green, *The Family of Green of Youghal*, 1902, Ir. 9292 g 15

Greene: Lt Col J. Greene, *Pedigree of the Family of Greene*, 1899, Ir. 9292 g 6

Gregory: V. R. T. Gregory, *The House of Gregory*, 1943, Ir. 9292 g 12

Grubb: G. W. Grubb, *The Grubbs of Tipperary*, 1972, Ir. 9292 g 13

Guinness: (1) R. Linn, *Pedigree of the Magennis (Guinness) family of New Zealand and Dublin*, Christchurch, 1897, Ir. 9292 g 7
(2) F. Mullally, *The silver salver: the story of the Guinness family*, London, 1981, Ir. 9292 g 21
Gunning: I. Gantz, *The pastel portrait: the Gunnings of Castlecoote and Howards of Hampstead*, London, 1963, Ir. 9292 g 23

H

Hagerty: J. L. Grady, *From Ireland . . .*, 1984, Ir. 9292 g 24
Halloran: M. L. Resch, *The descendants of Patrick Halloran of Boytonrath, Co. Tipperary*, Baltimore, 1987, Ir. 9292 r 12
Hamilton: (1) E. G. S. Reilly, *Historical anecdotes of the families of Boleyn, Carey, Mordaunt, Hamilton, and Jocelyn . . .*, Newry, 1825, Ir. 9292 b 14
(2) E. Hamilton, *Hamilton Memoirs*, Dundalk, 1920, Ir. 9292 h 1
Hanrahan: P. L. Hanrahan, *Hanrahan, family history*, Oregon, 1983, Ir. 9292 h 10
Harrigan: J. A. King, *The Irish lumberman-farmer: Fitzgeralds, Harrigans and others*, California, 1982, Ir. 9292 f 17
Harvey: G. H. Harvey, *The Harvey families of Inishowen, Co. Donegal, and Maen, Cornwall*, Folkestone, 1927, Ir. 9292 h 3
Hassard: Rev. H. B. Swanzy, *Some account of the Family of Hassard*, 1903, Ir. 9292 h 3
Haverty: R. V. Spear, *The descendants of Redmond Peter Fahey and Cecilia Haverty, and John Sweeney and Mary Dineen, 1810–1894*, US, 1984, Ir. 9292 s 21
Hawksby: L. C. Downey, T*he Hawksby family of Leitrim and Sligo*, 1931, Ir. 9292 d 13
Hayes: D. H. Crofton, *The children of Edmonston Park*, Peterhead, 1980, Ir. 9292 h 12
Heffernan: Patrick Heffernan, *The Heffernans and their times*, 1940, Ir. 9292 h 9
Hervey: D. A. Ponsonby, *Call a Dog Hervey*, London, 1949, Ir. 9292 h 14
Higginson: T. B. Higginson, *Descendants of Rev. Thomas Higgenson*, London, 1958, Ir. 9292 h 13, 15
Ho(a)re: Edward Hoare, *Account, from 1330, of the families of Hoare and Hore (. . .)*, 1883, Ir. 9292 h 5
Hogan: M. J. Culligan-Hogan, *The quest for the galloping Hogan*, New York, 1979, Ir. 9292 h 11
Holians: D. Regan, *The Holians, a Galway family in Australia*, 1984, Ir. 9292 r 10
Hollingsworth: Harry Hollingsworth, *The Hollingsworth Register*, 1965 to date, Ir. 9292 h 21
Hovenden: *Lineage of the family of Hovenden (Irish branch) by a member of the family*, 1892, Ir. 9292 h 6

J

Jacob: (1) A. H. Jacob and J. H. Glascott, *Historical and genealogical narration of the families of Jacob*, 1875, Ir. 9292 j 1

    (2) H. W. Jacob, *History of the Families of Jacob of Bridgewater. Tiverton and Southern Ireland*, 1929, Ir. 9292 j 4

Jellett: C. S. Gould, *Great trees from little saplings*, New York, 1931, Ir. 9292 j 3

Jephson: Brigadier M. D. Jephson, *An Anglo-Irish Miscellany: Some Records of the Jephsons of Mallow*, 1964, Ir. 9292 j 2

Jocelyn: E. G. S. Reilly, *Historical anecdotes of the families of Boleyn, Carey, Mordaunt, Hamilton, and Jocelyn . . .*, Newry, 1825, Ir. 9292 b 14

Joyce: K. Nutting, *The Joyces of Overflow and Eidsvold*, Brisbane, 1961, Ir. 9292 p 23 (2)

K

Kelly: (1) Turquet de la Boisserie, *Kelly of Nenton*, Ir. 9292 k 8

    (2) P. O'Kelly d'Aghrim, *Annales de la maison d'Hy Many*, La Haye, 1830, Ir. 9292 o 2

    (3) 'Notes on the O'Kellys and other families of Kilkeerin parish, Co. Roscommon' (typescript), Ir. 9292 k 5

    (4) J. D. Williams, *History of the name O'Kelly*, Dublin, 1977, Ir. 9292 p 14 (3)

Keeffe: B. Brodee, *Keeffe and Toner Families in Ireland and the U.S.*, Iowa, 1984, Ir. 9292 b 61

Kennedy: F. M. E. Kennedy, *A family of Kennedy of Clogher and Londonderry, 1600–1938*, Taunton, 1938, Ir. 9292 k 1

Kernans: *The Utica Kernans, descendants of Bryan Kernan, gent, . . . Co. Cavan*, 1969, Ir. 9292 k 7

Kerr: H. C. Kerr, *History of the Gabriel and George Kerr families, and other Kerr families from Enniskillen*, Quebec, 1976, Ir. 9292 k 9

Kirkpatrick: A. Kirkpatrick, *Chronicles of the Kirkpatrick family*, 1897, Ir. 9292 k 3

Kirwan: *Pedigree of the Kirwan family*, Ir. 9292 k 2

Knox: A. K. [sic] *Notes on some of the Ranfurly Knoxes*, 1950, Ir. 9292 k 10

L

Lally: D. P. O'Mullally, *History of O'Mullally and Lally Clans*, 1941, Ir. 9292 o 19

La Touche: *Genealogy of the La Touche Family of France*, Strasbourg, 1883, Ir. 9292 l 3

Le Fanu: T. Le Fanu, *Memoir of the Le Fanu Family*, 1924, Ir. 9292 l 4 ,

Lefroy: Sir J. H. Lefroy, *Notes and Documents relating to the Lefroy family (. . .) of Carrickglas, Co. Longford*, 1868, Ir. 9292 l 18

Lenox-Conyngham: M. Lenox-Cunningham, *An old Ulster house, and the people who lived in it*, 1946, Ir. 9292 l 14

Le Poer Trench: 2nd Earl of Clancarty, *Memoir of the Le Poer Trench family*, Dublin, 1874, Ir. 9292 l 5

Leslie: (1) P. Leslie Pielou, *The Leslies of Tarbert, Co. Kerry, and their forebears*, 1935, Ir. 9292 l 12
  (2) Seymour Leslie, *Of Glaslough in the kingdom of Oriel, and of noted men who have dwelt there*, 1913, Ir. 9292 l 6
Levinge: Sir Richard Levinge, *Jottings for the Early History of the Levinge Family*, 1873, Ir. 9292 l 7 and 15
Lindsay: (1) J. C. and J. A. Lindsay, *The Lindsay Memoirs* (Lisnacrieve and Belfast), 1884, Ir. 9292 l 8
  (2) E. H. Godfrey, *The Lindesays of Loughry, Co. Tyrone*, 1949, Ir. 9292 l 16
  (3) Daryl Lindsay, *The leafy tree, my family*, Cheshire, 1967, Ir. 9292 l 21
Lloyd: A. R. Lloyd, *Genealogical Notes*, n.d., Ir. 9292 l 13
Loftus: *Adam Loftus and the Ely Family*, n.d., Ir. 9292 l 17
Londonderry: H. M. Hyde, *The Londonderrys, a family portrait*, London, 1979, Ir. 9292 l 20
Lowther: Sir Edmund Bewley, *Lowthers in Ireland in the 17th century*, 1902, Ir. 9292 l 9
Lynch: (1) E. C. Lynch, *Lynch Record*, New York, 1925, Ir. 9292 l 10
  (2) Martin J. Blake, 'Lynch of Galway', 1912–17, Ir. 9292 l 19
Lyster: E. Alinor-Lyster, *Lyster Pioneers of Lower Canada*, British Columbia, 1984, Ir. 9292 l 22

Mc

McCann: A. Mathews, *Origins of the Surname McCann*, Dublin, 1968, Ir. 9292 m 37 (2)
McCarthy: (1) A. MacCarthy, *A historical pedigree of the MacCarthys of Gleannacrain*, Exeter, 1855, Ir. 9292 m 1
  (2) S. T. McCarthy, *A McCarthy Miscellany*, Dundalk, 1928, Ir. 9292 m 1
  (3) S. T. McCarthy, *The McCarthys of Munster*, 1927, Ir. 9292 m 1
  (4) P. Louis Laine, *Généalogie de la maison McCarthy*, Ir. 9292 m 1
  (5) M. J. O'Brien, *The McCarthys in early American history*, New York, 1921, Ir. 9292 o 25
  (6) J. D. Williams, *History of the Name MacCarthy*, Dublin, 1978, Ir. 9292 w 21 (3)
McClusky: W. H. McClusky, *A tree of four ancient stocks*, Iowa, 1984, Ir. 9292 m 44
McDermot: The McDermot, *The McDermots of Moylurg and Coolavin*, 1985, Ir. 9292 m 58
McDonald: A. B. MacDonald, *A romantic chapter in family history*, 1911, Ir. 9292 m 16
McDonnell: (1) G. Hill, *A historical account of the MacDonnells of Antrim*, Belfast, 1873 (repr. 1978), Ir. 9292 m 2
  (2) A. McDonnell, *The Antrim McDonnells*, Belfast, 1979, Ir. 9292 m 42
  (3) B. W. Kelly, *The Fate of Glengorry*, Dublin, 1905, Ir. 9292 m 41

McGillycuddy: W. B. Mazier, *The MacGillicuddy Papers*, 1867, Ir. 9292 m 3
McGready: S. McGready and S. Jennett, *A Family of Roses*, London, 1971, Ir. 9292 m 35
McGuinness: A. Mathews, *Origins of the Surname McGuinness*, Dublin, 1968, Ir. 9292 m 32 (3)
McGuire: B. Patterson, *Pat and Rose Anne McGuire and their descendants*, Madison, 1980, Ir. 9292 m 53
McKee: R. W. McKee, *The Book of McKee*, Dublin, 1959, Ir. 9292 m 26
McKenna: (1) C. E. Sweezy, *The MacKennas of Truagh*, 1977, Ir. 9292 s 20
    (2) A. Mathews, *Origins of the Surname McKenna*, Dublin, 1968, Ir. 9292 m 37 (3)
McKinney: B. M. Walker, *Sentry Hill: an Ulster farm and family*, Belfast, 1981, Ir. 9292 w 19
McKittrick: F. L. McKittrick, *The McKittricks and the roots of Ulster Scots*, Baltimore, 1979, Ir. 9292 m 45
McLysaght: E. MacLysaght, *Short study of a transplanted family in the seventeenth century*, Dublin, 1935, Ir. 9292 m 18
McNamara: (1) R. W. Twigge, *The pedigree of John McNamara Esq.*, pr. pr. 1908, Ir. 9292 m 19
    (2) E. Forgnes, *Histoire d'un sept irlandais*, 1901, Ir. 9292 m 22
McRory: R. F. Cronnelly, *A History of the Clanna-Rory*, 1921, Ir. 9292 r 1
MacSweeny: P. Walsh, *An account of the MacSweeny families in Ireland*, 1920, Ir. 9292 m 5

M

Madden: (1) F. Madan, *The Madan family and Maddens of England and Ireland*, Oxford, 1930, Ir. 9292 m 15
    (2) T. M. O'Madden, *The O'Maddens of Hy Many*, 1894, Ir. 9292 o 6
Magan: J. Lentaigne, *Pedigree of the Magan family of Ennoe, Co. Westmeath*, Dublin, 1868, Ir. 9292 m 17
Magee: F. J. Biggar, *The Magees of Belfast and Dublin*, 1916, Ir. 9292 m 6
Mahony: S. T. McCarthy, *Three Kerry Families: Mahonys, Conways and Spotiswoods*, Folkestone, 1923, Ir. 9292 m 7
Malenfont: A. V. Malenfont, *Malenfont families*, New South Wales, Ir. 9292 m 51
Marshall: G. F. Marshall, *Marshall of Manor Cunningham*, Fleet, 1931, Ir. 9292 m 21
Martin: (1) A. E. S. Martin, *Genealogy of the Family of Martin of Ballinahinch Castle, Co. Galway*, 1890, Ir. 9292 m 8
    (2) S. Clark, *The genealogy of the Martins of Ross*, Inverness, 1910, Ir. 9292 m 34
    (3) G. V. Martyn, *Historical notes on the Martyns of the west of Ireland*, n.d., Ir. 9292 p 9 (3)

(4) M. J. Blake, *Martyn of Cregans, Co. Clare, 1613–1927*, Ir. 9292 c 19

(5) B. E. Martin, *Parsons and Prisoners*, 1972, Ir. 9292 m 36 and m 39

Massey: *A genealogical account of the Massey family from the time of the conquest*, Dublin, 1890, Ir. 9292 m 28

Maunsell: E. P. Statham, *History of the Family of Maunsell*, 1917, Ir. 9292 m 9

Maxwell: W. G. Maxwell, *The annals of one branch of the Maxwell family*, Malaya, 1959, Ir. 9292 m 27

Meade: H. J. Peet, *Chaumiere papers . . . the descendants of David Meade*, n.d., Ir. 9292 m 23

Meagher: N. A. Meagher, *The Meaghers*, New York, 1980, Ir. 9292 m 47

Meares: M. and G. Meares, *Pedigree of the family of Meares of Co. Westmeath*, Dublin, 1905, Ir. 9292 m 38

Monck: E. Batt, *The Moncks and Charleville House*, Dublin, 1979, Ir. 9292 b 46

Monroe: Horace Monroe, *Foulis Castle and the Monroes of Lower Iveagh*, 1929, Ir. 9292 m 10

Montgomery: (1) W. Montgomery, *The Montgomery Manuscripts, 1603–1706*, Belfast, 1869, Ir. 9292 m 11

(2) E. J. S. Reilly, *A genealogical history of the Montgomerys . . . of Mount Alexander and Grey-Abbey*, 1942, Ir. 9292 m 24

Moore: (1) T. J. G. Bennett, *North Antrim Families*, 1974, Ir. 9292 b 23

(2) J. Hore, *The Moores of Moore Hall*, London, 1939, Ir. 9292 M 20

(3) The Countess of Drogheda, *The family of Moore,* Dublin, 1906, Ir. 9292 m 12

Moran: A. J. Moran, *Your father is a Moran and your mother was a Murphy*, 1987, Ir. 9292 m 61

Mordaunt: E. G. S. Reilly, *Historical anecdotes of the families of Boleyn, Carey, Mordaunt, Hamilton, and Jocelyn . . .*, Newry, 1825, Ir. 9292 b 14

Morris: E. Naomi Chapman, *Memoirs of my Family, together with some researches into the Early History of the Morris Families of Tipperary, Galway, and Mayo*, 1928, Ir. 9292 m 13

Mulock: Sir Edmund Bewley, *The Family of Mulock*, 1905, Ir. 9292 m 14

Murphy: (1) B. and M. Doyle, *Murphy: a family history*, US, 1981, Ir. 9292 m 46

(2) J. D. Williams, *History of the name Murphy*, Dublin, 1977, Ir. 9292 p 14 (1)

N

Nash: (1) E. F. Nash, *The Nash Family of Farrihy Co. Cork, etc.*, Ir. 9292 n 3

(2) A. C. S. Pabst, *Nashes of Ireland*, Ohio, 1963, Ir. 9292 n 9

Nangle: (1) F. R. and J. F. T. Nangle, *A short account of the Nangle family of Downpatrick*, 1986, Ir. 9292 n 8

(2) *A genealogical memoir of the extinct Anglo-Norman Catholic family of Nangle of Garisker, Co. Kildare*, 1869, Ir. 9292 n 2

Neill: I. Wilson, *Neills of Bangor*, Coleraine, 1982, Ir. 9292 n 6

Nesbitt: A. Nesbitt, *History of the family of Nesbitt in Scotland and Ireland*, Torquay, 1898, Ir. 9292 n 1

Nixon: Rev. H. B. Swanzy, *The Families of French of Belturbet and Nixon of Fermanagh and their Descendants*, 1908, Ir. 9292 f 15

O

O'Brien: (1) D. G. Holland, *The Fitzwilliam, O'Brien and Watson families: history and genealogy*, 1973, Ir. 9292 f 11

    (2) J. D. Williams, *History of the name O'Brien*, Dublin, 1977, Ir. 9292 p 14 (2)

    (3) J. O'Donoghue, *The O'Briens*, 1860, Ir. 9292 o 1

    (4) D. O'Brien, *History of the O'Briens*, London, 1946, Ir. 9292 o 24

    (5) *Playfair's Family Antiquities* (Earls of Thomond), 2 vols, Ir. 9292 o 29

    (6) H. Weir, *O'Brien people and places*, Whitegate, 1983, Ir. 9292 o 44

O'Byrne: (1) *The O'Byrnes and their descendants*, Dublin, 1879, Ir. 9292 o 22

    (2) P. L. O'Toole, *History of the clan O'Byrne and other Leinster septs*, Dublin, 1890, Ir. 9292 o 42

O'Cleirigh: P. Walsh, *The O'Cleirigh family of Tir Conaill*, Dublin, 1938, Ir. 9292 o 17

O'Connell: Basil O'Connell, *O'Connell Family Tracts*, Dublin, 1950, Ir. 9292 o 26

O'Conor: (1) Charles O'Conor, *The O'Conors of Connaught*, Dublin, 1891, Ir. 9292 o 2

    (2) Roderick O'Conor, *A history and genealogical memoir of the O'Conors of Connaught and their descendants*, Dublin, 1861, Ir. 9292 o 32

    (3) Roderick O'Conor, *The Anonymous Claim of Mr Arthur O'Connor*, Dublin, 1859, Ir. 9292 O 33

    (4) Roderick O'Conor, *Lineal Descent of the O'Conors of Co. Roscommon*, Dublin, 1862, Ir. 9292 o 34

O'Daly: E. R. O'Daly, *History of the O'Dalys*, New Haven, 1937, Ir. 9292 o 14

O'Dempsey: T. Mathews, *An account of the O'Dempseys*, Dublin, 1903, Ir. 9292 o 3

O'Devlin: J. C. Devlin, *The O'Devlins of Tyrone*, US, 1938, Ir. 9292 o 15

O'Doherty: A. Mathews, *Origins of the Surname O'Doherty*, Dublin, 1968, Ir. 9292 m 37 (4)

O'Donnell: E. T. Cook, *John O'Donnell of Baltimore, his forebears and descendants*, 1934, Ir. 9292 o 13

O'Donoghue: (1) M. O'Laughlin, *O'Donoghues*, 1980, Ir. 9292 p 23 (5)

    (2) A. Mathews, *Origins of the Surname O'Donoghue*, Dublin, 1968, Ir. 9292 m 37 (5)

O'Doyne: K. W. Nicholls (ed.), *The O'Doyne Mss*, IMC, Dublin, 1983, Ir. 9292 o 46

O'Dwyer: (1) Sir M. O'Dwyer, *The O'Dwyers of Kilnamanagh*, London, 1933, Ir. 9292 o 4

    (2) M. Callanan, *Records of Four Tipperary Septs: the O'Kennedys, O'Dwyers, O'Mulryans, and O'Meaghers*, Galway, 1938, Ir. 9292 o 16

O'Flaherty: A. Mathews, *Origins of the Surname O'Flaherty*, Dublin, 1968, Ir.
9292 m 32 (2)
O'Gowan: *A memoir of the name of O'Gowan or Smith, by an O'Gowan*, Tyrone,
1837, Ir. 9292 o 12
O'Kelly: A. Mathews, *Origins of the Surname O'Kelly*, Dublin, 1968, Ir. 9292 m
32 (1)
O'Kennedy: M. Callanan, *Records of Four Tipperary Septs: the O'Kennedys,
O'Dwyers, O'Mulryans, and O'Meaghers*, Galway, 1938, Ir. 9292 o 16
Oliver: H. O. Rea, *Henry (William) Oliver 1807–1888: ancestry and descendants*,
Dungannon, 1959, Ir. 9292 o 28
O'Madden: T. M. O'Madden, *The O'Maddens of Hy Many*, 1894, Ir. 9292 o 6
O'Mahoney: (1) J. B. O'Mahoney, *A history of the O'Mahony septs of Kinalmeaky
and Iveragh*, Cork, 1912, Ir. 9292 o 20
(2) *The O'Mahony Journal*, Vol. 1, 1971–, Ir. 9292 o 38
O'Malley: *Genealogy of the O'Malleys of the Owals*, Philadelphia, 1913, Ir. 9292 o 21
O'Meagher: (1) J. C. O'Meagher, *The O'Meaghers of Ikerrin*, 1886, Ir. 9292 o 7
(2) M. Callanan, *Records of Four Tipperary Septs: the O'Kennedys, O'Dwyers,
O'Mulryans, and O'Meaghers*, Galway, 1938, Ir. 9292 o 16
O'Mullally: D. P. O'Mullally, *History of O'Mullally and Lally Clans*, 1941, Ir.
9292 o 19
O'Mulryan: M. Callanan, *Records of Four Tipperary Septs: the O'Kennedys,
O'Dwyers, O'Mulryans, and O'Meaghers*, Galway, 1938, Ir. 9292 o 16
O'Neill:(1) T. Mathews, *The O'Neills of Ulster*, 1907, Ir. 9292 o 8
(2) D. Braly, *Ui Neill: a history of Western Civilization's oldest family*, 1976, Ir.
9292 o 35
(3) Anne O'Neill, *Odds and ends about Shane's castle and some of its inhabitants*,
London, 1904, Ir. 9292 o 39
(4) P. Walsh (ed.), *The will and family of Hugh O'Neill, Earl of Tyrone*, Dublin,
1930, Ir. 9292 o 41
(5) M. Westacott, *The Clan Niall in Ireland, 379–1030*, Sydney, 1970, Ir. 9292
n 5
(6) A. Mathews, *Origins of the Surname O'Neill*, Dublin, 1968, Ir. 9292 m 37 (1)
(7) J. D. Williams, *History of the Name O'Neill*, Dublin, 1978, Ir. 9292 w 21 (1)
O'Reilly: (1) E. M. O'Hanluain, *The O'Reillys of Temple Mills, Celbridge*, Dublin,
1940, Ir. 9292 o 18
(2) J. J. O'Reilly, *The history of Breifne O'Reilly*, New York, 1975, Ir. 9292 o 36
(3) J. Carney (ed.), *A genealogical history of the O'Reillys*, 1959, Ir. 9292 o 18
(4) A. Mathews, *Origins of the Surname O'Reilly*, Dublin, 1970, Ir. 9292 o 31 (2)
Orpen: Goddard H. Orpen, *The Orpen Family*, 1930, Ir. 9292 o 9
O'Rourke: (1) J. C. Smith, *The Children of Master O'Rourke*, London, 1978, Ir.
9292 o 37
(2) B. McDermott, *O'Ruairc of Breifne*, 1983, Ir. 9292 o 45
(3) A. Mathews, *Origins of the Surname O'Rourke*, Dublin, 1970, Ir. 9292 o 31 (1)

Osborne: J. Osborne, *The Osbornes of Co. Louth and Nicollot County, Wisconsin,* US, 1978, Ir. 9292 o 40

O'Sullivan: (1) M. R. O'Sullivan, *The Beginning of the O'Sullivan Sept,* New Jersey, 1975?, Ir. 9292 p 12 (5)

(2) M. R. O'Sullivan, *Sullivan Sept: Inter Sept,* Ir. 9292 p 12 (6)

(3) J. D. Williams, *History of the Name O'Sullivan,* Dublin, 1978, Ir. 9292 w 21 (2)

O'Toole: (1) P. L. O'Toole, *History of the Clan O'Toole, and other Leinster septs,* Dublin, 1890 (4 vols), Ir. 9292 o 10

(2) C. P. Meehan, *The O'Tooles, anciently lords of Powerscourt,* Dublin, 1911, Ir. 9292 o 10

(3) C. D. Comte O'Kelly-Farrell, *Notice sur le clan des O'Toole . . .,* La Reole, 1864, Ir. 9292 o 49

(4) L. O'Tuathalain, *Notes of the genealogy of the O'Tuathalains of Cloonyquin, Clontarf, and Clara,* 1985, Ir. 9292 o 47

Ouseley: R. J. Kelly, *The Names and family of Ouseley,* 1910, Ir. 9292 o 11

Owen: H. Owen, *Owen and Perrin family histories,* 1981, Ir. 9292 o 43

P

Palmer: T. Prime, *Some account of the Palmer family of Rahan, Co. Kildare,* New York, 1903, Ir. 9292 p 4

Palatines: (1) R. Hayes, *The German Colony in Co. Limerick,* 1937, Ir. 9292 h 8

(2) Hank Jones, *The Palatine Families of Ireland,* San Leandro, 1965, Ir. 9292 p 6

Patterson: B. Patterson, *Edmund and Margaret (Leamy) Patterson and their descendants,* Madison, 1979, Ir. 9292 p 18

Peel: B. B. Peel, *In search of the Peels and the Bradens,* Edmonton, 1986, Ir. 9292 p 23 (4)

Pentheny: *Memoir of the Ancient Family of Pentheny or De Pentheny of Co. Meath,* 1821, Ir. 9292 p 13

Penrose: C. Penrose, *The Penrose family of Halston, Wheeldrake, and Co. Wicklow,* New York, 1975, Ir. 9292 p 11

Perrin: H. Owen, *Owen and Perrin family histories,* 1981, Ir. 9292 o 43

Pilkington: *Harland's history of the Pilkingtons, from the Saxon times (. . .) to the present,* 1882, Ir. 9292 p 1

Pim: F. B. Pim, *A Pim genealogy,* n.d., Ir. 9292 p 21

Poe: Sir E. T. Bewley, *Origin and Early History of the Family of Poe, with full Pedigrees of the Irish Branch . . .,* 1906, Ir. 9292 p 2

Pooles: Rosemary ffolliott, *The Pooles of Mayfield, Co. Cork and Other Irish Families,* 1956, Ir. 9292 p 5

Power: B. Patterson, *Patrick, Margaret, Jeffrey and Ellen Power and their descendants,* Madison, 1980, Ir. 9292 p 17

Pratt: (1) John Pratt, *The Family of Pratt of Gawsworth, Carrigrohane, Co. Cork*, 1925,
    Ir. 9292 p 3
    (2) John Pratt, *Pratt Family records: an account of the Pratts of Youghal and
    Castlemartyr and their Descendants*, 1931, Ir. 9292 p 15

R
Ranahans: J. P. M. Feheny, *The Ranahans of Iverus, Co. Cork*, 1987, Ir. 9292 r 14
Rea: (1) H. O. Rea, *Samuel Rea, 1725–1811: his heritage and descendants*, 1960, Ir.
    9292 r 6
    (2) J. H. Rea, *The Rea Genealogy*, Banbridge, 1927, 1971, Ir. 9292 r 8
    (3) *A Belfast Man: memoirs of the Rea family, 1798–1857*, London, 1857, Ir.
    9292 r 11
Reagan: Hugh Peskett, 'Presented to the Hon. Ronald Reagan on behalf
    of . . . Ballyporeen', Ir. 9292 p 19
Reeves: L. T. Fleming, *Fleming and Reeves of Co. Cork*, 1975, Ir. 9292 p 12 (4)
Roberts: E. J. A. Impey, *A Roberts Family, quondam Quakers of Queen's Co.*, 1839,
    Ir. 9292 r 3
Rochfort: R. R. Forlong, *Notes on the history of the family of Rochfort*, Oxford,
    1890, Ir. 9292 r 4
Rudkin: Sir E. T. Bewley, *The Rudkins of the Co. Carlow*, 1905, Ir. 9292 r 2

S
Saunderson: Henry Saunderson, *The Saundersons of Castle Saunderson*, 1936, Ir.
    9292 s 10
Savage: G. F. Savage-Armstrong, *The Savages of the Ards*, 1888, Ir. 9292 s 1
Seaver: Rev. G. Seaver, *History of the Seaver Family*, 1950, Ir. 9292 s 12
Segrave: C. W. Segrave, *The Segrave Family, 1066–1935*, 1936, Ir. 9292 s 9
Shannon: J. Shannon (ed.), *The Shannon Saga*, New South Wales, 1972, Ir.
    9292 p 9 (1)
Shaw: N. Harris, *The Shaws*, London, 1977, Ir. 9292 s 18
Shirley: E. P. Shirley, *Shirlieana, or Annals of the Shirley Family*, 1873, Ir. 9292 s 2
Sinnett: C. N. Sinnett, *Sinnet genealogy . . . records of Sinnets, Sinnots etc. in Ireland
    and America*, 1910, Ir. 9292 s 3
Slacke: H. A. Crofton, *Records of the Slacke Family in Ireland*, 1900–1902, Ir. 9292
    s 4
Smeltzer: (1) M. R. Smeltzer, *The Smeltzers of Kilcooley and their Irish-Palatine
    kissing cousins*, Baltimore, 1981, Ir. 9292 s 19
    (2) M. R. Smeltzer, *Irish-Palatine Smeltzers around the world*, Baltimore, 1987,
    Ir. 9292 s 23
Smith: (1) *A memoir of the name of O'Gowan or Smith, by an O'Gowan*, Tyrone,
    1837, Ir. 9292 o 12
    (2) G. N. Nuttall-Smith, *The chronicle of a Puritan family in Ireland*, Oxford,
    1923, Ir. 9292 s 5

(3) *Memoir of the descendants of William Smith in New Hampshire*, 1903, Ir. 9292 s 24

Spotiswood: S. T. McCarthy, *Three Kerry Families: Mahonys, Conways and Spotiswoods*, Folkestone, 1923, Ir. 9292 m 7

Standish: J. Richard Houston, *Numbering the Survivors: a history of the Standish family of Ireland, Ontario and Alberta*, 1980, Ir. 9292 s 22

Stewart: G. Hill, *The Stewarts of Ballintoy, with notices of other families in the district in the seventeenth century*, Ballycastle, 1976, Ir. 9292 p 20 (2)

Stoney: F. S. Stoney, *Some old annals of the Stoney family*, n.d., Ir. 9292 s 11

Stopford: L. O'Broin, *Protestant nationalists in revolutionary Ireland: the Stopford connection*, Dublin, 1985, Ir. 9292 s 15

Stuart: A. G. Stuart, *A genealogical and historical sketch of the family of Stuart of Castlestuart in Ireland*, Edinburgh, 1854, Ir. 9292 s 6

Studdert: R. H. Studdert, *The Studdert Family*, 1960, Ir. 9292 s 13

Sullivan: T. C. Armory, *Materials for a family history of John Sullivan of Bewick, New England and Ardee*, 1893, Ir. 9292 s 7

Sweeney: R. V. Spear, *The descendants of Redmond Peter Fahey and Cecilia Haverty, and John Sweeney and Mary Dineen, 1810–1894*, US, 1984, Ir. 9292 s 21

Synan: (1) Mannanaan Mac Lir [*sic*], *The Synans of Doneraile*, 1909, Ir. 9292 s 17

(2) Rev. J. A. Gaughan, *The family of Synan*, 1971, Ir. 9292 s 16

T

Taaffe: Count E. F. J. Taaffe, *Memoirs of the family of Taaffe*, 1856, Ir. 9292 t 1

Tiernan: C. B. Tiernan, *The Tiernans and other families*, 1901, Ir. 9292 t 2

Tone: F. J. Tone, *History of the Tone family*, New York, 1944, Ir. 9292 t 11

Toner: B. Brodee, *Keeffe and Toner Families in Ireland and the U.S.*, Iowa, 1984, Ir. 9292 b 61

Toolan: L. O'Tuathalain, *Notes of the genealogy of the O'Tuathalains of Cloonyquin, Clontarf, and Clara*, 1985, Ir. 9292 o 47

Trant: S. Trant McCarthy, *The Trant Family*, Folkestone, 1924, Ir. 9292 t 3

Travis/Travers: A. Casey, *Southern Travis, Travers and Traverse families*, 1978, Ir. 9292 t 10

Trench: (1) T. R. F. Cooke-Trench, *A Memoir of the Trench Family*, 1896, Ir. 9292 t 5

(2) Henry Trench, *Trench Pedigree*, 1878, Ir. 9292 t 8

Tweedy: Owen Tweedy, *The Dublin Tweedys: The Story of an Irish Family*, 1956, Ir. 9292 t 9

Tyrrell: J. H. Tyrrell, *Genealogical History of the Tyrrells of Castleknock in Co. Dublin, Fertullagh in Co. Westmeath and now of Grange Castle, Co. Meath*, 1904, Ir. 9292 t 6

U

Ussher: Rev. W. B. Wright, *The Ussher Memoirs . . .*, 1889, Ir. 9292 u 1

W

Wall: Hubert Gallwey, *The Wall family in Ireland, 1170–1970*, 1970, Ir. 9292 w 14

Walsh: (1) *Une famille royaliste irlandaise et française*, Nantes, 1903, Ir. 9292 w 1

(2) M. de Courcelles, *Généalogie de la maison de Walsh*, Paris, 1825, Ir. 9292 w 13

(3) J. C. Walsh, *The lament for John McWalter Walsh, with notes on the history of the family of Walsh, 1170–1690*, New York, 1925, Ir. 9292 w 20

Stoker Wallace: E. G. Brandt, *Memoirs of the Stoker Wallaces*, Chicago, 1909, Ir. 9292 w 25

Warren: C. O'Boyle, *The Warren Saga*, Derry, 1946, Ir. 9292 w 8

Washington: George Washington, *The Irish Washingtons*, 1898, Ir. 9292 w 24

Waters: E. W. Waters, *The Waters or Walter Family of Cork*, 1939, Ir. 9292 w 5

Watson: D. G. Holland, *The Fitzwilliam, O'Brien and Watson families: history and genealogy*, 1973, Ir. 9292 f 11

Wauchope: G. M. Wauchope, *The Ulster Branch of the Family of Wauchope*, 1929, Ir. 9292 w 7

White: John D. White, *The History of the Family of White of Limerick, Knocksentry, etc.*, 1887, Ir. 9292 w 10

Williams: J. F. Williams, *The Groves and Lappan: Co. Monaghan . . . in search of the genealogy of the Williams Family*, 1889, Ir. 9292 w 2

Wilson: A. Wilson, *Fragments that remain*, Gloucester, 1950, Ir. 9292 w 9

Winter Cooke: G. J. Forth, *Report on the English and Irish background of the Winter Cooke family*, 1980, Ir. 9292 w 18

Wogan: Count O'Kelly, *Mémoire historique et généalogique sur la famille de Wogan*, Paris, 1896, Ir. 9292 w 3

Wolfe: Major R. Wolfe, *The Wolfes of Forenaghs, Co. Kildare*, 1885, Ir. 9292 w 4, 17, 23

Woods: J. R. Woods and L. C. Baxter, *William and Eliza Woods of Co. Antrim, their descendants, and some allied families*, Baltimore, 1984, Ir. 9292 w 22

Wray: C. V. Trench, *The Wrays of Donegal, Londonderry and Antrim*, 1945, Ir. 9292 w 6

Wyly: D. A. A. Wyly, *Irish Origins: a family settlement in Australia*, 1976, Ir. 9292 w 15, 16

Y

Young: Amy Young, *300 Years in Inishowen, being . . . and account of the Family of Young of Culdaff with short accounts of many other families connected with them*, 1929, Ir. 9292 y 1

Z

Zlatover: M. Berman and M. Zlatover, *Zlatover story: a Dublin story with a difference*, Dublin, 1966, Ir. 9292 z 1

PART 2

Appleton, E. G., *A family 'tapestry: the interwoven threads of some Anglo-Irish and French families*, Cambridge, 1948, Ir. 9292 a 10

Black, J. A., *Your Irish Ancestors*, London, 1974, Ir. 9292 b 51, 53

The Clans of Ireland, Dublin, 1956, Ir. 9292 c 17

Clare, W., *Guide to copies and abstracts of Irish wills*, 1930, Ir. 9292 c 5

Cronnelly, R. F., *Irish Family History*, n.d., Ir. 9292 c 11

Cronnelly, R. F., *A history of Clan Eoghan*, 1964, Ir. 9292 c 16

Cronnelly, R. F., *A simple guide to Irish Genealogy*, 1966, Ir. 9292 c 12

de Breffny, Brian, *Bibliography of Irish Family History and Genealogy*, Cork, 1974, Ir. 9292 d 10

de Courcy, B. W. (ed.), *A genealogical history of the Milesian families of Ireland*, 1880, Ir. 9292 d 6

Edwards, R. D., *Irish Families: the archival aspect*, Ir. 9292 p 10 (1)

Falley, M. J., *Irish and Scotch-Irish Ancestral Research*, Illinois, 1962, Ir. 9292 f 9

Family Links, Vol. 1, 1981–, Ir. 9292 f 19

Grehan, Ida, *Irish Family Names*, London, 1973, Ir. 9292 g 14

Griffith, M. C., *How to use the records of the Republic of Ireland*, Salt Lake City, 1969, Ir. 9292 p 8 (2)

Henchy P., *Three centuries of emigration from the British Isles: Irish emigration to North America . . .*, Salt Lake City, 1969, Ir. 9292 p 8 (1)

L'Estrange, A. G. K., *Connor and Desmond*, 1897, Ir. 9292 g 16

Gaelic Gleanings, Vol. 1, 1981–, Ir. 9292 g 22

Irish Family History Society Newsletter, Vol. 1, 1978–, Ir. 9292 i 3

Kearsley's Peerage, 1796 (3 vols), Ir. 9292 k 4

Laffan, T., *Tipperary's Families: Hearth Money Rolls, 1665–7*, Dublin, Ir. 9292 l 11

MacCarthy, C. J. F., 'Cork Families' (typescript), 1973, Ir. 9292 p 9 (4)

Mac Giolla Domhnaigh, P., *Some Ulster Surnames*, Dublin, 1923 (repr. 1975), Ir. 9292 p 12 (3)

MacLysaght, E., *Irish Families*, Dublin, 1966, Ir. 9292 m 25

MacLysaght, E., *More Irish Families*, Dublin, 1968, Ir. 9292 m 25

MacLyaght, E., *Supplement to Irish Families*, Dublin, 1970, Ir. 9292 m 25

MacLyaght, E., *Bibliography of Irish Family History*, Dublin, 1981, Ir. 9292 m 52

Magee, Peggy, *Tracing your Irish Ancestors*, US, 1986, Ir. 9292 m 59

Mayo, H. N., *The McDonnell, Simpson, McLaughlin and Arnold families and early paper-making in the U.S. . . .*, 1986, Ir. 9292 p 23 (1)

Mullen, T. H., *The Ulster Clans: O'Mullen, O'Kane, OMellan*, Belfast, 1966, Ir. 9292 m 29

Mullen, T. H., *Roots in Ulster soil: a family history*, Belfast, 1967, Ir. 9292 m 54

Mullen, T. H., *Families of Ballyrashane*, Belfast, 1969, Ir. 9292 m 33

Murphy, H., *Families of Co. Wexford*, Dublin, 1986, Ir. 9292 m 60

Newport Macra an Tuaithe, *Newport Local Names*, 1981, Ir. 9292 p 20 (4)

Ni Aonghusa, Nora, *How to trace your Irish roots*, Dublin, 1986, Ir. 9292 n 10

O'Hart, John, *Historic Princes of Tara*, 1873, Ir. 9292 o 5

Rooney, John, *A genealogical history of Irish families*, New York, 1895, Ir. 9292 r 7

Ryan, J. G., *A guide to tracing your Dublin ancestors*, Dublin, 1988, Ir. 9292 r 15

Smythe-Wood, P. (ed.), *Index to Clonfert and Kilmacduagh Wills*, 1977, Ir. 9292 p 12 (2)

Sweezy, C. E., *The Irish Chiefs: a directory*, New York, 1974, Ir. 9292 p 10 (6)

Ulster Genealogical and Historical Guild Newsletter (continued as *Familia*), Ir. 9292 u 3

Ulster Genealogical and Historical Guild: Subscribers' interest list, Ir. 9292 u 2

Williams, A. H. D., *Read about your Irish roots* (16 parts), Ir. 9292 r 13 (1–16), covering Burke, Byrne, Carroll, Daly, Doherty, Doyle, Fitzgerald, Kennedy, Lynch, Murray, O'Connor, O'Donnell, O'Reilly, Ryan, Smith, Walsh

14

Church of Ireland Parish Records in Dublin Repositories

What follows is a listing of all Church of Ireland parish registers, originals, copies and extracts to be found at present (1991) in Dublin repositories, as well as those which have been published. It is *not* a complete list of all surviving records. In particular, no attempt has been made to cover those records for which copies are only available in the Public Record Office of Northern Ireland, in effect the records of all parishes in the six counties of Northern Ireland which survived 1922, or records which are still only available locally. Only records of baptisms, marriages and burials are included (i.e. no vestry records, preachers' lists etc. are given). Where only extracts from the relevant records are available, this is indicated. Where 'RCBL' appears, the original records are deposited in the Representative Church Body Library. The microfilm copies in the RCBL are from the Public Record Office of Northern Ireland. National Archives 'M' numbers may be either original records or transcripts. National Archives microfilms cover both originals and copies made locally before the originals were deposited in the Public Record Office, and destroyed in 1922. For this reason the National Archives' own list showing records destroyed in 1922 is not always an accurate guide to what is actually available. It should be remembered that for microfilm copies of parish records in the dioceses of Kildare, Glendalough and Meath, particularly those with registers extending up to the 1980s, written permission is required from the local clergyman before the Archives can allow research.

Parish	Baptisms	Marriages	Burials	Location
Co. Antrim				
Belfast Cathedral	–	1874–93	–	RCBL (mf)
also:	–	1745–99	–	IMA, Vol. 12/13
Jordanstown	1878–1974	–	–	RCBL (mf)
Co. Armagh				
Newtownhamilton	1622–1826	1622–1826	1622–1826	NL MS. 2669 (Leslie transcript)
Newry	1784–1864	1784–1864	1784–1864	NL MSS. 2202–34 (Leslie transcript)
Mullaghbrack	1622–1826	1622–1826	1622–1826	NL MS. 2669 (Leslie transcript)
Co. Carlow				
Bilboa	–	1846–1956	–	RCBL
Carlow	1695–1885	1695–1915	1698–1894	RCBL
also:	1744–1816	1744–1816	1744–1816	GO 578 (extracts)
	1698–1835	1698–1835	1698–1835	NA ref. 1073
Cloonegoose	–	1846–1954	–	RCBL
Clonmish	–	1846–1934	–	RCBL
Dunleckney	1791–1837	1791–1957	1791–1837	RCBL
Kellistown	–	1854–1917	–	RCBL
Killeshin (see Carlow)				
Kiltennel	1837–75	1837–1950	1837–1957	RCBL
Lorum	–	1845–1954	–	RCBL
Nurney	–	1845–1954	–	RCBL
Old Leighlin	1781–1813	1790–1855	1781–1813	RCBL
Painstown (St Ann)	1859–1919	1864–1913	–	RCBL
also with Carlow records in NA				
Tullow	1696–1844	1700–1843	1700–1844	RCBL
Wells	1870–1957	1803–1915	1802	RCBL
Co. Cavan				
Annagh (see Cloverhill)	1803–1985	1801–1916	1803–1985	RCBL (mf)
Ashfield (see also Kilsherdoney)	1821–1907	1845–1956	1818–1985	RCBL (mf)
also:	1821–76			NA M.5077–80
Arvagh	1877–1905	1845–1941	1877–1921	RCBL (mf)
Baillieboro (see also Knockbride)	1824–1985	1824–1985	1809–1915	RCBL (mf)
Ballintemple	1880–1955	1845–1952	1880–1971	RCBL (mf)
Ballyjamesduff	1877–1986	1845–1955	1879–1985	RCBL (mf)
Ballymachugh	1816–1932	1815–1901	1816–1986	RCBL (mf)
Billis	–	1851–1900	–	RCBL (mf)

Castlerahan	1879–1986	1846–1956	1879–1982	RCBL (mf)
Cloverhill	1860–1985	1860–1956	–	RCBL (mf)
Crosserlough	1801–78	1801–1949	1803–1938	RCBL (mf)
(Kildrumferton)				
Denn	1879–1982	1845–1954	1879–1986	RCBL (mf)
Dernakesh	1837–1905	1838–1942	1837–1985	RCBL (mf)
Derryheen	1879–1984	1846–1917	1879–1983	RCBL (mf)
Derrylane	1845–1917	1846–1945	1875–1958	RCBL (mf)
Dowra	1877–91	–	–	RCBL (mf)
Drumgoon	1802–1909	1825–1957	1825–1915	RCBL (mf)
Drumlane	1874–1985	1845–1932	1877–1982	RCBL (mf)
(see also Quivy)				
Kildallon	1856–1986	1845–1923	1877–1985	RCBL (mf)
Killeshandra	1735–1982	1735–1955	1735–1955	RCBL (mf)
Killoughter	1827–1982	1827–43	1827–1905	RCBL (mf)
(Redhills)				
Killinagh	1877–1941	–	1877–1956	RCBL (mf)
Killinkere	1878–99	1845–98	1877–1901	RCBL (mf)
(see also Billis)				
Kilmore	1702–1950	1702–1930	1702–1970	RCBL (mf)
Kilsherdoney	1796–1982	1796–1845	1797–1929	RCBL (mf)
(Kildrumsherdan)				
Kinawley	1761–1972	1761–1935	1761–1966	RCBL (mf)
Kingscourt	–	1845–1949	–	RCBL
Knockbride	1825–1917	1827–1930	1866–1971	RCBL (mf)
Loughan	–	1880–91	–	RCBL (mf)
Lurgan	1831–1902	1831–1900	1831–1901	RCBL (mf)
Moybologue	–	1878–1956	–	RCBL
(Baillieboro)				
Mullagh	1877–1984	1946–48	1877–1986	RCBL (mf)
Munterconnaght	1857–1901	1845–99	1857–1901	RCBL (mf)
Quivy	1854–1938	1857–1940	–	RCBL (mf)
Shercock	1881–1979	1846–1955	1881–1976	RCBL (mf)
Swanlinbar	1798–1863	1798–1952	1798–1883	RCBL
Tomregan	1797–1984	1802–1913	1805–1986	RCBL (mf)
Templeport	1837	1845–1954	1878–1906	RCBL
Urney	1804–1940	1804–1946	1804–1916	RCBL (mf)

Co. Clare

Clare Abbey	–	1845–1901	–	RCBL
Clondegad	–	1845–85	1882–1915	RCBL
Clonlea	1879–1947	1845–1946	1877–1951	RCBL
Drumcliff (Ennis)	1744–1870	1744–1845	1744–1869	NA MFCI 1, M5222
Kildysert	1881–1920	1847–1918	1882–1915	RCBL
Kilfarboy	–	1845–1957	–	RCBL
Kilfenora	–	1853–1918	–	RCBL

Kilferagh	–	1845–1954	–	RCBL
also:	1829	1829	–	NA M5244
Kilfinaghty	–	1862–1969	–	RCBL
Killard	–	1848–1933	–	RCBL
Killaloe	1679–1872	1682–1845	1683–1873	NA MFCI 5, M5222
Kilmanaheen	1886–1972	1845–1920	–	RCBL
Kilmurry	1889–1972	1845–1905	1892–1954	RCBL
Kilnaboy	1799–1831	1802–1961	1821–31	RCBL
Kilnasoolagh	1731–1874	1799–1844	1786–1876	NA MFCI 2, 5, M5222
also:	1731–1829	1746–1954	1739–1829	RCBL
Kilrush	1741–1872	1760–1845	1742–1873	NA MFCI 4, 5, M5240, 5235
also:	1741–1840	1766–1841	1742–1841	RCBL
Kilseily	1881–1915	1848–1905	1877–1951	RCBL
Ogonnelloe	1807–70	1807–65	1836–75	NA MFCI 5
Quin	1907–54	1845–1915	1906–27	RCBL

Co. Cork

Abbeymahon	1782–1852	1738–1852	1732–1852	RCBL (transcript)
also:	1827–73	–	–	NA MFCI 18 & 20
Abbeystrewery	1788–1915	–	–	NA MFCI 32
Aghabulloge	–	1808–43	–	O'K, Vol. 14
also:	1808–77	1808–43	1808–79	NA M.5067
Aghada	1730–1921	1730–1915	1730–1924	NA M.6075–77a, 6201, MFCI 20, 30, 36
Ballyclogh	1831–1900	1831–1948	1831–1900	NA M.5047
Ballymartle	1799–1868	–	1800–76	NA M.5081
Ballymodan	1695–1878	1695–1958	1695–1878	RCBL, also NA
Ballymoney	1805–71	1805–54	1805–73	NA MFCI 19
Ballyvourney	–	1845–1935	–	O'K, Vol. 11
Berehaven (Killaconenagh)	1787–1872	1784–1844	1796–1873	NA M.6051, MFCI 25
Blackrock	1828–97	1828–1981	1830–1946	RCBL
also:	1828–72	1828–44	1828–71	NA MFCI 19
Bridgetown & Kilcummer	1859–71	–	–	NA M.5083
Brigown	1751–1870	1775–1848	1775–1871	NA MFCI 21, M6044
Brinny	1797–1884	1797–1844	1797–1884	RCBL (transcript)
also:	1797–1884	1797–1844	1797–1884	NA MFCI 28
Buttevant	1873–1900	–	–	O'K, Vol. 11
Caheragh	1836–71	1837–43	1860–78	NA MFCI 19
Caherlog	–	1870–1955	–	RCBL
Carnaway	–	1845–71	–	RCBL

Carrigaline	1724–1871	1791–1871	1808–79	NA MFCI 19
				NA M.6001, 6028
also:	1724–56	1726–92	–	RCBL
Carrigleamleary	–	1848–71	–	O'K, Vol. 14
Carrigtohill	1776–1875	1779–1844	1776–1843	NA MFCI 24
also:	–	1848–1955	–	RCBL
Castletownroche	1728–1928	1728–1893	1733–1803	NA M.5048, 5083
Clondrohid	–	1848–84	–	RCBL
also:	–	1848–1984	–	O'K, Vol. 11
Clonfert	–	1845–47	–	O'K, Vol. 14
Clonmel (Cobh)	1761–1870	1761–1845	1761–1870	NA MFCI 28 & 29
Clonpriest	–	1851–70	–	NA M.5114
Cloyne	1708–1871	1708–1845	1708–1871	NA MFCI 30,
				M.6072, 6036
Cork City				
Holy Trinity	1664–1871	1643–1845	1644–1885	NA MFCI 21, 22
St Anne	1772–1871	1772–1845	1779–1882	NA MFCI 25, 26,
				27; M.6053, 6059
(Garrison Chapel & Foundling Hospital)				
St Luke	1837–74	–	–	NA MFCI 27
St Mary	1802–78	1802–40	1802–78	NA MFCI 22,
				M6049, 5064
St Nicholas	1725–1870	1726–1845	1726–1870	NA MFCI 23, 24,
				25, M.6047
Corkbeg	1836–72	1838–50	1836–74	NA MFCI 36
Cullen	1779–1876	1775–1851	1779–1873	NA MFCI 6
Desertserges	1811–71	1811–45	1811–72	NA MFCI 27, 28
Doneraile	1869–1952	–	–	O'K, Vol. 14
Douglas	1789–1818	1792–1893	1790	RCBL
also:	1789–1872	1792–1845	1789–1871	NA MFCI 29
Drimoleague	1802–71	1802–11	1802–72	NA MFCI 31,
				M6086
Dromtarriffe	–	1849–1913	–	O'K, Vol. 11
Dungourney	1850–1954	–	–	RCBL
Fanlobbus	1855–71	–	1853–71	NA M5110
Fermoy	1802–73	1803–45	1805–71	NA MFCI 25
Frankfield	–	1847–1955	–	RCBL
Glengarriff	1863–1913	–	–	NA M5113
Inch	–	1847–1948	–	NA M6077b
Inchigeelagh	1900	1845–65	–	RCBL
Iniscarra	1820–71	1820–44	1820–72	NA MFCI 25
also:	1870–1901	1845–1903	1852–1901	O'K, Vol. 14
Inishannon	1693–1844	1693–1911	1693–1844	RCBL
also:	1696–1871	1693–1844	1693–1879	NA MFCI 28, 29
Kilbritain	1832–76	1830–68	–	RCBL (transcript)
Kilbrogan	1752–1871	1753–1845	1707–1877	NA MFCI 29,
				M6065

Killanully	1831–74	–	1836–77	NA M6029, 6030
Killeagh	1782–1870	1776–1879	1782–1884	NA M5114
also:	1782–1863	1778–1840	1787–1868	RCBL (extracts)
Killowen	1833–74	–	1851–1972	NA MFCI 28
Kilmahon	–	1808–1944	–	NA M6046
Kilroan	1885–1920	1846–1920	–	RCBL
Kilshannig	1731–1877	1731–1846	1731–1876	NA MFCI 18, M6031
also:	1731–1965	1845–1925	1855–1958	O'K, Vols 11, 14
Kinneigh	1794–1877	1814–44	1815–70	NA M6038
Kinsale	1684–1871	1688–1864	1685–1872	NA MFCI 30, 31, M6071
Knockavilly	1837–83	1844–48	–	NA MFCI 28
also:	1837–83	1844–48	1837–83	RCBL (transcript)
Leighmoney	1869–1943	–	–	RCBL
Lislee	1809–90	1809–44	1823–89	NA MFCI, 18, 20, M6041
Macroom	1727–1837	1737–1835	1727–1835	NA M5138
also:	1727–1913	1727–1913	1727–1913	O'K, Vols 8, 14
Magourney	1757–1876	1756–1844	1758–1876	NA M5118
Mallow	1793–1871	1793–1863	1793–1871	NA MFCI 18, 19
also:	1783–1965	1845–1936	–	O'K, Vols 11, 14
Marmullane	1801–73	1797–1843	1801–73	NA MFCI 29, 32
also:	1801–73	1802–1954	1803–73	RCBL
Middleton	1810–83	1811–81	1809–83	NA M5119
also:	1699–1881	1728–1823	1696–1877	RCBL (extracts)
Monkstown	1842–72	1841–44	1842–1903	NA MFCI 30
Murragh	1750–1876	1739–1876	1784–1876	NA MFCI 27, M6056, 6060, 6063
Nohaval	1846–70	–	1846–75	NA M6033, 6039
Rahan	1773–1833	1773–1833	1773–1833	NA, no ref.
also:	–	1847–59	–	O'K, Vol. 14
Rathclaren	1780–1875	1780–1849	1792–1875	RCBL (transcript)
Rathcooney	1750–1871	1749–1849	1750–1853	NA MFCI 24, 25
also:	1750–1897	1749–1854	1750–1853	RCBL
Ringcurran	1793–1870	1793–1829	1849–72	NA MFCI 30, M6070
Rosscarbery (Ross)	1690–1871	1704–1845	1696–1870	NA MFCI 19
Rushbrook	1866–72	–	–	NA M6073
Schull	1826–73	–	–	NA MFCI 25
Templemartin	1845–79	–	1845–79	NA MFCI 24, M6048
Templemichael	1845–53	–	–	RCBL
Templenacarriga	–	–	1883–1932	RCBL
Timoleague	1827–78	–	–	RCBL (transcript)
Youghal	1665–1871	1666–1842	1665–1871	NA MFCI 19, 20, M6034/5, 6042

Co. Derry

Culmore	1867–1920	1865–1935	–	RCBL (mf)
Templemore (Derry Cathedral)	1642–1703	1669–1800	1669–1800	PRS

Co. Donegal

Ardara	1829–1954	1845–1956	1876–1984	RCBL (mf)
Aughanunshin	1878–94	1845–1971	1878–90	RCBL
Burt	1829–1913	1829–1929	1829–1941	RCBL (mf)
Clondahorky	1871–1906	1845–1915	1884–1926	RCBL (mf)
Clonleigh	1872–1983	1845–1956	1877–1984	RCBL (mf)
Convoy	1871–1981	1845–1902	1881–1981	RCBL (mf)
Conwal	1876–1971	1845–1988	1878–1906	RCBL
Craigadooish	–	–	1871–1907	RCBL (mf)
Culedaff	1875–1911	1845–1921	1876–1980	RCBL (mf)
Desertegney	–	1848–1929	1879–1981	RCBL (mf)
Donaghmore	1818–1902	1817–1955	1824–92	RCBL (mf)
Dunlewey	–	1853–82	–	RCBL (mf)
Fahan Upper	1762–1921	1814–1909	1832–1934	RCBL (mf)
Fahan Lower	1817–1980	1818–1939	1822–1983	RCBL (mf)
Gartan	1881–1959	1845–1946	–	RCBL
Glenalla	1871–1983	1871–1951	1906–1981	RCBL (mf)
Glencolumbkille	1827–1984	1845–1954	1828–1975	RCBL (mf)
Gleneely	1872–1981	1859–1954	–	RCBL (mf)
Glenties	1898–1972	–	1898–1982	RCBL (mf)
Gweedore	1880–1980	1855–1952	1881–1982	RCBL (mf)
Inch	1868–1951	1846–1946	1868–1965	RCBL (mf)
Inniskeel	1818–64	1818–64	1818–64	NA M5749
also:	1699–1700	1699–1700	1699–1700	NA M5749
also:	1852–1948	–	1852–1983	RCBL (mf)
Kilcar	1819–1957	1819–1938	1818–1930	RCBL (mf)
Killea	1877–1922	1845–1931	–	RCBL (mf)
Killybegs	1809–1983	1810–1944	1806–1984	RCBL (mf)
Kilteevoge	1818–1979	1845–96	1825–1921	RCBL (mf)
Lettermacaward	1889–1982	–	1890–1981	RCBL (mf)
Leck	1878–1975	1846–1959	1878–1900	RCBL
Meenglass	–	1864–1963	–	RCBL (mf)
Milford	1880–1981	1860–1949	1902–76	RCBL (mf)
Muff	1837–1986	1837–1956	1847–75	RCBL (mf)
Newtowncunningham	1877–1937	1845–97	1820–1955	RCBL (mf)
Raymochy	1844–1986	1845–1982	1878–1986	RCBL (mf)
Stranorlar	1802–70	1821–93	1821–1976	RCBL (mf)
Tullyaughnish	1798–1983	1798–1935	1798–1983	RCBL (mf)
Taughboyne	1820–1983	1836–1906	1836–1982	RCBL (mf)
Templecarn	1825–1936	1825–1906	1825–1905	RCBL (mf)
Templecrone	1878–1982	–	1879–1980	RCBL (mf)

Co. Down

Blaris (Lisburn)	1637–1873	1639–1832	1629–1868	RCBL (mf)

Co. Dublin

Castleknock	1709–1959	1710–1956	1710–1963	RCBL
also:	1768–1865	1768–1865	1772–1865	GO 495 (ph.stat)
Clonsilla	1830–1901	1831–1956	1831–1902	RCBL
also:	1827–65	1827–65	1826–45	GO 495 (ph.stat)
Clontarf	1816–49	1811–52	1812–60	NA MFCI 13, M5967
Cloughran	1782–1870	1738–1839	1732–1870	NA M5084
also:	1870–91	1858–75	1871–1938	RCBL
also:	1782–1852	1738–1852	1732–1852	RCBL (extracts)
Crumlin	1740–1863	1764–1863	1740–1862	NA M5088–91
also:	–	–	1740–1830	IMA, Vol. 12/13
Dunganstown	1782–1984	1787–1862	1783–1954	NA MFCI 79
Finglas	–	–	1664–1729	IMA, Vol. 11
also:	–	–	1877–1956	RCBL
also:	1685–1818	1667–1780	1685–1727	GO 578 (extracts)
Monkstown	1669–1800	1669–1800	1669–1800	PRS, Vol. 6
Mulhuddert	–	1871–1944	–	RCBL
Newcastle Lyons	1768–1982	1773–1859	1776–1982	NA MFCI 88

Dublin City

Arbour Hill Barracks	1848–1922	–	1847–84	RCBL
Baggotrath	1865–1923	1882–1923	–	RCBL
Beggar's Bush Barracks	1868–1922	–	–	RCBL
Christ Church	1740–1886	1717–1826	1710–1866	LC
Donnybrook	1712–1857	1712–1956	1712–1873	RCBL
Donnybrook	–	1712–1800	–	IMA
Female Penitentiary	1898–1907	–	–	RCBL
Free Church	1902–87	–	–	RCBL
Grangegorman	1816–1990	1830–1990	1833–34	LC
Irishtown	1812–1973	1824–1956	1712–1873	RCBL
Kilmainham	1857–1982	1861–1981	–	RCBL
Mission to Seamen	1961–81	–	–	RCBL
Molyneux Chapel	1871–1926	–	–	RCBL
North Dublin Union	1906–18	–	–	RCBL
Pigeon House Fort	1872–1901	–	–	RCBL
Portobello Barracks	1857–69	–	–	RCBL
Richmond Barracks	1857–1922	–	–	RCBL
Rathmines (Holy Trinity)	1850–75	–	–	With St Peter's
Royal Hospital, Kilmainham	1826–79	–	1849–79	LC*
St Aidan	1910–61	–	–	RCBL

St Andrew	–	1672–1800	–	PRS, Vol. 12
also:	–	1672–1819	–	NA M.5135
also:	1694–1803	1695–1802	1694–1796	TCD MS. 2062 (extracts)
also:	–	1801–19	–	IMA, Vol. 12/13
St Anne	1719–1813	1799–1822	1722–1822	GO 577 (extracts)
also:	–	1719–1800	–	PRS, Vol. 11
also:	1873–1938	1845–1973	1780–1816	RCBL
St Audoen	1672–1916	1673–1947	1673–1885	RCBL
also:	–	1672–1800	–	PRS, Vol. 11
also:	–	–	1672–92	IMA, Vol. 12/13
St Augustine	1911–65	–	–	RCBL
St Bride	–	1845–87	–	RCBL
also:	–	1639–1800	–	PRS, Vol. 11
St Catherine	1699–1966	1679–1966	1679–1898	RCBL
also:	1636–1715	1636–1715	1636–1715	PRS, Vol. 5
also:	–	1715–1800	–	PRS, Vol 12
St George	1784–1875	1794–1956	1824–1908	RCBL
St James	1730–1963	1742–1963	1742–1989	RCBL
also:	1730–1836	1742–1834	1742–1834	NL mf, Pos. 6014
St John	1619–1878	1619–1878	1619–1850	RCBL
also:	1619–99	1619–99	1619–99	PRS, Vol. 1
also:	–	1700–98	–	IMA, Vol. 11
also:	–	–	1620–1850	GO 577
St Kevin	1883–1908	1884–1977	–	RCBL
St Luke	1713–1974	1716–1963	1716–1974	RCBL
also:	–	1716–1800	–	PRS, Vol. 12
St Mark	1730–1971	1730–1971	1733–1923	RCBL
also:	–	1730–50	–	NL MS. 18319
St Mary	1697–1972	1697–1880	1700–1858	RCBL
also:	–	1697–1800	–	PRS, Vol. 12
also:	1831–70	1831–70	1831–70	NA, 1A.45.59
St Mathias	1867–1955	1873–1955	–	RCBL
St Michael	1674–86	1663–1765	1678–1750	RCBL (extracts)
also:	1749–1872	1750–1852	1750–1804	printed in *The Irish Builder*, 1890/91
also:	–	1656–1800	–	IMA, Vol. 11
St Michan	1701–87	1706–1809	1727–45	RCBL (extracts)
also:	1636–1701	1636–1701	1636–1701	PRS, Vols 3, 7
also:	1700–24	–	1700–24	GO MS. 577
also:	–	1700–1800	–	IMA, Vol. 11
St Nicholas Within	1671–1866	1671–1865	1671–1863	RCBL
also:	–	1671–1800	1671–1823	IMA, Vol. 11
also:	–	–	1825–63	IMA, Vols 12/13
St Nicholas Without	1694–1861	1699–1861	1694–1875	RCBL
also:	1694–1739	1694–1739	1694–1739	PRS, Vol. 10

St Patrick	1677–1990	1677–1990	1677–1990	LC
also:	1677–1800	1677–1800	1677–1800	PRS, Vol. 2
also:				GO 701 (extracts)
St Paul	1698–1987	1699–1982	1702–1892	RCBL
also:	–	–	1702–18	IMA, Vol. 12/13
also:	–	–	1719–1821	NA, IA.37.52
also:	–	–	1718–30	GO MS. 577
St Peter	1669–1974	1670–1975	1670–1883	RCBL
also:	1669–1771	1669–1771	1669–1771	PRS, Vol. 9
St Philip, Milltown	1844–76	–	–	LC*
St Stephen	1837–1912	1862–1956	–	RCBL
St Thomas	1750–1931	1750–1957	1762–1882	RCBL
St Victor	1897–1954	1916–56	–	RCBL
St Werburgh	1704–1913	1704–1956	1704–1843	RCBL
also:	–	1627–1800	–	PRS, Vol. 12
Sandymount	1850–61	–	–	RCBL
Santry	1754–1875	1754–1831	1753–1876	RCBL
Trinity	1871–1918	1874–1915	–	RCBL

Co. Fermanagh

Aghalurcher	1867–1983	1845–1924	1870–1927	RCBL (mf)
Aghavea	1857–83	1853–1907	1859–1986	RCBL (mf)
Belleek	1820–1918	1823–1912	1822–50	RCBL (mf)
Cleenish	1886–1947	1845–1934	1886–1922	RCBL (mf)
Clones (Aghadrimsee)	1829–1927	1829–1935	1829–90	RCBL (mf)
Drumkeeran	1873–1944	1845–1904	–	RCBL (mf)
Enniskillen	1667–1789	1668–1794	1667–1781	RCBL (extracts)
also:	1666–1826	1666–1826	1666–1826	GO 578 (extracts)
Garrison	1879–1924	1849–1935	1877–1924	RCBL (mf)
Inishmacsaint	1660–72	1660–72	1660–72	NA M5148
also:	1800–66	1800–66	1800–66	NA M5148
also:	1660–72	1660–72	1660–72	GO 578
Mullaghadun	1819–36	1819–1921	1819–1927	RCBL (mf)
Mullaghfad	1878–1971	1906–62	–	RCBL (mf)

Co. Galway

Ahascragh	1785–1872	1785–1859	1787–1875	NA MFCI 6, M5354
Ardrahan	1804–71	–	1857–79	NA M5253/4
Athenry	1796–1828	1796–1827	1795–1827	NA M5147B
Aughrim	1814–75	1815–42	1822–72	NA MFCI 6
Ballinakill	1775–1814	1792–1928	1803–1951	RCBL
also:	1852–72	–	1852–78	NA MFCI 31
Ballinasloe (Creagh)	1809–73	1808–45	1824–71	NA MFCI 6, M5360

* Registers which survived 1922 in local custody, but whose whereabouts now
appear uncertain.

Castlekirke	1879–1925	–	1879–1963	RCBL
Clifden (Omey)	1831–87	1831–44	1832–1900	NA MFCI 35, M6088
Clontuskert	–	–	1843–70	NA M5353
Dunmore	1884–1914	1846–1903	1887–1938	RCBL
Eyrecourt				GO 701 (extracts)
Headford	1888–1941	1845–1920	1885–1975	RCBL
Inniscaltra	1851–76	–	1851–74	NA MFCI 4, M5234
Kilcummin	1812–76	1812–76	1812–76	NA MFCI 33
Kilconla	–	1846–1906	–	RCBL
Killaraght	–	1846–1936	–	RCBL
Killererin	1811–28	1818–28	1818	RCBL (extracts)
Kilmoylan	1866	–	–	RCBL
Loughrea	1808–73	1819–45	1819–72	NA MFCI 5, M5222
Moylough	1762–1804	1828	–	NL MS. 7924
also:	1826–1922	1823–44	1843–1940	RCBL
also:	1827–1922	1826–44	1847–1919	NA MFCI 35
Moyrus	1841–71	1845–75	1844–71	NA MFCI 35
Renvyle	1884–1918	1869–1910	1871–1932	RCBL
Ross	–	1856–1950	–	RCBL
Sellerna	1897–1913	1857–1906	–	RCBL
Taughmaconnell	1852–88	–	1845–79	NA M5279
Tuam	1818–71	1831–40	1829–75	NA MFCI 7, M5351/2

Co. Kerry

Aghadoe	1838–78	1840–61	1838–81	NA M5974
Ballybunion (Liselton)	1840–81	–	1840–75	NA MFCI 17
Ballymacelligot	1817–56	1817–56	1817–56	NA MFCI 17, M5991
Ballyseedy	1830–78	–	1831–78	NA MFCI
Caher	1878–1947	1847–76	–	RCBL
Castleisland	1835–71	1836–48	1836–75	NA M5986
Dromod & Prior	–	1822–42	–	NA M5093
Kenmare	1818–73	1819–1950	1818–49	RCBL
Kilcrohane	–	1846–1930	–	RCBL
Kilgarvan	1811–50	1812–1947	1819–1960	RCBL
Killorglin	1840	1837–40	1837	NA TAB 12/63
Kilmore	1826–1960	1850–1925	–	RCBL
Kilnaughtin	1785–1871	1785–1845	1786–1873	NA MFCI 17
Listowel	1835–72	1835–45	1836–71	NA MFCI 17, M5970
Templenoe	–	1849–1920	–	RCBL
Tralee (Ratass)	1771–1872	1796–1850	1805–80	NA MFCI 14
Valentia	1826–72	–	1826–77	NA M5988/9

Co. Kildare

Athy	1669–1880	1675–1891	1669–1850	NA MFCI 78
Ballinafagh	1876–1954	1851–1957	1877–1964	RCBL
Ballymore Eustace	1838–79	1840–79	1832–79	NA MFCI 86
Ballysax	1830–1939	1841–59	1834–1982	NA MFCI 71
also:	–	1859–1903		NA M5140–5
Castlecarbery	1804–1902	1805–45	1805–48	NA MFCI 66
Celbridge	1777–1977	1777–1975	1787–1882	RCBL
also:	1777–1881	1777–1843	1787–1882	NA MFCI 88
Clane	1802–46	1804–81	1804–1906	NA M5953
also:	–	1850–1956	1906–47	RCBL
Clonaslee	1814–1982	1814–44	1816–1982	NA MFCI 69
Clonsast	1805–1983	1804–57	1806–1983	NA MFCI 63
Curragh Camp & Newbridge Garrison	1856–98	1890–1914	1869–1912	NA M5050–5
Donadea	1890–1968	1846–1939	1892–1920	RCBL
Edenderry (Monasteroris)	1678–1754	1678–1754	1678–1754	NA M5111
Fontstown	1814–40	1811–56	1811–69	RCBL
Kilcullen	1778–1982	1779–1839	1778–1982	NA MFCI 71
Kildare	1801–1962	1801–45	1801–69	NA MFCI 70
Kill	1814–84	1820–44	1814–79	NA MFCI 68
Lackagh	1829–82	1829–64	1829–79	NA MFCI 70
Lea	1830–52	1841	1842–86	RCBL
Leixlip	1778–1879	1781–1876	1778–1879	NA MFCI 90
Maynooth	–	1839–70	–	NA MFCI 42
Monasterevin (Harristown)	1666–1917	1799–1883	1802–1983	NA MFCI 67
Naas	1679–1882	1742–1848	1679–1891	NA MFCI 68
Newbridge Garrison	1867–1922	–		RCBL
Straffan	1838–81	1838–1950	1841–1940	RCBL
also:	1838–81	1838	1841–1940	NA MFCI 88
Timolin	1802–74	1800–97	1803–1984	NA MFCI 84

Co. Kilkenny

Burnchurch	1881–1942	–	1882–1980	RCBL
Callan	1892–1966	1846–1954	1894–1982	RCBL
Castlecomer	1799–1839	1799–1845	1799–1901	RCBL
Castlecomer Colliery	1838–58	1839–44	–	RCBL
Clonmore	1817–1906	–	1822–1921	NA M5086
Gowran	1885–1977	1845–1956	–	RCBL
Graiguenamanagh	1804–5	1846–1933	–	RCBL
Grangesilva	–	1850–1921	–	RCBL
Kilmocahill	–	1848–64	–	RCBL
Knocktopher	1884–1959	1849–1940	1887–1983	RCBL
Mothel	1810–43	1811–1950	1817–42	RCBL
Powerstown	–	1854	–	RCBL

Rathcool	1836–44	1842	–	RCBL
Rower	1888–1943	1849–1937	1883–1985	RCBL
Shankill	–	1845–1950	–	RCBL
Tiscoffin	–	1853–80	–	RCBL
Thomastown	1895–1965	1845–1949	1870–1987	RCBL
Ullard	–	1857	–	RCBL

Co. Laois (Queen's Co.)

Coolbanagher	1802–90	1802–45	1803–72	NA MFCI 69
Durrow	1731–1841	1731–1836	1731–1836	RCBL (transcript)
also:	1731–41	1731–41	1731–41	NL MS. 2670 (transcript)
also:	1808–75	1808–75	1808–75	NA M5056–8
Mountmellick	1840–1982	1840–56	1840–1982	NA MFCI 69
Lea	1801–90	1801–69	1801–69	NA MFCI 72
Portarlington	1694–1972	1694–1812	1694–1983	NA MFCI 72
Roscrea	1784–1878	1792–1845	1792–1872	NA MFCI 3, M5222
Rosenallis	1801–1976	1801–71	1801–1972	NA MFCI 69

Co. Leitrim

Ballaghmeehan	1877–1985	1859–1986	1877–1986	RCBL (mf)
Carrigallen	1883–1986	1845–1941	1874–1936	RCBL (mf)
Clooneclare	1816–1972	1816–1921	1816–1972	RCBL (mf)
Drumkeeran	1873–1944	1845–1904	–	RCBL (mf)
Inishmagrath	1877–1985	–	1877–1983	RCBL (mf)
Killargue	1877–1985	1859–1986	1877–1986	RCBL (mf)
Killasnet	1877–1984	1846–1950	1863–1956	RCBL (mf)
Killenummery	1884–1961	1845–1905	1356–1945	RCBL (mf)
Newtowngore	1877–1921	1847–1950	1877–1981	RCBL (mf)

Co. Limerick

Abington	1811–98	1813–45	1810–92	NA MFCI 2, M5222
Adare	1845–89	–	–	NL Pos. 1994
Ardcanny & Chapelrussel	1802–48	1802–44	1805–44	NL Pos. 2761
also:	1802–1927	1802–1920	1805–1940	NA M5072–5
Ballingarry	1785–1872	1809–46	1809–75	NA MFCI 16
also:				GO 701 (extracts)
Ballinlanders	–	1852–77	–	RCBL
Bruff	1859–71	–	1859–71	NA M5975/6
Cahernarry	1855–77	–	–	NA M5112
Corcomhide	1805–95	1805–95	1805–95	NA MFCI 16, M5987
Fedamore	1840–91	–	–	NA M5112
Kilfergus	1812–58	1815–43	1836–49	NA MFCI 17

Kilfinane	1804–71	1804–41	1798–1871	NA MFCI 16
Kilmeedy	1805–95	1805–95	1805–95	NA MFCI 16, M5987
Kilscannell	1824–74	1825–59	1860–87	NA MFCI 16, M5987
Limerick City				
Garrison	1858–71	–	1865–71	NA MFCI 17, M5789/80
St John's	1697–1883	1697–1845	1697–1876	NA MFCI 14, 15
St Mary's	1726–1871	1726–1845	1726–1942	NA MFCI 15, M5978
St Michael's	1803–71	1803–45	1803–89	NA MFCI 17, M5991
Mahoonagh	–	–	1861–64	NA M5977
Mungret	1852–56	–	1843–72	NA M5981, 5986
Newcastle	1848–70	–	1848–76	NA M5983/4
Particles	1841–71	–	–	NA MFCI 16, M5987
Rathkeale	1781–1871	1781–1836	1781–1871	NA MFCI 16, M5987, M5120/1
Rathronan	1818–71	–	1824–71	NA MFCI 16, M5987
Stradbally	1792–1881	1787–1844	1791–1850	NA MFCI 3, M5222, M5249–52

Co. Longford

Columbkille	1894–1985	1845–1934	1896–1983	RCBL (mf)
Forgney	1808–1918	1804–71	1804–1914	NA MFCI 61
Shrule	1854–63	–	–	RCBL
Templemichael	1796–1835	1777–1838	1796–1838	NA M5724–6

Co. Louth

Ardee	1799–1868	1802–49	1801–1981	RCBL (mf)
Baronstown	1878–1952	1846–1951	1878–1956	RCBL (mf)
Charlestown	1822–1936	1824–45	1823–80	RCBL (mf)
Clogher	1811–91	1792–1910	1810–1986	RCBL (mf)
Collon	1790–1969	1790–1845	1791–1950	RCBL (mf)
Darver	–	1870–75	–	RCBL (mf)
Drogheda	1654–1886	1654–1956	1653–1864	RCBL (mf)
also:	1747–72	1747–72	1747–72	NA M5127
Dundalk	1729–1924	1750–1929	1727–1985	RCBL (mf)
Dunleer	1787–92	1738–96	1729–95	RCBL (extracts)
Faughart	–	1848–64	–	RCBL (mf)
Heynestown	1865–1984	1855–1951	1871–1983	RCBL (mf
Killincoole	1877–1954	1849–1944	1886–1965	RCBL (mf)
Louth	1889–1904	1849–1944	1886–1965	RCBL (mf)
Omeath	1883–1936	1845–1930	1883–1936	RCBL (mf)

Co. Mayo

Aasleagh	–	1849–1956	–	RCBL
Achill	1854–96	1855–1936	–	RCBL
also:	–	–	1854–77	NA MFCI 33
(see also Dugort)				
Aughagower	1825–92	1828–46	1828–93	NA MFCI 33
Aughaval	1801–87	1802–54	1820–1903	RCBL
also:	1801–72	1802–45	1820–1908	NA MFCI 33
Ayle	1825–92	1828–1904	1828–93	RCBL
Ballinakill	1852–73	–	1852–78	NA MFCI 31
Ballinchalla	1831–35	1832–1917	1831–36	RCBL
Ballinrobe	1796–1912	1809–62	1809–1974	RCBL
also:	1796–1872	1809–46	1809–75	NA MFCI 35
Ballycroy	–	1855–98	1883–1962	RCBL
Ballyovey	1879–1951	1854–1954	1880–1966	RCBL
Ballysakeery	1802–71	1802–63	1802–75	NA MFCI 32
Bulnahinch	–	1854–73	–	RCBL
Castlebar	1835–72	1835–72	1834–67	NA MFCI 33
Castlemore	1890–1911	1847–1908	–	RCBL
Cong	1746–1863	1745–1849	1736–1872	NA MFCI 32
also:	1746–1863	1745–1956	–	RCBL
Crossboyne	1877–1924	1854–1937	1879–1963	RCBL
Crossmolina	1768–1872	1775–1851	1779–1873	NA MFCI 6
Dugort	1838–1864	1838–89	1838–74	NA MFCI 33/4
also:	–	1845–88	–	RCBL
Kilcolman	1877–1932	1846–1949	1878–1969	RCBL
Kilcommon	1921–26	1845–1937	1920–59	RCBL
Killalla	1757–1871	1759–1842	1758–1877	NA MFCI 31/2
Kilmainemore	1744–1927	1744–1891	1744–1958	RCBL
also:	1744–1927	1744–1891	1744–1908	NA MFCI 35, M6088
Kilmeena	1887–1904	1845–1917	–	RCBL
Kilmoremoy	1793–1874	1793–1846	1769–1875	NA MFCI 35/6
Knappagh	–	1855–1952	–	RCBL
also:	–	–	1855–71	NA MFCI 32
Louisburgh	–	1846–1952	–	RCBL
Mayo	–	1849–62	–	RCBL
Turlough	1821–72	1822–56	1822–73	NA MFCI 36

Co. Meath

Agher	1796–1874	1807–39	1798–1875	NA MFCI 51
Athboy	1736–1877	1736–1845	1736–1877	NA MFCI 53/4
Bective	1853–73	–	1857–79	NA MFCI 48
Castlerickard	1869–77	–	–	NA M5137
Clonard	1792–1880	1836–76	1838–90	NA M5232, 5233
also:	–	1846–50	–	RCBL
Clongill	1795–1804	–	1795–1804	NA MFCI 43/4

Drogheda (St Mary's)	1763–1871	1763–1845	1763–1872	NA MFCI 39
Drumconrath	1799–1983	1820–44	1821–98	NA MFCI 45
also:	1799–1826	1820–1956	1821–26	RCBL
Dunshaughlin	1839–74	–	1839–77	NA MFCI 41
Julianstown	1787–1869	1797–1837	1778–1873	NA MFCI 39
Kells	1773–1876	1773–1844	1773–1904	NA MFCI 46/7
Kilmainhamwood	1881–92	1852–76	–	RCBL
Kilmore	–	1834–42	1827–42	NA MFCI 42
Killachonagan (Ballivor)	1853–77	1853–62	1853–63	NA M5117
Loughcrew	1800–21	1800–21	1800–21	NA MFCI 51
Nobber	1828–68	1828–44	1831–61	NA M5062
also:	–	1850–1945	–	RCBL
Oldcastle	1814–84	1815–45	1814–90	NA MFCI 52
Painestown	1833–1917	1835–1919	1834–1908	RCBL
also:	1704–1901	1704–1901	1704–1901	NA MFCI 40/1 (extracts)
Rathcore	1810–1983	1811–35	1810–71	NA MFCI 51
Rathmolyon	1733–1876	1834–56	1834–77	NA MFCI 51
Syddan	1720–1983	1721–1865	1725–1983	NA MFCI 46
also:	1720–1825	1721–1949	1725–1824	RCBL
Trim	1782–1876	1792–1849	1792–1871	NA MFCI 49

Co. Monaghan

Carrickmacross	1797–1984	1798–1920	1831–1981	RCBL (mf)
Cooneen	1872–1975	1887–1935	–	RCBL (mf)
Clones (Aghadrimsee)	1829–1927	1829–1935	1829–90	RCBL (mf)
Clontibret	1864–65	–	–	RCBL (extracts)
Donaghmoine	–	–	1878–1969	RCBL (mf)
Kilmore	1826–1984	1826–1956	1826–1982	RCBL (mf)
Magheracloone	1806–1984	1813–1985	1806–1984	RCBL (mf)
Monaghan	1802–1907	1802–1910	1802–57	RCBL (mf)
Mullaghfad	1878–1971	1906–62	–	RCBL (mf)
Tydavnet	1822–83	1822–1950	1822–67	RCBL (mf)

Co. Offaly (King's Co.)

Ballyboy	1709–48	1709–48	1709	RCBL (transcripts)
Ballyboy	1797–1847	1806–19	1800–68	RCBL (extracts)
Birr	1760–1870	1760–1844	1786–1858	NA MFCI 2, 3, M5221
also:	1760–1806	1762–1804	1792–1856	GO 578 (extracts)
Borrisnafarney	1828–77	1827–51	1827–76	NA MFCI 4
Castlejordan	1702–1839	1707–1840	1704–1840	RCBL
also:	1702–1877	1707–1845	1704–1877	NA MFCI 50
Cloneyburke	1824–1982	–	1834–1983	NA MFCI 72
Clonmacnoise	1828–74	–	1818–1977	NA MFCI 57
Dunkerrin	1825–73	1826–45	1825–73	NA MFCI 4, M5222

Durrow	1816–83	1818–75	1817–83	NA MFCI 55
Ettagh	1825–67	1826–68	1826–73	NA MFCI 4, M5222
Ferbane (Whirry)	1819–75	–	1821–57	NA MFCI 57
also:	1797–1822	1797–1822	1797–1822	NL MS. 4122
Geashill	1713–1905	1713–1846	1713–1907	NA MFCI 65
Kilcoleman	1839–75	–	1839–72	NA MFCI 4, M5235
Killeigh	1808–23	1809–32	1808–35	NA M5115/6
also:	1808–35	1808–35	1808–35	NL MS. 7974 (transcript)
also:	1808–71	1808–82	1808–71	NA MFCI 65
Kinnitty	1850–78	–	1850–83	NA MFCI 57
Roscrea	1784–1878	1791–1845	1792–1872	NA MFCI 3, M5222
Shinrone	1741–1877	1741–1844	1741–1876	NA MFCI 4, M5222
Templeharry	1845–79	–	1845–79	NA MFCI 24, M6048
Tessauran	1819–77	–	1819–77	NA MFCI 57
Tullamore	1805–1902	1805–50	1805–70	NA MFCI 55

Co. Roscommon

Athlone (St Mary's)	1849–1903	1845–90	1849–1901	NL Pos. 5309
also:	1746–1903	1754–1860	1747–1892	NA MFCI 57
(St Peter's)	–	1845–70	–	NL Pos. 5309
Kiltoom	1797–1943	1802–1910	1801–1943	NL Pos. 5309
also:	1797–1943	1802–43	1801–73	NA MFCI 61

Co. Sligo

Ballysadare	–	1845–1954	–	RCBL
Castleconnor	1800–21	1800–21	1800–21	NA MFCI 33
Drumcliff	1805–87	1805–66	1805–58	NA M5094–5107
Easkey	1822–71	1822–45	1822–71	NA MFCI 33
Emlafad	1808–80	1831–73	1831–73	NA MFCI 33
also:	1762–1882	1762–1875	1762–1941	RCBL

Co. Tipperary

Ardfinnan	1877–1937	–	–	RCBL
Ardmayle	1815–71	–	1815–77	NA M5889, 5890
Ballingarry	1816–18	–	–	NA M5131
Ballintemple	1805–71	1805–43	1805–75	NA MFCI 13, M5880, 5931
Borrisnafarney	1828–77	1827–51	1827–76	NA MFCI 4
Cahir	1805–73	1802–48	1825–72	NA MFCI 9, M5366
Carrick-on-Suir	1803–74	1804–65	1803–75	NA MFCI 9

Cashel	1668–1842	1654–1842	1668–1842	NA MFCI 7, M5366
also:	1668–1786	1654–1842	1668–1786	NL Pos. 1390
Castletownarra	1802–72	1803–46	1802–79	NA MFCI 5
Clonmel	1766–1874	1768–1847	1767–1873	NA MFCI 8, 9
also:	1791–1807	–	–	RCBL
Clonoulty	1817–92	1817–92	1817–92	NA MFCI 13
Cloughjordan	1846–72	–	–	NA MFCI 4
Corbally	1834–49	–	–	NA MFCI 4
Donoghill	1856–74	–	1859–78	NA M5887, 5888
Dunkerrin	1825–73	1826–45	1825–73	NA MFCI 4, M5222
Fethard	1804–50	1804–43	1804–50	NA MFCI 12
Holy Cross	1800–80	–	1876–80	NA M5930
Killenaule	1742–1801	–	–	NL MS. 2048 (ph.stat)
Magorban	1804–78	1804–14	1805–73	NA M5278, 5280/1
Mealiff	1851–84	–	–	NA M5930
Modreeny	1842–73	1841–44	1842–1903	NA MFCI 30
Newport (St John's)	1755–1842	1789–1872	1783–1836	NA MFCI 2, M5222
Roscrea	1784–1878	1791–1845	1792–1872	NA MFCI 3, M5222
Templemore	1791–1877	1812–45	1791–1891	NA MFCI 7, M5364
Templetouhy	1787–1835	1793–1835	1794–1834	NA MFCI 7
Terryglass	1809–62	1809–1916	1809–82	RCBL
also:	1809–77	1809–53	1809–77	NA MFCI 3, M5222
Tipperary	1779–1873	1779–1845	1779–1875	NA MFCI 6
Toem	1802–66	1804–45	1803–77	NA M5130
Tubrid	1892–1905	–	–	RCBL
Tullamellin	1818–77	1831–40	1829–75	NA MFCI 7, M5351/2

Co. Tyrone

Barr	1880–1982	1845–1934	1885–1921	RCBL (mf)
Clogherny	1859–75	–	–	NA M5049
Donacavey	1878–1936	1845–1902	1878–1903	RCBL (mf)
Newtownsaville	1877–1901	1860–1935	1877–1933	RCBL (mf)

Co. Waterford

Clonegam	1741–1870	1742–1845	1743–1875	NA MFCI 13, 15
Clonmore	1828–76	–	–	NA M5085
Dungarvan	1741–1875	1741–1875	1741–1875	NA MFCI 10, M5056–8

Kill (St Nicholas)	1730–1864	1730–1864	1730–1864	NA MFCI 8
Killea	1816–54	1816–49	1849–52	NA M5363
Killrossanty	1838–76	1838–41	1843–71	NA M5952
Kilwatermoy	1860–72	–	1858–80	NA M5355, 5350
Lismore	1693–1841	1692–1847	1711–1841	NA MFCI 1, 18, M5222, 5982
Rossmire	1866–71	–	1866–71	NA M5370
Tallow	1829–74	–	1831–73	NA MFCI 9, M5357
Templemichael	1801–72	1804–65	1823–1920	NA M5065/6, 5356
Waterford City				
Holy Trinity	1655–1857	1655–1850	1655–1892	NA MFCI 12, 13
St Olave's	1741–1872	1742–1845	1744–1838	NA MFCI 10, 11, M5366, 5368/9
St Patrick's	1723–1872	1725–1845	1723–1855	NA MFCI 10, 11

Co. Westmeath

Almorita	–	1846–1937	–	RCBL
Ardnurcher	–	1819–76	–	NA MFCI 62
Athlone (St Mary's)	1849–1903	1845–90	1849–1901	NL Pos. 5309
also:	1746–1903	1754–1860	1747–1892	NA MFCI 57
(St Peter's)	–	1845–70	–	NL Pos. 5309
(see also Willbrook)				
Bunowen	1820–1941	1820–1941	1820–1941	NL Pos. 5309
also:	1819–76	–	1829–77	NA MFCI 61
Castletownkinadelan	1850–77	–	–	NA MFCI 54
Collinstown	1838–1963	1818–51	1837–1960	NA MFCI 51
Delvin	1817–1947	1817–50	1817–1943	NA MFCI 51
Drumcree (Kilcumney)	1816–75		1816–81	NA M5108/9
Enniscoffey	1881–1953	1845–1925	1891–1976	RCBL
Kilkenny West	1762–83	1762–83	–	NL Pos. 5309
also:	1783–1956	1783–1855	1784–1945	NA MFCI 61
Killucan	1696–1863	1787–1857	1700–1888	RCBL
also:	1696–1786	1696–1786	1696–1786	NL MS. 2049 (ph.stat)
also:	1696–1778	–	1700–72	GO 578
Kinnegad	1892–1917	1845–94	1895–1956	RCBL
Leney	1840–72	–	1860–71	NA MFCI 62
also:	1840–43	–	–	RCBL
Mayne	1808–70	1809–70	1808–70	NA MFCI 51
Moyliscar	–	1845–1956	–	RCBL
Mullingar	–	1845–1956	–	RCBL
Portnashangan	–	1846–1979	1880–1977	RCBL
Rathconnell	–	–	1881–95	RCBL
Stonehall	1814–57	1814–54	1915–54	NA MFCI 62
also:	1878–1941	–	–	RCBL

Willbrook (Moydrum)	1756–83	1763–75	–	NL Pos. 5309
also:	1756–83	–	–	NA MFCI 62

Co. Wexford

Carne	–	–	1815–76	NA M1451
Churchtown	–	–	1835–77	NA M1451
Inch	1726–1866	1726–1887	1726–1896	NA M5059 / 60
also:	1866–1984	–	1896–1984	NA MFCI 82
Killinick	1804–20	1804–20	1805–19	NA M5063
Kilmeaden	1693–1873	1683–1847	1683–1882	NA MFCI 13, M5965
Kilpatrick	–	–	1834–64	NA M1451
Templeshanbo	1827–75	1827–91	1827–91	NA M5729
Whitechurch				GO 701 (extracts)

Co. Wicklow

Aghold	1714–1863	1714–1863	1714–1863	GO 578 (extracts)
Ballinaclash	1839–1989	1843–51	1842–1984	NA MFCI 76
Ballintemple	1823–51	1823–54	–	NA MFCI 76
Blessington	1695–1985	1683–1878	1683–1985	NA MFCI 87
Castlemacadam	1720–1904	1719–1860	1719–1979	NA MFCI 76
Delgany	1666–1985	1666–1845	1666–1985	NA MFCI 75
Donard	–	1848–1955	1888–1965	RCBL
Donoughmore	1720–1888	1720–1856	1720–1929	RCBL
also:	1720–1888	1720–1853	1720–1874	NA MFCI 89
Dunlavin	1697–1934	1697–1956	1697–1934	RCBL
also:	1697–1879	1698–1844	1698–1879	NA MFCI 86
Enniskerry	1662–1874	1662–1852	1662–1874	NL Pos. 5484
Glenely	1808–80	1808–64	1817–71	NA MFCI 77
Kilbride	1834–1970	1845–76	1834–1984	NA MFCI 82
Killiskey	1818–1905	1818–44	1824–77	NA MFCI 83
Newcastle	1698–1954	1697–1846	1699–1881	NA MFCI 85
Powerscourt	1677–1874	1662–1860	1663–1873	NA MFCI 91
Rathdrum	1706–1865	1706–1855	1706–1916	NA MFCI 77
Redcross	1830–52	–	–	NA MFCI 79
Wicklow	1655–1983	1729–1869	1729–1909	NA MFCI 83

15

Research Services, Societies and Repositories

SECTION 1. RESEARCH SERVICES

A. Professional Associations

Two associations of professional researchers exist, the Association of Ulster Genealogists and Record Agents (AUGRA), based exclusively in Northern Ireland, and the Association of Professional Genealogists in Ireland (APGI), with members north and south. Both bodies are principally concerned with upholding research standards, rather than undertaking commercial research in their own right. The secretaries of both associations will supply a list of members on request:

The Secretary, AUGRA, Glen Cottage, Glenmachan Road, Belfast BT4 2NP, Northern Ireland.
The Secretary, APGI, c/o The Genealogical Office, 2 Kildare St, Dublin 2.

B. Research Agencies

The following are research agencies whose staff are members of the two professional associations:

Gorry Research, 16 Hume St, Dublin 2.
Hibernian Research Co. Ltd, P.O. Box 3097, Dublin 6.
    Telephone (01) 966522 (24 hours); Fax 973011 (24 hours)
Historical Research Associates, 7 Lancastrian Street, Carrickfergus BT38 7AB, Co. Antrim, Northern Ireland.

Irish Heritage Association, 162a Kingsway, Dunmurry, Belfast BT17 9AD. Telephone (0232) 629595

Irish Research Services, 111 South Parade, Belfast BT7 2GN, Northern Ireland.

Research Ireland, Fair View, Kindelstown Hill, Delgany, Co. Wicklow.

C. The Irish Genealogical Project

In the early 1980s, as part of a series of government-sponsored youth employment and training schemes in the Republic of Ireland, local history and heritage societies and other interested bodies began to organise the indexing of local parish records. With some exceptions, at the outset little thought was given to the potential value of these records. However, in the mid-1980s, as the number of areas covered by the indexing projects grew, their efforts were co-ordinated by an umbrella body, the Irish Family History Council, later to become the Irish Family History Foundation. An ambitious plan was drawn up under the aegis of this body to transcribe and computerise not only all the parish records of all denominations for the entire country, but also all other sources of major genealogical interest: the Tithe Books, Griffith's Valuation, the civil records of births, marriages and deaths, the 1901 and 1911 census returns, and local gravestone inscriptions. Expanded government funding was secured for this plan, known as the Irish Genealogical Project, and in 1990, with the adherence of four centres in Northern Ireland, the International Fund for Ireland also became involved.

Thirty-five geographical catchment areas have been identified, and, as of mid-1991, centres have been designated for thirty-one of these. Each centre is to computerise the records for its area, and provide a commercial genealogical research service using these records. Ultimately this service will be co-ordinated by two central agencies, north and south, acting as signposts to the relevant centre. The computerised records are to remain exclusively in the custody of the local centres, and it is not envisaged that the public will have direct access to them.

As well as those working in the local heritage centres, the Project also aims to include professional genealogists, in particular the members of the two professional bodies named above. When the computerisation of the records is complete, currently anticipated for 1994, a comprehensive research service will exist, combining the experience and expertise of the professionals with the speed and accuracy of the local databases. For the moment, the situation is less clear, with centres at different points on the road to full computerisation. What follows is a listing of the centres currently involved, together with some comments on their progress.

MEMBER CENTRES OF THE IRISH FAMILY HISTORY FOUNDATION
The comments given on the centres reflect the situation in mid-1991; obviously, as the Project develops their positions will change. The comments concentrate on the indexing of parish records, since this was their first priority and the area in which most progress has been made. Apart from parish records, however, the majority of centres also hold copies of the other major genealogical sources. Not all the centres offer a research service. For the moment, the only centres to carry out full commissioned research are those in Clare, Leitrim, Limerick, Laois/Offaly, Roscommon and Waterford. Most of the centres which have completed a substantial amount of indexing will check the records they have covered, though this varies from centre to centre. Again, as the Project progresses the services offered and fees charged will be standardised.

Catchment Area	*Centre*	*Comment*
Antrim/Down	Ulster Historical Foundation, 66 Balmoral Avenue, Belfast BT9 6NY	The UHF is a long-established, highly reputable research and publishing agency. Its indexing activities as part of the IGP date from 1990 and are, as yet, at an early stage.
Armagh	Armagh Records Centre, Ara Coeli, Armagh BT61 7QY	This was originally part of the archives of the Catholic Archdiocese of Armagh, and has computerised the Catholic records for this area, which also includes parts of Cos Tyrone, Louth and Down.
Carlow	No centre designated as yet	
Cavan	Cavan Heritage & Genealogy Centre, c/o Cavan Co. Library	The centre has indexed, on cards, almost all the Catholic records for the county, as well as Griffith's Valuation and the Tithe Books.

Clare

The Clare Genealogy Centre, Corofin, Co. Clare	One of the longest-established centres, this has completed indexing of all church records for the county, as well as a substantial proportion of the other major sources.

Cork North

Mallow Heritage Centre, 27–8 Bank Place, Mallow, Co. Cork	The centre has completed the indexing, on card, of most of the Catholic records of north Cork and a substantial proportion of the Church of Ireland records. At the moment (1991) two further centres to cover the rest of Co. Cork have yet to be designated.

Derry

Inner City Trust Genealogy Centre, 8 Bishop St, Derry BT48 6PW	The centre is long-established and has completed indexing of Griffith's, Tithe Books and emigration records, as well as almost half the Catholic records, and a number of Presbyterian registers.

Donegal

Donegal Genealogical Committee, Letterkenny, Co. Donegal	The various groups represented on the Committee have indexed almost all the Presbyterian and Church of Ireland records for the county, and the Catholic records for the Inishowen peninsula.

Down

See Antrim

Dublin North

The Fingall Heritage Centre,	The centre has indexed a substantial number of the

10 North St,   Catholic records of north
Swords, Co. Dublin   Co. Dublin.

Dublin City

Dublin Heritage   The group has indexed
Group,   church records for West
Clondalkin Library,   Dublin, and a small
Clondalkin,   proportion of the Dublin
Co. Dublin   City records.

Dublin South

Dun Laoghaire   Indexing of the Catholic
Heritage Centre,   records of Dun Laoghaire
Moran Park House,   is complete, with work
Dun Laoghaire,   continuing on the records
Co. Dublin   of adjoining parishes.

Fermanagh/Tyrone

Irish World,   The efforts of this centre
26 Market Sq,   have been concentrated
Dungannon BT70 1AB,   so far on Griffith's, Tithe
Co. Tyrone   Books, and gravestone
                                inscriptions; the inscriptions
                                are particularly extensive,
                                covering more than 300
                                graveyards throughout
                                Northern Ireland.

Galway East

Woodford   About half the Catholic
Heritage Centre,   records of East Galway
Woodview House,   have been indexed, along
Woodford,   with a small proportion
Co. Galway   of the Church of Ireland
                                records.

Galway West

Co. Galway Family   The Society has indexed
History Society, 4 New   almost half the Catholic
Docks, Galway   records of west Galway.

Kerry

No centre designated
as yet

Kildare

| | Kildare Genealogical Committee, Co. Library, Newbridge, Co. Kildare | Slightly less than half the Catholic records for the county have been indexed. |

Kilkenny

| | Kilkenny Archaeological Society, Rothe House, Kilkenny | Almost half the Catholic records for the county have been indexed, along with a small proportion of the Church of Ireland records, and a large number of gravestone inscriptions. |

Laois/Offaly

| | Family History Research Centre, Charleville Road, Tullamore, Co. Offaly | Over three-quarters of all church records have been indexed. The centre also holds a large number of other sources, and is very active in local history. |

Leitrim

| | Leitrim Heritage Centre, Co. Library, Ballinamore, Co. Leitrim | The centre has completed indexing of all church records for the county, as well as Griffith's, Tithe Books, and other sources. |

Limerick

| | Limerick Archives, The Granary, Michael St, Limerick | All church records for the county are indexed, along with a wide range of other sources. |

Longford

| | Longford Genealogical Centre, Barrack Road, Longford. | Over half the Catholic records for the county are indexed on cards. |

Louth

See Meath

Mayo North

| | Mayo North Family History Research | Virtually all the church records for north Mayo |

	Centre, Enniscoe, Crossmolina, Co. Mayo	have been indexed.
Mayo South	Family Research Centre, Town Hall, Ballinrobe, Co. Mayo	Almost all the Catholic and Church of Ireland records for the south of the county are indexed. The centre also has a large collection of indexed school rolls.
Meath/Louth	Meath Heritage Centre, Trim, Co. Meath	Most of the surviving Church of Ireland records for the area are indexed. The Catholic records completed are mainly for Co. Meath, and come to less than half the total.
Monaghan	Monaghan Ancestral Research Centre, 6 Tully, Monaghan	The centre has indexed a little less than half the total church records for the county. It also holds a wide range of other sources.
Offaly	See Laois	
Roscommon	Roscommon Heritage & Genealogical Centre, Strokestown, Co. Roscommon	The Centre has virtually completed indexing of Catholic records for the county, and has covered a large proportion of the Church of Ireland records.
Sligo	Sligo Heritage & Genealogical Centre, Stephen's St, Sligo	Indexing of all church records is complete. The centre has also indexed almost all the gravestone inscriptions for the county.

Tipperary North

	Nenagh District Heritage Society, Governor's House, Nenagh, Co. Tipperary	The centre holds indexes to more than half the Catholic and Church of Ireland records for the north of the county.

Tipperary South

	Bru Boru Heritage Centre, Cashel, Co. Tipperary	Access to Catholic records is limited, though the centre holds a wide range of other sources.

Tyrone

See Fermanagh

Waterford

	Waterford Heritage Survey Ltd, St John's College, Waterford	The Survey has indexed almost all the parishes in the diocese of Waterford and Lismore.

Westmeath

	Dun na Si Heritage Centre, Moate, Co. Westmeath	A number of Catholic and Church of Ireland registers have been indexed, but the project is still in its early stages.

Wexford

	Tagoat Community Council, Tagoat, Rosslare, Co. Wexford	More than half the Catholic records for the county have been indexed.

Wicklow

	Wicklow Heritage Centre, Court House, Wicklow	Almost all the Catholic records in the county have been indexed.

SECTION 2. SOCIETIES

A. Ireland

Dublin Family History Society, c/o 36 College Drive, Templeogue, Dublin 6

Huguenot Society of Great Britain and Ireland, c/o Nora Fahie, 47 Ailesbury Road, Dublin 4

Irish Family History Society, P.O. Box 36, Naas, Co. Kildare
Publishes *Irish Family History*

Irish Genealogical Research Society, 6 Eaton Brae, Orwell Road, Dublin 14
Publishes *The Irish Genealogist*

Irish Heritage Association, 162a Kingsway, Dunmurry, Belfast BT17 9AD
Publishes *Irish Family Links*

North of Ireland Family History Society, 29 Grange Park, Dunmurry, Belfast BT17 OAN
Publishes *North Irish Roots*

Ulster Historical and Genealogical Guild, Ulster Historical Foundation, 66 Balmoral Ave, Belfast BT9 6NY
Publishes *Familia: Ulster Genealogical Review*

B. Abroad

Family History Association of Canada, P.O. Box 91398, West Vancouver, BC V7V 3P1, Canada

Federation of Family History Societies, 96 Beaumont Street, Mile House, Plymouth PL2 3AQ, England

Irish Family Names Society, P.O. Box 2095, La Mesa, CA 92044, USA

Irish Genealogical Research Society, c/o Challoner Club, 59/61 Port Street, Knightsbridge, London SW1X 0BG, England
Publishes *The Irish Genealogist*

Irish Genealogical Society, P.O. Box 16585, St Paul MN 55116, USA
Publishes *Septs*

New Zealand Society of Genealogists, P.O. Box 8785, Auckland 3, New Zealand

The Society of Australian Genealogists, Richmond Villa, 120 Kent St, Sydney, N.S.W. 2000, Australia
Publishes *Descent*

SECTION 3. RECORD REPOSITORIES

A. Northern Ireland

Area libraries
North-east Area Library, Demesne Avenue, Ballymena BT49 7BG, Co. Antrim. Telephone (0266) 41531

Southern Area Library, Brownlow Row, Legahory, Craigavon BT65 8DP,
Co. Armagh. Telephone (0238) 562639
South-East Area Library, Windmill Hill, Ballynahinch BT24 8DH, Co.
Down. Telephone (0861) 341946
Western Area Library, 41 Dublin Road, Omagh BT78 1HG, Co. Tyrone.
Telephone (0662) 244821
Belfast Central Library, Royal Avenue, Belfast BT1 1EA. Telephone (0232)
243233 (Open 9.30 a.m. – 8 p.m. Mon. & Thurs.; 9.30 a.m. – 5.30 p.m.
Tues., Wed., Fri.; 9.30 a.m. – 1 p.m. Sat.)

OTHER REPOSITORIES
Church of Jesus Christ of Latter-day Saints Family History Centre,
Hollywood Road, Belfast. Telephone (0232) 643998. (Open Wednesday
evenings)
General Register Office, Oxford House, 49–55 Chichester St, Belfast BT1
4HL. Telephone (0232) 235211 (Only the indexes are open for public
research, and by appointment only)
Linen Hall Library, 17 Donegal Square North, Belfast BT1 5GD.
Presbyterian Historical Society, Room 218, Church House, Fisherwick Place,
Belfast BT1 6DW. Telephone (0232) 323936 (Open 10 a.m. – 12.30 p.m.
Mon. – Fri.; 10 a.m. – 12.30 p.m. and 2 p.m. – 4 p.m. Wed.)
Public Record Office of Northern Ireland, 66 Balmoral Avenue, Belfast BT9
6NY. Telephone (0232) 661621 (Open 9.15 a.m. – 4.45 p.m. Mon. – Fri.)
Society of Friends Library, Meeting House, Railway Street, Lisburn, Co.
Antrim (Postal queries only)

B. Republic of Ireland

COUNTY LIBRARIES
Carlow: Dublin St, Carlow. Telephone (0503) 31126
Cavan: Farnham St, Cavan. Telephone (049) 31799
Clare: Mill Road, Ennis, Co. Clare. Telephone (065) 21616
Cork: Farranlea Road, Cork. Telephone (021) 546499
Donegal: High Road, Letterkenny, Co. Donegal. Telephone (084) 24950
Dublin: (1) Gilbert Library, 138–142 Pearse St, Dublin 2. Telephone (01)
777662 (2) Central Library, The ILAC Centre, Henry St, Dublin 1.
Telephone (01) 734333
Galway: Island House, Cathedral Square, Galway. Telephone (091) 62471
Kerry: Moyderwell, Tralee, Co. Kerry. Telephone (066) 21200
Kildare: Athgarvan Road, Newbridge, Co. Kildare. Telephone (045) 31145
Kilkenny: 6 John's Quay, Kilkenny. Telephone (056) 22021
Laois: County Hall, Portlaoise, Co. Laois. Telephone (0502) 21993

Leitrim: The Courthouse, Ballinamore, Co. Leitrim. Telephone (078) 44012
Limerick: 58 O'Connell St, Limerick. Telephone (061) 318692
Longford: Annelly Car Park, Longford. Telephone (043) 41124
Louth: Crowe St, Dundalk, Co. Louth. Telephone (042) 35457
Mayo: Mountain View, Castlebar, Co. Mayo. Telephone (094) 21342
Meath: Railway St, Navan, Co. Meath. Telephone (046) 21134
Monaghan: The Diamond, Clones, Co. Monaghan. Telephone (047) 51143
Offaly: O'Connor Sq., Tullamore, Co. Offaly. Telephone (0506) 21419
Roscommon: Abbey St, Roscommon. Telephone (0903) 26100
Sligo: The Courthouse, Teeling St, Sligo. Telephone (071) 42212
Tipperary: Castle Avenue, Thurles, Co. Tipperary. Telephone (0504) 21555
Waterford: Lismore, Co. Waterford. Telephone (058) 54128
Westmeath: Dublin Rd, Mullingar, Co. Westmeath. Telephone (044) 40781
Wexford: County Hall, Abbey St, Wexford. Telephone (053) 22211
Wicklow: Greystones, Co. Wicklow. (01) 2874387

OTHER REPOSITORIES

Church of Jesus Christ of Latter-day Saints Family History Centre, Finglas
    Road, Glasnevin, Dublin 11. Telephone (01) 309960 (Open Wednesday
    and Friday (evening), Saturday (morning))
Cork Archives Institute, Christ Church, South Main St, Cork. Telephone
    (021) 277809 (Open 10 a.m. – 1 p.m., 2.30 p.m. – 5 p.m. Mon. – Fri).
The Genealogical Office: 2 Kildare St, Dublin 2. Telephone (01) 618811
    (Open 10 a.m. – 4.30 p.m. Mon. – Fri.)
The General Register Office, Joyce House, 8–11 Lombard St E., Dublin 2.
    Telephone (01) 711000 (Open 9.30 a.m. – 12.30 p.m., 2.15 p.m. – 4.30 p.m.)
Land Valuation Office: 6 Ely Place, Dublin 2. Telephone (01) 763211 (Open
    9.30 a.m. – 12.30 p.m., 2 p.m. – 4.30 p.m. Mon. – Fri.)
National Archives: Four Courts, Dublin 7. Telephone (01) 783711. Due to
    move to Bishop St, Dublin 8, by January 1992. (Open 10 a.m. – 5 p.m.
    Mon. – Fri.)
National Library: Kildare St, Dublin 2. Telephone (01) 618811 (Open 10 a.m. –
    9 p.m. Mon.; 2 p.m. – 9 p.m. Tues., Wed.; 10 a.m. – 5 p.m. Thurs., Fri.;
    10 a.m. – 1 p.m. Sat.)
Registry of Deeds: Henrietta St, Dublin 1. Telephone (01) 733300
    (Open 10 a.m. – 4.30 p.m. Mon. – Fri.)
Society of Friends Library: Swanbrook House, Morehampton Road,
    Donnybrook, Dublin 4. Telephone (01) 683684 (Open Thursdays 10.30
    a.m. – 1 p.m.)
Representative Church Body Library: Braemor Park, Rathgar, Dublin 14.
    Telephone (01) 979979 (Open 9 a.m. – 1 p.m., 1.45 p.m. – 5 p.m. Mon. –
    Fri.)